Steven Claydon

Culpable Earth

firstsite

firstsite

Published by firstsite on the occasion
of the exhibition Steven Claydon, *Culpable Earth*,
4 February – 7 May 2012

firstsite, Lewis Gardens
High Street, Colchester
Essex CO1 1JH
www.firstsite.uk.net
+44 (0)1206 577067
info@firstsite.uk.net
Registered Charity Number 1031800

Chair: Chris Paveley
Director: Katherine Wood
Senior Curator: Michelle Cotton
Assistant Curator: Laura Earley
Curatorial Assistant: Asana Greenstreet
Programmes Intern: Daisy Courtauld
Technical Manager: Philip Gardner
Gallery Technician: Simon Newby

Edited by Michelle Cotton. Texts by Martin Clark,
Steven Claydon, Michelle Cotton and Patrizia
Dander © the authors and firstsite, 2012.

Design: Secondary Modern

Printing: Healeys

ISBN 978-0-948252-33-4

Distributed by Cornerhouse Publications
70 Oxford Street, Manchester
M1 5NH England
www.cornerhouse.org/publications
+44 (0)1612 001 503
publications@cornerhouse.org

Steven Claydon would like to thank James
Cahill, Martin Clark, Michelle Cotton, Max Craig,
Patrizia Dander, Joe Hill, Kevin Hill, Karl Otto
Karl, Sebastian Lloyd Rees, Hannah Sawtell and
Clarrie Wallis.

firstsite would also like to thank Arts Council
England, Colchester Borough Council and Essex
County Council and the Henry Moore Foundation
for their support.

Image credits:
p14-17 LIAF
p18-23, p54-55, p74, p75 (right), p76, p81,
p82-85, p86 (left) Kimmerich, New York
p24-27 La Salle de bains, Lyon
p28-29 Hayward Touring
p30-35, p38 (no.3), p39-42, p45, p75 (left),
p88-89 Hotel, London
p36-37, p38 (no.s 1&2), p43 Haus der Kunst,
Munich
p46-47 Tate St Ives
p48-51 Massimo De Carlo, Milan
p52-53 Galerie Rüdiger Schöttle, Munich
p60-63 Camden Arts Centre, London
p64 Arnolfini, Bristol
p65 David Kordansky Gallery, Los Angeles
p75 (left) Sadies Coles HQ, London
p86 (right) The Approach, London
p87 KAI10 | Raum für Kunst, Düsseldorf
p110 performed by Steven Claydon, Steffany
George, Joe Hill, Daniel Lipp, Kieron Livingstone
p111 performed by Steven Claydon, Steffany
George, Joe Hill, Simon Ling and Sebastian Lloyd
Rees. Hayward Touring
p112-113 performed by Mark Blower, Paul
Clinton, Daniel Lipp, Maximilian Mugler, Leo
Whetter, and 6 italian actors from Scuola del
Teatro Stabile di Torino. Artissima, Turin

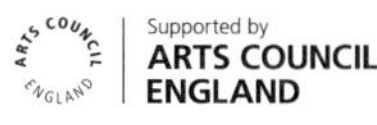
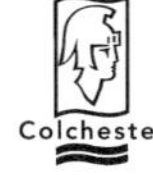
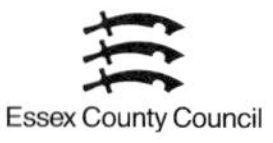

The Henry Moore Foundation   HEALEYS PRINT GROUP

Steven Claydon

Culpable Earth

Contents

Foreword

Michelle Cotton

Over the last decade Steven Claydon's sculpture, print, painting, film and performance have been worrying away at the taxonomies and values integral to the Western canon. His exhibitions with their hessian grounds, stacked pedestals, frames within frames, portrait busts and eccentric artefacts both emulate and debunk the nature of the museum. Like many artists of his generation, Claydon's work evidences the weight of historical precedence, quoting from art and literature amongst other creative fields. More than points of departure, passing references or asides, Claydon has adopted these fragments of culture – past and present – and made them his subject and material. His work explores what Martin Heidegger might describe as the 'thingly' character of an object – its 'self-sustaining and self-containing nature', its most evident, salient reality.

At the centre of *Culpable Earth*, Steven Claydon's exhibition for Firstsite, there is a huge ceramic vessel (part modern barrel, part Roman funerary urn) embellished with a likeness of Alfred Russel Wallace. A founding father of evolutionary theory (his own work on natural selection is said to have prompted Charles Darwin to publish *The Origin of Species* in 1859), Wallace is the latest in a long line of unglorified, bearded faces to appear in Claydon's work. Mounted on a series of grey, Formica plinths and positioned between two rails and four wheels (three ceramic, one cut from a wicker effigy of a Harley Davidson motorbike), he looks on grimly from this vehicle-like assemblage that appears to merge the design of a 19th century steam engine with that of a Roman chariot. The references and associations borne by this sculpture, *The passage of differentiated substance* (2012), with its accent on the great technological and scientific breakthroughs of the industrial revolution, appear progressive and dynamic. In the gallery, its bulk-weight and steel-pallor seems to establish it as a monument to obsolescence.

Obsolescence is a recurrent theme in Claydon's work, perhaps the end-point in what he has described as 'the passage of materials' – the journey of an object 'from base matter to cultural artefact'. Articles are re-made and stripped of their utility; plastic barrels manufactured to ship olives around the world are cast as solid objects, tin cans are replicated from blocks of turned wood, wine glasses and bottles are reproduced in solid aluminium. An ancient vessel is hybridised with a modern Alessi teapot – a copy, in a sense, of an object that never existed. Yet more are cut-up, dismantled, broken or affected by a process not normally associated with art; there are pots that after firing have been shot at (with a pistol) and prints that have been 'cooked' in an oven. These fragments circulate in what Claydon describes as 'atmospheres' or 'climates' of stuff; forging alliances through material, formal or anecdotal associations, they link one to another whilst individually eluding categorization.

This book gathers documentation, ideas and influences from the last six years, featuring the body of work created for the exhibition in Colchester alongside major exhibitions at Haus der Kunst in Munich and Camden Arts Centre in London as well as sculpture, painting, posters, performance and film made for solo presentations and other exhibitions. Designed by Claydon in close collaboration with Secondary Modern, it includes previously unpublished texts and source material in addition to scripts written for performances and films. We would like to thank Martin Clark and Patrizia Dander for their insightful contributions and the galleries and curators who helped collate this material, and especially Sadie Coles HQ, Massimo De Carlo, Hotel, Kimmerich, David Kordansky Gallery and Galerie Rüdiger Schöttle for their assistance. We are also grateful for the support of Arts Council England and the Henry Moore Foundation and to the individuals who have committed their time and energy in particular; my colleagues at Firstsite, Joe Hill, and not least Steven who undertook the unprecedented challenge to produce the first solo exhibition in our new galleries.

firstsite, Colchester

Culpable Earth

Fourteen exhibitions

2

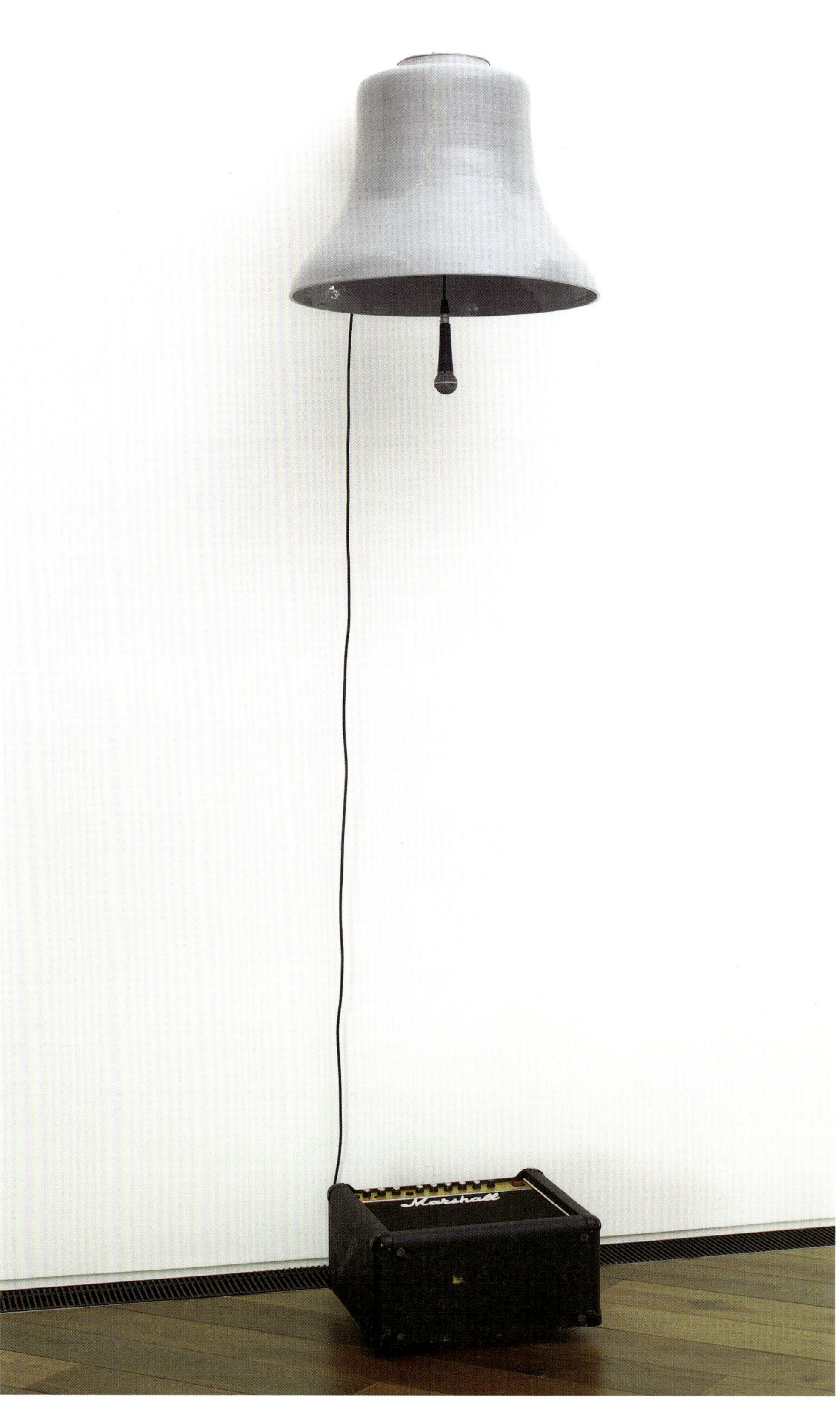

1

1- *Carrier*
2012
Ceramic, microphone, amplifier, powder coated steel
Dimensions variable
Photo: Andy Keate

2- *Culpable Earth*, installation view
2012
Photo: Andy Keate

3- *Energetic Recesses*
2012
Digital prints on Somerset paper
Each 60 x 60 cm
Photo: Andy Keate

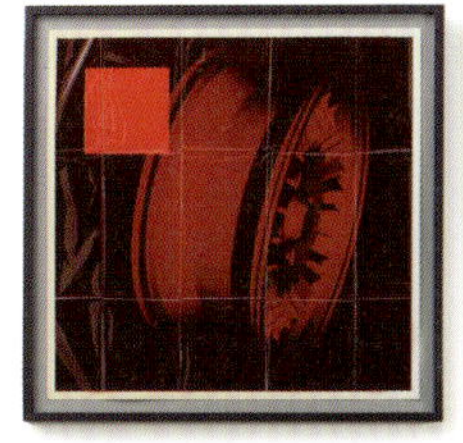 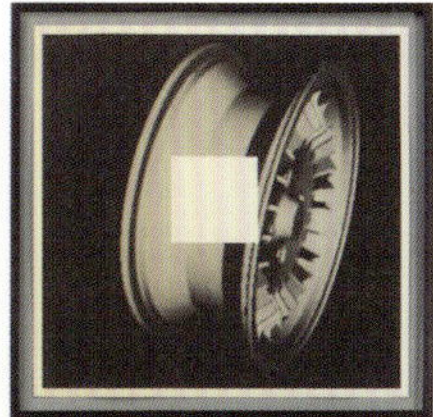
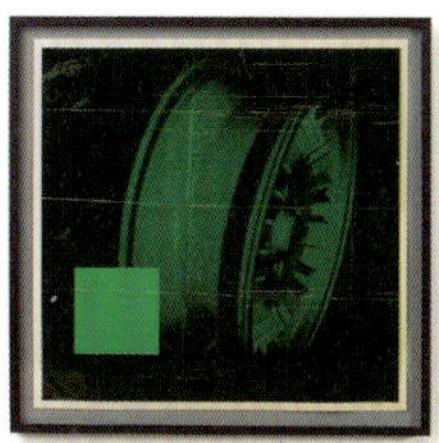 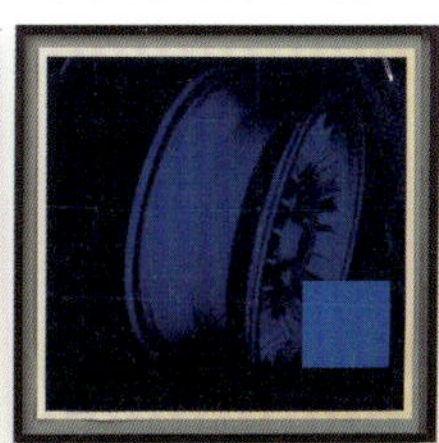

2

3

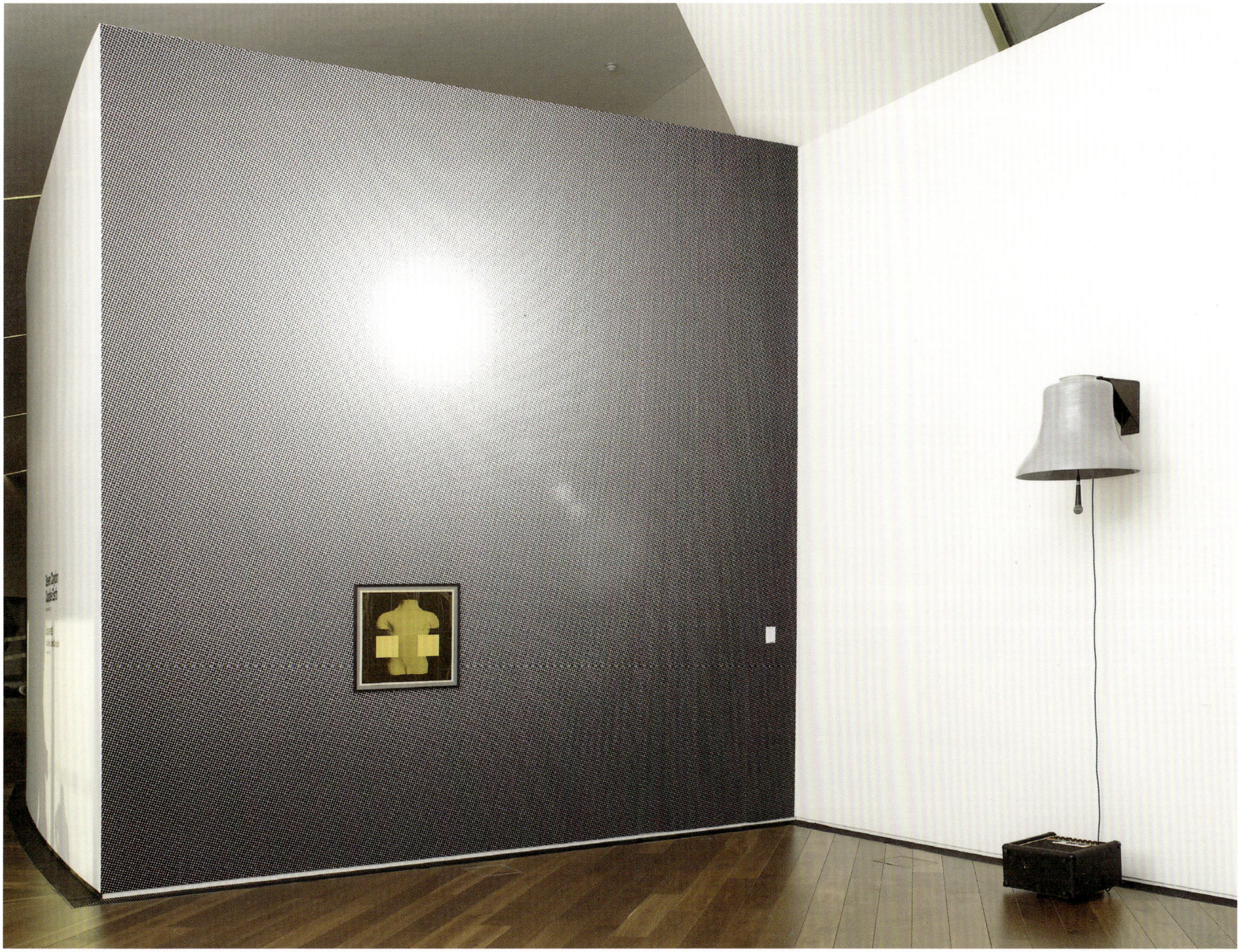

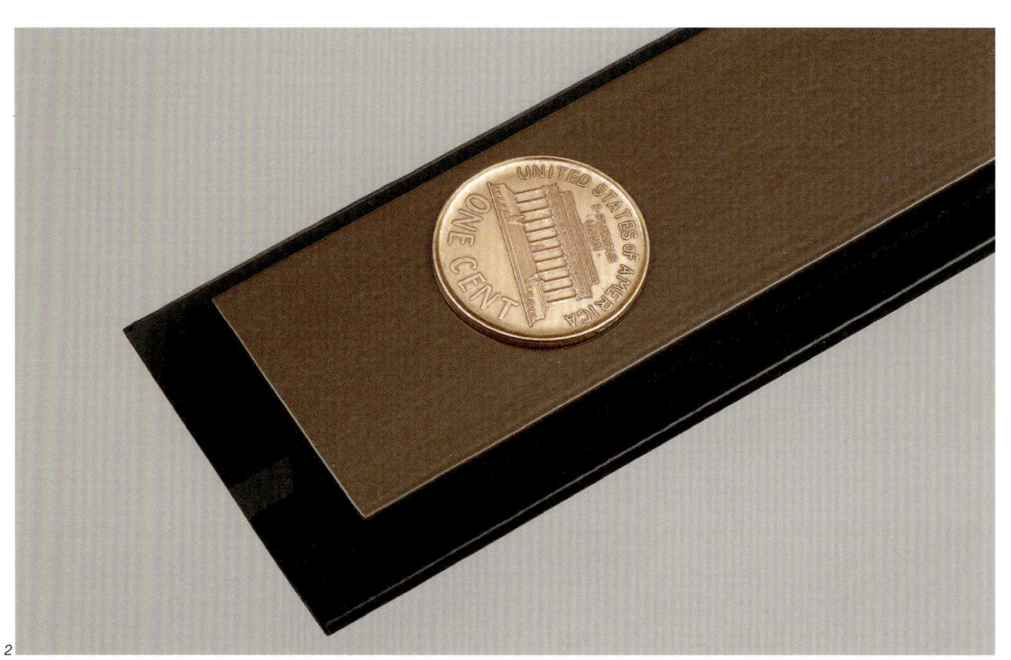

2

1

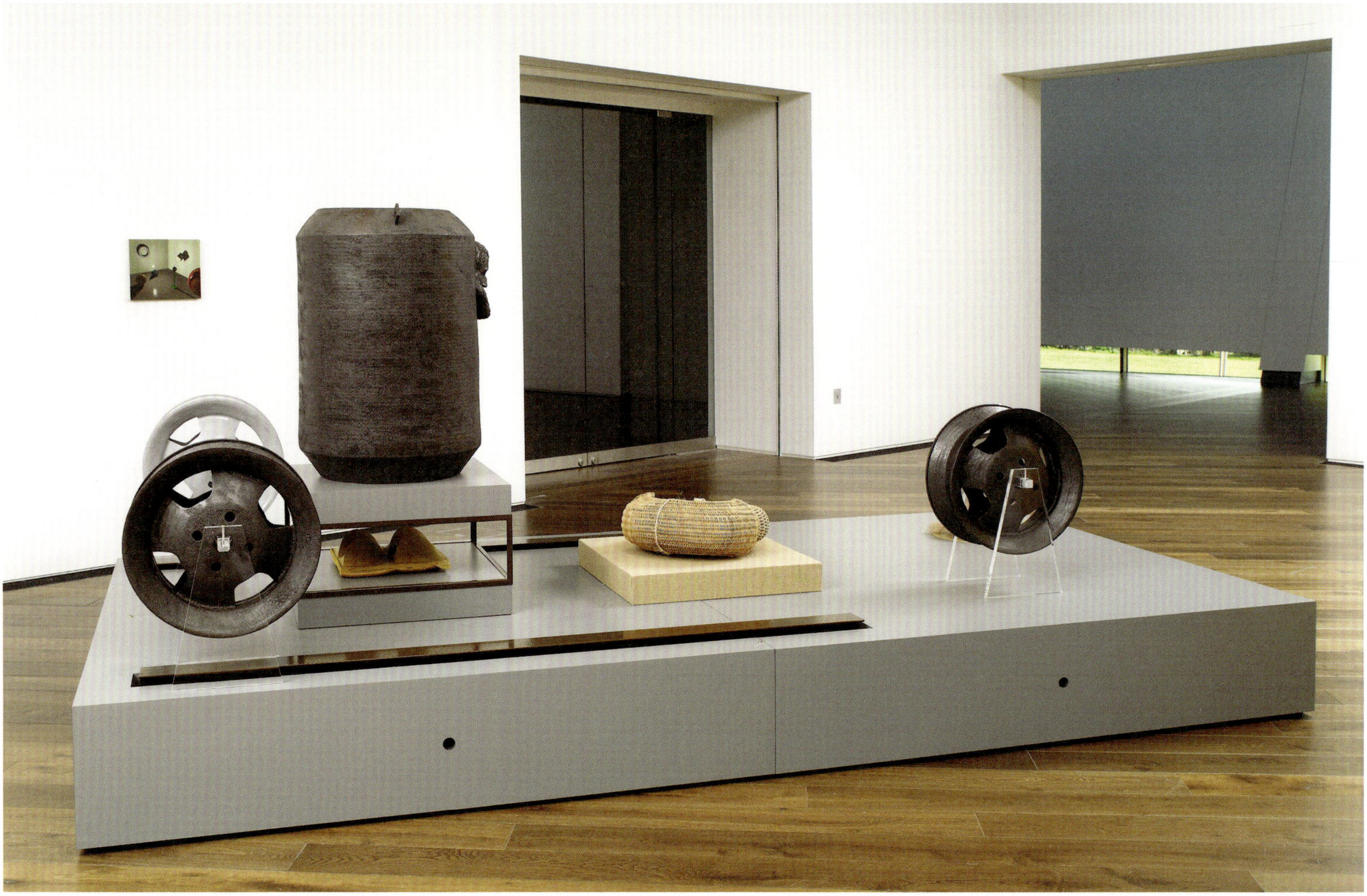

4

1- Culpable Earth, installation view
2012
Photo: Andy Keate

2-3 - The passage of differentiated substance, detail
2012
Ceramic, wicker, Formica, acrylic, powder coated
steel, copper, polyurethane foam, hessian, string,
peacock feathers, gum rubber, wood, brass
178 x 200 x 400 cm
Photo: Andy Keate

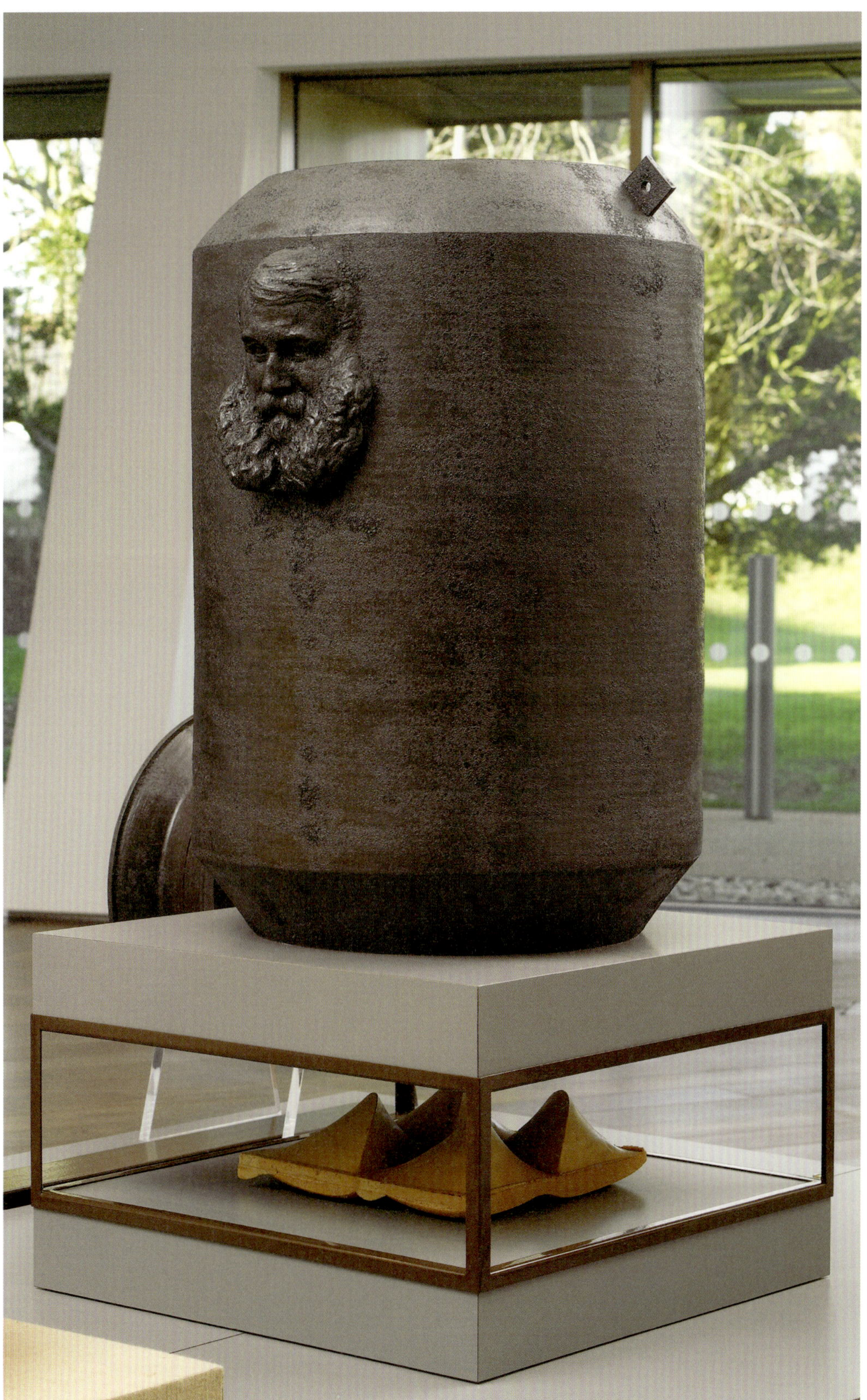

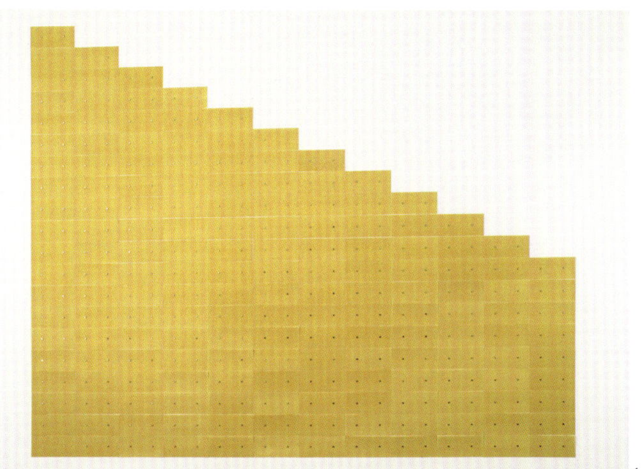

1

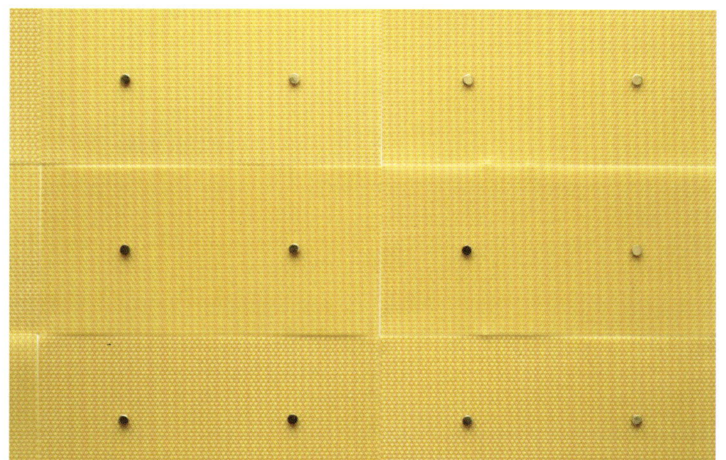

2

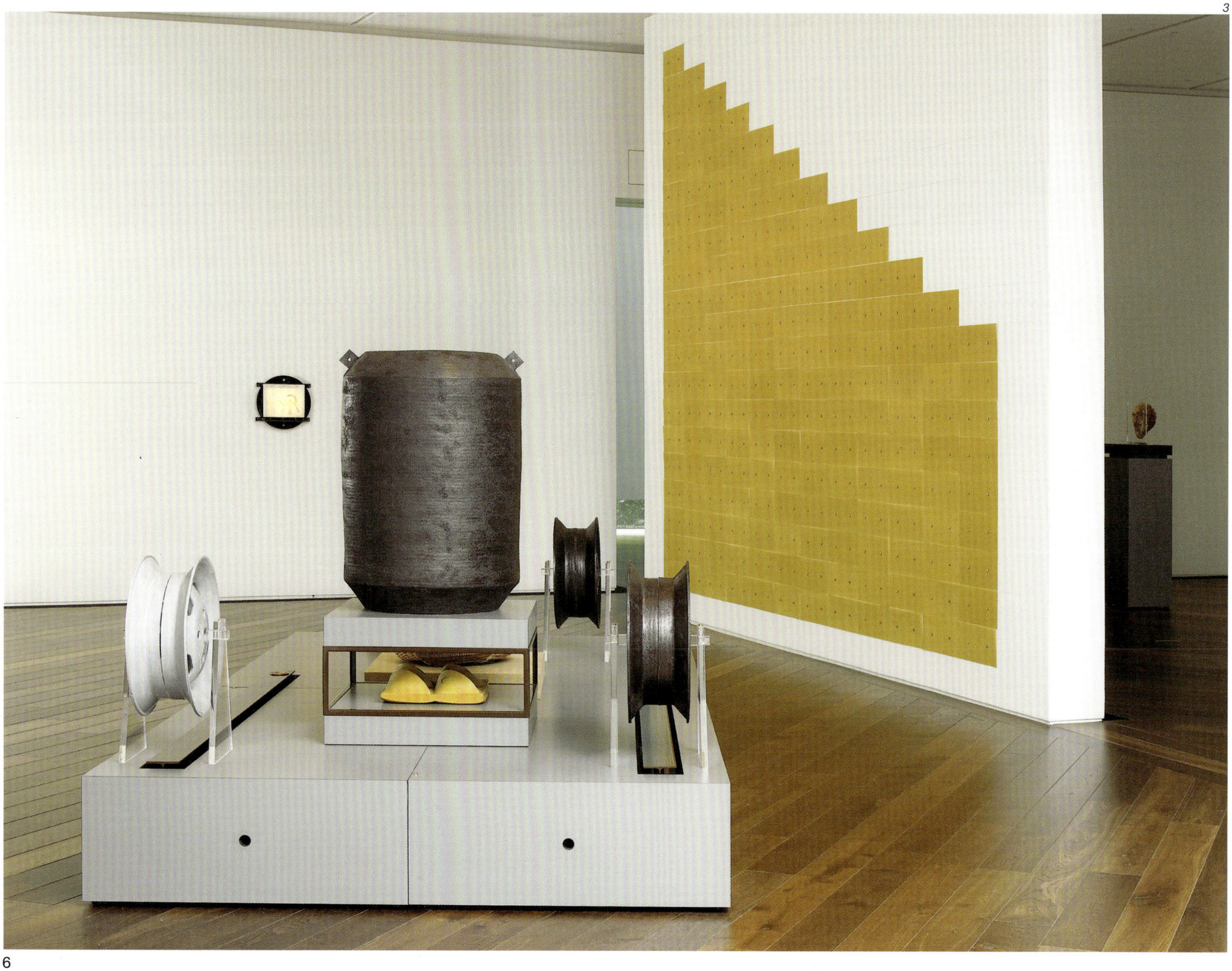

3

6

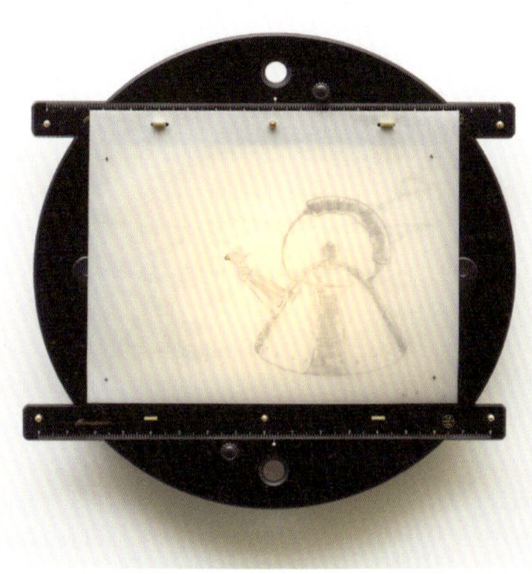

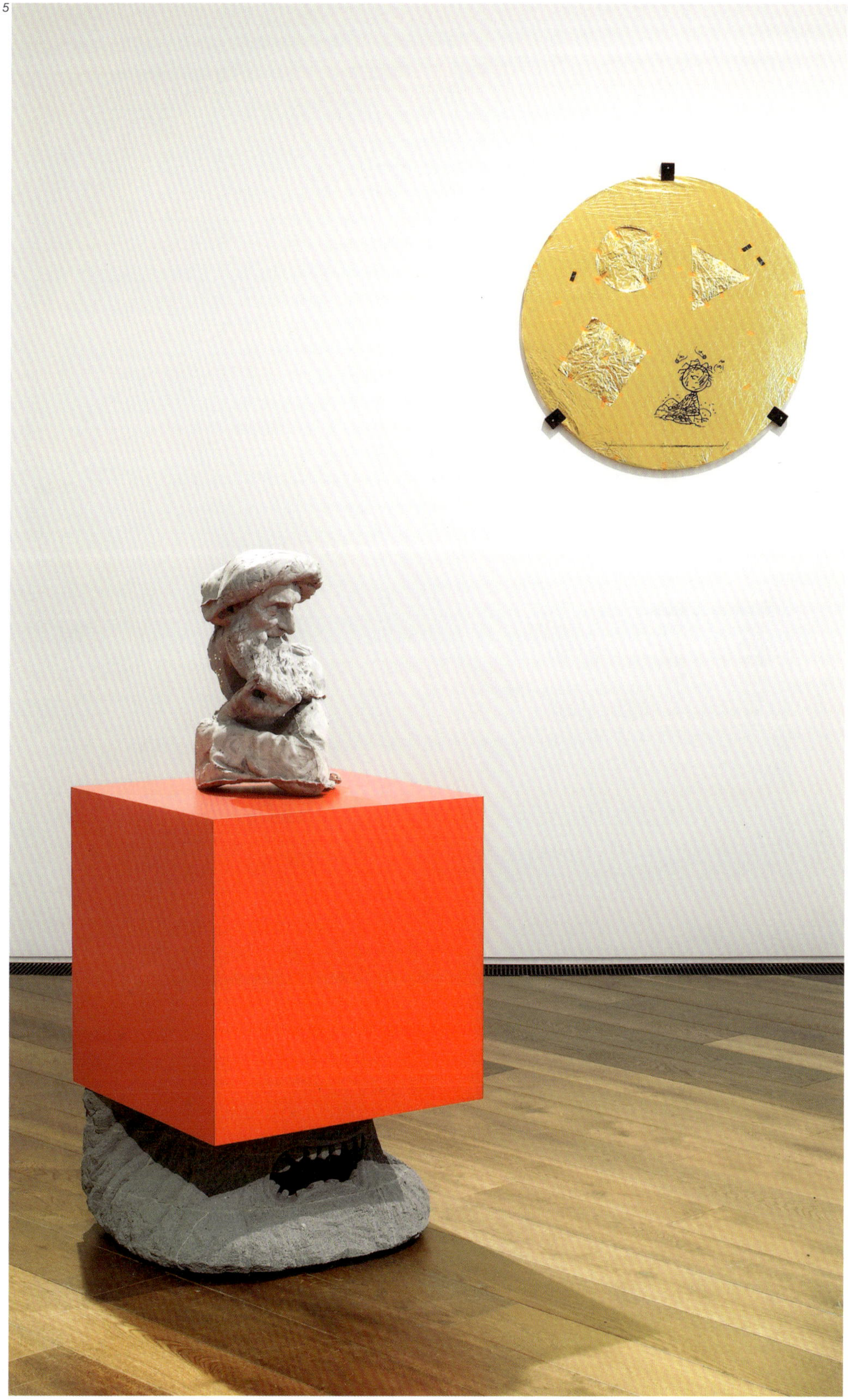

1- Alias
(because the pixels are arranged in an array...)
2012
Beeswax, brass fittings, pencil
174 panels, each 4.04 x 20 cm
Photo: Andy Keate

2- Alias
(because the pixels are arranged in an array...), detail
2012
Beeswax, brass fittings, pencil
174 panels, each 4.04 x 20 cm
Photo: Andy Keate

3,5 - Culpable Earth, installation view
2012
Photo: Andy Keate

4- Cell anima
(we need to look again at our kettles and tables)
2012
Acrylic animation wheel, felt-tip pen, pencil, paper,
tracing paper
44 x 44 x 5.5 cm
Photo: Andy Keate

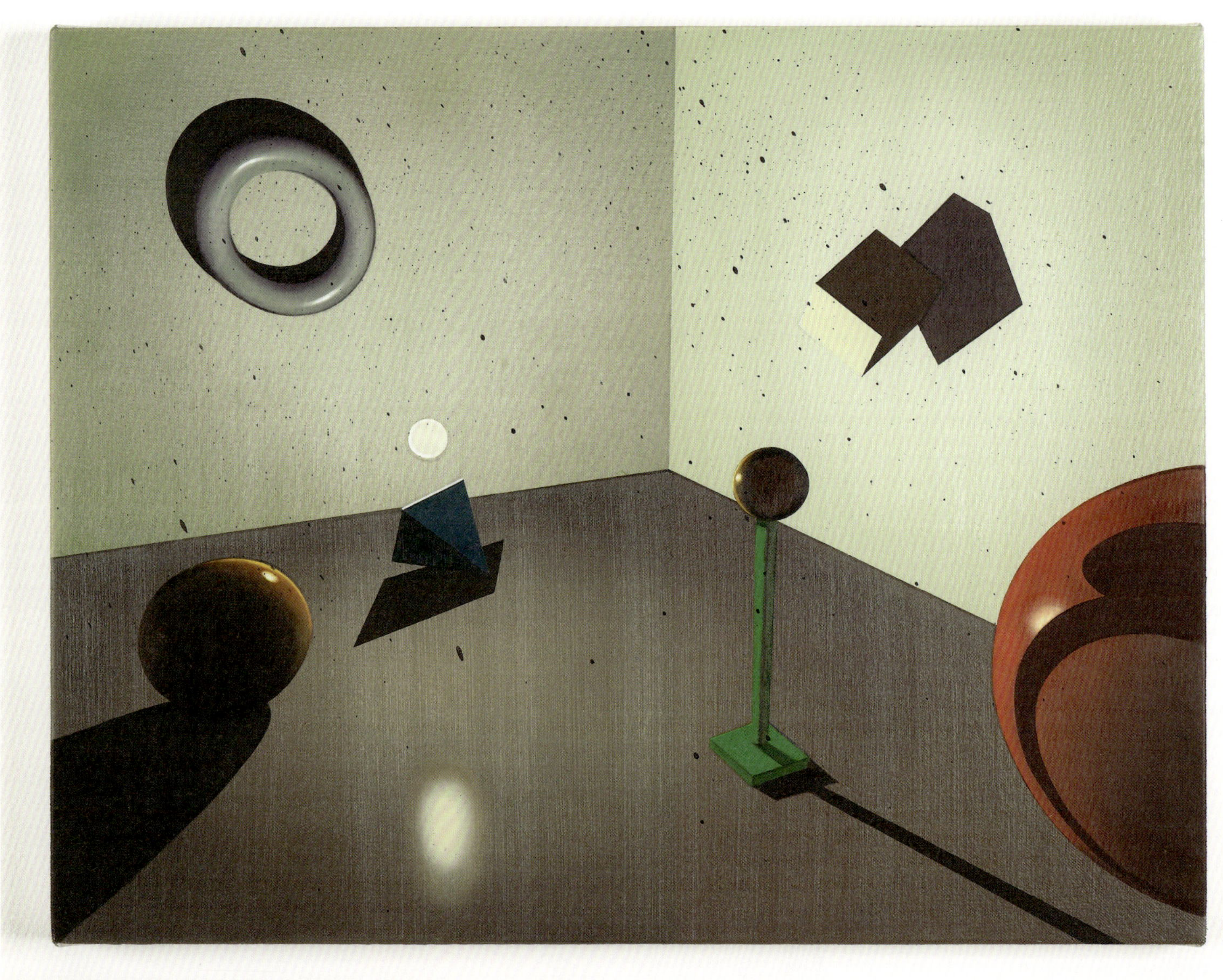

1- *The darkling interior of thingly space*
2012
Oil and spray paint on canvas
32 x 40 x 5 cm
Photo: Andy Keate

2- *Confections in orbit*
(mailbox, spider, gumdrop)
2012
Formica, aluminium, gum rubber, brass, acrylic,
polyurethane foam, Kapton tape, Mylar, ceramic, wood,
brick-kiln slag, buckshot bauxite, powder coated steel,
resin, hessian, silicone, towelling
Dimensions variable / plinth 200 x 200 x 240 cm
Photo: Andy Keate

3- *Confections in orbit*
(mailbox, spider, gumdrop), detail
2012
Formica, aluminium, gum rubber, brass, acrylic,
polyurethane foam, Kapton tape, Mylar, ceramic, wood,
brick-kiln slag, buckshot bauxite, powder coated steel,
resin, hessian, silicone, towelling
Dimensions variable / plinth 200 x 200 x 240 cm
Photo: Andy Keate

2

3

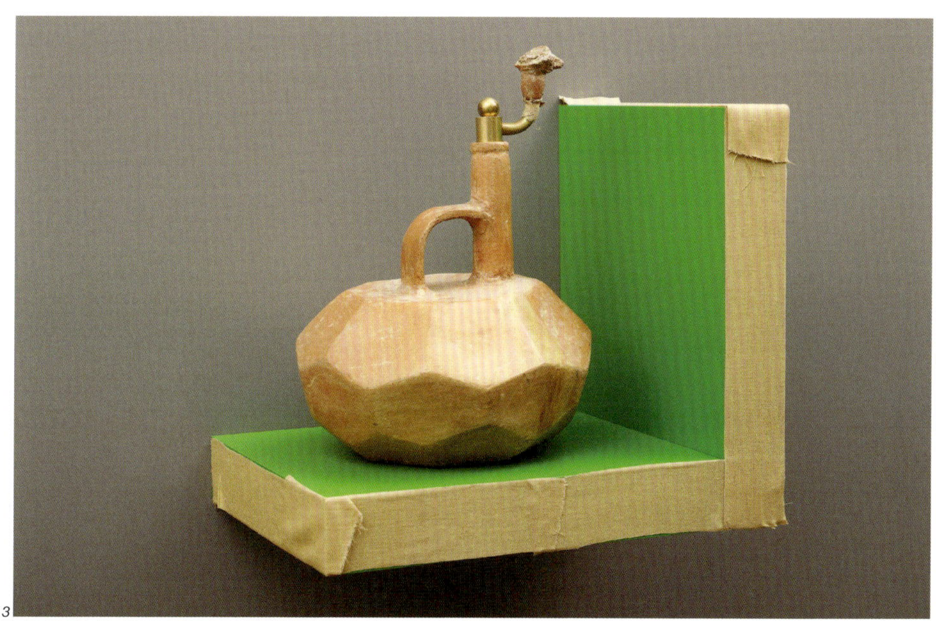

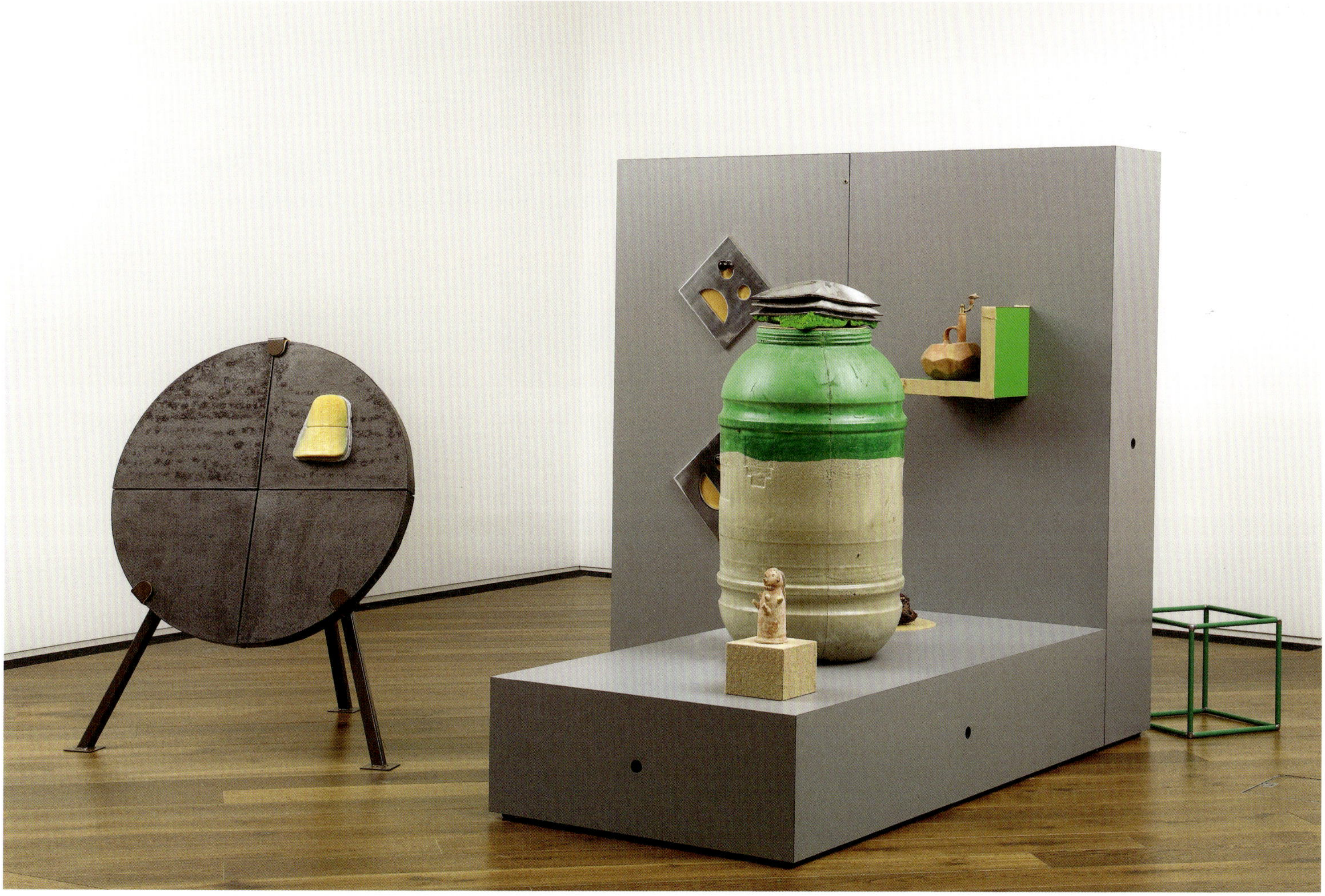

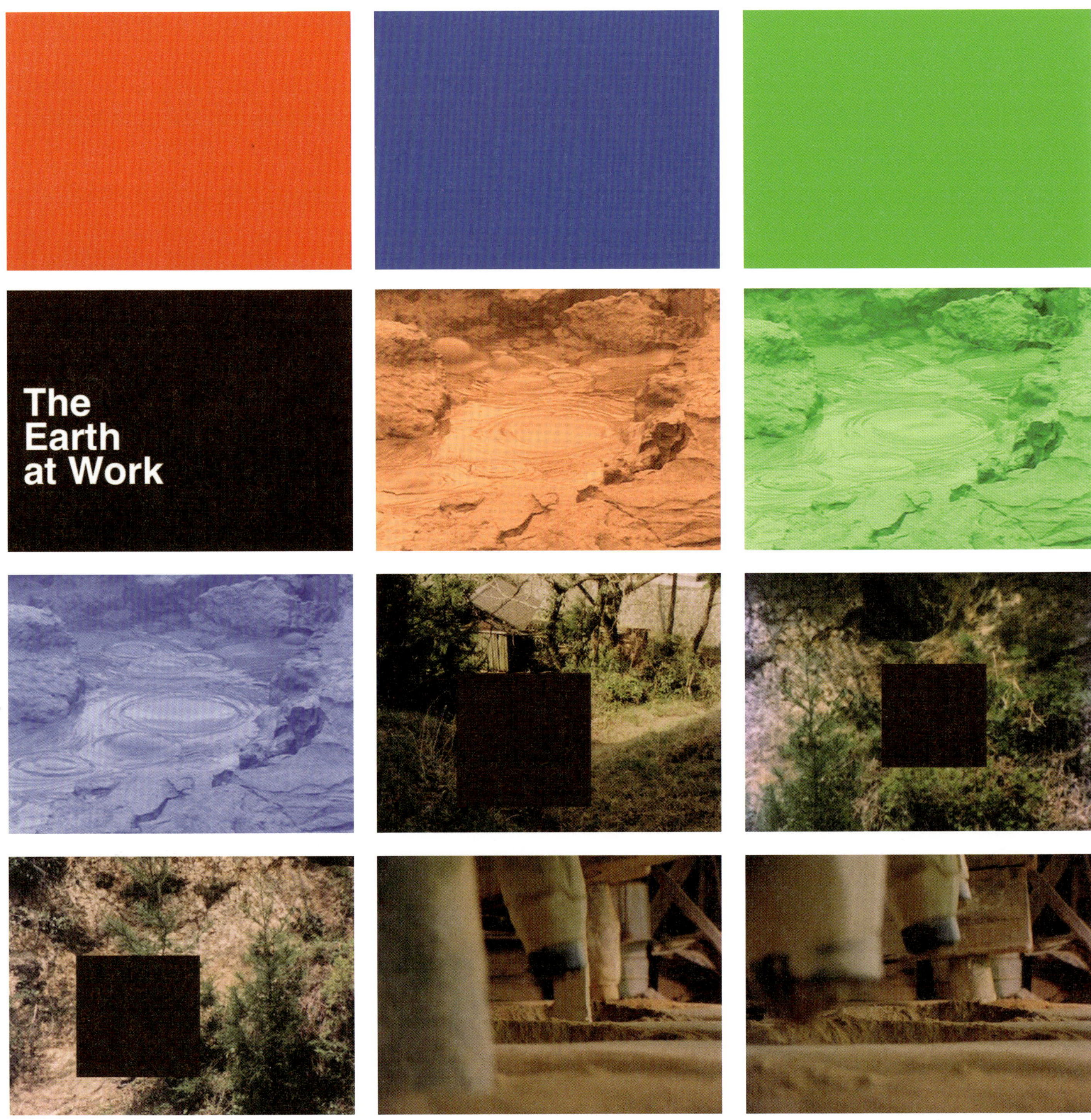

The
Earth
at Work

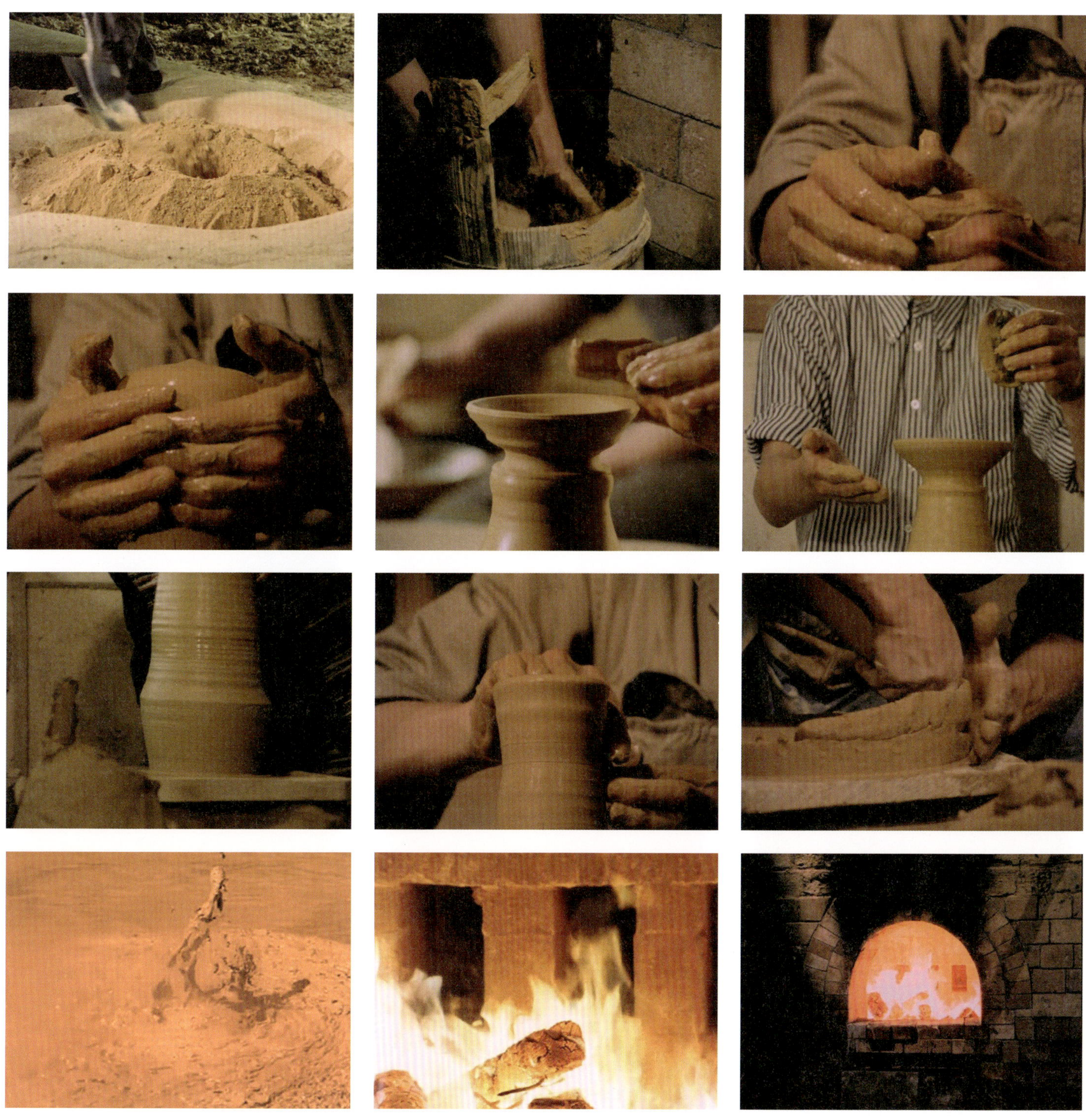

The Earth at Work
2012
Video (13 minutes) on Sony cube monitors, flight cases,
powder coated steel, ceramic, wood, parcel tape
Dimensions variable

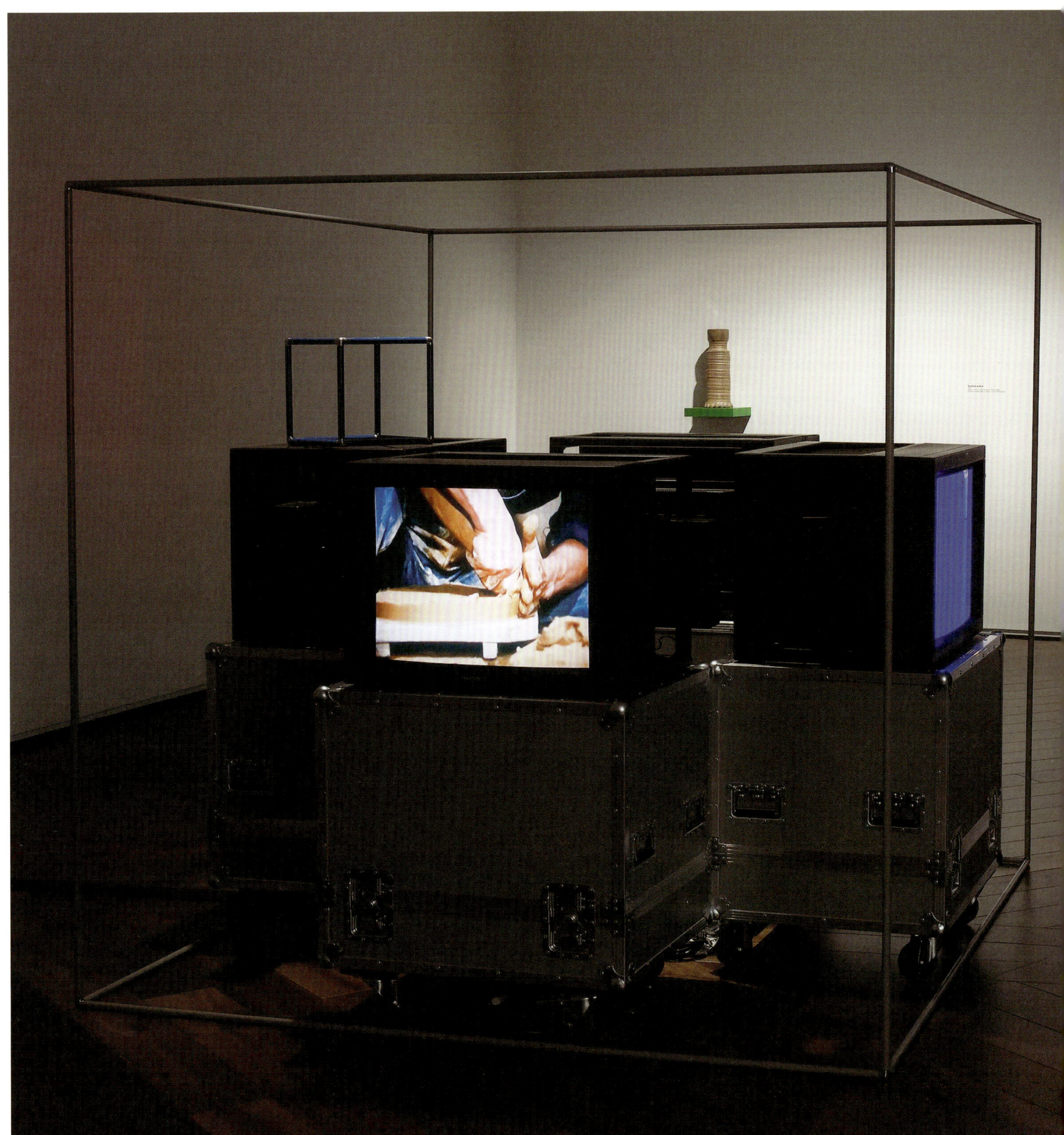

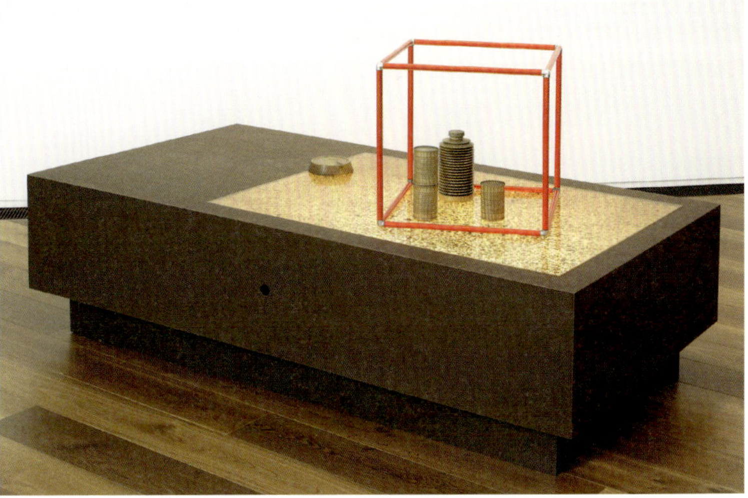

1- Whence things derive their coming into being
2012
Wood, Formica, shredded money in resin, powder
coated steel, aluminium, fluorescent tubes
55 x 100 x 200 cm
Photo: Andy Keate

2- Culpable Earth, installation view
2012
Photo: Andy Keate

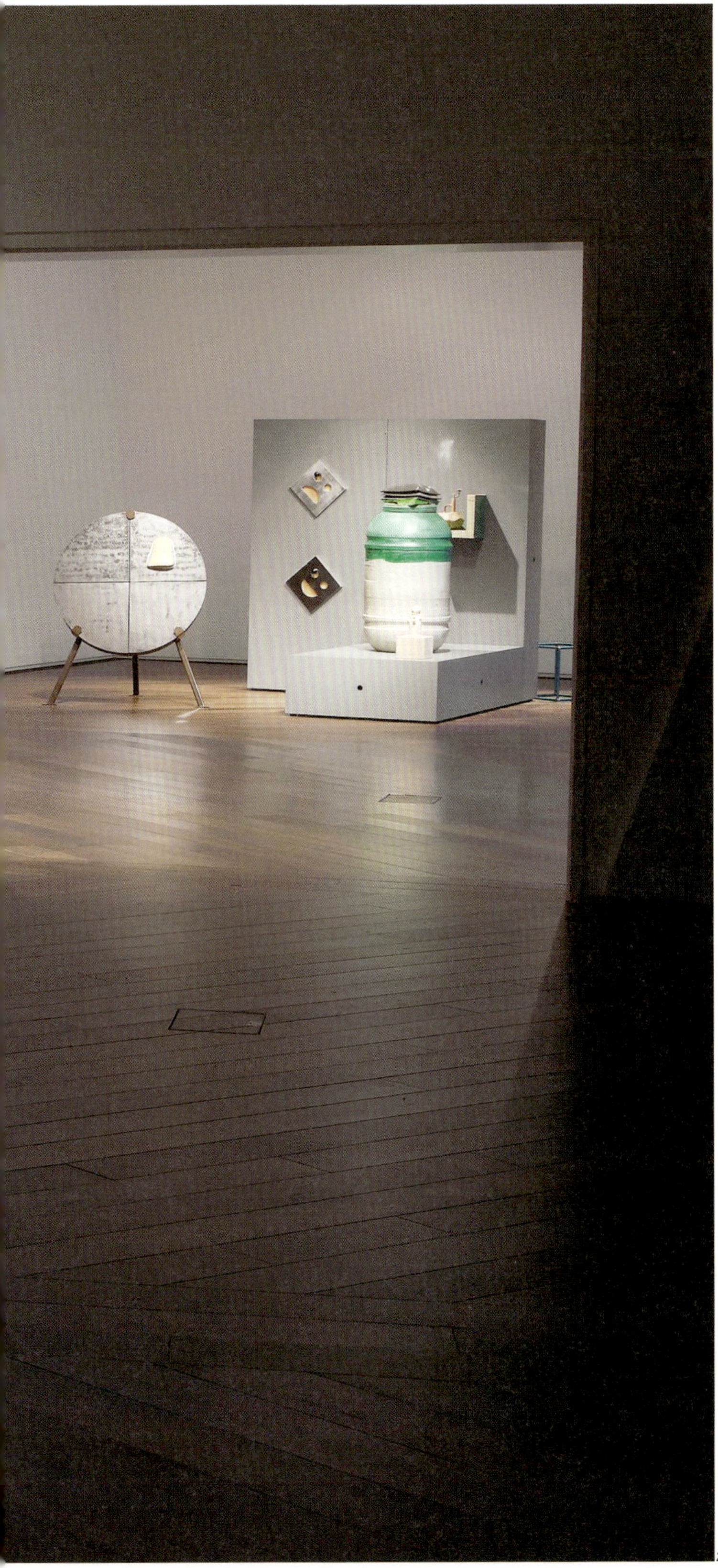

LIAF, Kabelvag

Something in the way

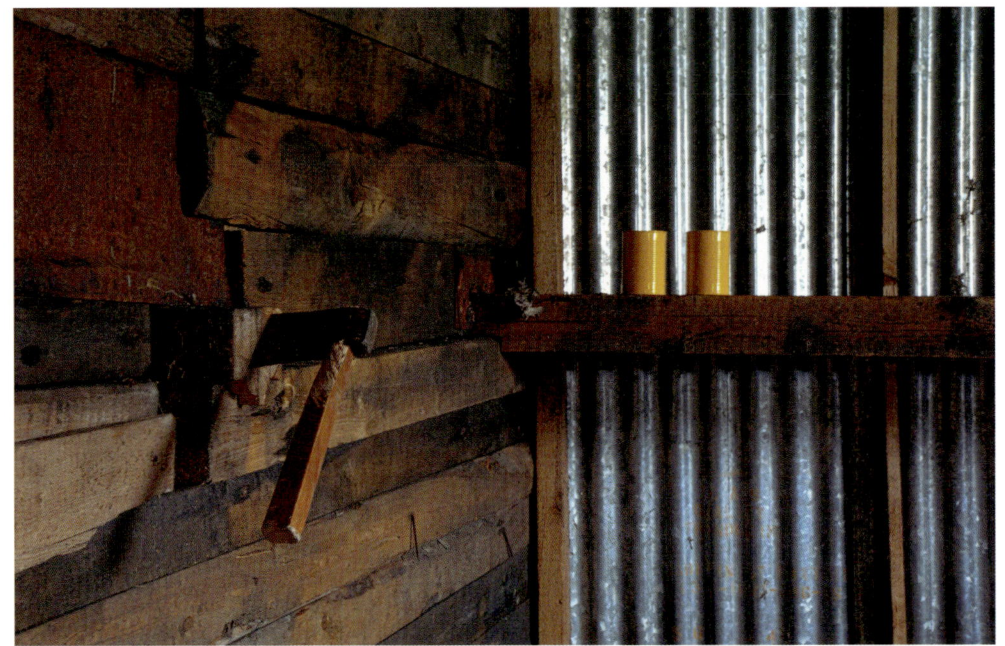

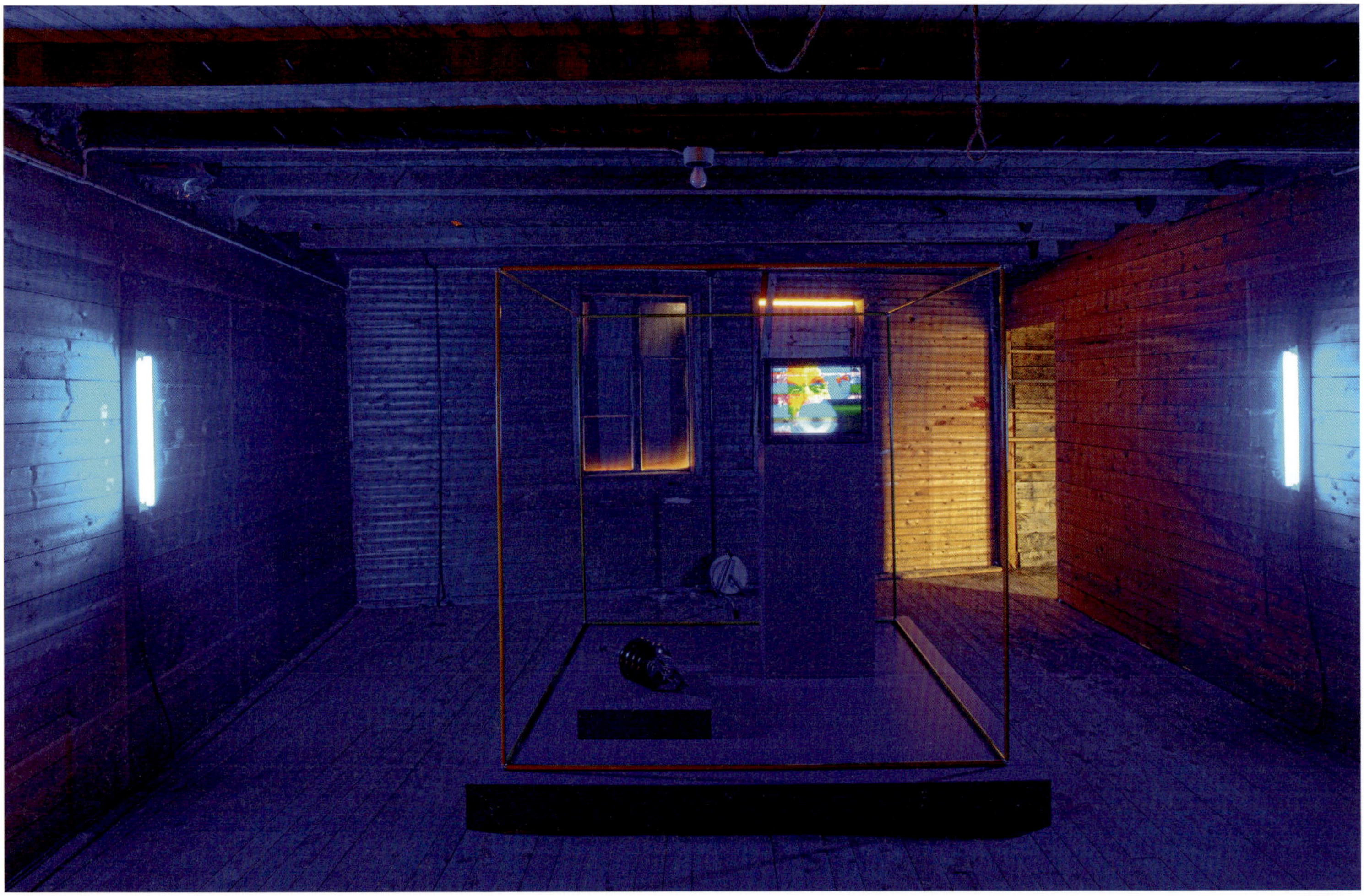

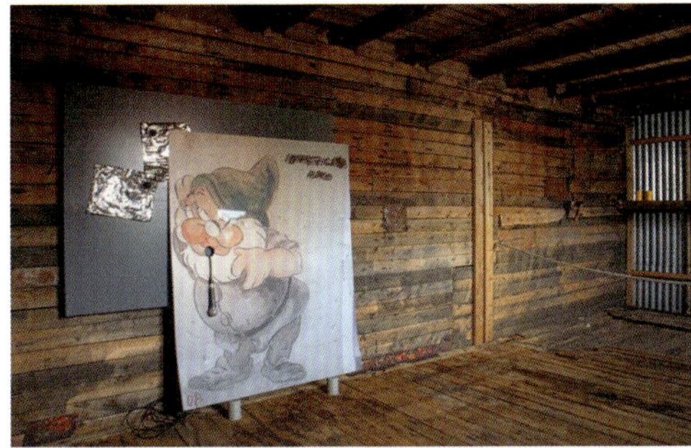

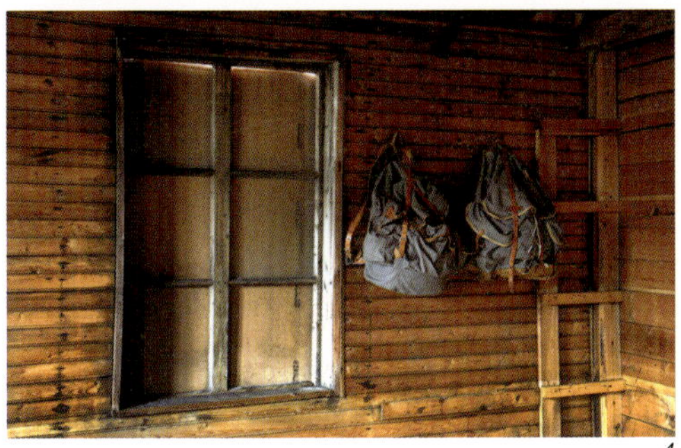

3
4
5

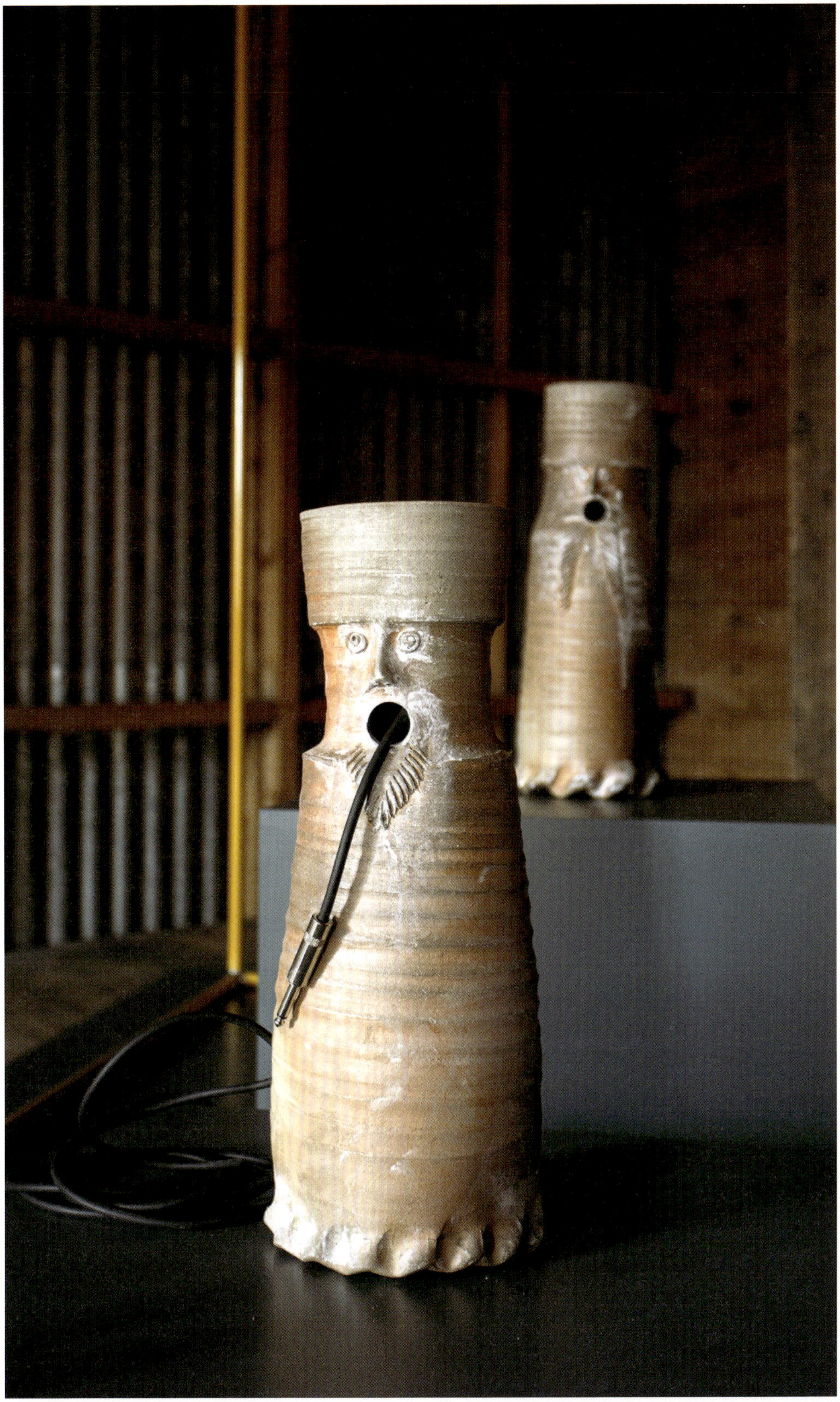

1- Whistle while you work, detail
2011
Mixed media installation
Dimensions variable
Photo: Jason Havneraas

2- The ancient set deployed
2008/11
Mixed media installation
200 x 200 cm
Photo: Jason Havneraas

3-4 - Whistle while you work, detail
2011
Mixed media installation
Dimensions variable
Photo: Jason Havneraas

5- The thingly vehicle (Migrated and in array), detail
2011
Mixed media installation
Dimensions variable
Photo: Jason Havneraas

Following pages:
Whistle while you work, detail
2011
Mixed media installation
Dimensions variable
Photo: Jason Havneraas

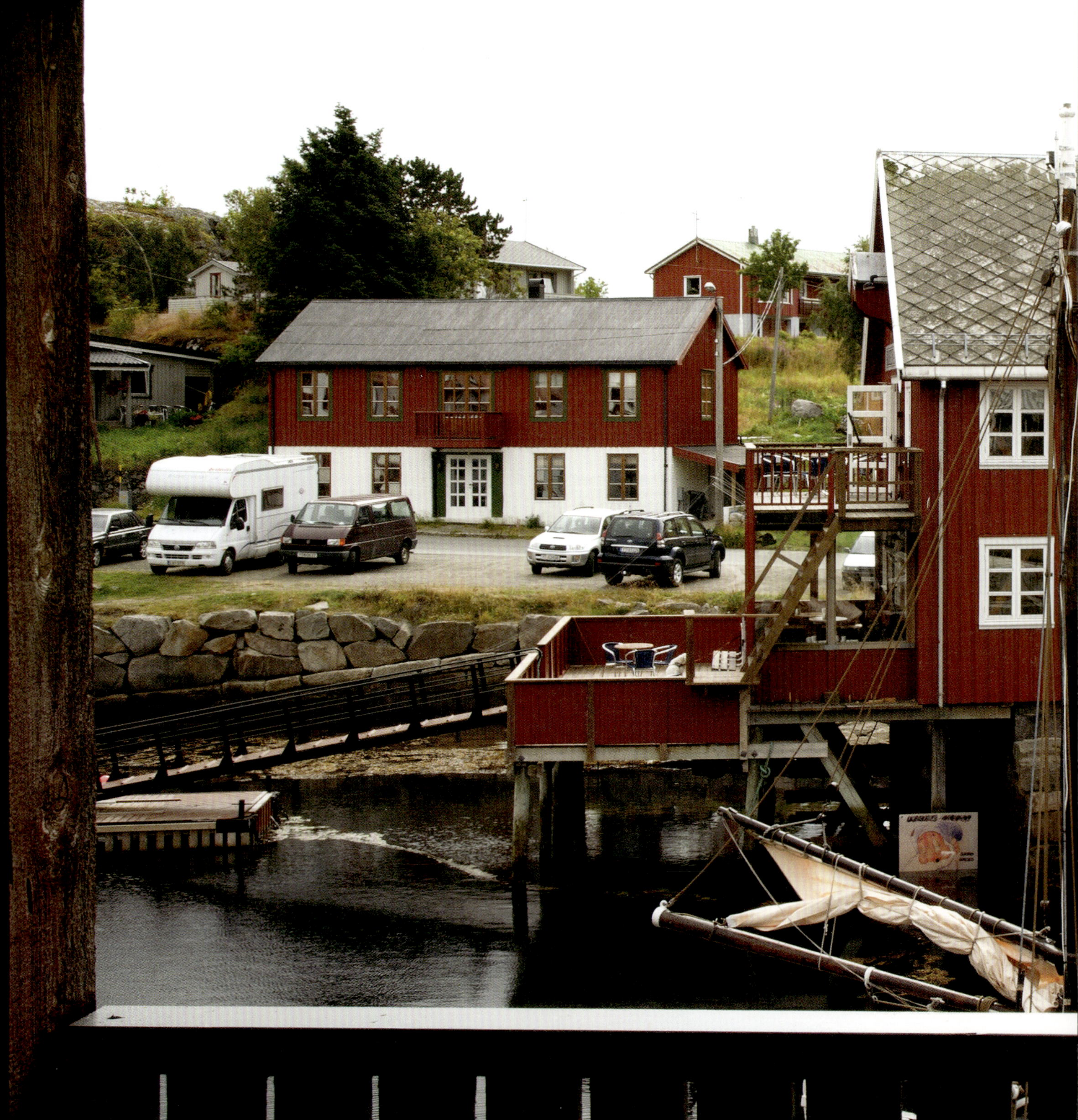

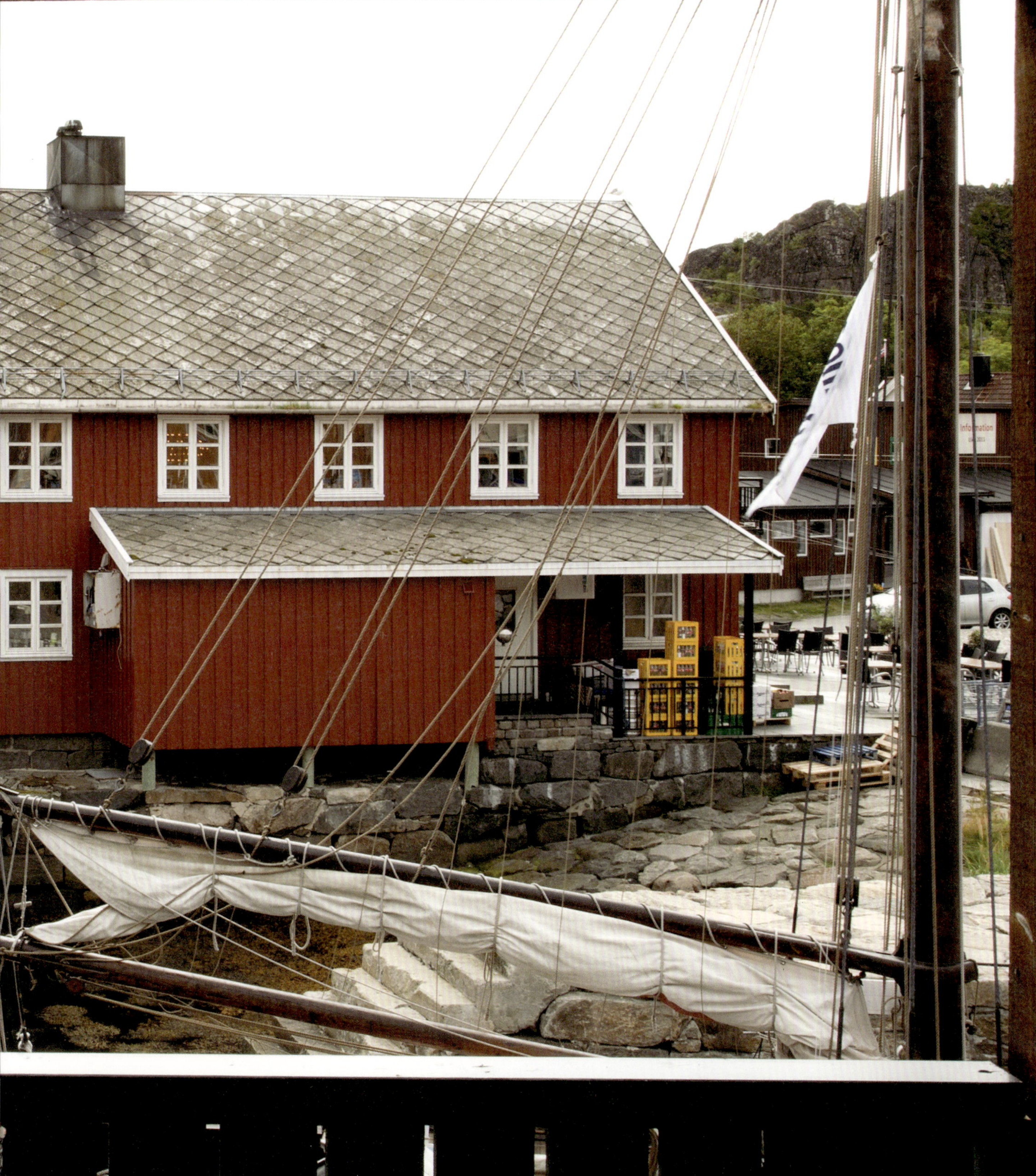

Kimmerich, New York

Twickenham Garden

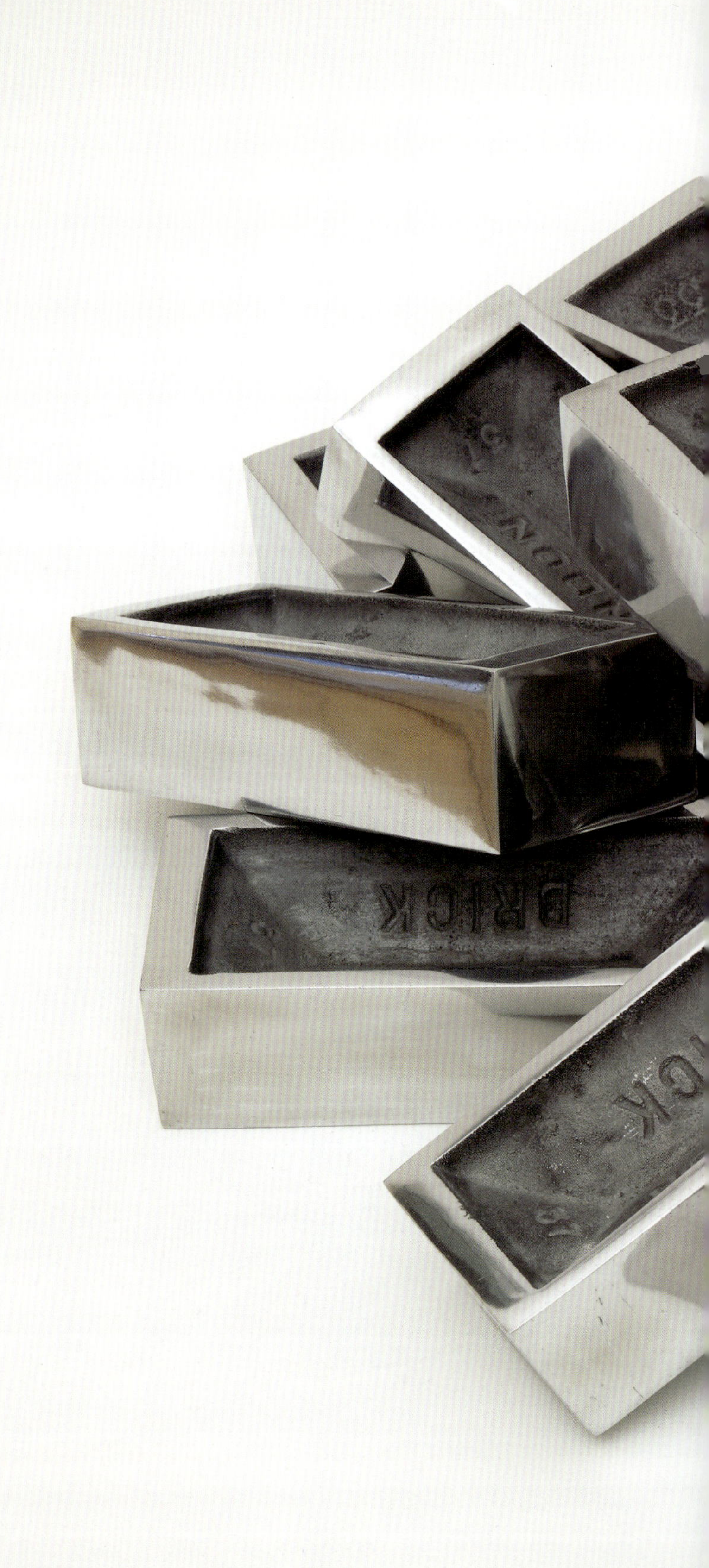

London Pixel
2010
Aluminium
Dimensions variable
Photo: Thomas Müller

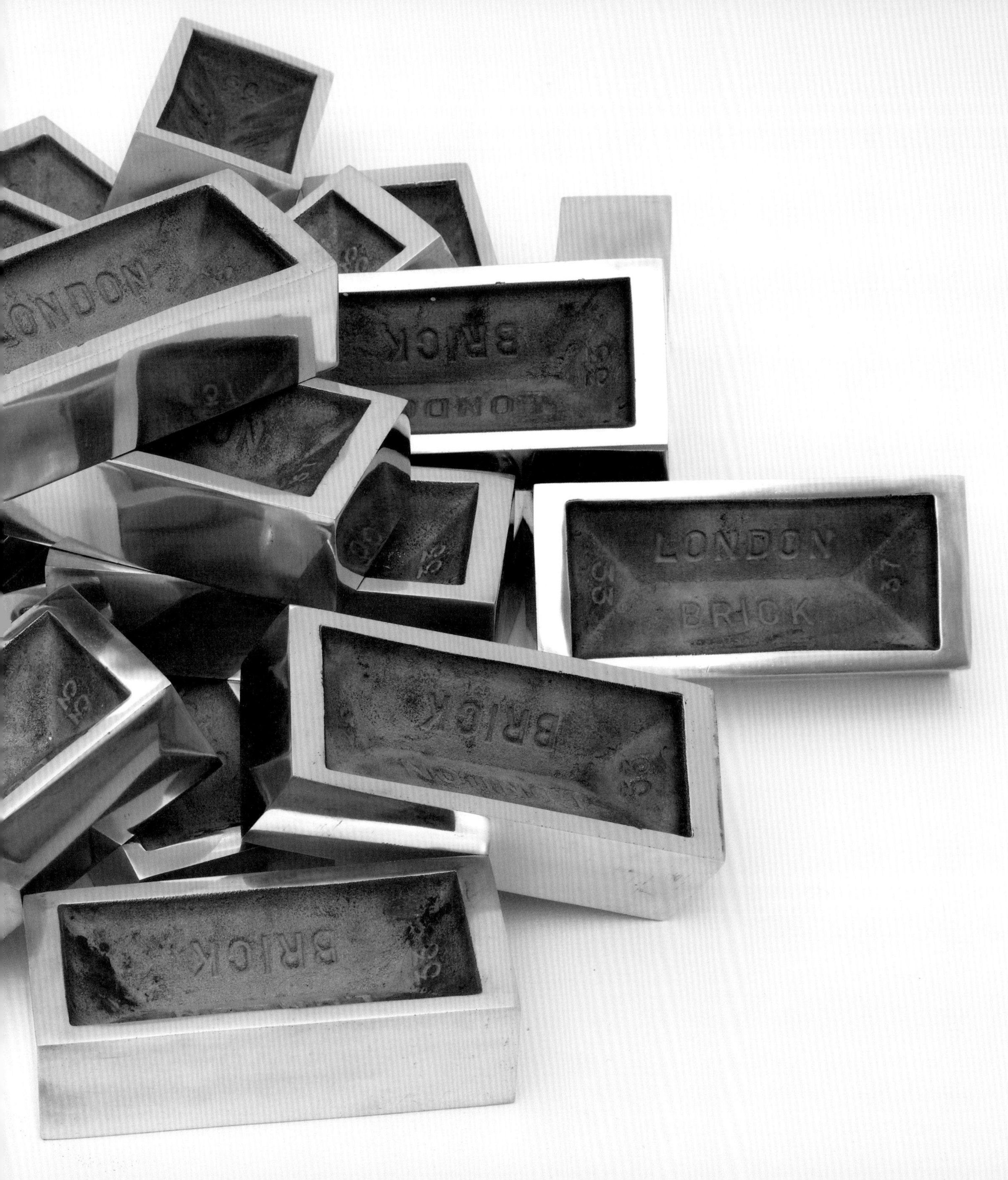

LONDON
BRICK
BRICK
LONDON
LONDON
BRICK
BRICK

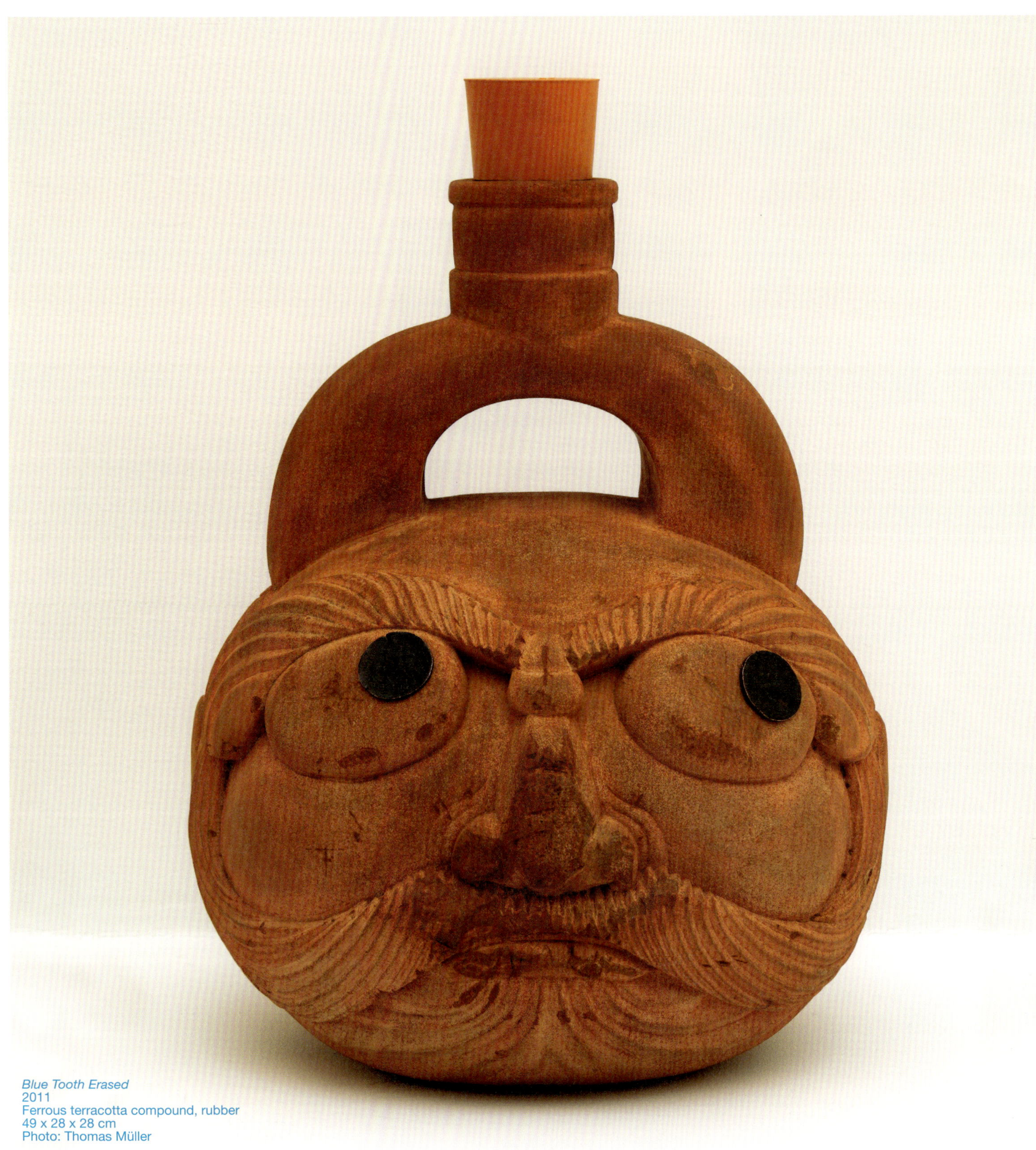

Blue Tooth Erased
2011
Ferrous terracotta compound, rubber
49 x 28 x 28 cm
Photo: Thomas Müller

20

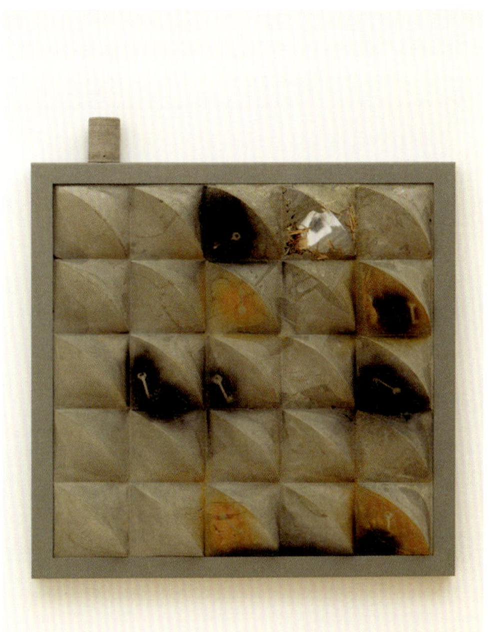

1

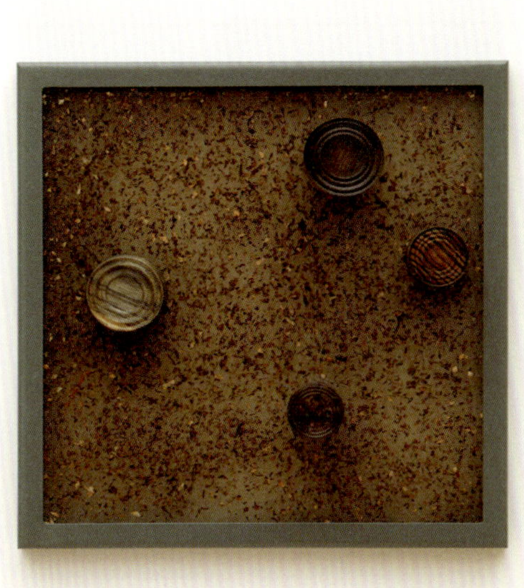

3

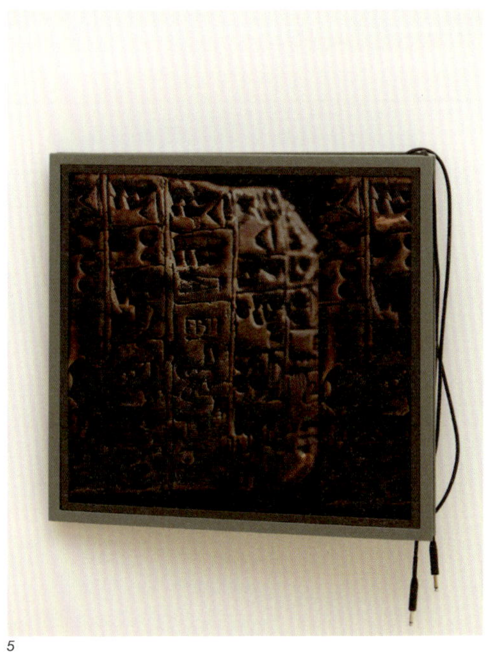

5

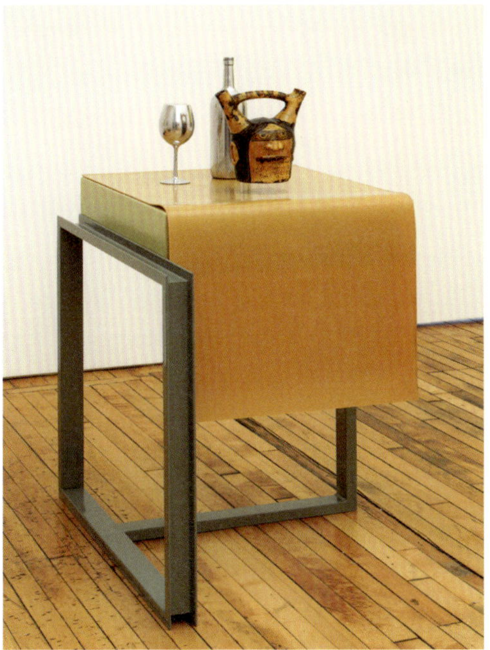

2

4

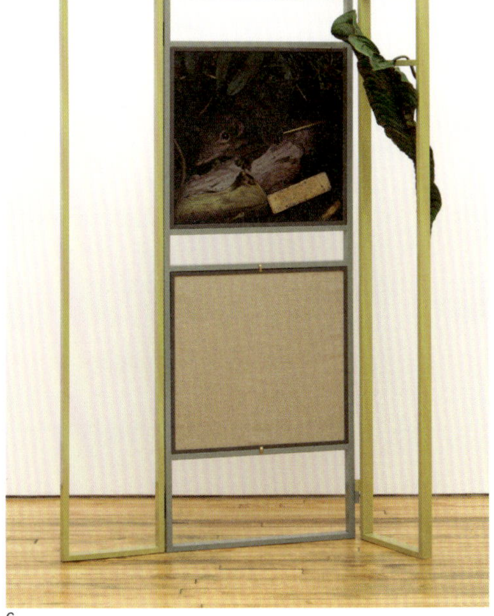

6

1- Trom, Trom, Trom
2010
Powder coated steel, aluminium, foam, spray paint,
straw, concrete
97 x 97 x 16 cm
Photo: Thomas Müller

2- Concorde
2011
Powder coated steel, natural gum rubber, ceramic,
aluminium, Plexiglas
124.5 x 90.2 x 67.3 cm
Photo: Thomas Müller

3- Corpuscles in Climate
2011
Powder coated steel, wood, resin, paper currency
62 x 62 cm
Photo: Thomas Müller

4- Drawing
2011
Powder coated steel
140 x 140 cm
Photo: Thomas Müller

5- Purple List
2011
Powder coated steel, oil on canvas, 1/4" audio cable,
Plexiglas, brass
64 x 64 x 18.5 cm
Photo: Thomas Müller

6- A Twickenham Garden
2011
Powder coated steel, oil on canvas, ceramic, hessian,
plastic, brass
185.4 x 38 x 114 cm
Photo: Thomas Müller

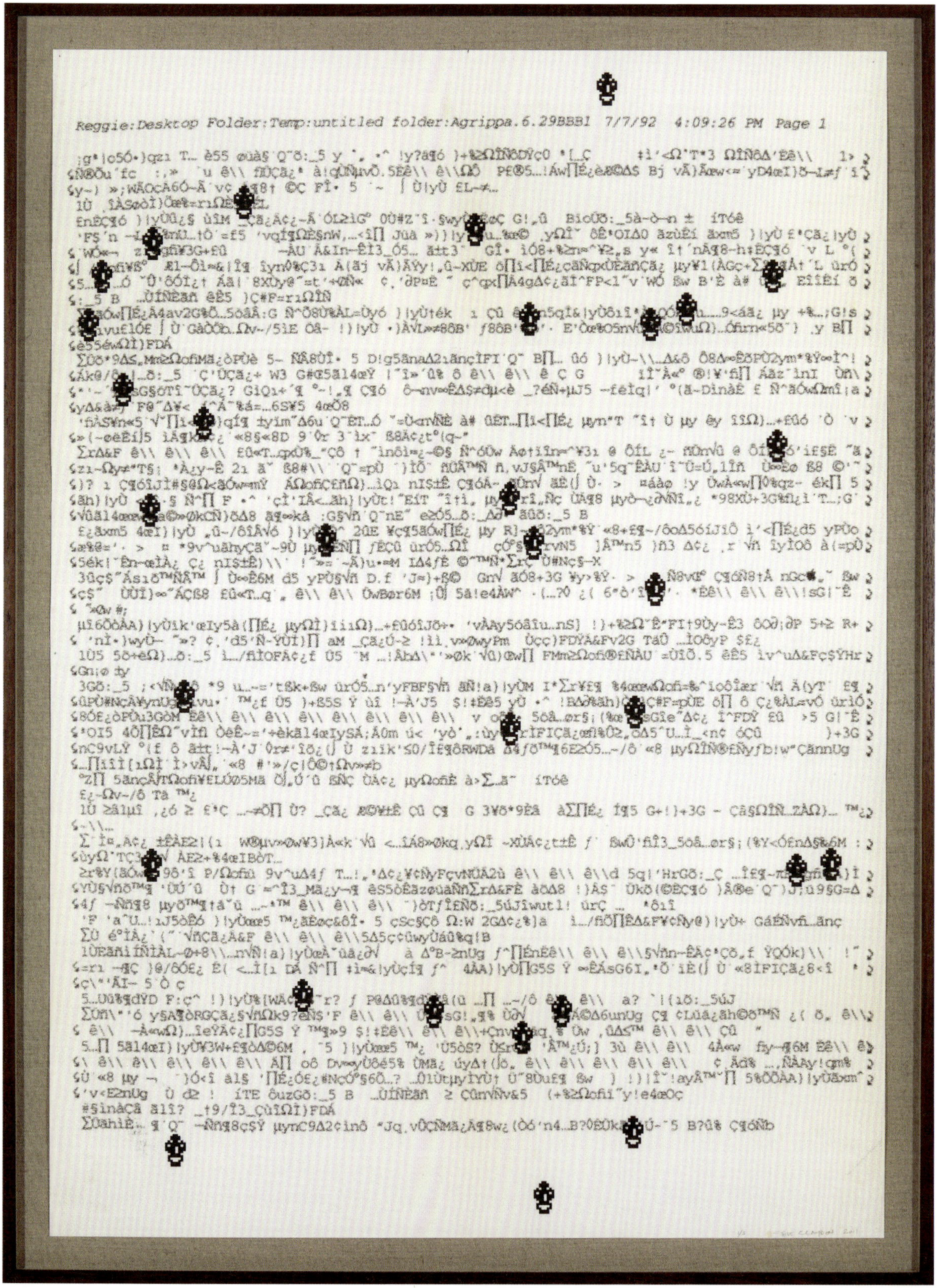

Reggie:Desktop Folder:Temp:untitled folder:Agrippa.6.29BBB1 7/7/92   4:09:26 PM Page 1

Poisoned Orchard
2011
Cooked carbon print mounted on linen
118 x 82 cm
Photo: Thomas Müller

Elements in Perfidy
2011
Carbon print mounted on linen
118 x 82 cm
Photo: Thomas Müller

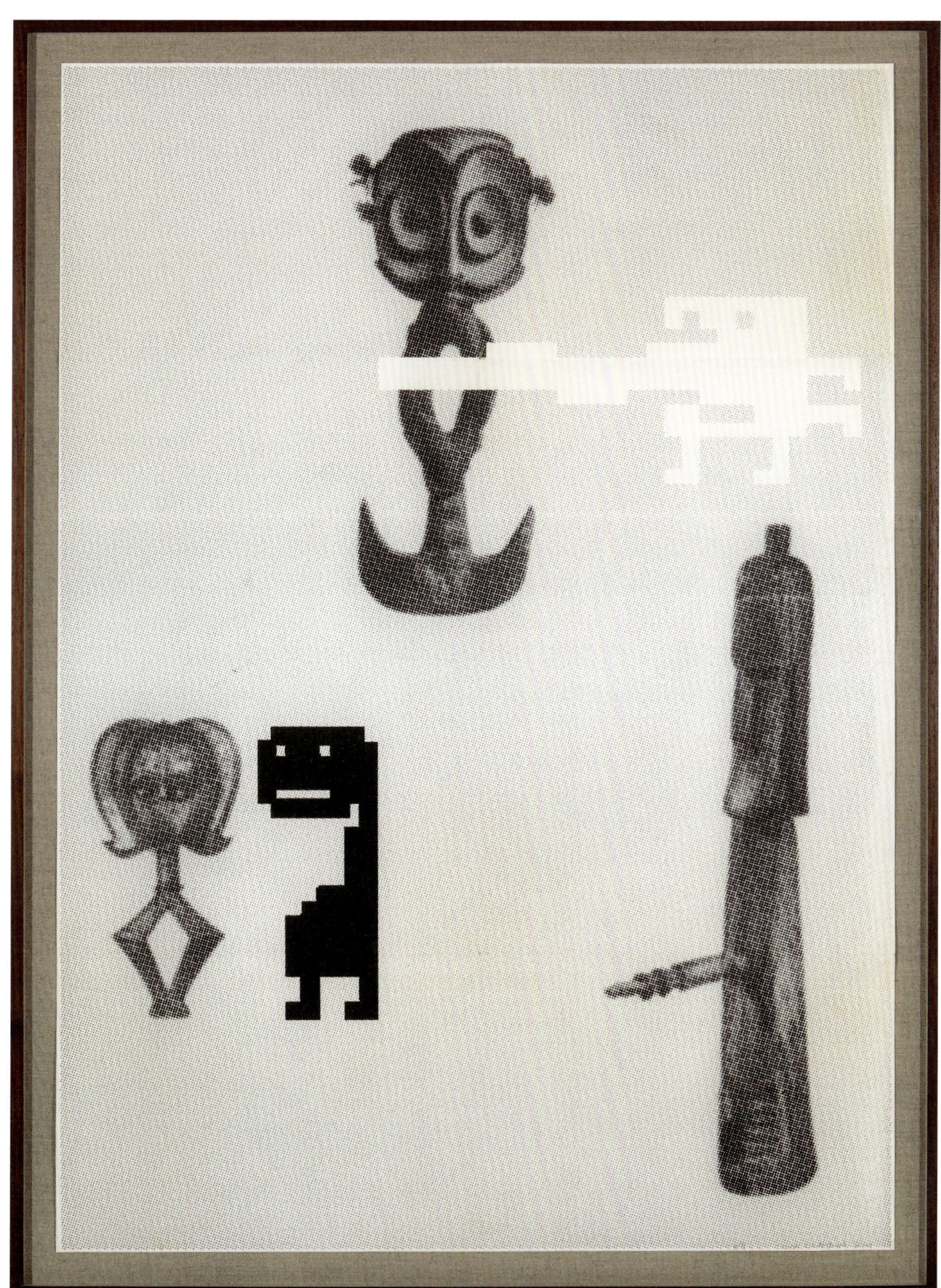

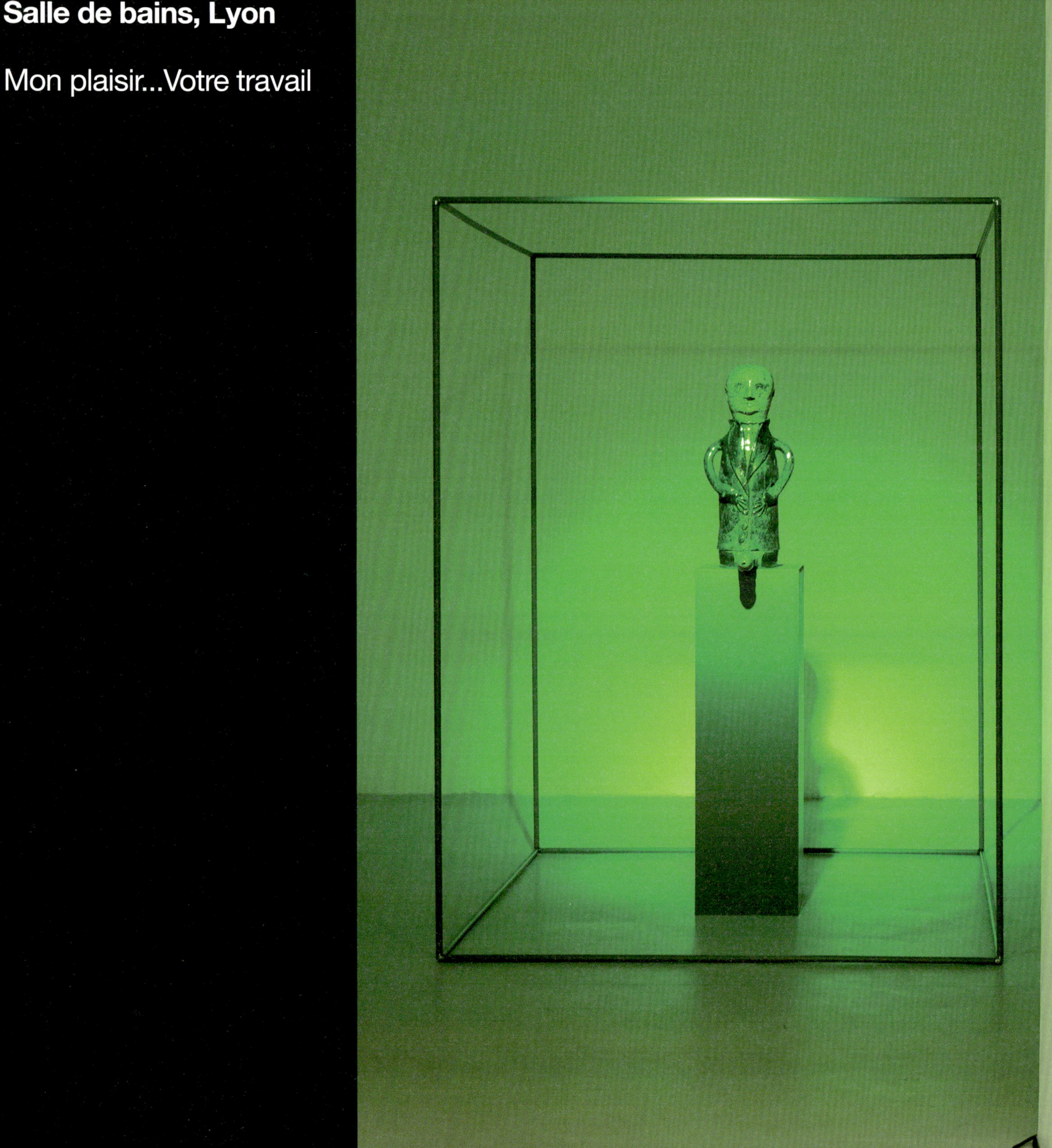

Salle de bains, Lyon
Mon plaisir...Votre travail

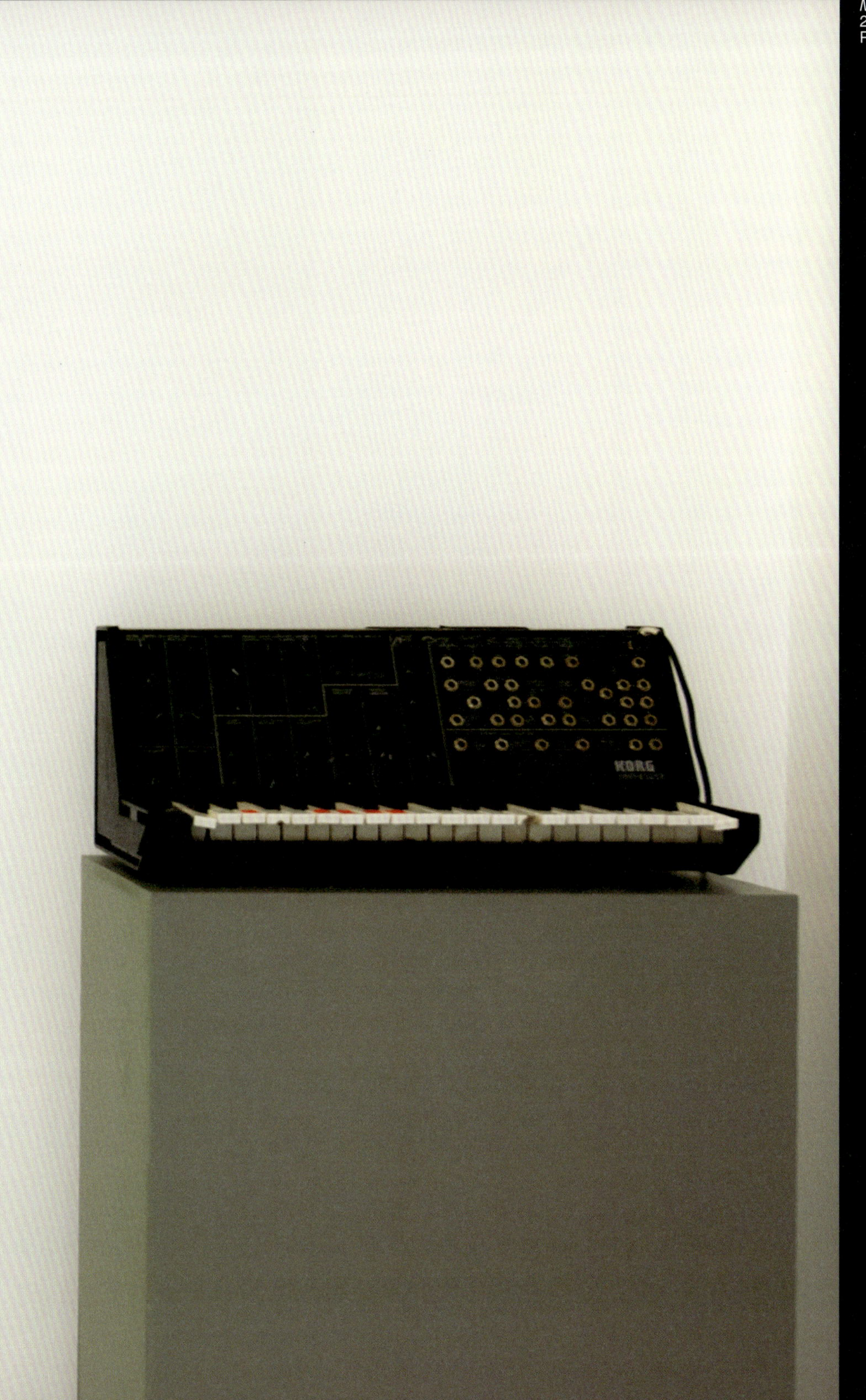

Mon plaisir...Votre travail, installation view
2011
Photo: Aurélie Leplatre

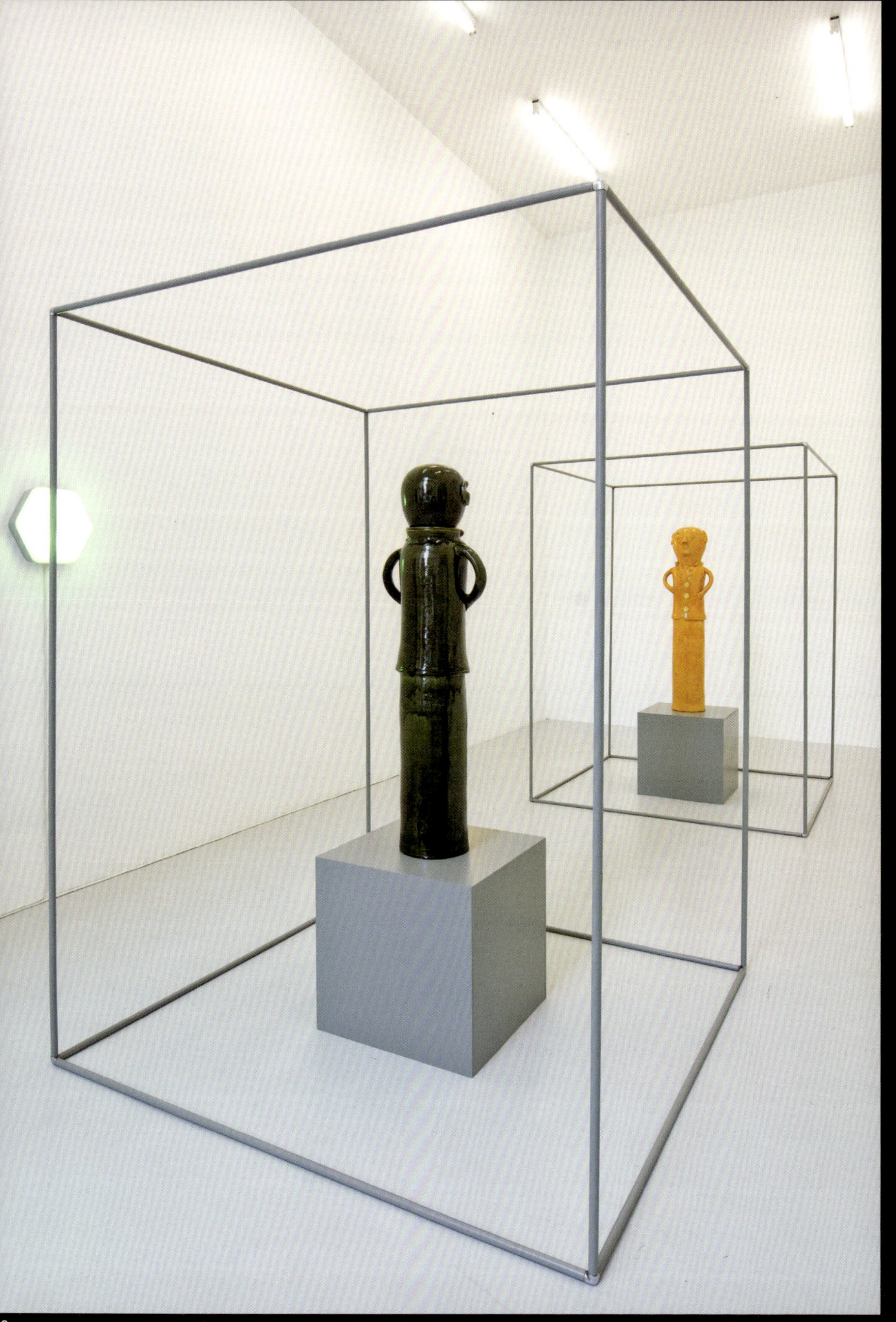

Mon plaisir...Votre travail, installation views
2011
Photo: Aurélie Leplatre

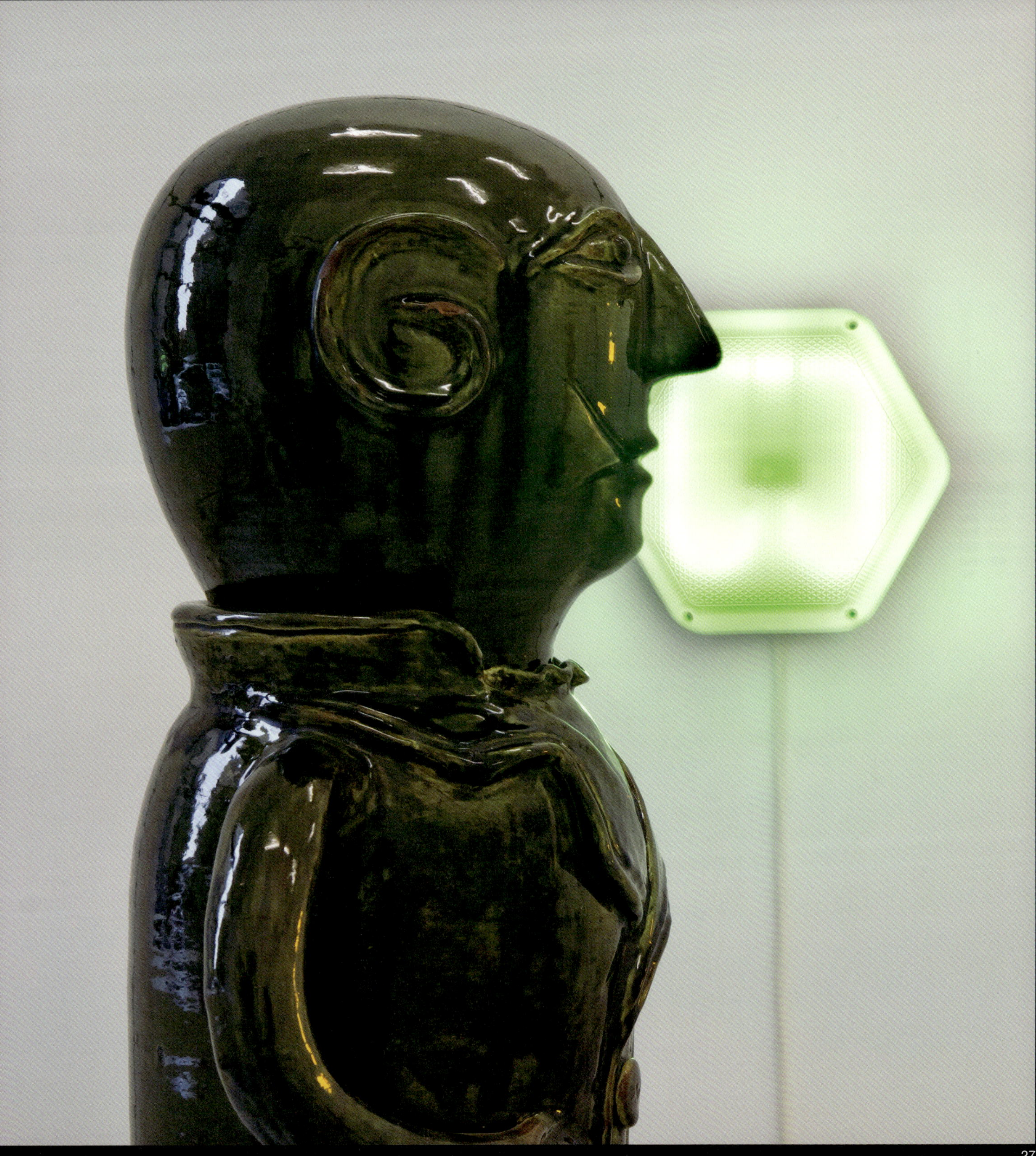

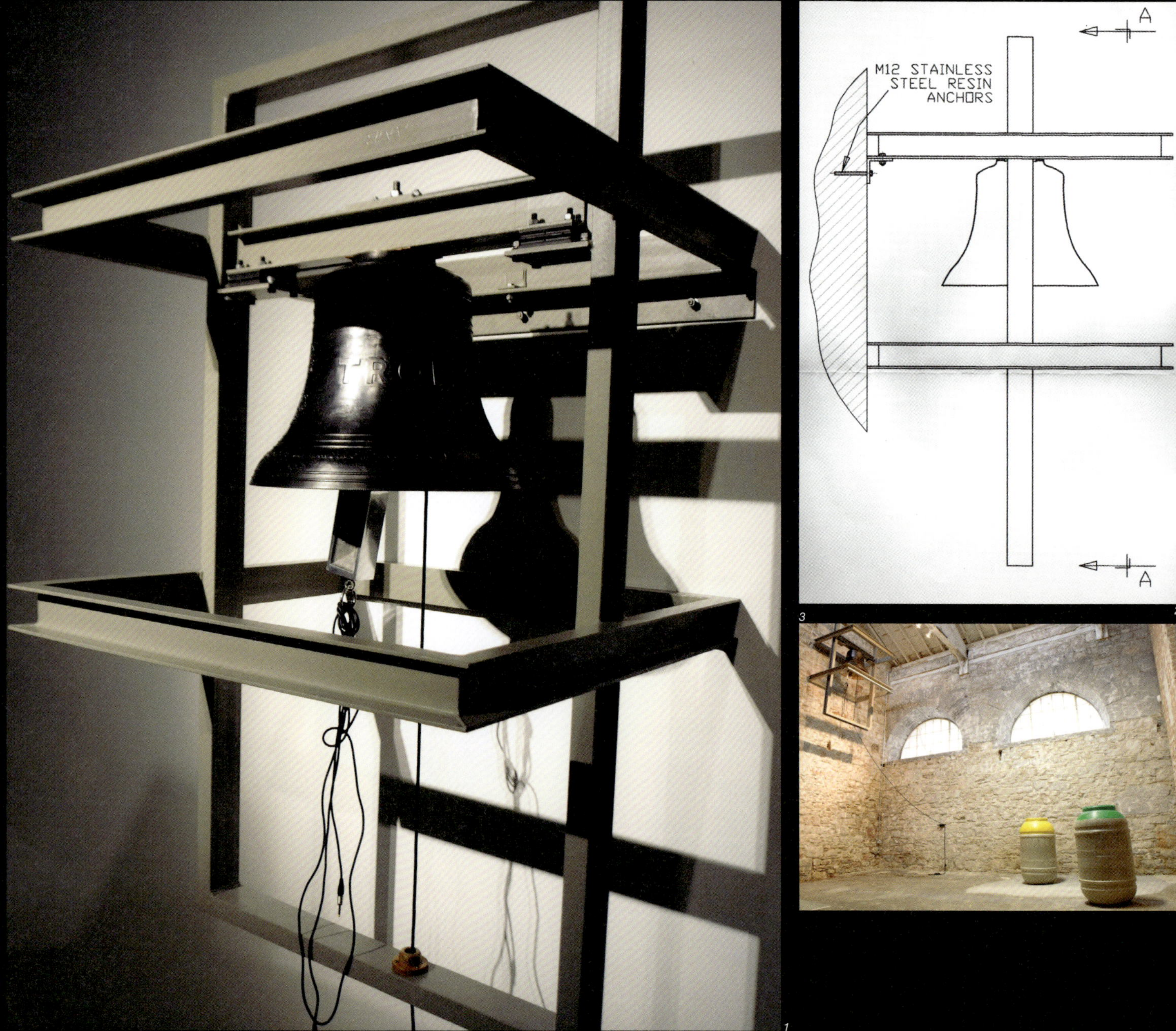
M12 STAINLESS
STEEL RESIN
ANCHORS
A
A
1
2
3

B   B

614
(24.2" dia.)

2000

1000

4 @ 230
M12 STAINLESS STEEL
RESIN ANCHORS

1100

1000

1000

1100

1200

VIEW ON B-B

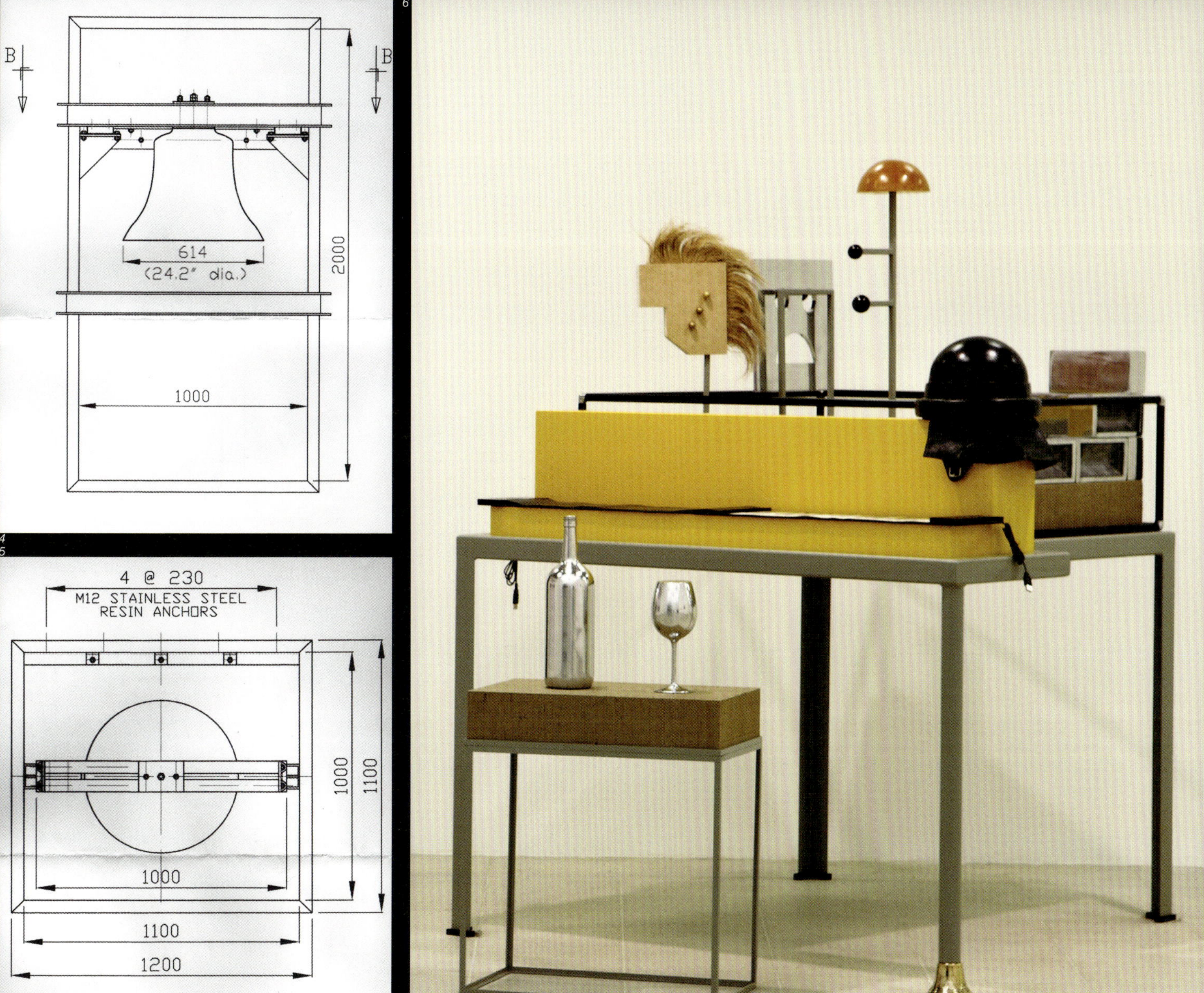

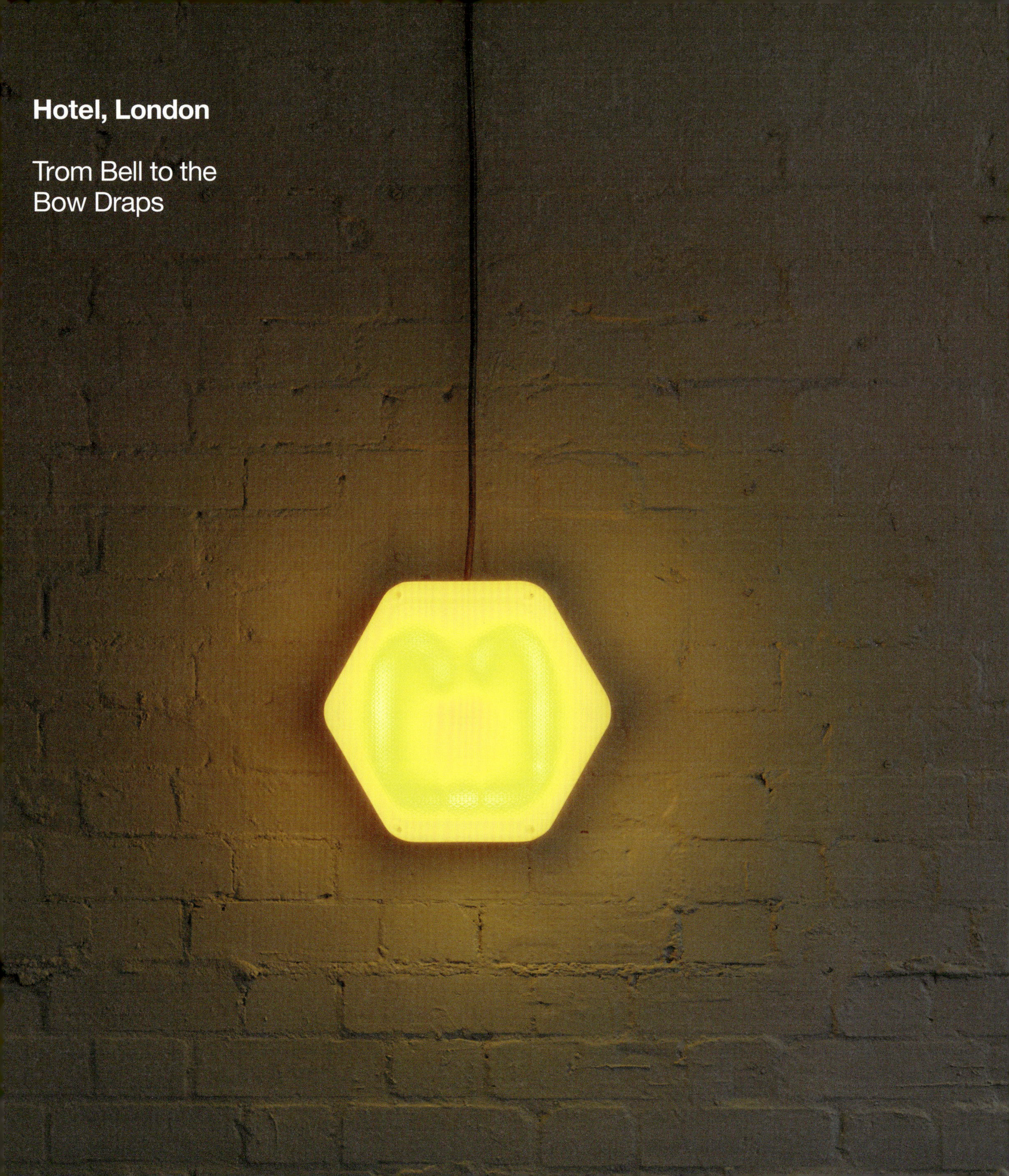

Hotel, London

Trom Bell to the
Bow Draps

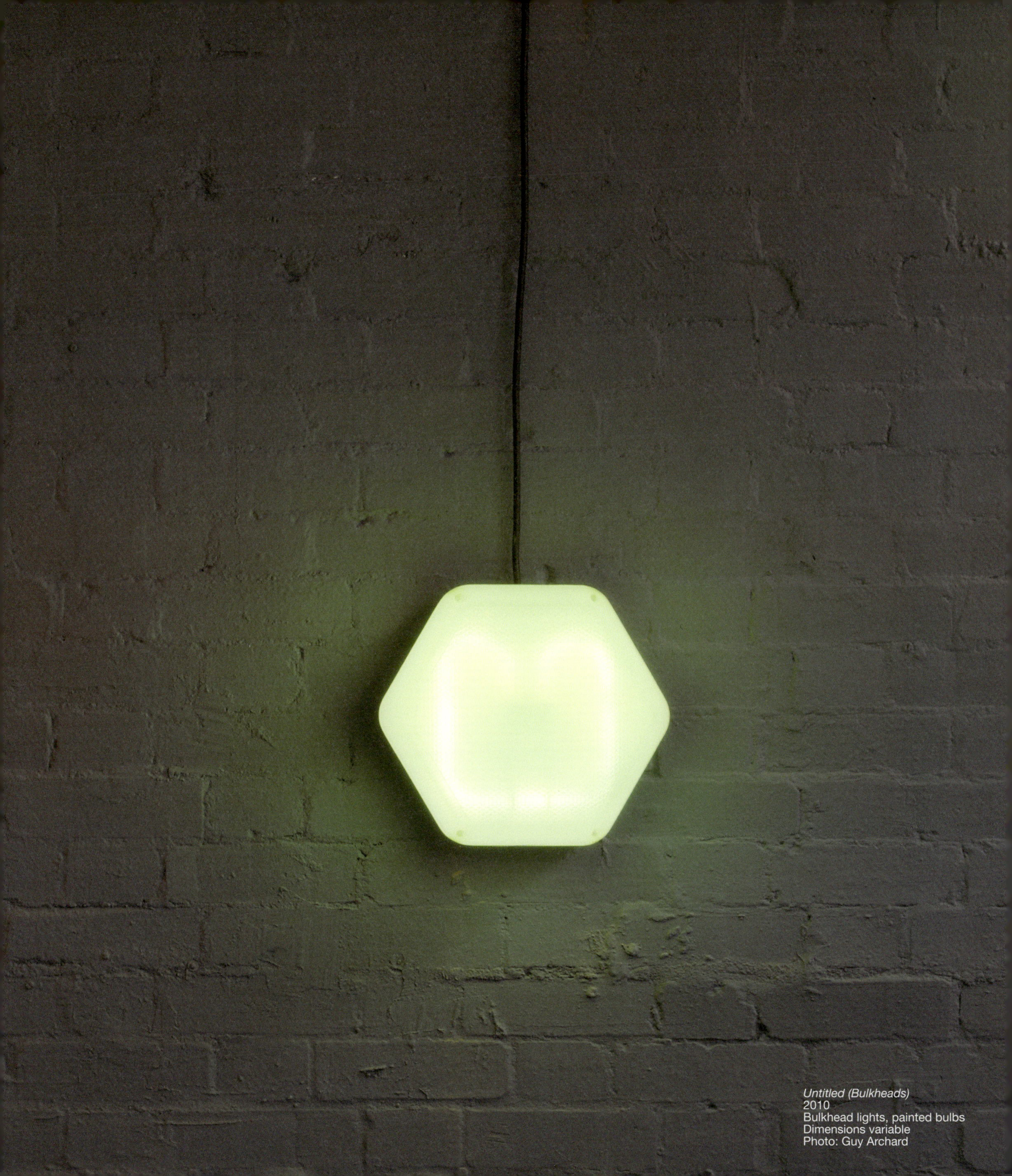

Untitled (Bulkheads)
2010
Bulkhead lights, painted bulbs
Dimensions variable
Photo: Guy Archard

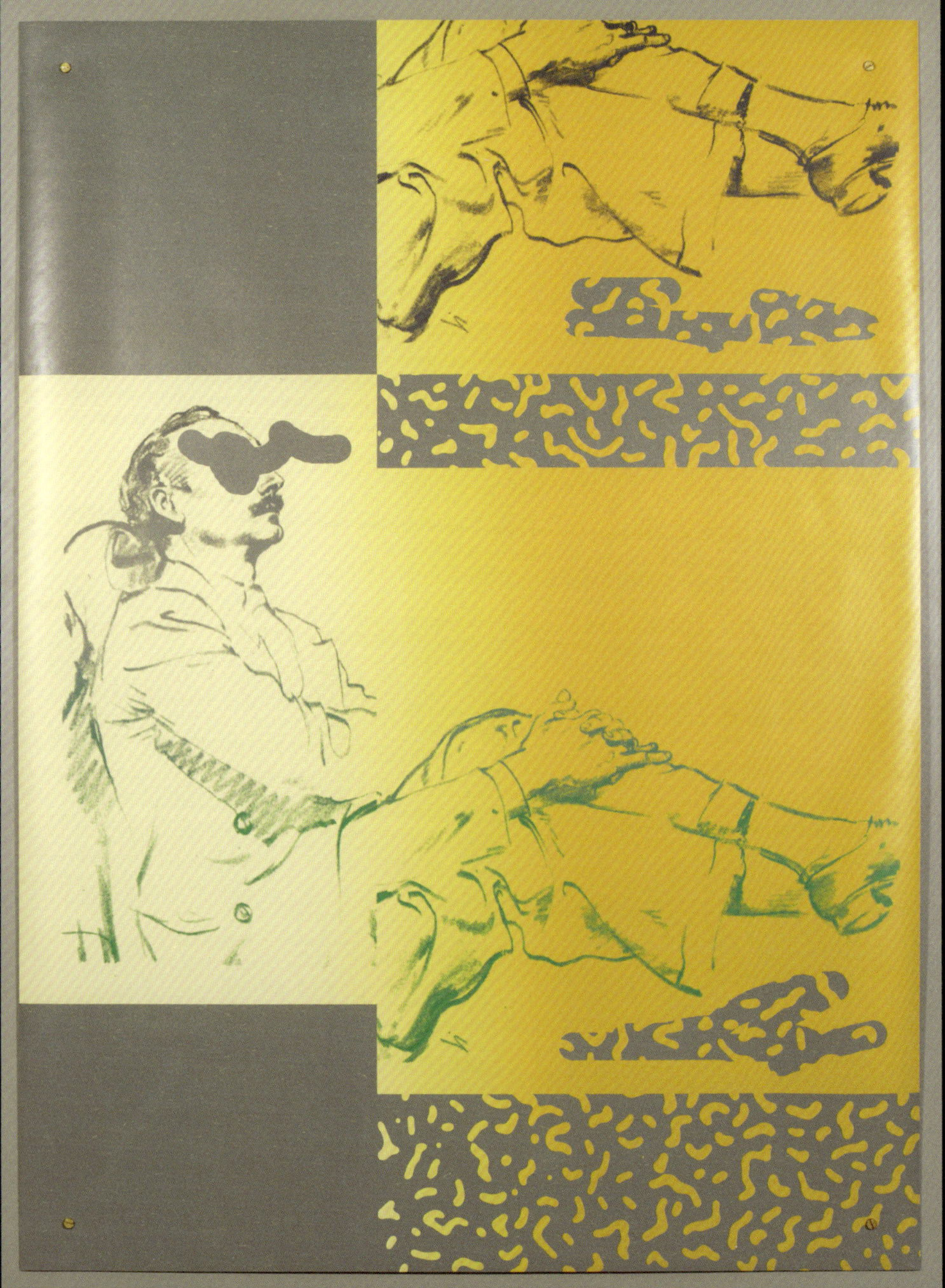

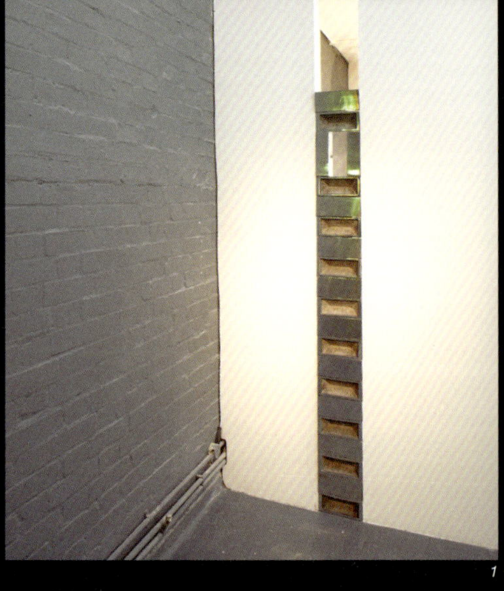

1

3

32

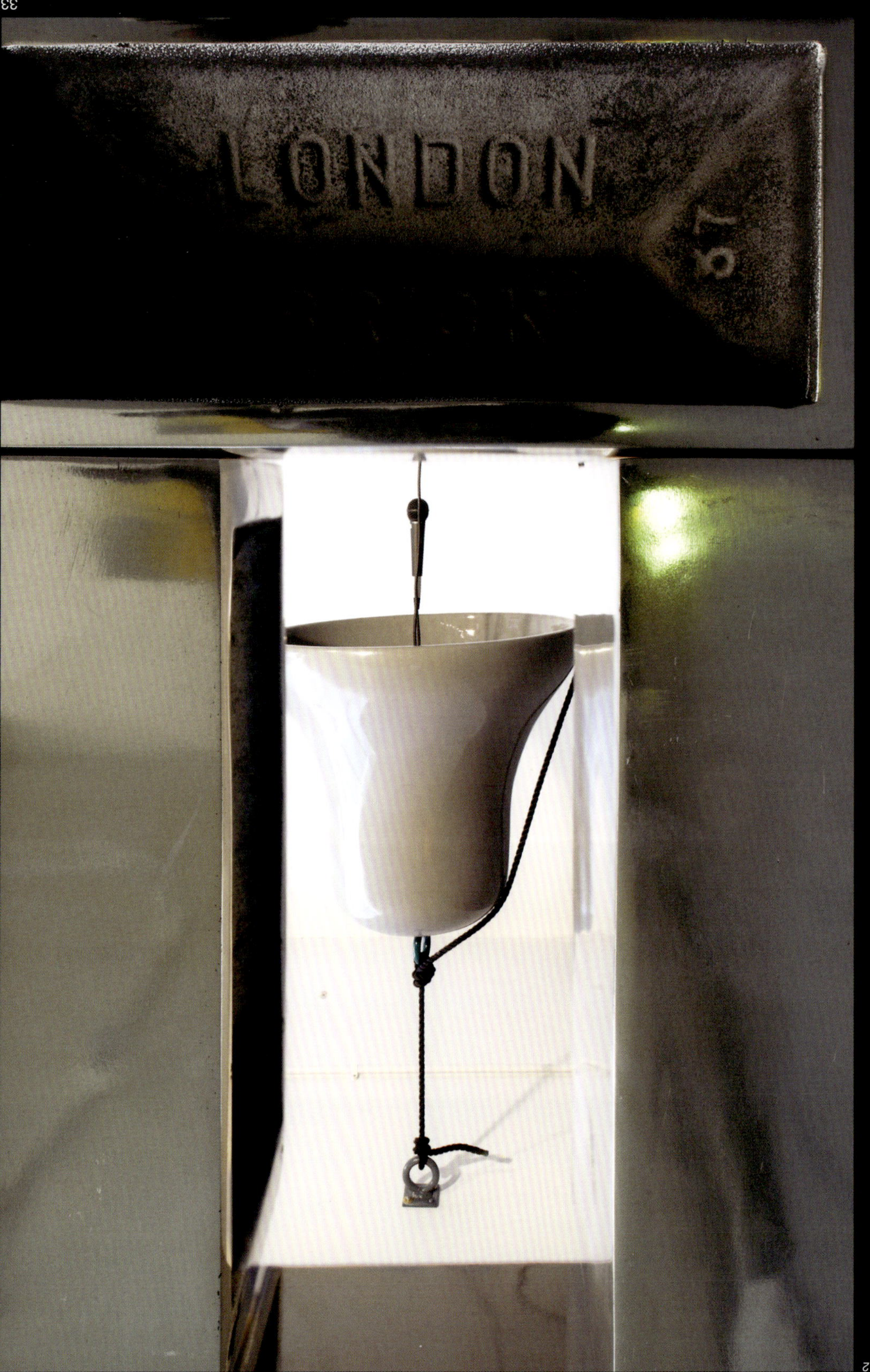

LONDON
19

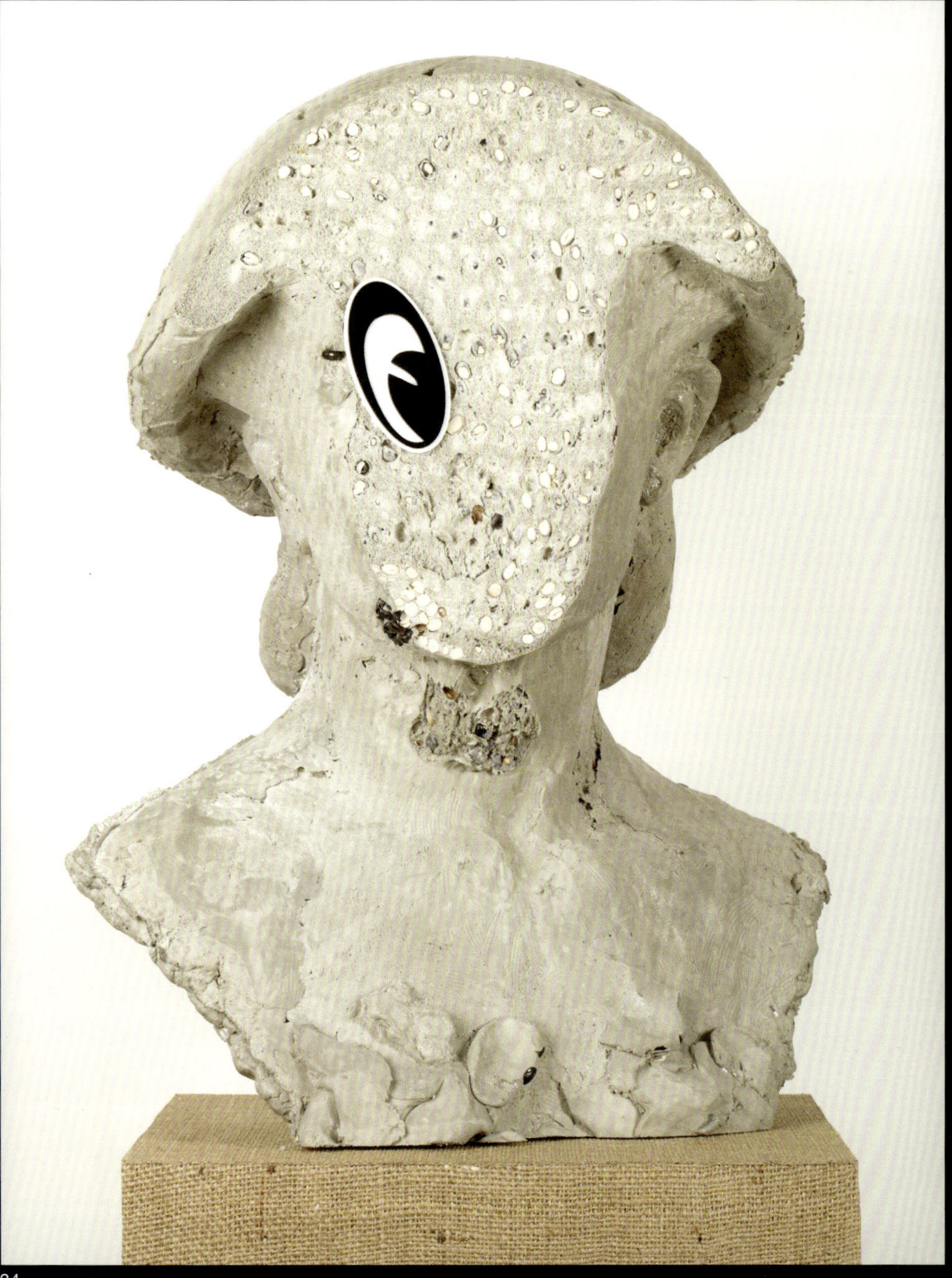

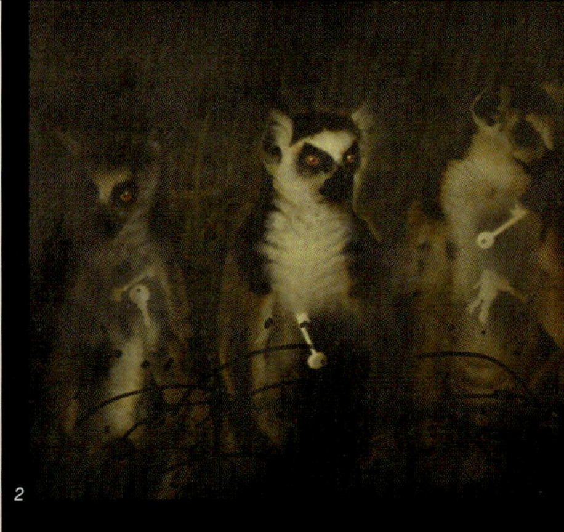

2

1

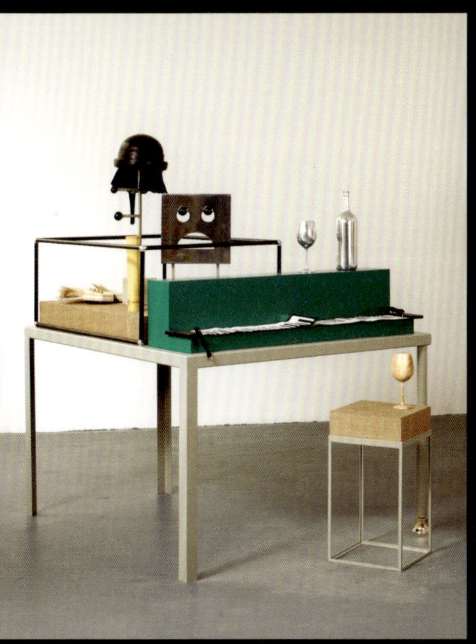

3
4

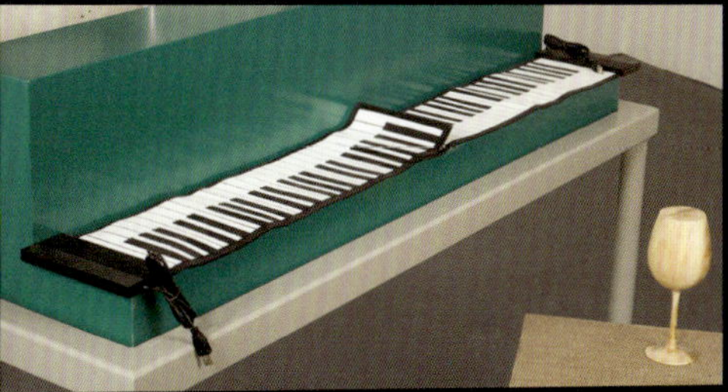

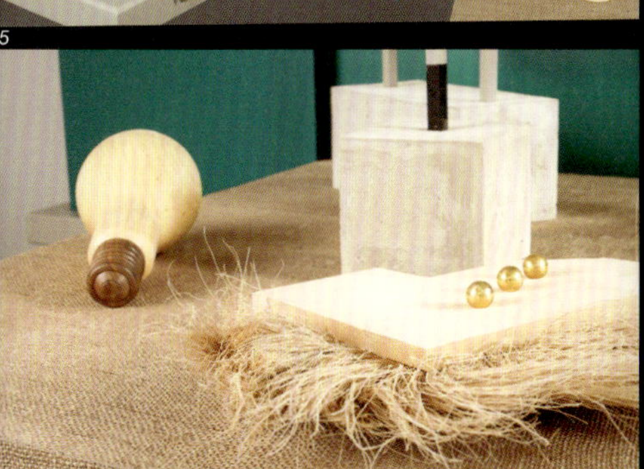

5

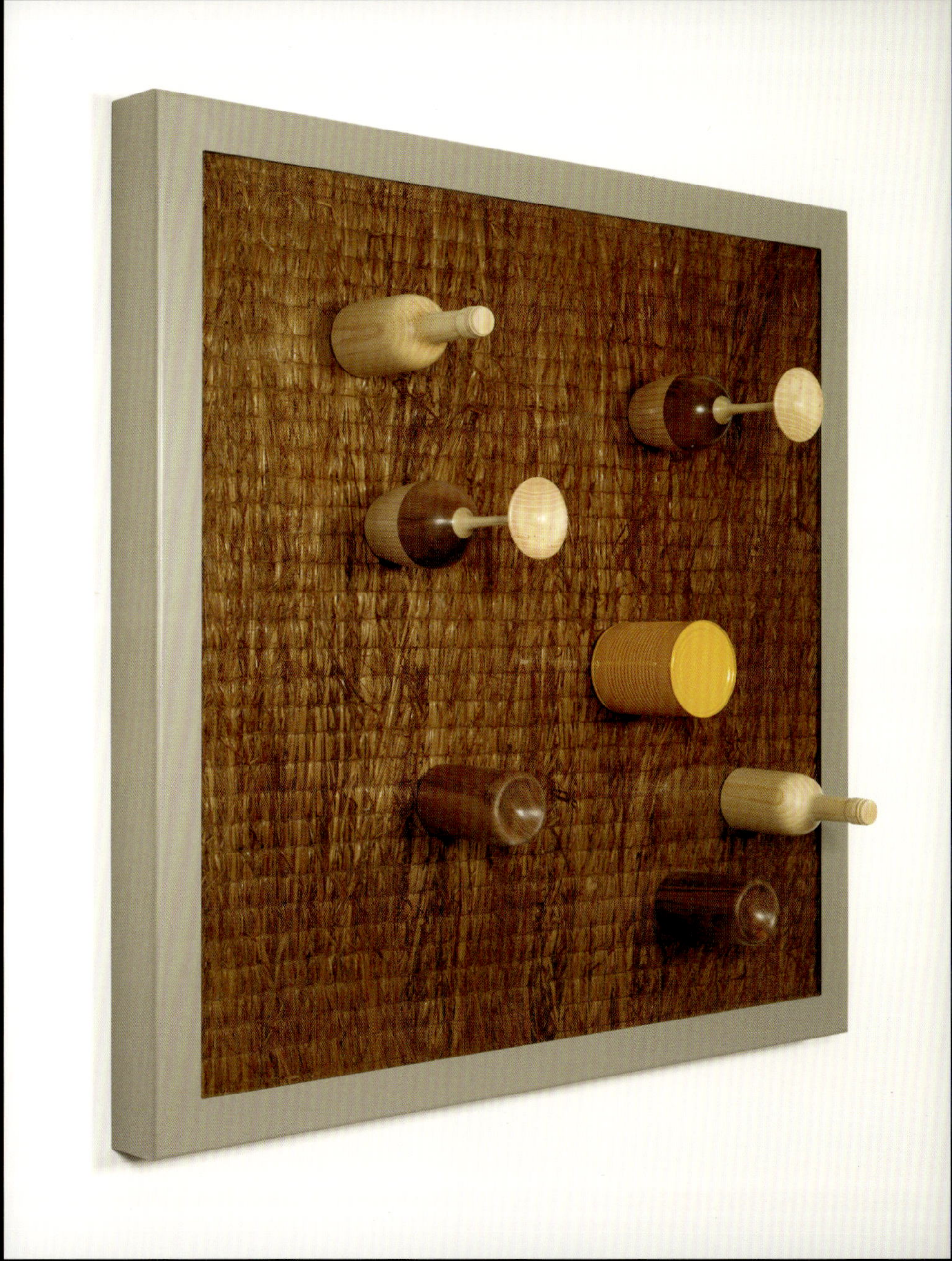

6

3- *(Joanna) The Concealment and the Showing Forth*
2010
Powder coated steel, aluminium, peacock feathers,
wood, buckram, MDF, concrete, leather
150 x 124 x 75 cm
Photo: Guy Archard

4-5 - *(Joanna) The Concealment and the Showing Forth,*
detail
2010
Powder coated steel, aluminium, peacock feathers,
wood, buckram, MDF, concrete, leather
150 x 124 x 75 cm
Photo: Guy Archard

6- *A Gathering of Vessels (Towards Material Indefinity)*
2010
Powder coated aluminium and steel frame, Perspex,
aluminium, straw matting, wooden objects
97.5 x 97.5 x 7.5 cm
Photo: Guy Archard

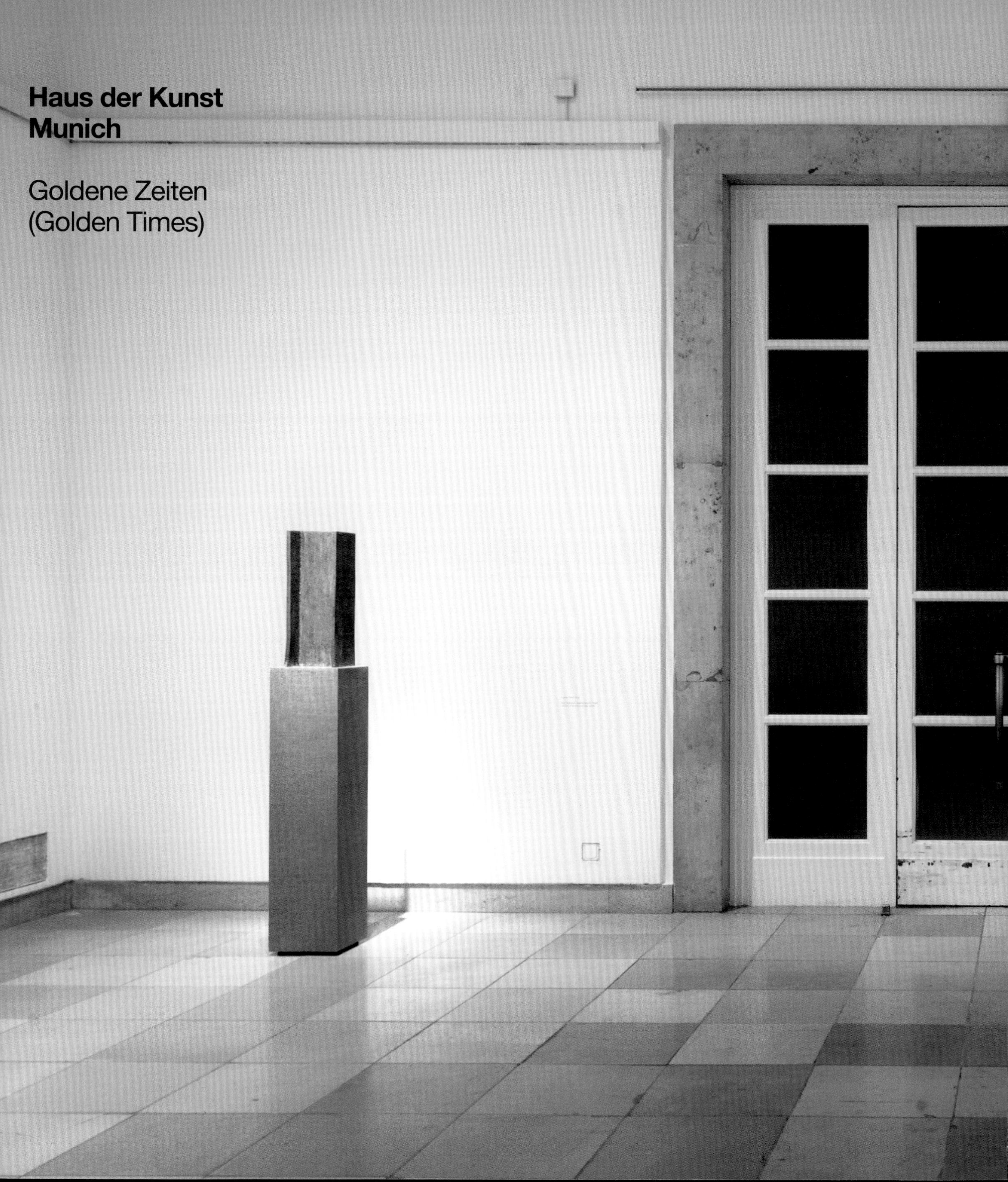
Haus der Kunst
Munich

Goldene Zeiten
(Golden Times)

Previous pages- *Goldene Zeiten (Golden Times),* installation view
2010
Photo: Wilfried Petzi

1- Like a Potted Vessel
2009
Hessian, wood, powder coated steel, aluminium, plastic, copper,
Roman vessel, rubber
204 x 105 x 105 cm
Photo: Guy Archard

2 - Goldene Zeiten (Golden Times), installation view
2010
Photo: Wilfried Petzi

3 - Funerary Pixel, detail
2009
ceramic, hessian, wood
188 x 30 x 30 cm
Photo: Guy Archard

4 - Hostile Pavilions
2009
Powder coated steel, plastic, nickel-plated cast iron
150 x 250 x 40 cm
Photo: Guy Archard

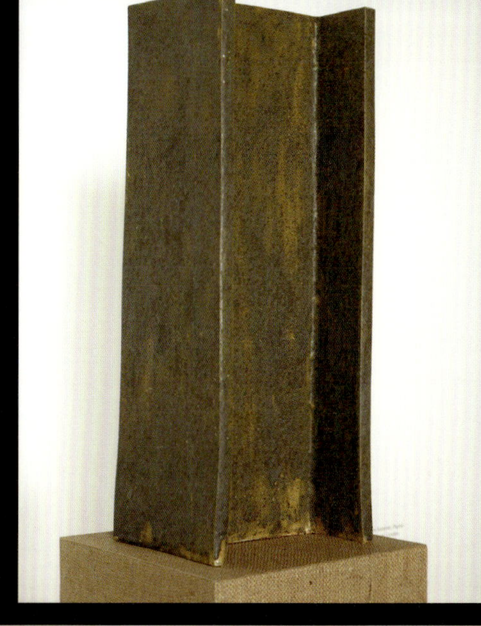

1   2

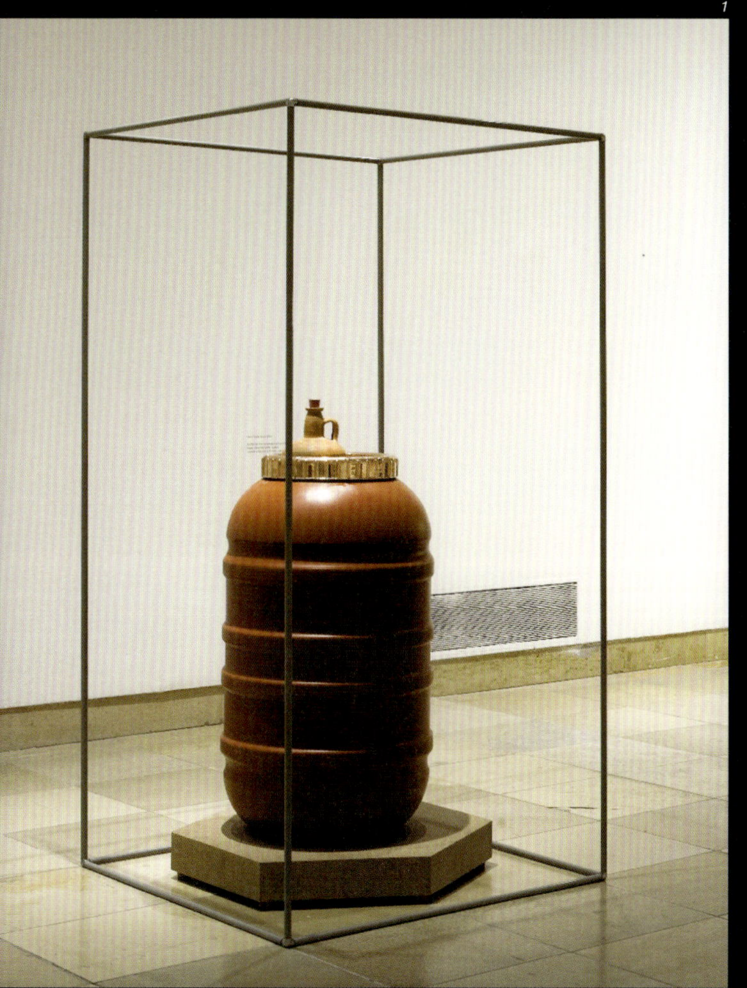

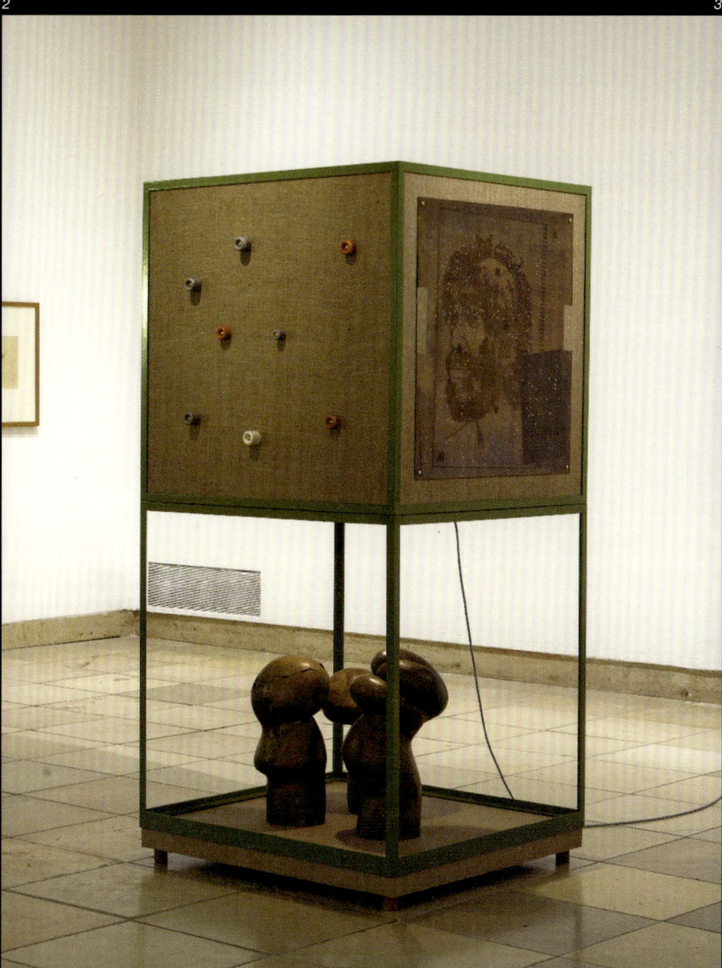

3

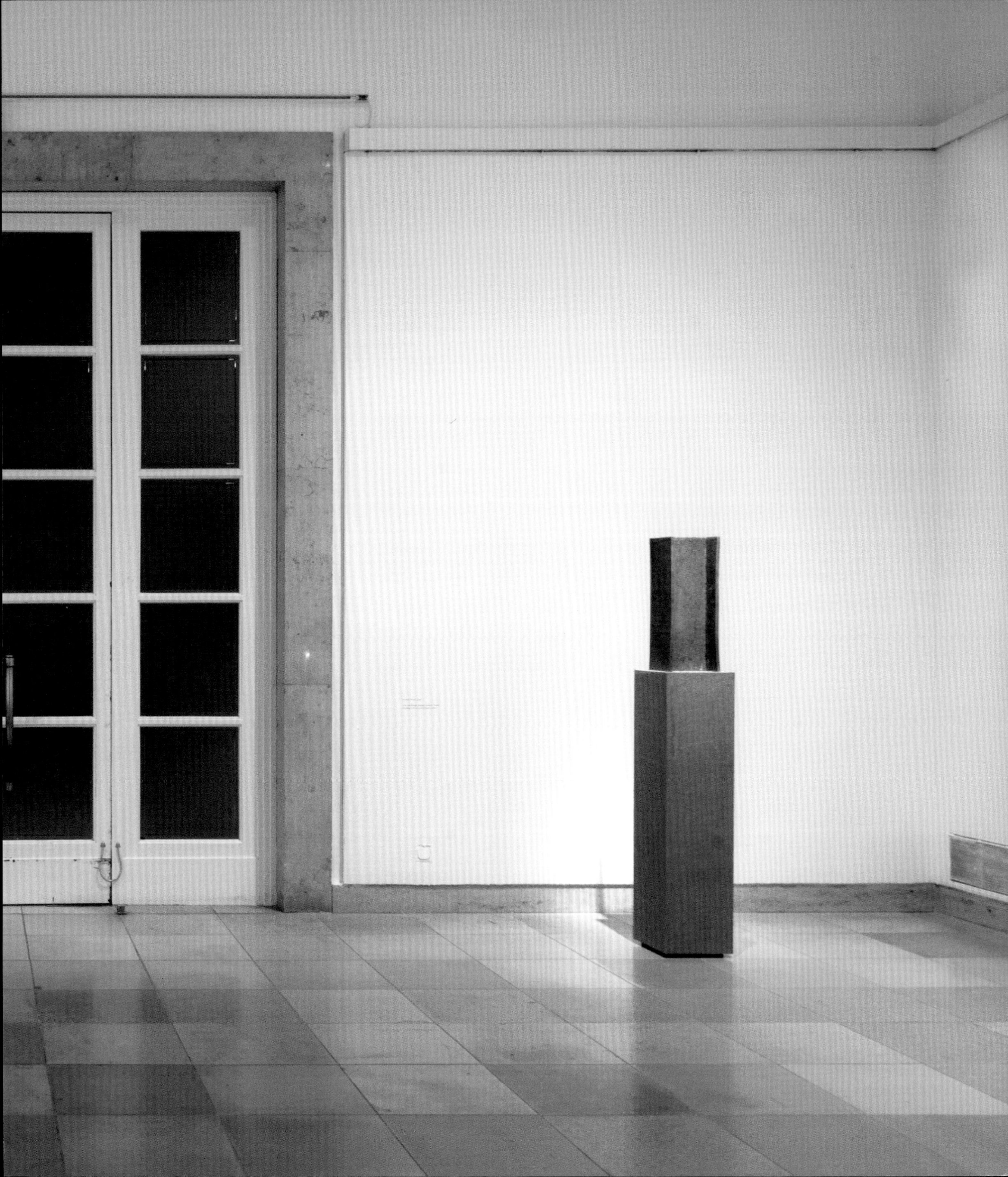

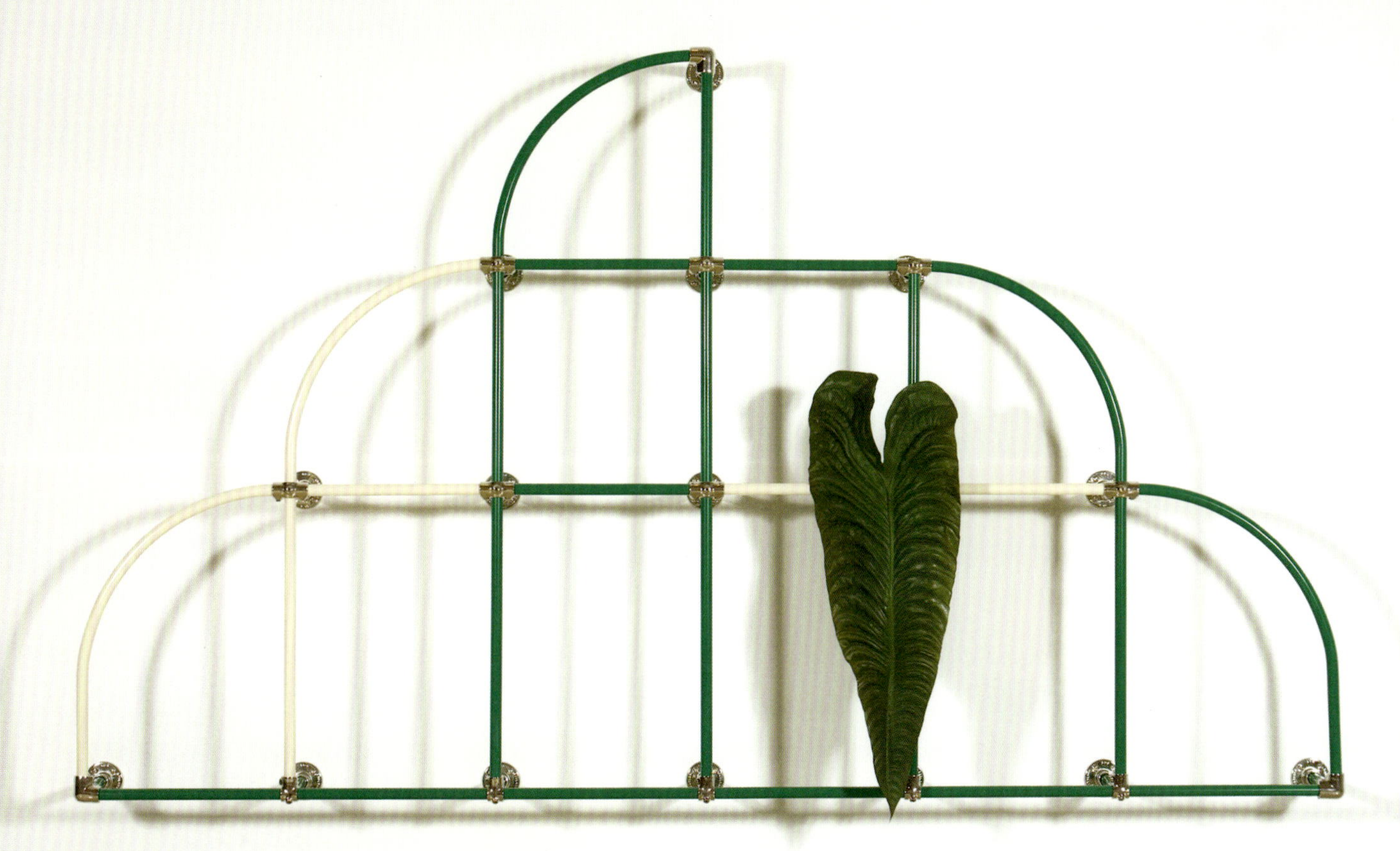

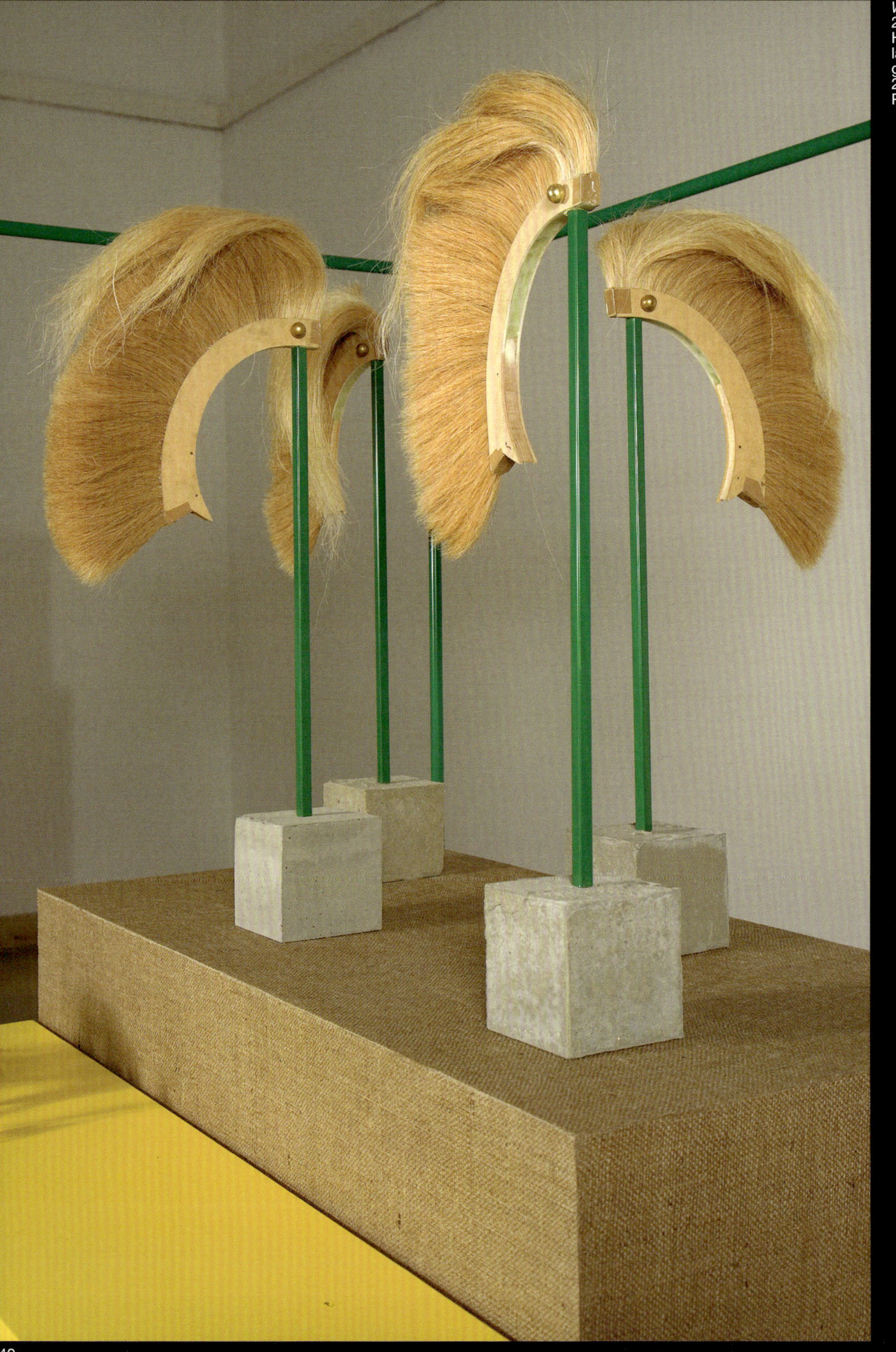

Western Plan (Commuted), detail
2009
Hessian, wood, powder coated steel,
lacquered wood, horse hair, concrete
gold-plated resin, piano keys, brass
206 x 120 x 120 cm
Photo: Guy Archard

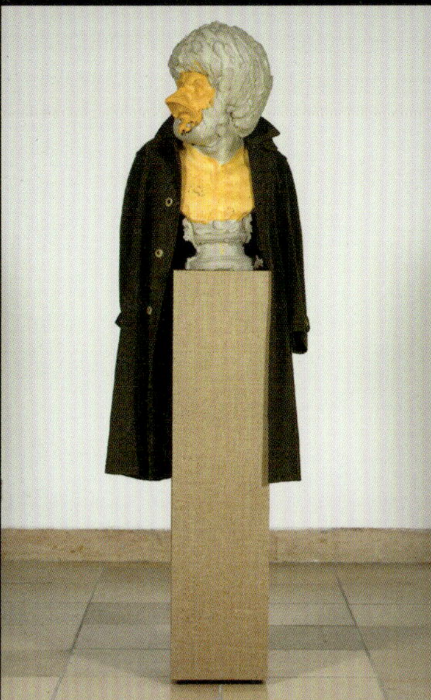

Atop the Loam (A Forester)
2009
Wood, hessian, Loden coat, casting foam,
glitter, black beans, pigment, plastic
205 x 65 x 45 cm
Photo: Guy Archard

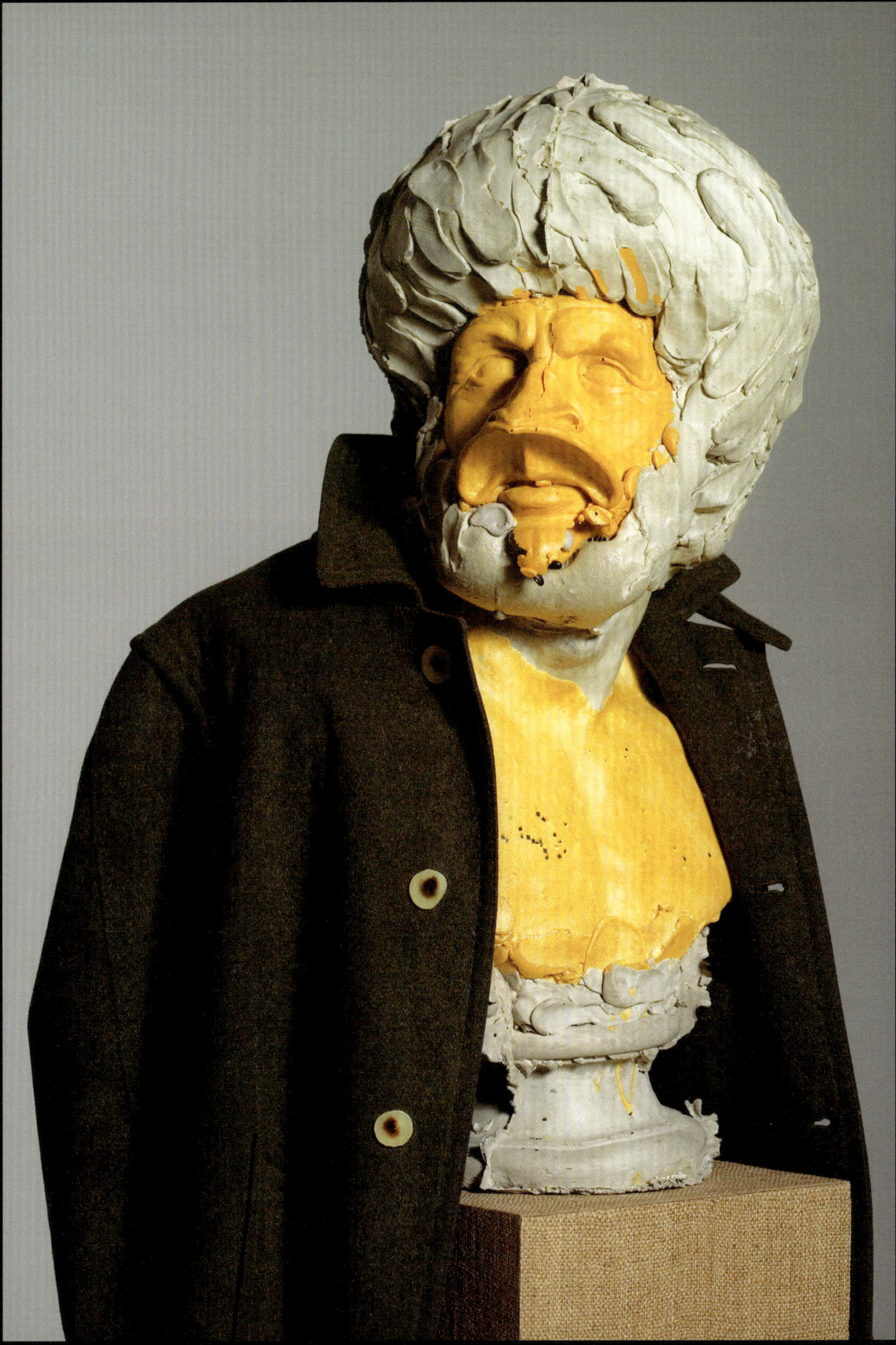

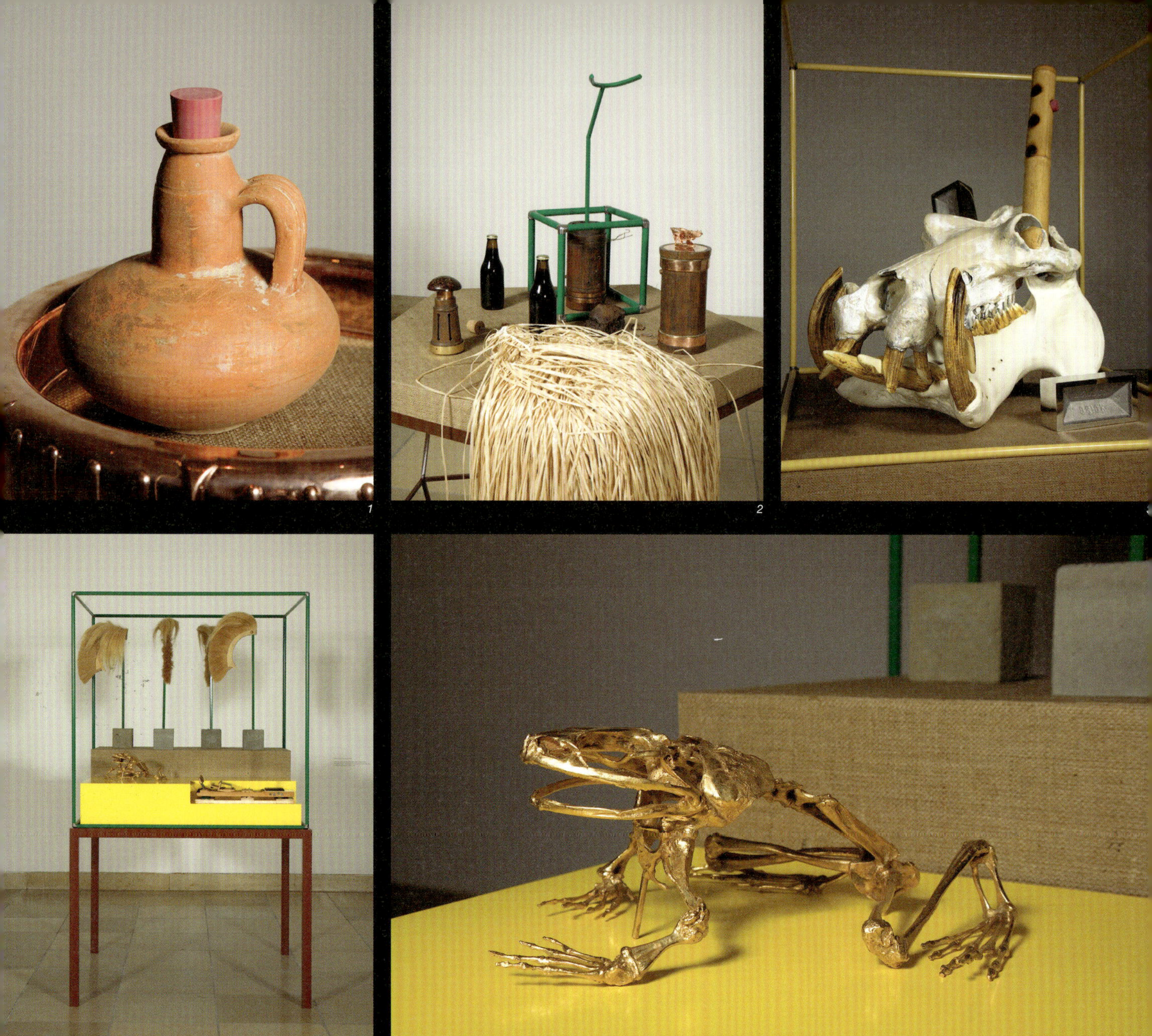

1
2

1- Like a Potted Vessel, detail
2009
Hessian, wood, powder coated steel, aluminium, plastic,
copper, Roman vessel, rubber
204 x 105 x 105 cm
Photo: Guy Archard

*2- Renaissance Malt - A Demonstrative Equivalence of
the Coarseness of Converse Properties,* detail
2009
Hessian, wood, powder coated steel, resin, acrylic,
plastic, brass, copper, Bakelite, glass, liquid, cork,
aluminium, raffia grass-skirt
93 x 96 x 96 cm
Photo: Guy Archard

3- The World Alighted (Heavy Is), detail
2009
Hessian, wood, powder coated steel, polyester resin,
cast aluminium, plastic, bamboo, rubber, aluminium
paint, acrylic, zinc sunblock, toothpaste
188 x 109 x 109 cm
Photo: Guy Archard

4- Western Plan (Commuted)
2009
Hessian, wood, powder coated steel, lacquered wood,
horse hair, concrete, gold-plated resin, piano keys, brass
206 x 120 x 120 cm
Photo: Guy Archard

5- Western Plan (Commuted), detail
2009
Hessian, wood, powder coated steel, lacquered wood,
horse hair, concrete, gold-plated resin, piano keys, brass
206 x 120 x 120 cm
Photo: Guy Archard

6- Goldene Zeiten (Golden Times), installation view
2010
Photo: Wilfried Petzi

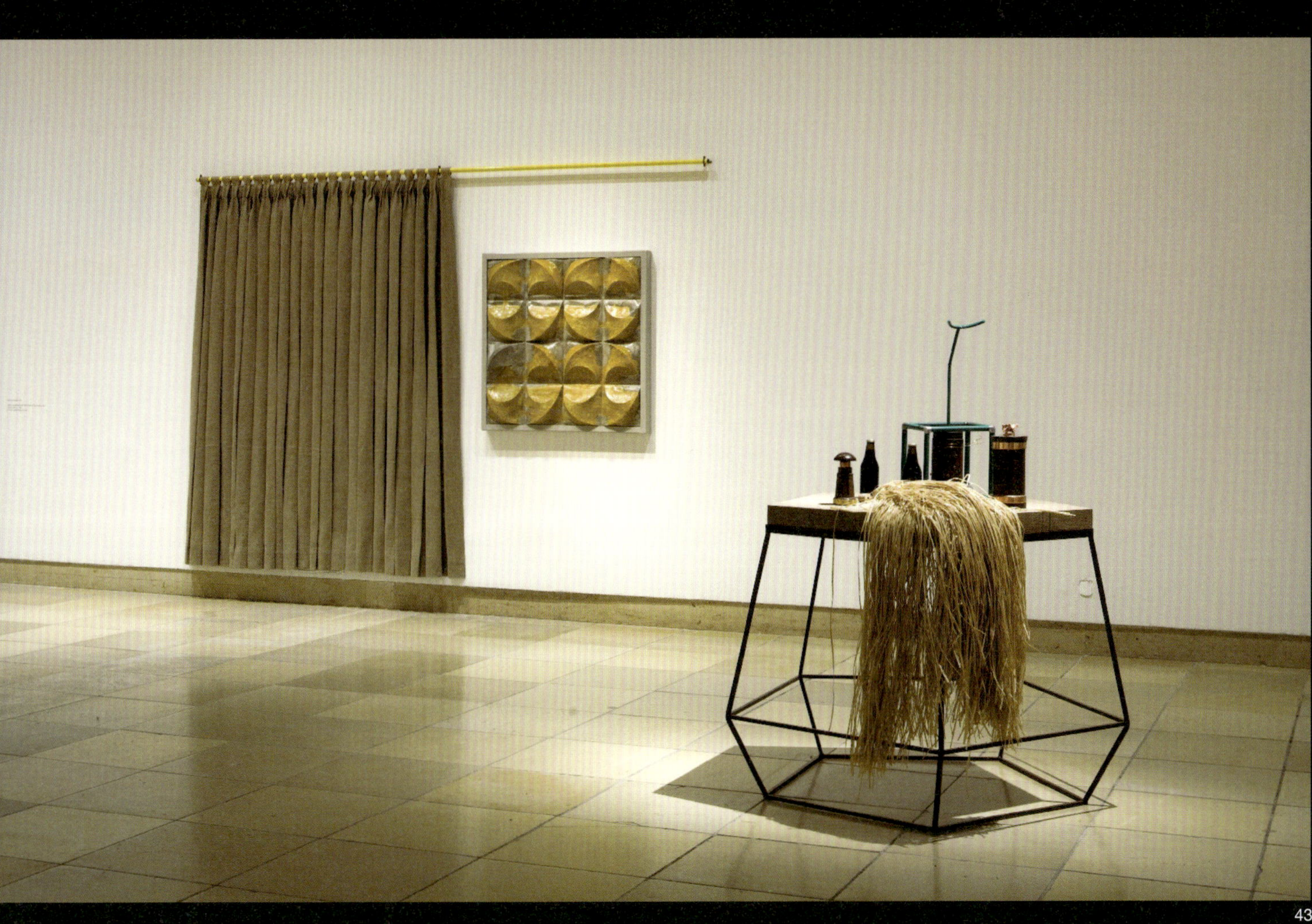

Golden Times

Patrizia Dander

For several years, Steven Claydon has been absorbed with Martin Heidegger's *The Origin of the Work of Art* (1935-6), a philosophical thesis questioning the nature of art. Heidegger attempts to determine what constitutes an artwork as such, and how it can be distinguished from ordinary objects. He writes, as Claydon says, 'about the schism between the art object and a craft object; amongst other things Heidegger seeks truth in the work of art – aspirations that seem hackneyed or redundant now – but the really interesting thing for me was this metamorphosis from a material 'thing' into a cultural object … about how an artwork can oscillate between its material earth-like quality and its cultural beingness.'[1] With regards to artworks, Heidegger considers two elements as inseparable yet united in their strife: the earth as something concealing, enclosing, material, and the world as towering, self-opening, spiritual. By bringing the material and spiritual together, the work as a cultural sign transcends the object as such, which Heidegger situates within the earth-like.[2]

The concepts used by Heidegger mirror categorical, if not hierarchical, thinking about culture, where the work is placed above the mere object and essentially also the world above the earth (although Heidegger tries to dissolve this hierarchy by perceiving them as mutually interdependent). A similar concept can be found in the generally prevalent dichotomies of mundane objects and sacrosanct art objects – of 'high' and 'low' – but also in categories such as logical and irrational. Claydon purposefully provokes such confrontations. In his works, he unites seemingly disparate elements and entangles them – to use Heidegger's expression – in a strife.

In terms of composition, Claydon's works seem to hybridise objects and plinths, or artefacts and display, whereby both elements appear to be of equal importance. This becomes apparent in, for example, *From the Foliage of Poor Judgement (A Prism)* (2009, adjacent), where three biomorphic clay sculptures – found objects – are grouped and lit from beneath a structure, which in turn exposes, amongst others, an etching by Claydon.

Also by combining 'everyday' objects and original artworks, values are played off against each other. *Like a Potted Vessel* (2009, p42), for instance, consists of an earthenware Roman pot, placed on top of a plastic vessel with a copper-coated cover, which has been set upon a low hexagonal pedestal. Both pot and vessel were originally defined by their use value, and even served the same purpose: transporting goods. Nevertheless, perhaps through the sheer passage of time, we are likely to assign more value to the Roman pot than to the plastic vessel – even though the latter has been refined by the artist with a noble metal. The question persists: when and how did the transition from commodity to historical artefact occur? These confrontations complicate any one-dimensional classification. Claydon thereby directs the gaze towards our habits of presenting and perceiving cultural products.

The precise use of materials also serves this purpose. His works recall idiosyncratic and partly contradictory impressions between the antiquated and hypermodern, and the sublime and disconcerting. Polyester resin or cast aluminium are on an equal footing to the traditional techniques used in the manufacture of ceramics or bronzes. Added to this are found items and artefact-like objects that Claydon treats with unorthodox means such as zinc-based sunblock or toothpaste – as is the case with the artificially aged, cast-resin hippo skull in *The World Alighted (Heavy Is)* (2009, p42). 'I'm interested in utilising the subversion of materials in order to catalyse a sense of dislocation from received ideas of venerability and engender a critical appraisal of the way we encounter things … I also work hard to employ contemporary materials and techniques, providing a forum … that destabilises any rose-tinted reading of the work and generates a suspicion of inherited notions of tradition and accepted modes of thought.'[3]

Critical distancing from accepted modes of thought is also decisive when considering his conceptualisation of the works' content. Starting points are often forgotten or little-noticed historical times of upheaval; moments when utopian visions were formulated as an alternative to the domineering view of the world and existing structures were to be broken up in favour of a radical substitute. Claydon sees them as alternative pathways to a linear evolutionary model of history, to which the past serves as derivation from and justification for the present: 'I think that it's necessary to disable and contradict the acknowledged historical machine as often as possible in order to perceive through the little wounds and holes the kind of intervals necessary to allow for breath and a less homogeneous and self-satisfied reading of 'past'. To instill a healthy scepticism that extends to all aspects of seductive models.'[4]

One of the infamously well-known 'seductive models' of the 20th century was National Socialism, of which the Haus der Kunst – with its sedate, neo-classical architecture – is also a product. Claydon took this architecture as a point of departure for *Golden Times*, not to confirm established stereotypes about the ideological nature of the building but rather to look back at its precursors, such as the liberal field of the Munich Secession movement.[5] He chose to reflect on the point of deviation and misinterpretation: 'The Secession likened its democratic impulse to that of classical Athens and identified itself with a Dionysian hedonism framed in the clean lines of neo-classicism that in retrospect seems something of a disjuncture. This kind of misappropriation is, of course, not uncommon, but we are all too happy to attribute all neo-classical architecture to the dark realms of Troost, Speer and the National Socialist movement, who colonised a pre-existing democratic aesthetic and turned it into a kitsch caricature that serviced a cynical regime.'[6]

Claydon does not deliver a coherent alternative reading of the historical canon, since this would merely be a repetition of history's problems. Rather, he opens up a complex 'a-historical, a-parallel'[7] field picking up on a variety of sidelines in terms of aesthetics and content: 'Here the language of the 19th century and early 20th century satire marches in step with whisperings of local mineral and fossil deposits. Flightless birds.

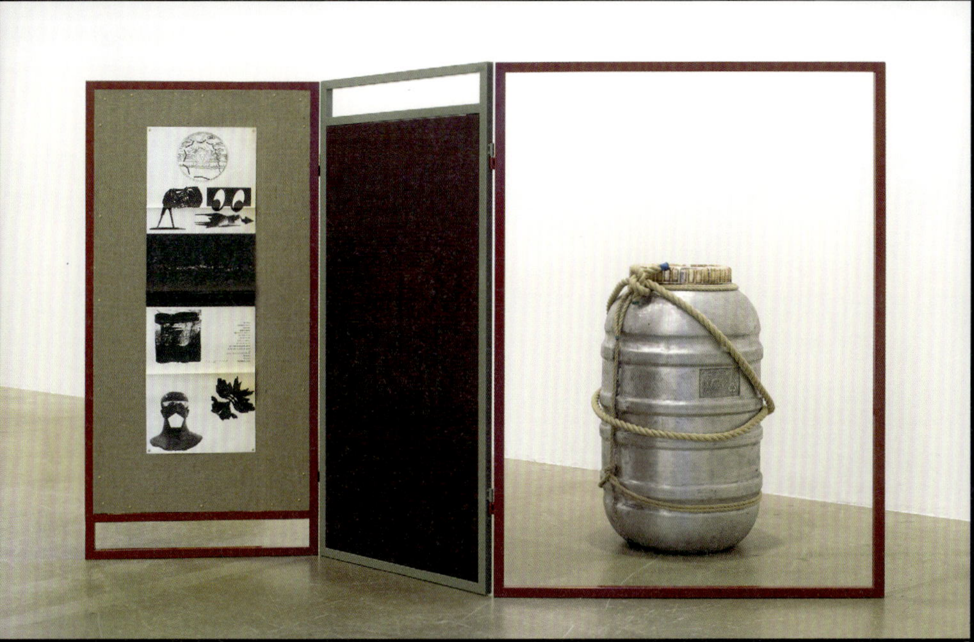

5

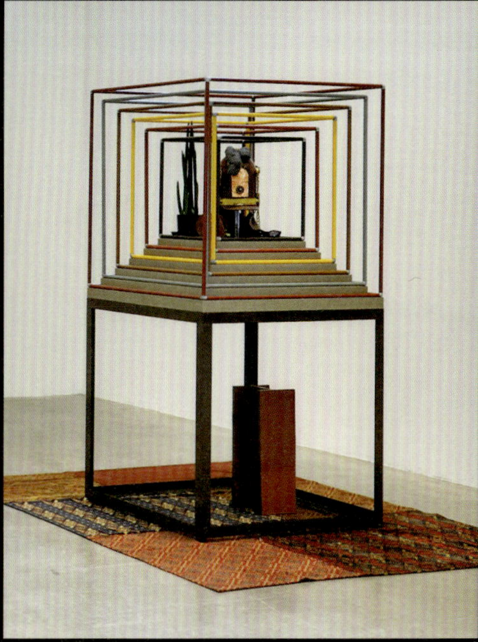

6
7

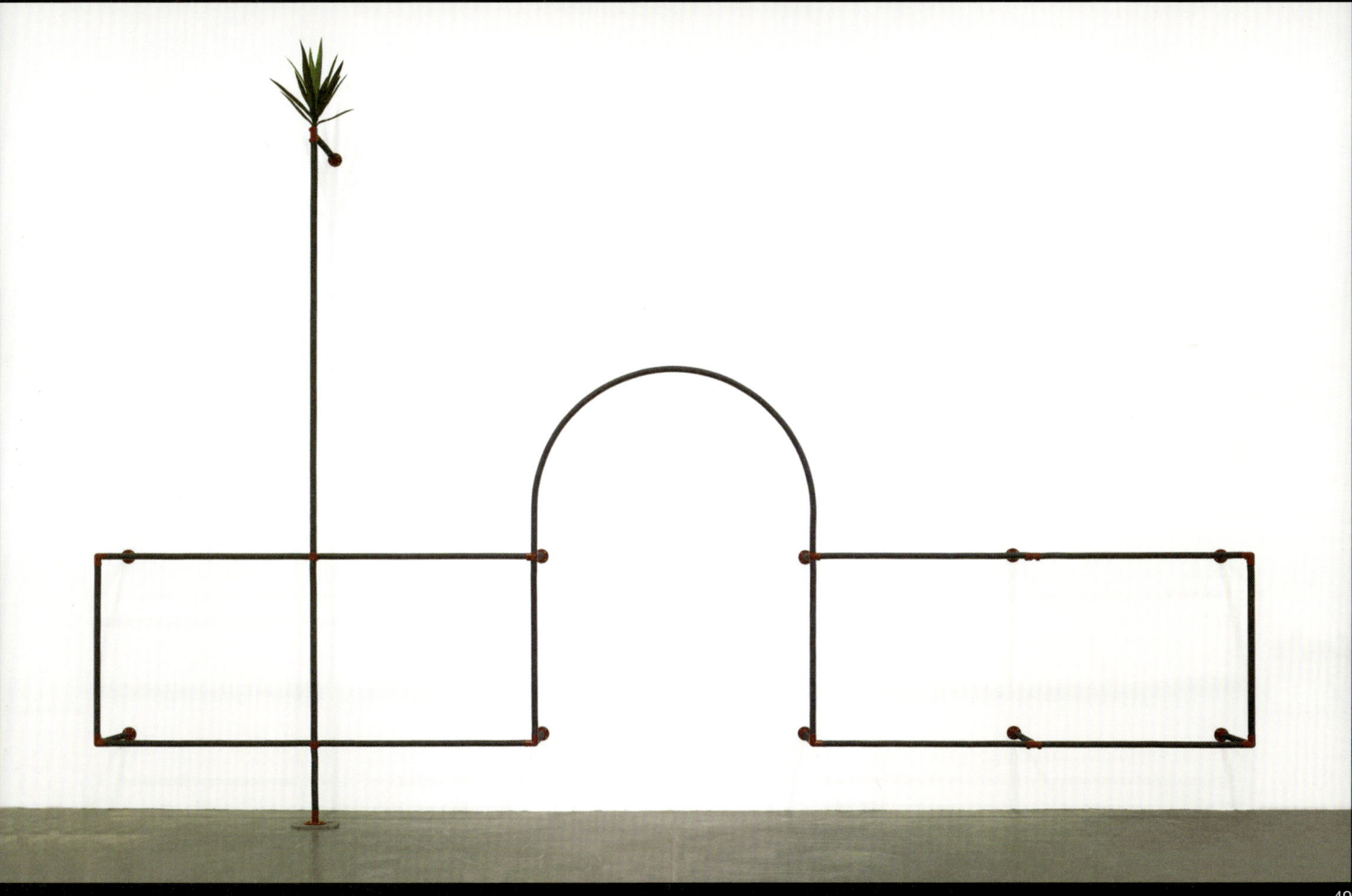

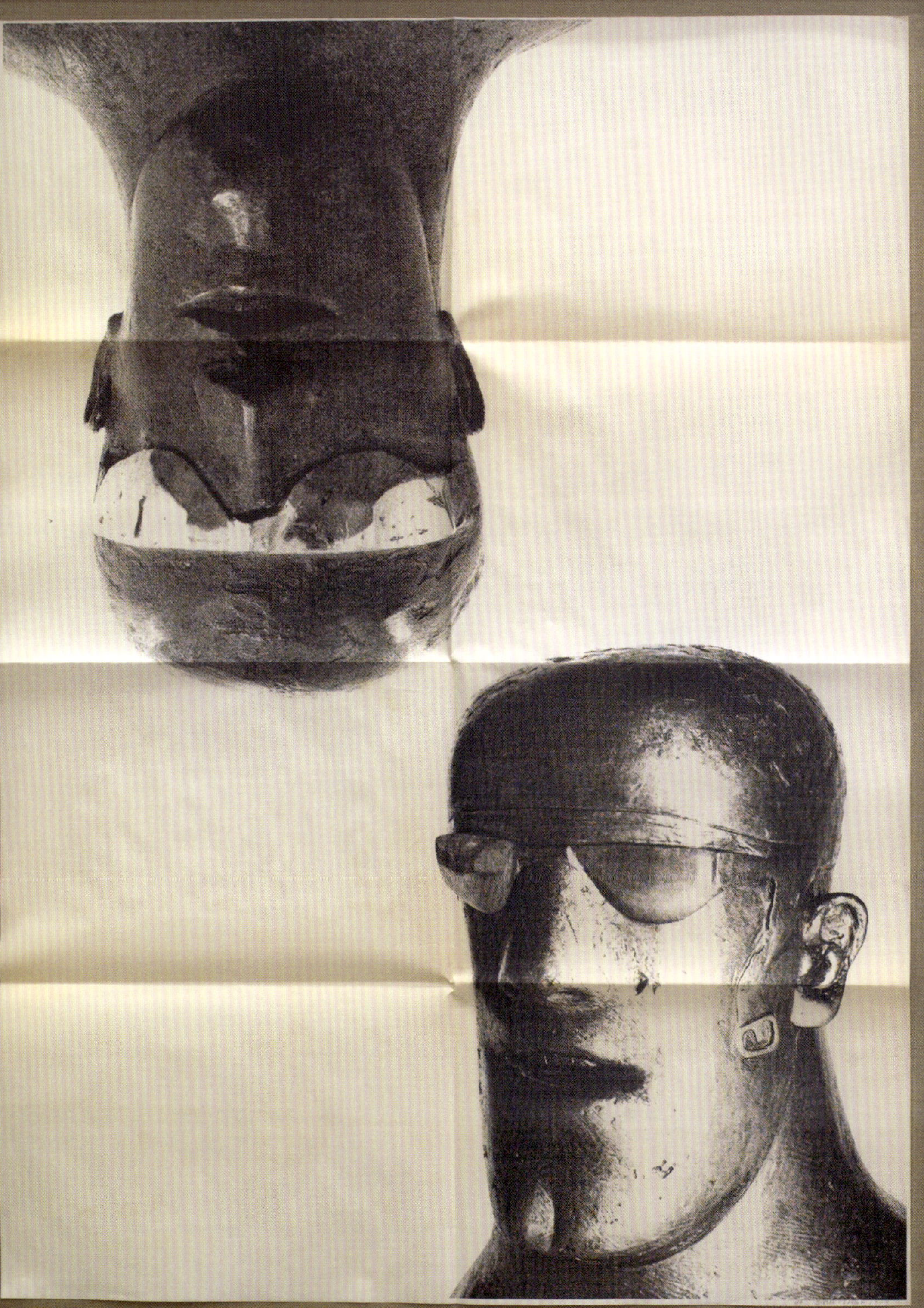

2009
Print on paper
327.7 x 243.8 x 12
Photo: Alessandro
Zambianchi

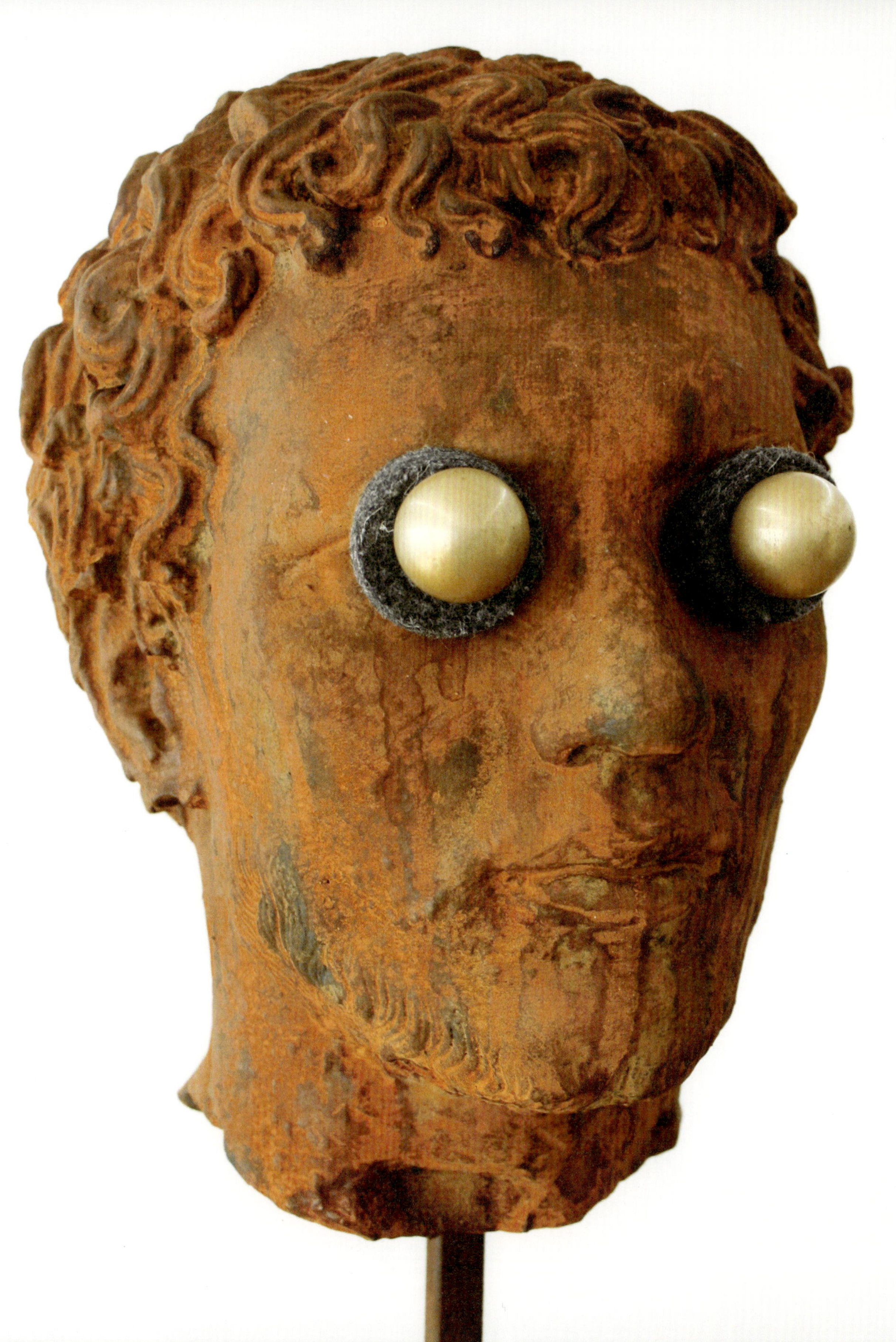

Kimmerich
Düsseldorf

A & not A

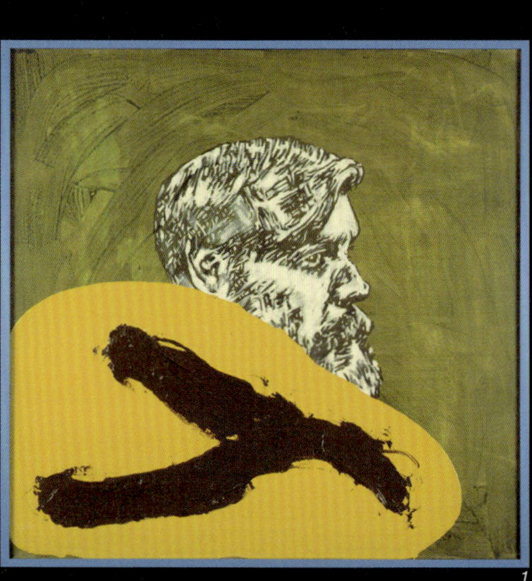

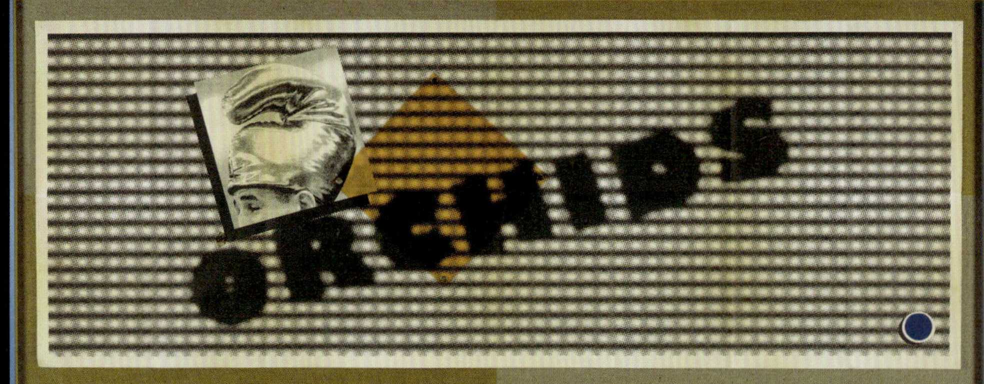

1- grün gelb
2008
Acrylic and road paint on canvas
91.5 x 91.5 cm
Photo: Ivo Faber

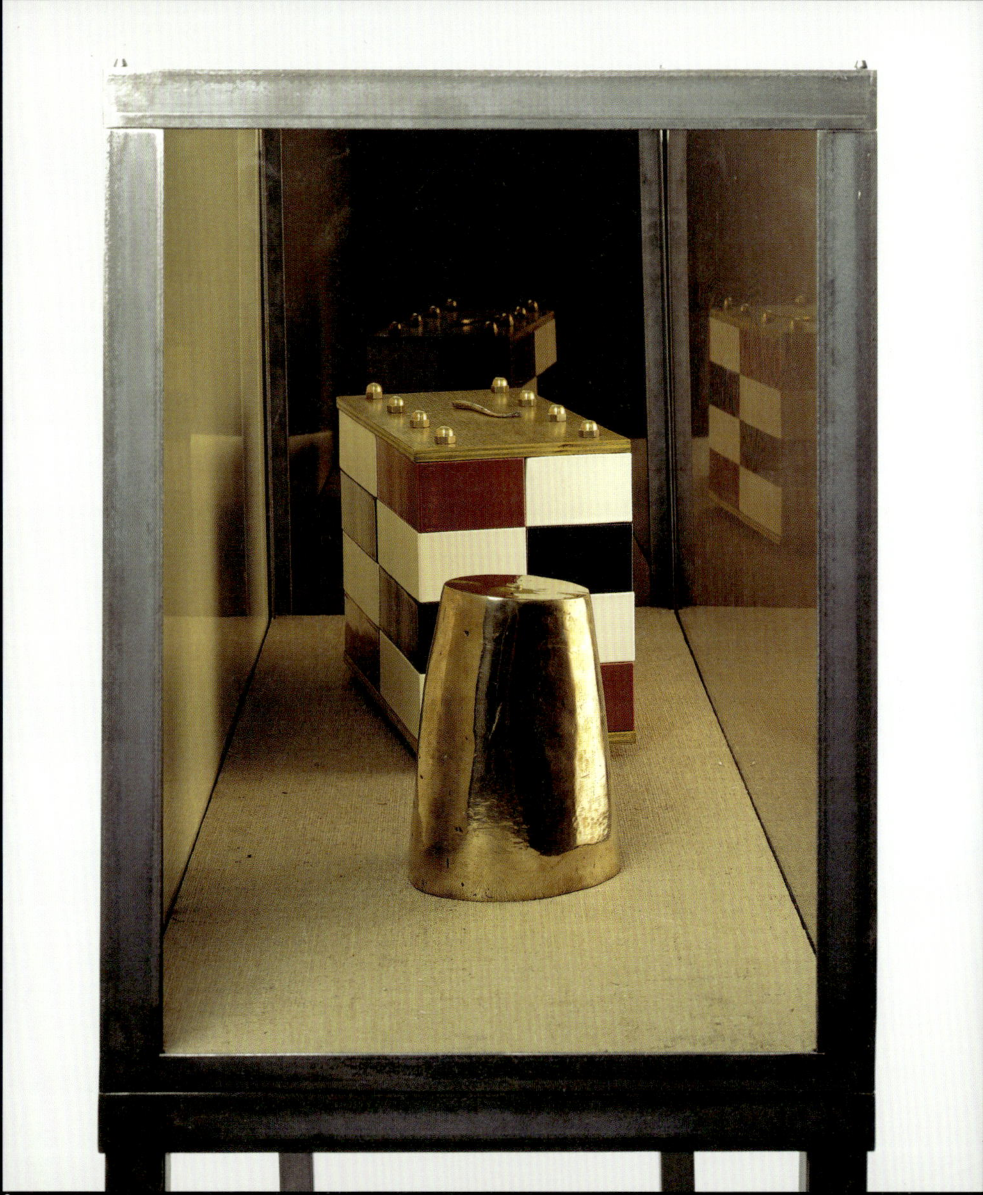

2- It and not It (I will untable myself)
2008
Steel, hessian, bronze, brass, glazed ceramic, acrylic
158 x 150 x 50 cm
Photo: Ivo Faber

3- Phrygian Orchids
2008
Screenprint, paint and Plexiglas
97 x 233 cm
Photo: Ivo Faber

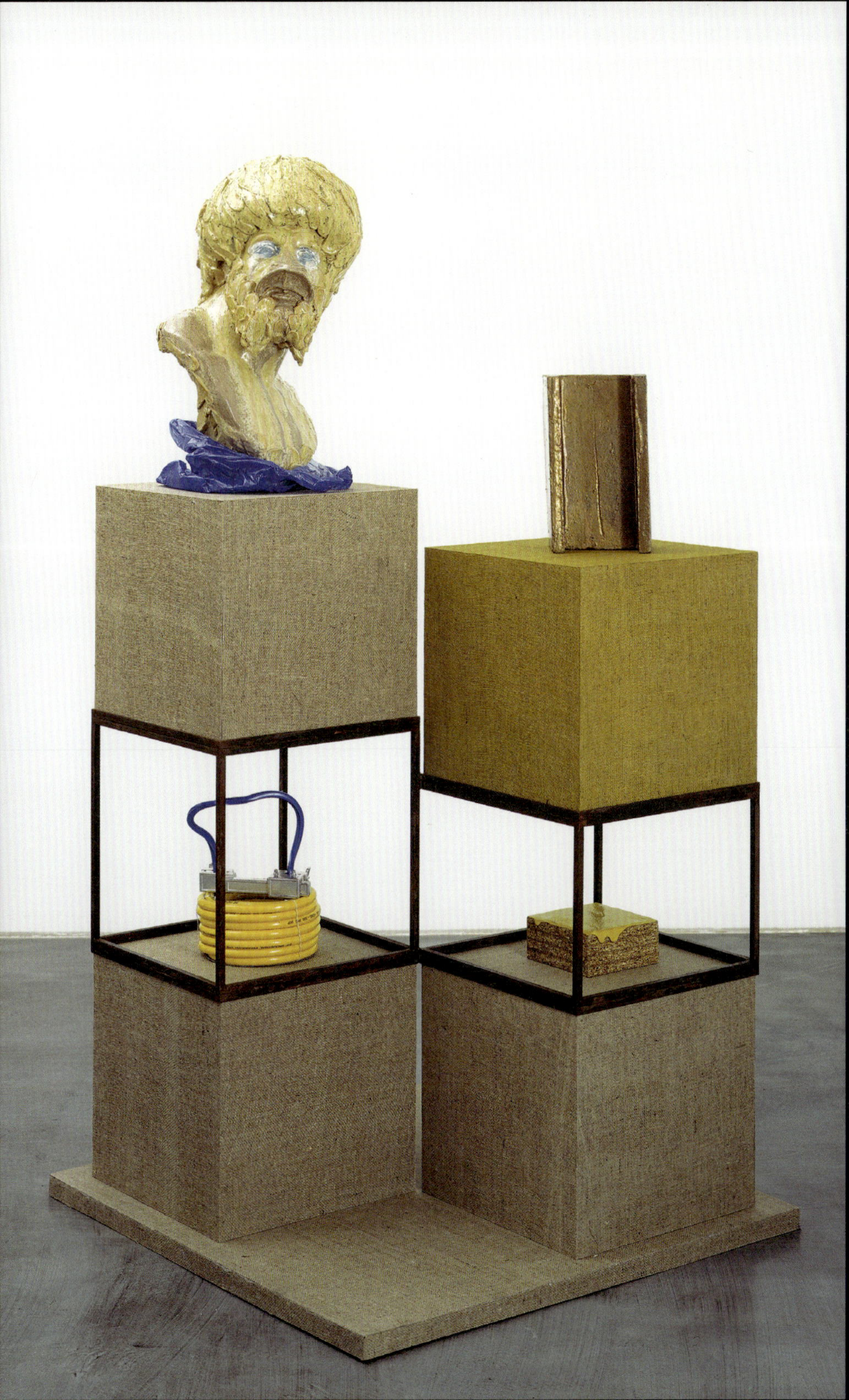

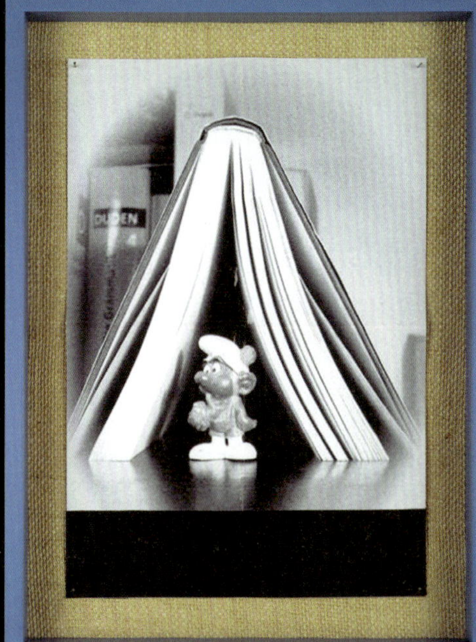

5
4

4- A lark descending (Preparations for Leda)
2008
Ceramic, hessian, powder coated steel, paint,
rubberised tubing
183 x 91 x 91.5 cm
Photo: Ivo Faber

5- Stocking cap in Bucholia
2008
Photography and tape
37 x 27 cm
Photo: Ivo Faber

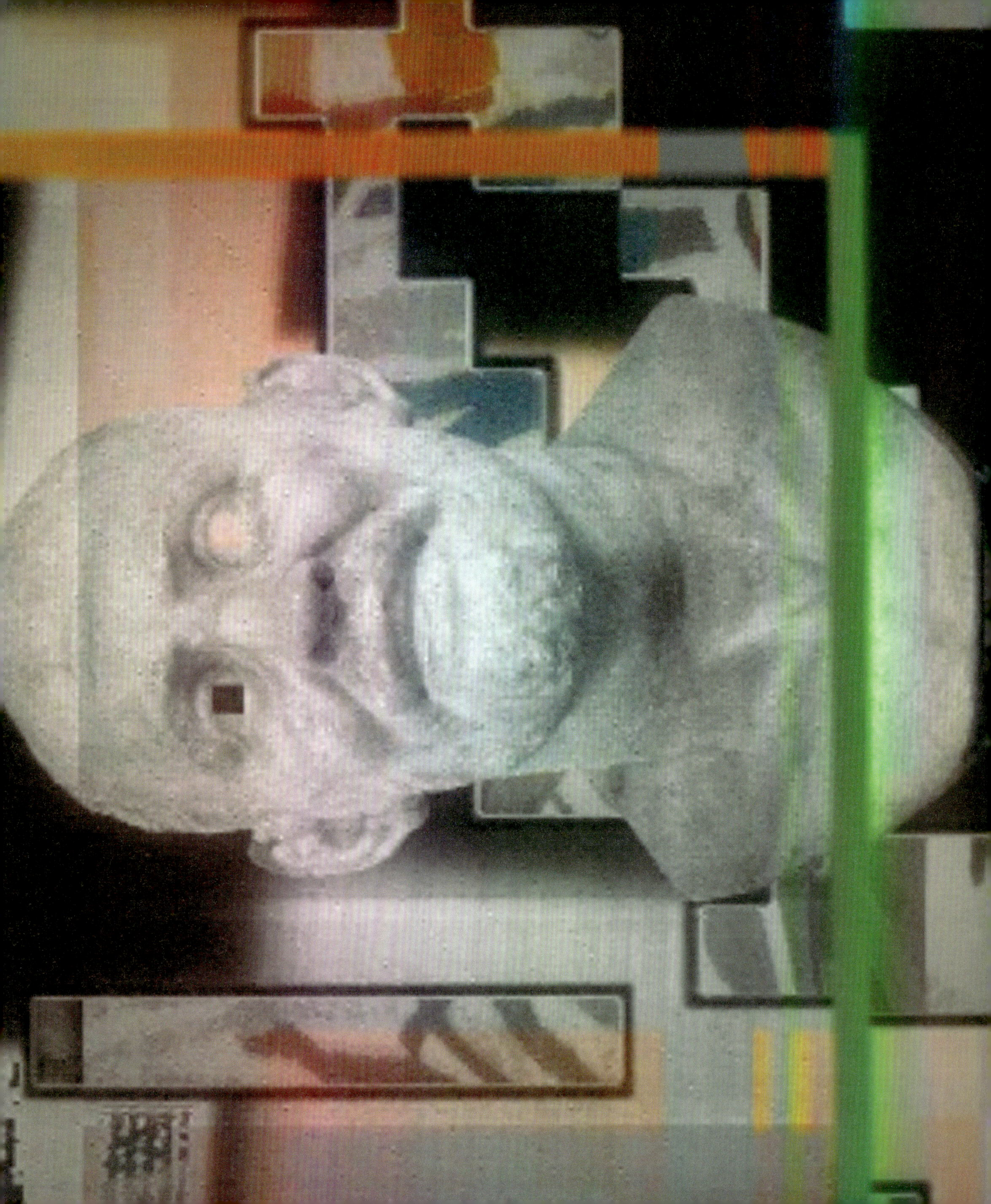

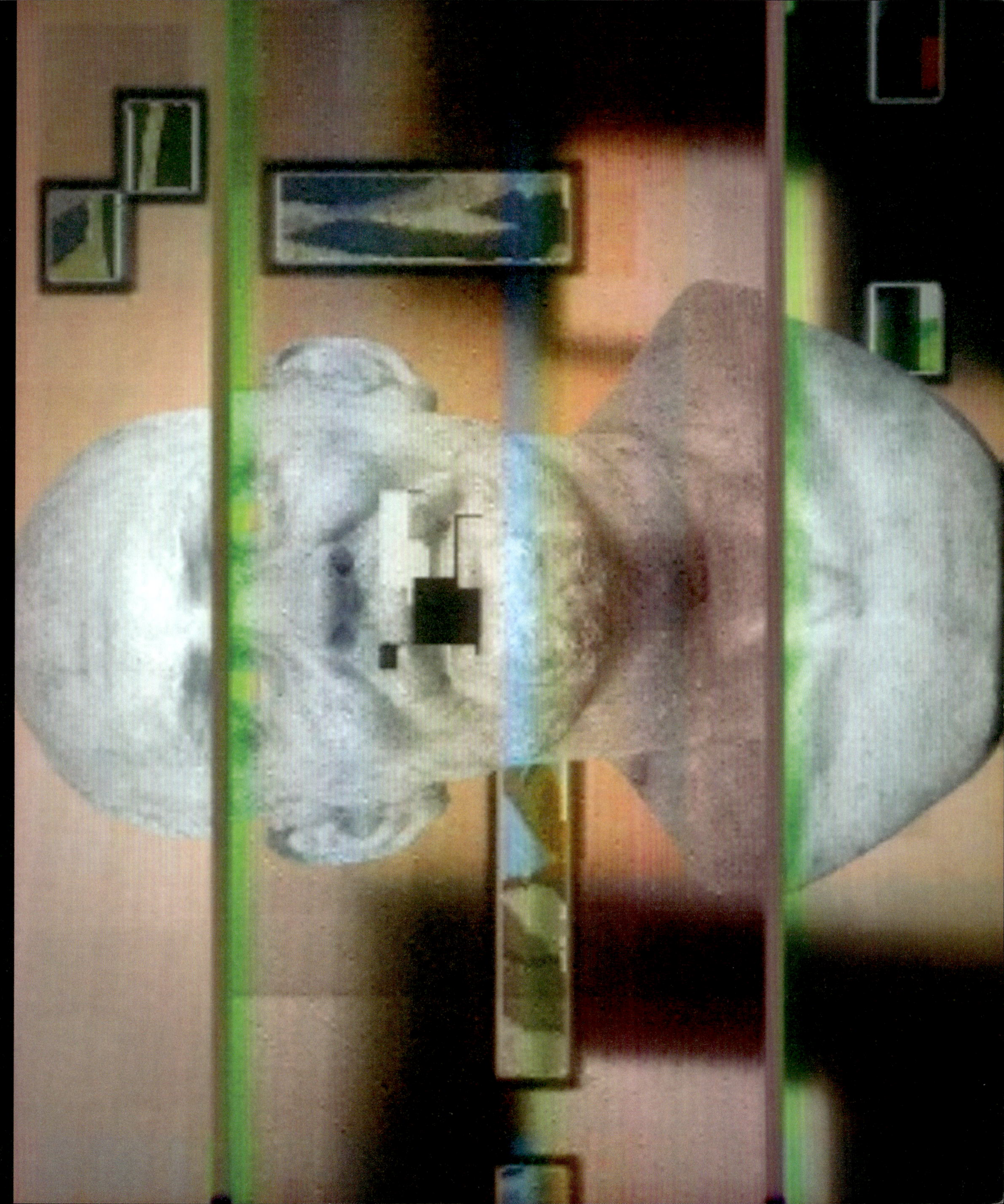

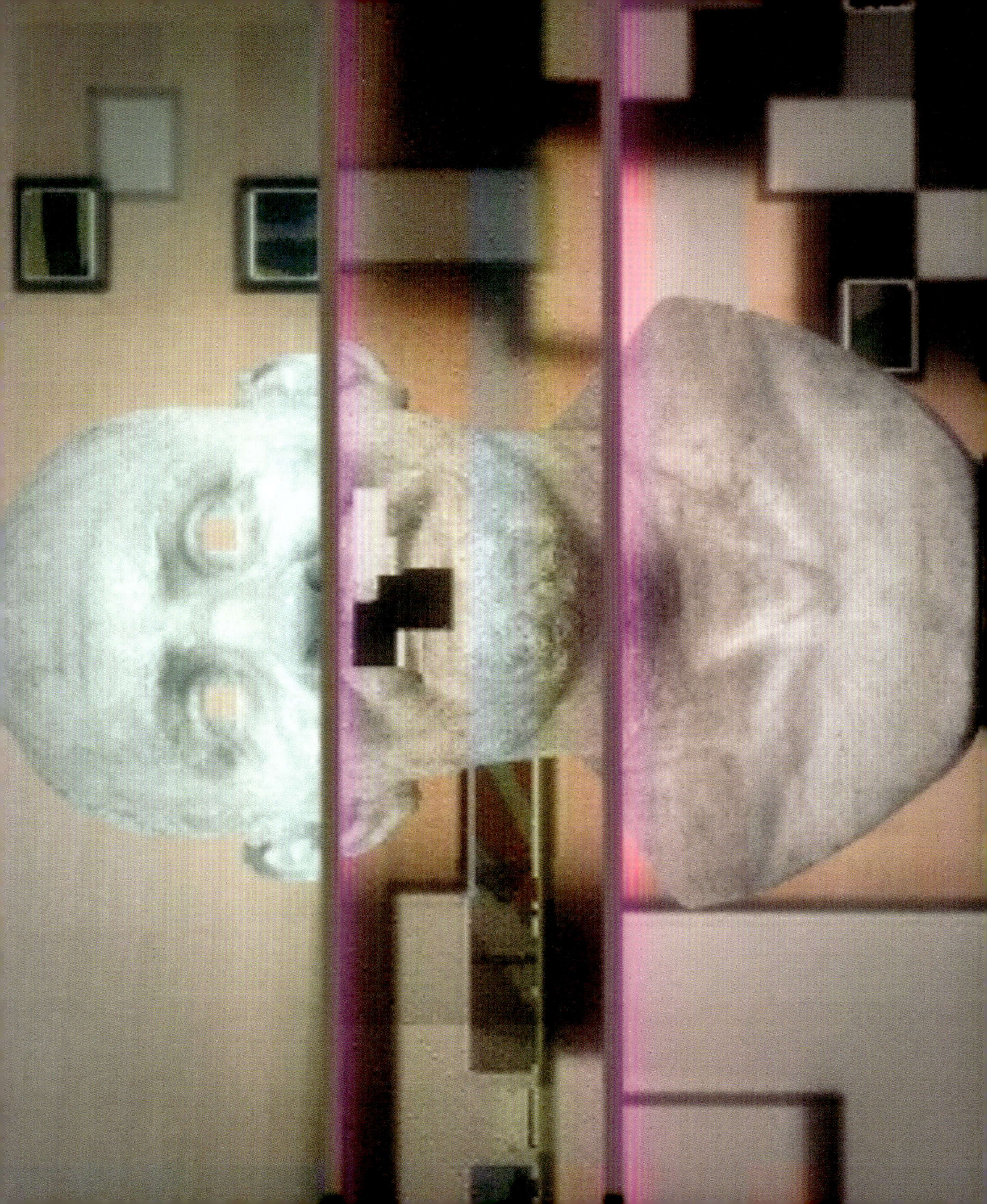

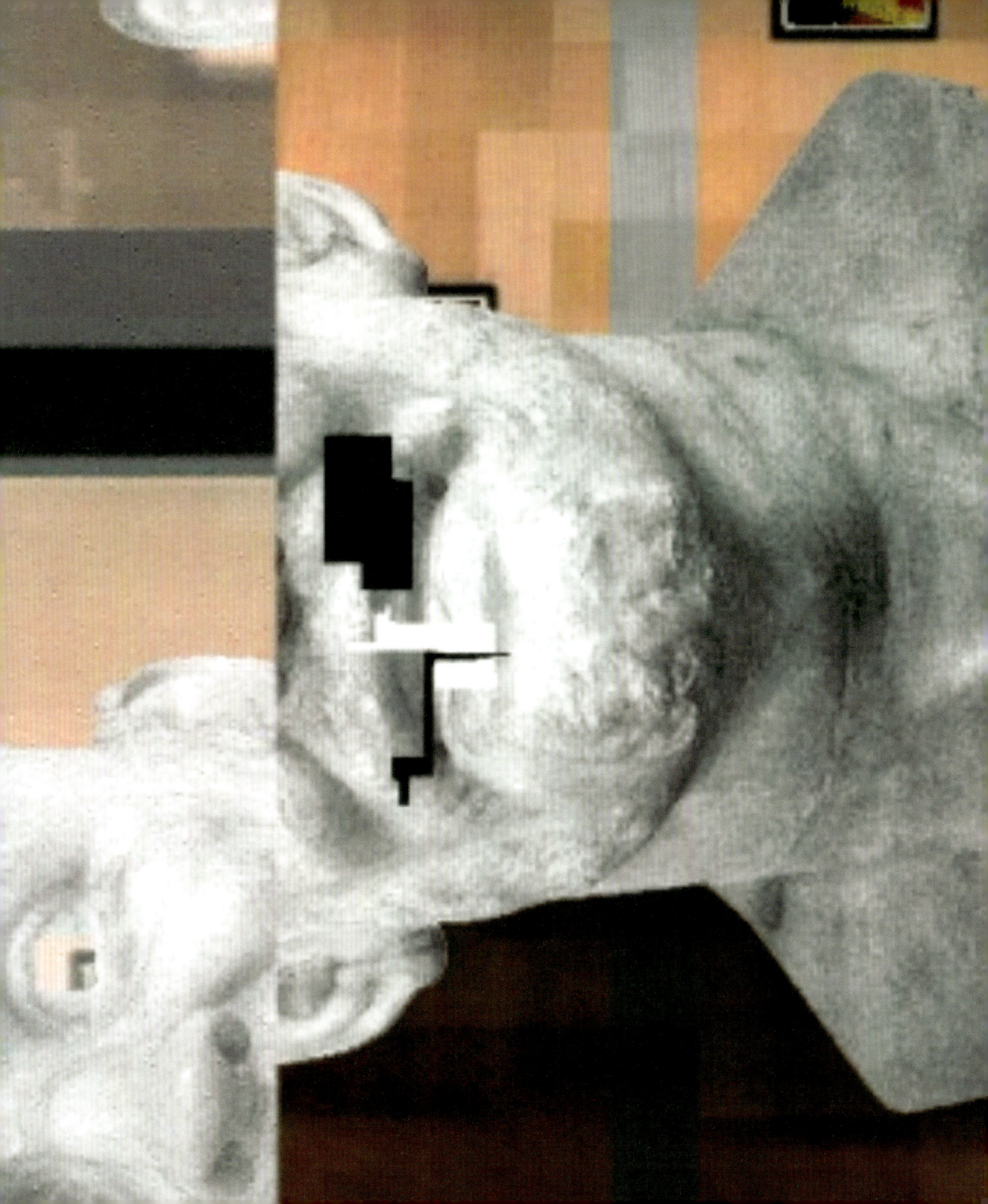

Camden Arts Centre
London

Strange Events Permit Themselves the Luxury of Occurring

The Coronation of Talu vii, Emperor of Ponukele
and King of Drelshkaf
" …three objects hanging in a row clearly displayed like lottery prizes. The first of these objects was nothing more nor less than a bowler hat with the French word 'PINCÉE' printed in white capitals on its white crown; the next one was a dark grey suede glove with the palm turned outwards and a large 'C' lightly marked on it with chalk; lastly there dangled from the string a fine sheet of parchment, covered with strange hieroglyphs and bearing as a heading the rather crude drawing of five figures, deliberately made to look absurd by their general posture and exaggerated features." [Raymond Roussel, *Impressions of Africa*, Paris 1910]

Raymond Roussel devotes the opening chapter of his novel to the description of a curious, eccentric, fanciful and opiate tableau set in a fictitious country in a continent he had not and would never visit. In a specially selected area, a complex series of constructions, objects and vignettes are arranged in oblique relation to one another. Each scenario is distinct, but a loose aura of commonality is provoked or inferred, partly through proximity and partly by design. The familiarity of the furniture of display (pedestals, plaques, frames, notices, vitrines, stages etc) leads one to suspect or impose some kind of fugitive logic on to the seemingly aimless constellation of absurd, anachronistic, cruel and redundant objects, artifacts, images and documents at once domestic and exotic, both practical and specialised beyond application or implementation. What unifies these things, scenes, texts and dysfunctional machines is not explained; Roussel leaves this to the ensuing chapters,

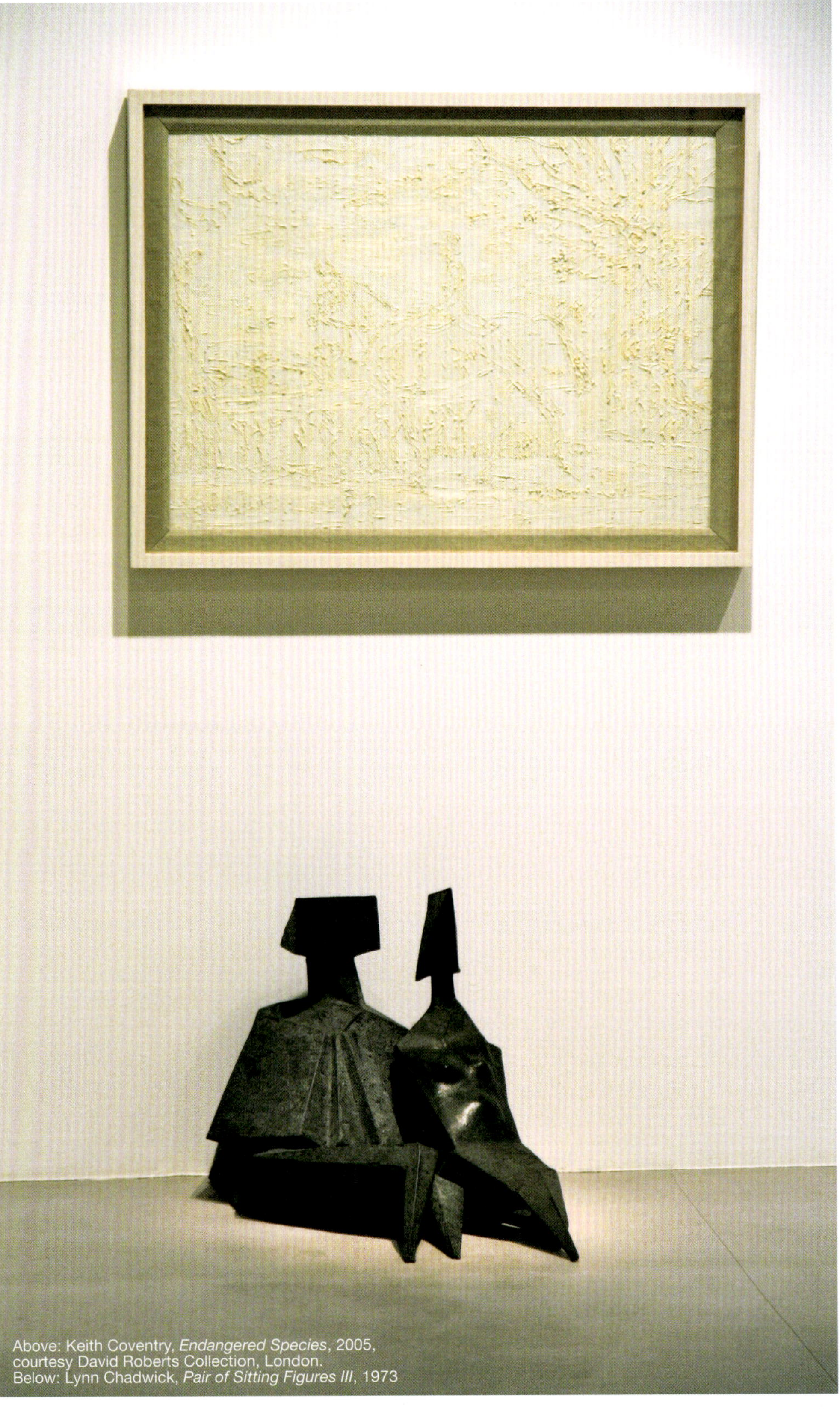

Strange Events Permit Themselves the Luxury of Occuring, installation views
2007-8
Photos: Andy Keate

where he proceeds to unravel this Sado-Dadaistic intestine of undigested possibility. It is Roussel's process of fictional observation and matter-of-fact illustration that lends these very strange objects and images gravity in spite of their idiosyncratic context, or because of it.

"IF YOU WANT TO HAVE YOUR OWN IDEAS CHANGE THEM AS OFTEN AS YOU WOULD A SHIRT" "Only useless things are indispensable" [Francis Picabia, *YES NO: Poems & Sayings* (from 1939, 1953, 1957), 1990]

Strange Events Permit Themselves the Luxury of Occurring concerns itself with certain exceptions, flaws, aberrations, yawning apertures and flowering discrepancies inherent in taxonomic, historical, and aesthetic groupings. In particular it considers the way in which the artefact, object and document behave within a shifting contextual climate with an emphasis on the 'thingly' character of the work of art and its constant attempts to struggle against definition, toward self-abnegation and self-cannibalisation.

"Beethoven's quartets lie in the publisher's storeroom like potatoes in the cellar" [Martin Heidegger, *The Origin of the Work of Art*, 1948]

Martin Heidegger dwells on this wrestling match between material 'Earth' and contextual 'World' in his 1948 text *The Origin of the Work of Art*. This semantic pugilism is for Heidegger the 'Work-Being' in the work of art, an oscillation between revealing and concealment necessary to distinguish the art object from 'equipment' (craft, utility). Heidegger argues that the craft object consumes its material in the service of the thing. The energy or work is expended in the manufacture of the 'equipment' which then conceals it, rendering the object superficial or decorative. Heidegger perceives the artist as conduit or medium who enables through spontaneous growth (*phusis*) the 'being' of the work, who sets the stage for the work's 'pure self subsistence', a unique and self-perpetuating (autonomous) encounter between substance and symbol that "holds open the Open of the world". This event for Heidegger is the Work-Being in the work of art. He leaves himself a failsafe by sneakily allowing the artwork the luxury (quite rightly) of a vacillation between concealment and revealing – what Nietzsche would identify as the Apollonian and Dionysian character of the artist straddling, in tandem, the artefact.

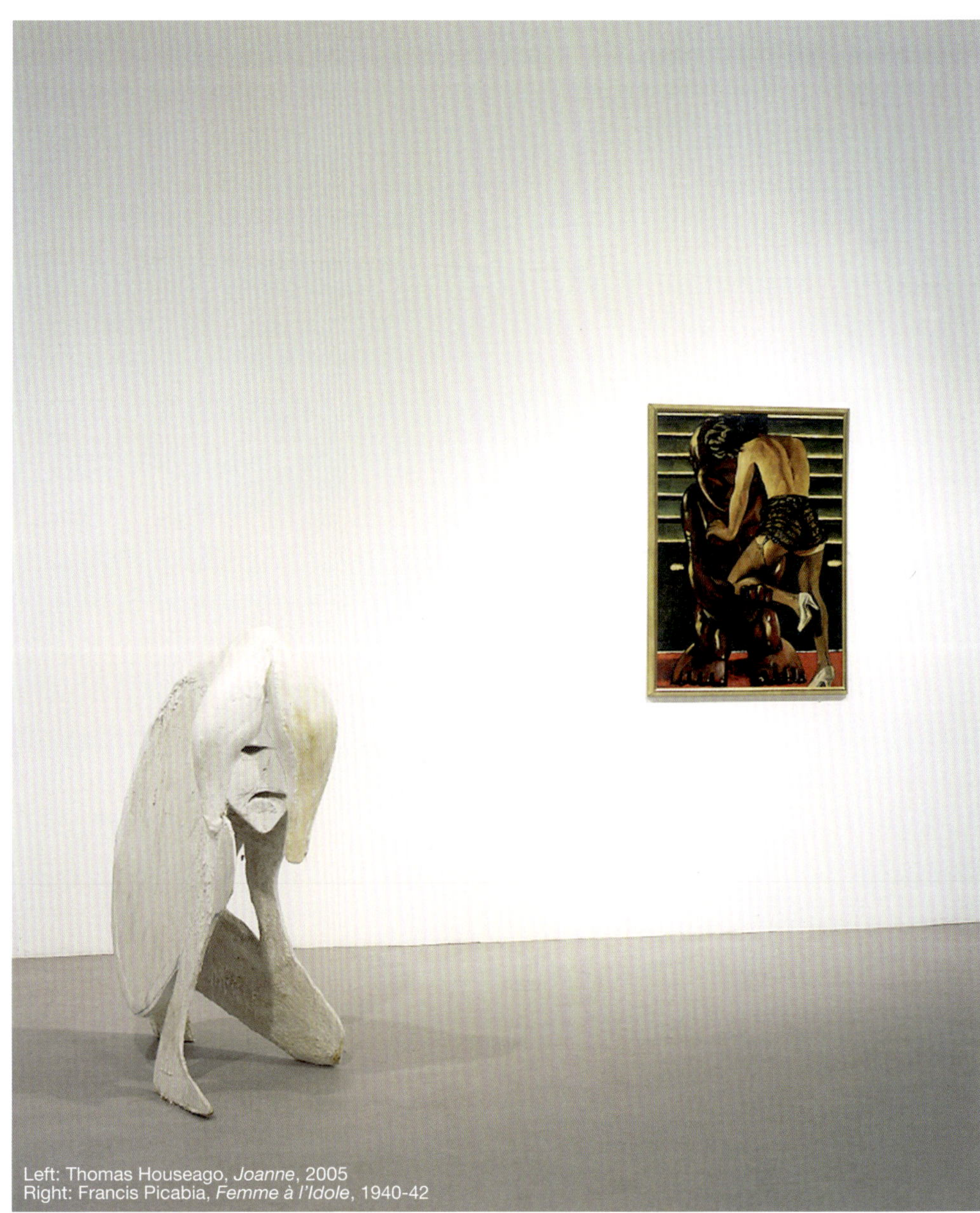

Left: Thomas Houseago, *Joanne*, 2005
Right: Francis Picabia, *Femme à l'Idole*, 1940-42

" The greatest monuments create the most dust." [Arthur Cravan, *Four Dada Suicides*, Selected Texts of Arthur Cravan, Jacques Rigaut, Julian Torma and Jacques Vache, 1995]

In my capacity as guest curator, I would like this exhibition (amongst other things) to shed some light on the curious and spurious hierarchy of materials (matter, earth, caca etc) and the venerable status endowed on the work of art, monument or relic. *Strange Events* attempts to loosely accrete artists whose practices betray a willful incongruity and a mercurial approach to such associative categorisations and establish a climate of practice that aggregates around the errant core of the 'thingly', whatever that may be. The show explores the problematic and elusive penumbra where the art object somehow distinguishes itself from the utilitarian or craft object through means of discretion or bombast.

*"The Pursuit of Fecality
There where it smells of shit
it smells of being.
Man could just as well not have shat,
not have opened the anal pouch,*

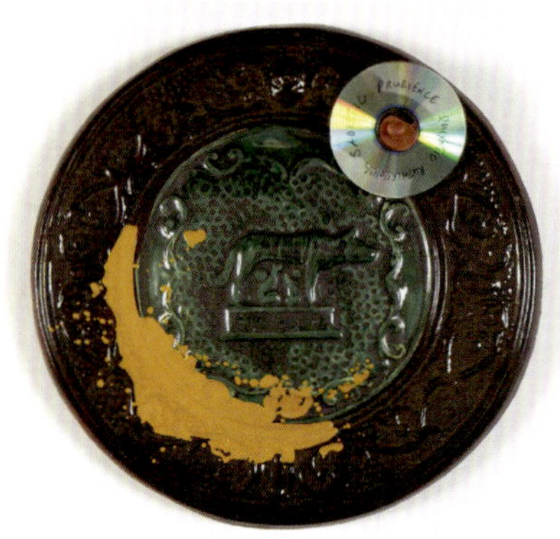

1- SPQR Series
2007
Ceramic, audio CD, grip fill
20cm Ø
Photo: Camden Arts Centre

2- Strange Events Permit Themselves the Luxury of Occuring, installation view
2007
Photo: Andy Keate

3-4 - Logs From The Black Forest detail,
2007
Bronze, powder coated steel, oil on canvas, wood, plastic
Dimensions variable
Photo: Andy Keate

5- Call From the Ruhr, detail
2007
Sunglasses, copper slate, resin, acrylic, canvas, steel, hessian
Dimensions variable
Photo: Andy Keate

6- Strange Events Permit Themselves the Luxury of Occuring, installation view
2007
Photo: Andy Keate

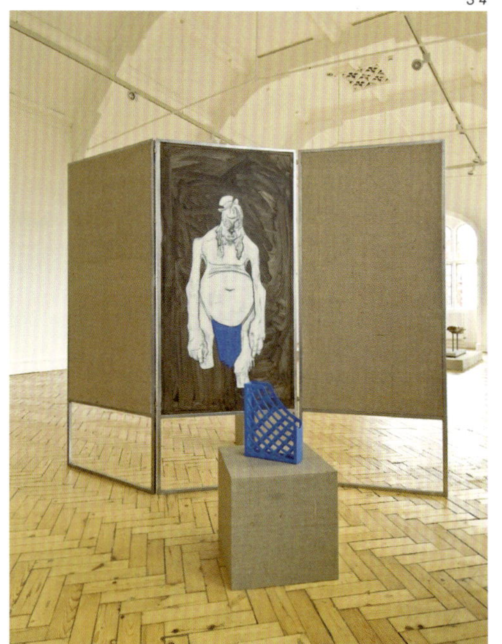

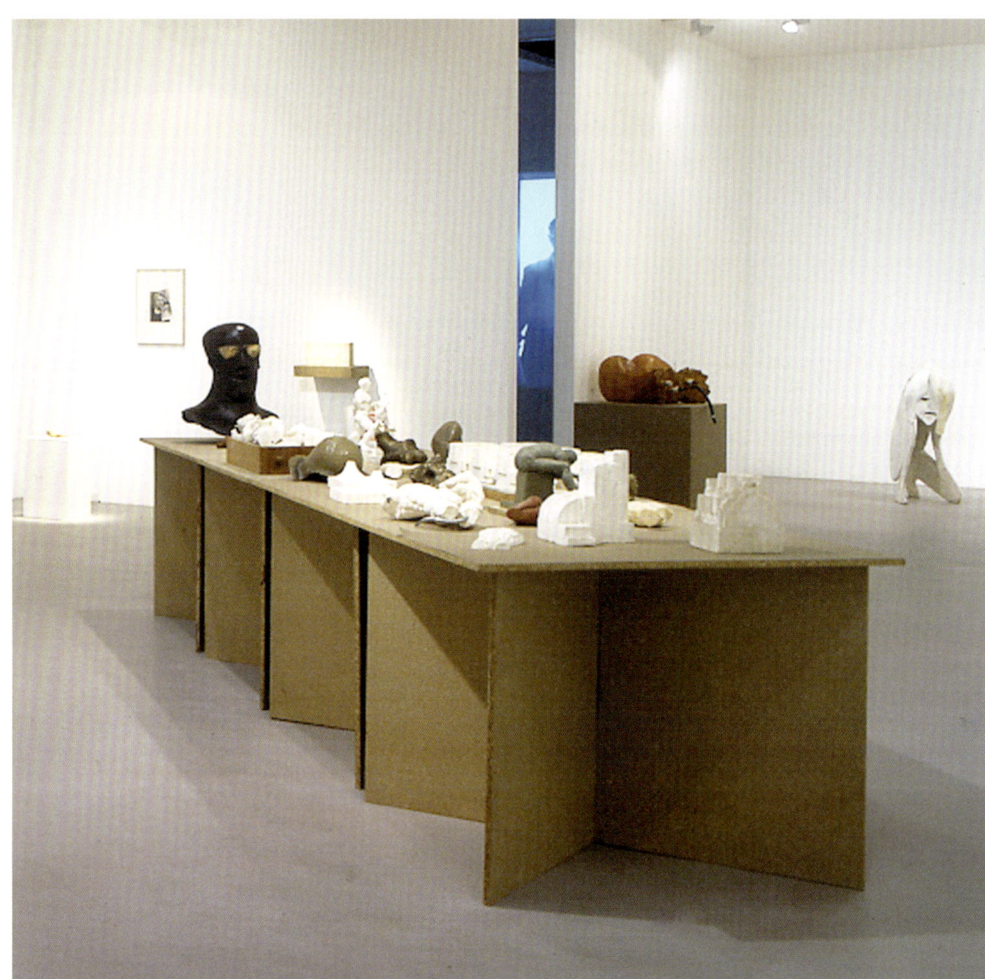

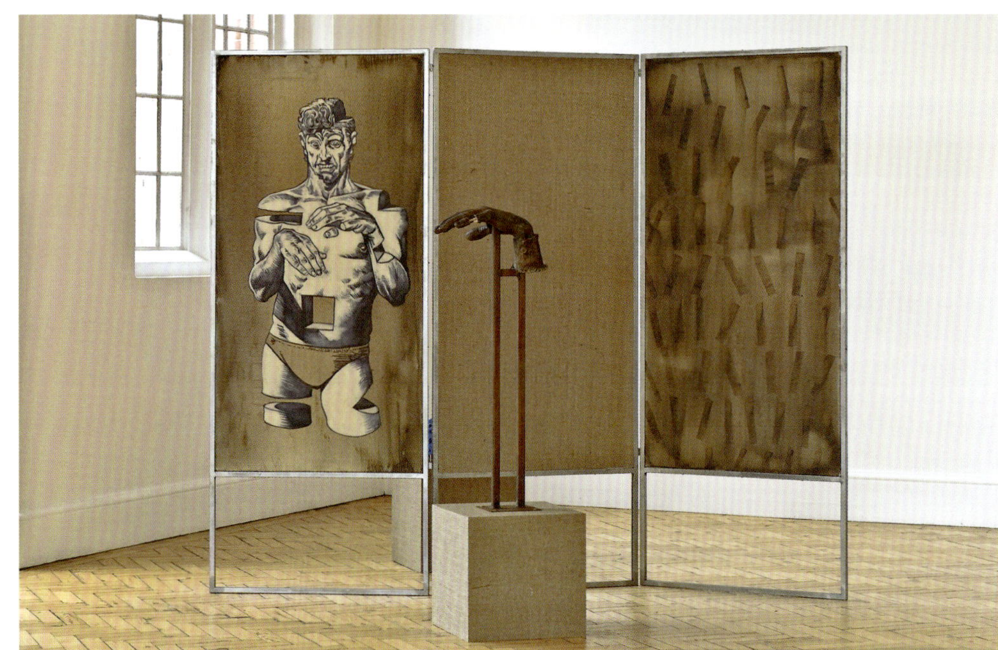

*but he chose to shit
as he would have chosen to live
instead of consenting to live dead.
Because in order not to make caca,
he would have had to consent
not to be,
but he could not make up his mind to lose
being,
that is, to die alive.
There is in being
something particularly tempting for man and this
something is none other than
CACA.
(Roaring here.)"*
[Antonin Artaud, *To Have Done With the Judgement of God*, (Pour en finir avec le jugement de dieu), a radio play, 1947]

Anomalies and free radicals have constantly referenced and cross-referenced one another, circumventing the labyrinth of categorisation. These artists have no time for governing principles, maintaining a scrupulous lack of scruples and embracing the territory between asceticism and suppurating grotesquery, even burrowing their way back to their swampy material genesis. Other artists ape utility or forge a spurious utilitarian provenance, doctoring the venerability heaped on posterity. Puncturing every timeline, there is an aberration that perverts lineal conceit and illuminates hermeneutics, history and the history of things to become an obscure and lateral mesh where exceptions challenge orthodoxy. These complex and contradictory elements spawn a panoply of exceptions and incongruity that threaten the already flimsy lineal dictates that sheepishly steward art production. The remnants of a litany of flawed utopian manifestos and spectres of proselytising modernist and postmodern pronouncements that replaced an equally ludicrous skeleton of theories and rhetoric before them. Here the document becomes the monument as the fragment cannibalises the whole (the periphery subsumes the academy) and the cycle continues.

"Laws are against the exception, I only like the exception."
"Morality is the dorsal spine of idiots."
[Francis Picabia, *YES NO: Poems & Sayings* (from 1939, 1953, 1957), 1990]

Associative groupings appear from this miasma of disparate processes and practices like survivors from a big fat disaster, an unlikely assembly of limbs and singularities bonded by expedience. This post-historical fallout leaves us frolicking in the void like imbeciles waiting for a really good fart. Like the subjects of Artaud's *The Pursuit of Fecality*, we find ourselves producing (caca) for production's sake, in lieu of the tangible, in lieu of manifesto, and that's fine with me. We know that tangibility was always a construct, the manifesto as a bombastic conceit and history – at best a kind of retrospective fiction – what Richard Dawkins describes as 'the conceit of hindsight'. So what? It may be that an acceptance of the polymorphic or a-parallel nature of histories and culture-context could lead us to better understand 'the thingliness of things', or perhaps as Charlie Chan, a character as fictional and preposterous as any in Roussel's *Impressions of Africa*, didn't once say, 'Strange events permit themselves the luxury of occurring.'

Steven Claydon, 2007.
Text reprinted from Camden Arts Centre File Note, published on the occasion of *Strange Events Permit Themselves the Luxury of Occurring*.

5

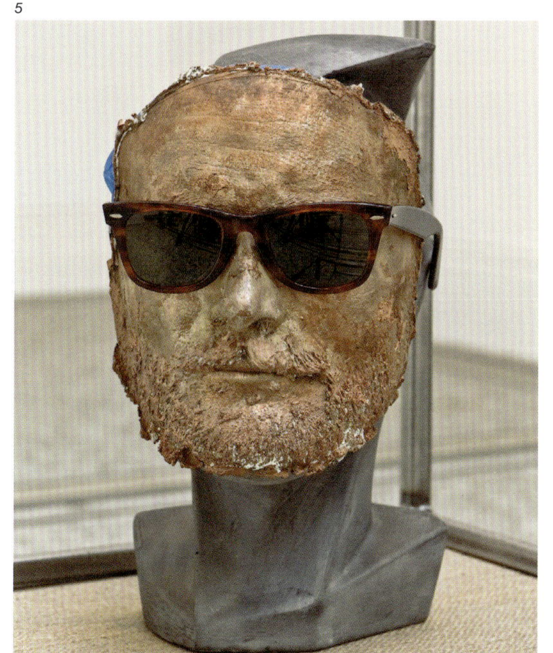

6

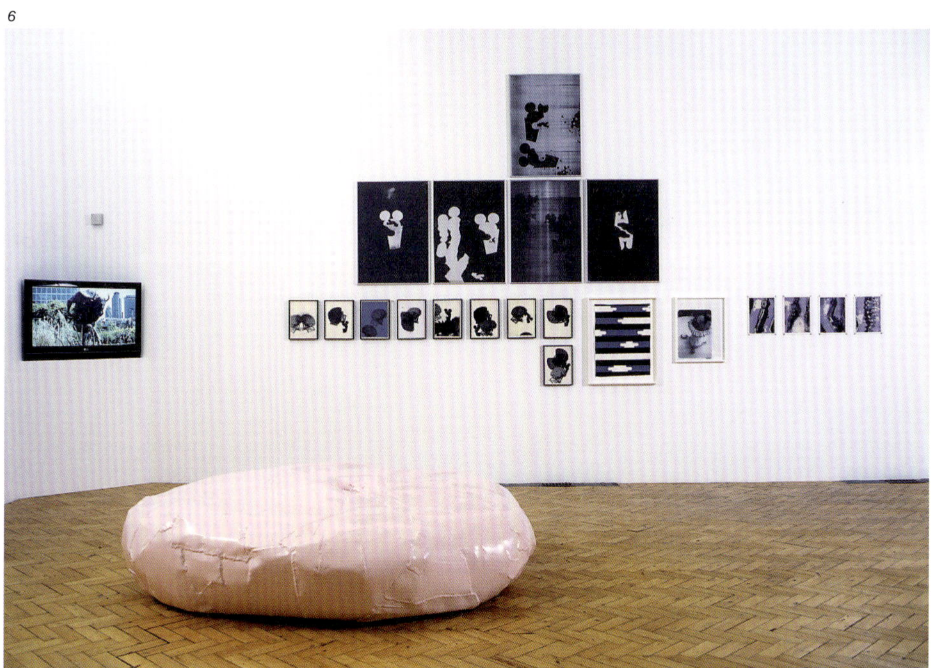

Arnolfini, Bristol

Pale Carnage

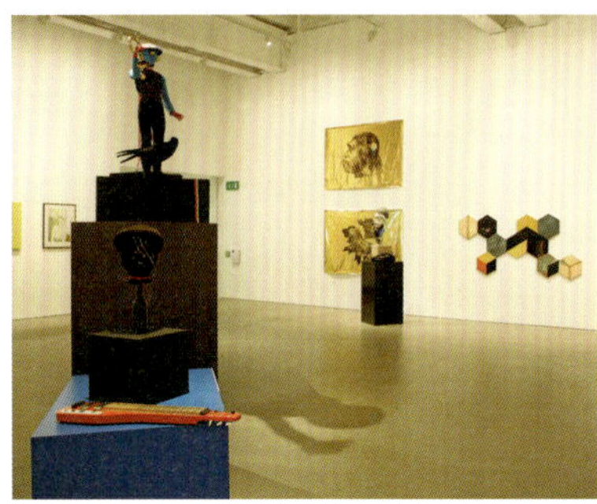

1-2- *Pale Carnage,*
installation view
2007

3- *A Monopoly On
Posterity
(Battering Ram)*
2007
Coffee and ink on Mylar
124.5 x 179.1 cm

*A Monopoly on Posterity
(book lungs)*
2007
Screenprint on Mylar,
sealing wax, bronze
123.8 x 178.4 cm

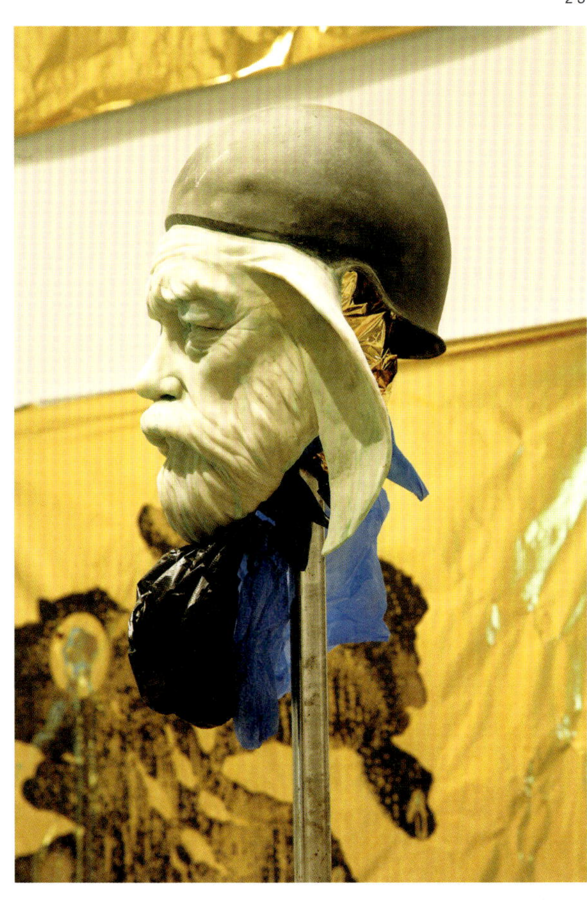

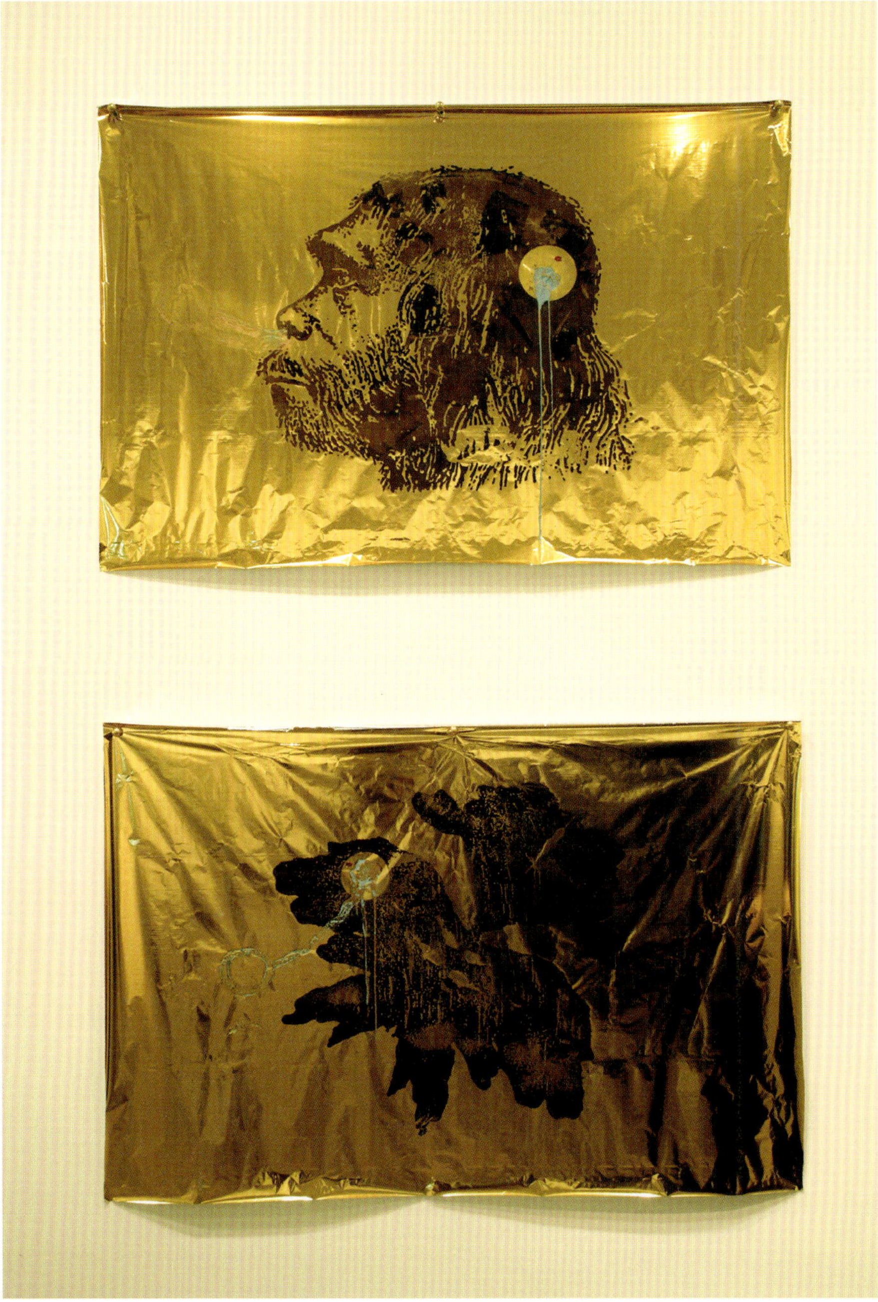

David Kordansky Gallery, New York

New Valkonia

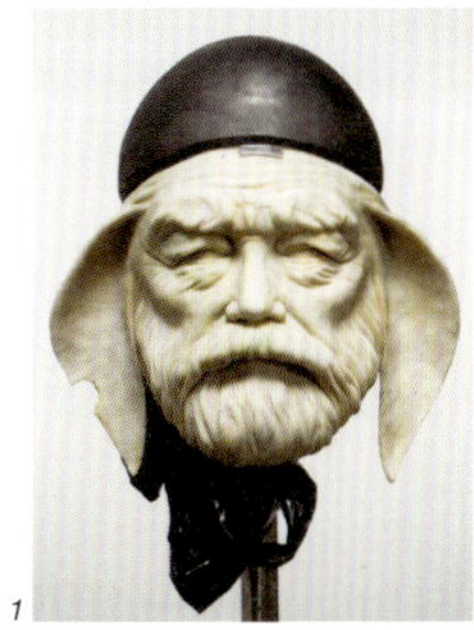

1- Spaka Spou
(Deposed Deity), detail
2007
Resin, graphite, marble
and steel, plastic, space
blanket
180.3 x 38.1 x 38.1 cm
Photo: Fredrik Nilson

2- New Valkonia,
installation views
2007
Photos: Fredrik Nilsen

3- Hornets (Mousterians
& Moderns), detail
2007
Acrylic, oil, copper and
bronze solution, sealing
wax on canvas, lead,
Plexiglas, bronze, found
object
782.5 x 351.8 x 76.2 cm

4- The Layman's Lot
2007
Pencil on found drawing
57.2 x 33 cm
Photo: Fredrik Nilsen

5- Lightbox Group
2007
Lightboxes, bronze, brass,
bull horn, plastic, steel,
quartz crystals, copper,
leather, paint
Dimensions variable
Photo: Fredrik Nilsen

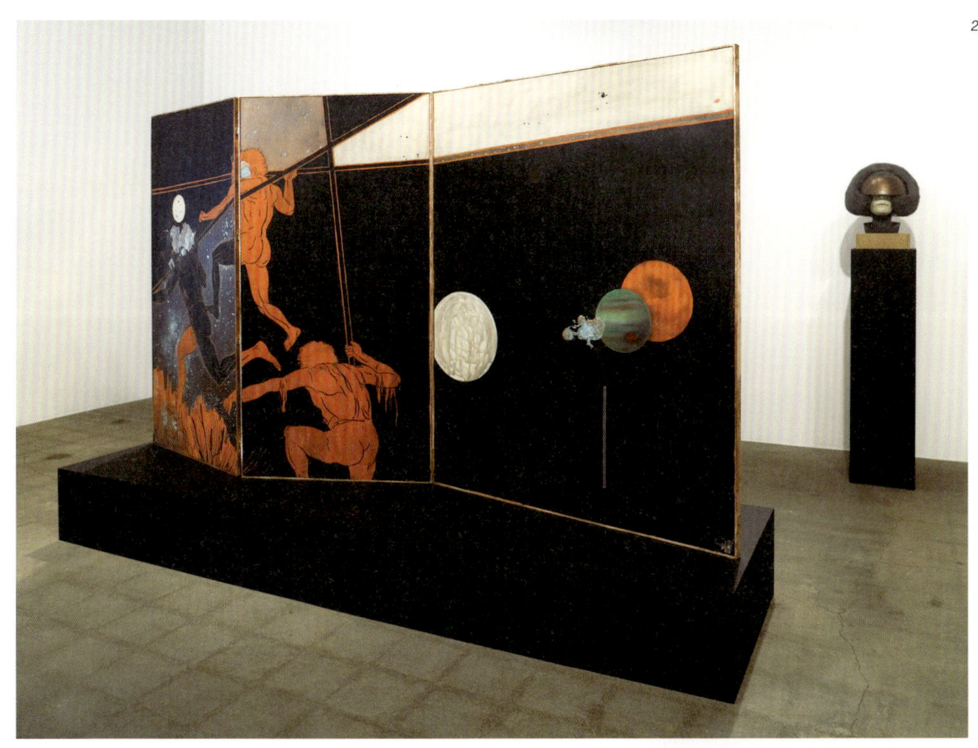

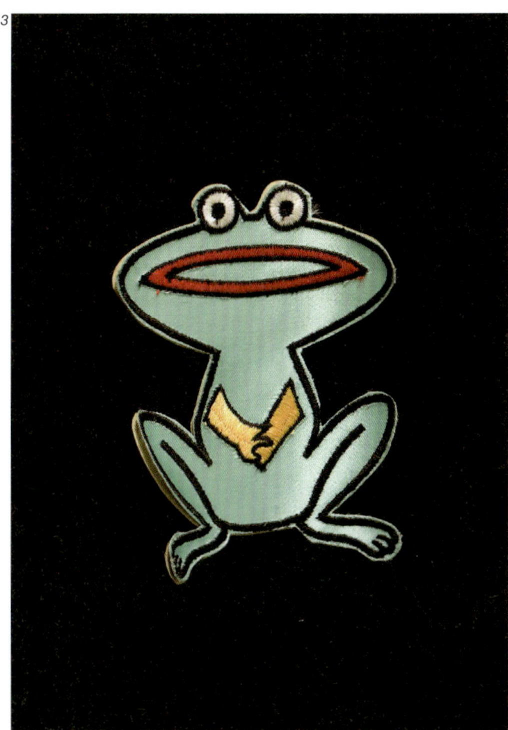

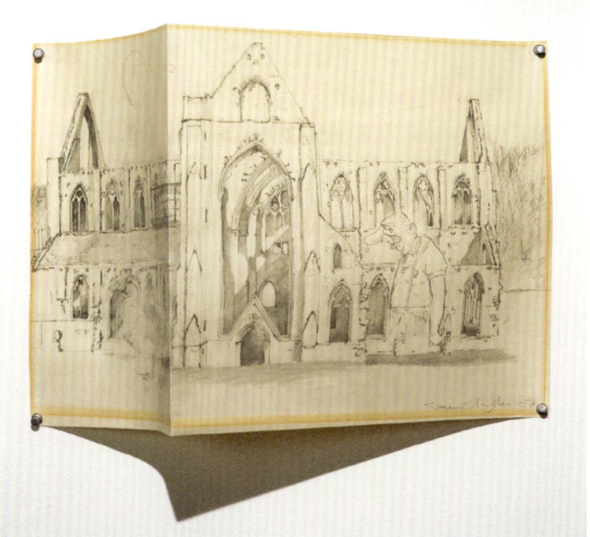

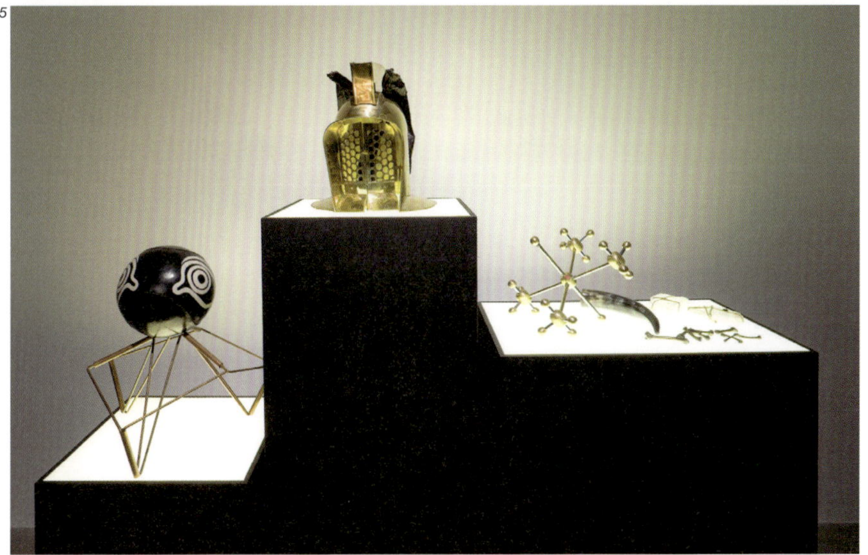

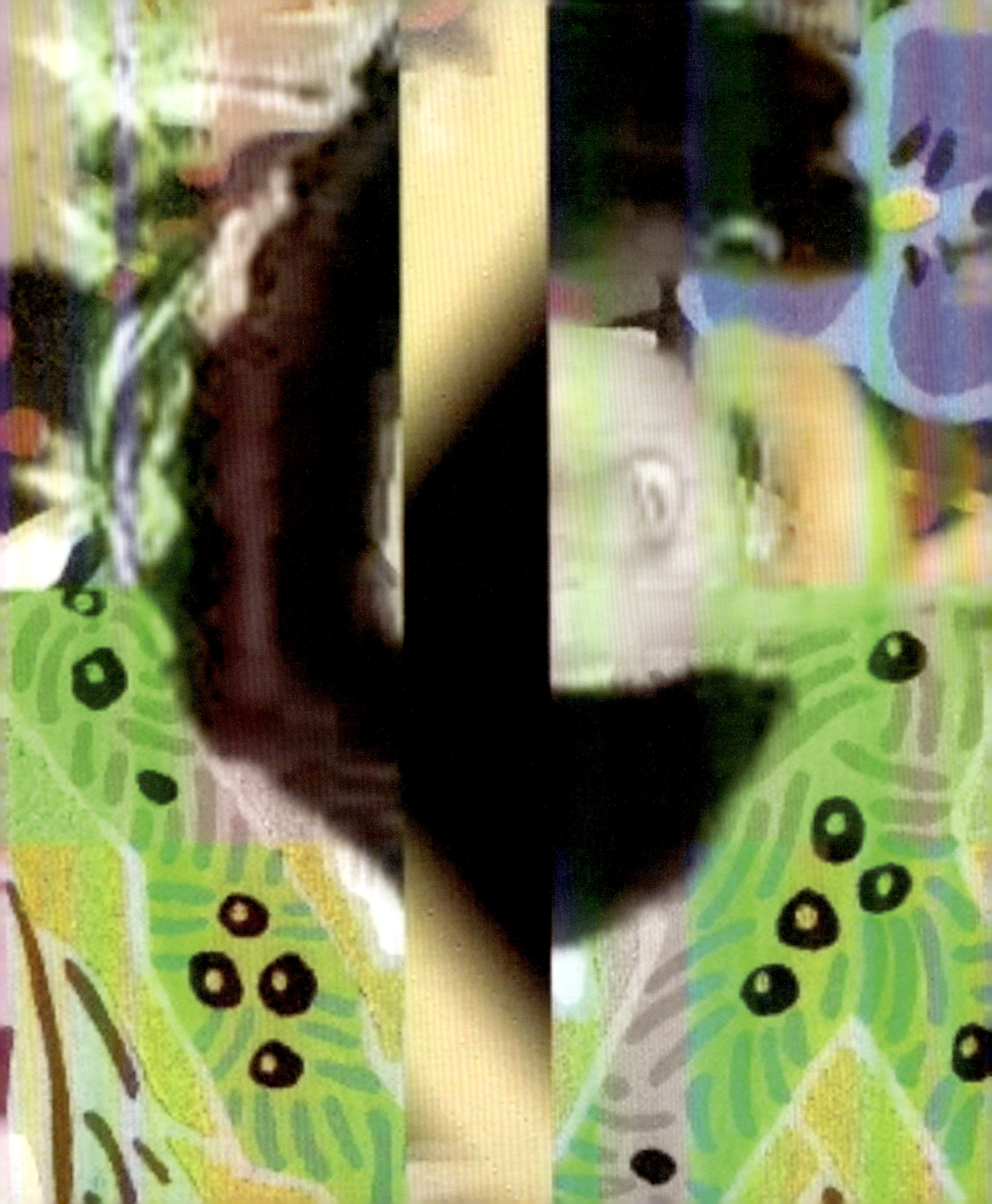

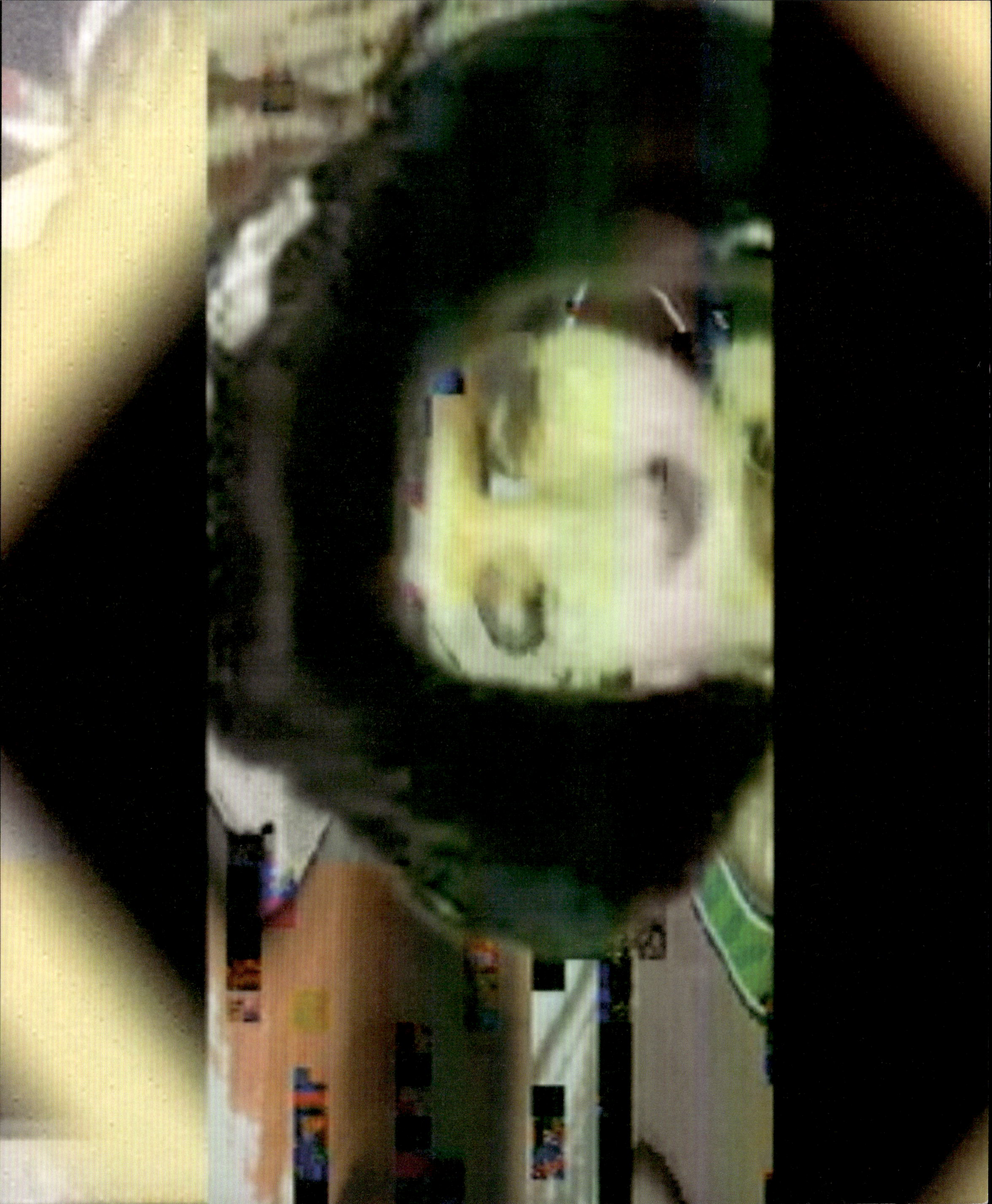

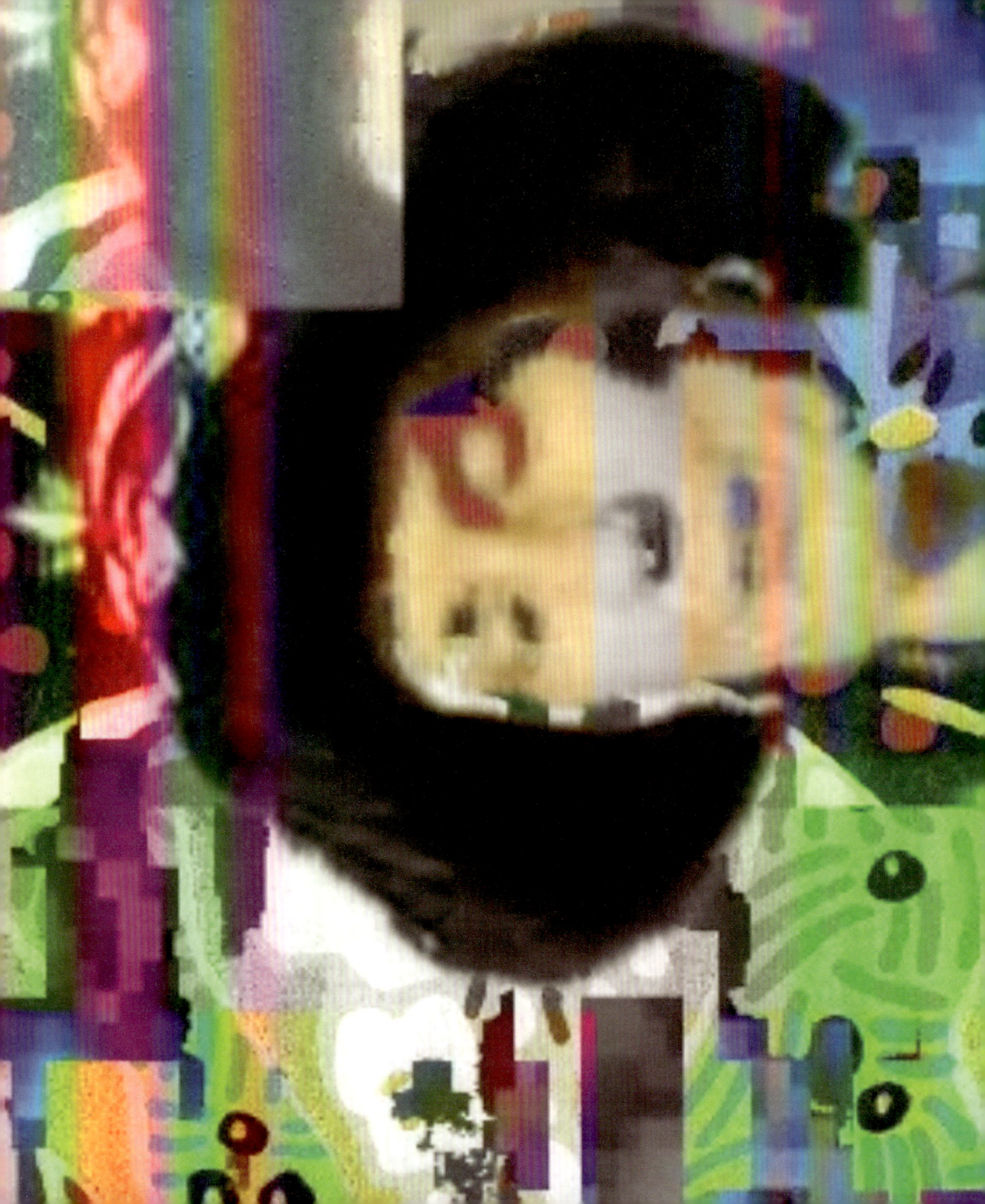

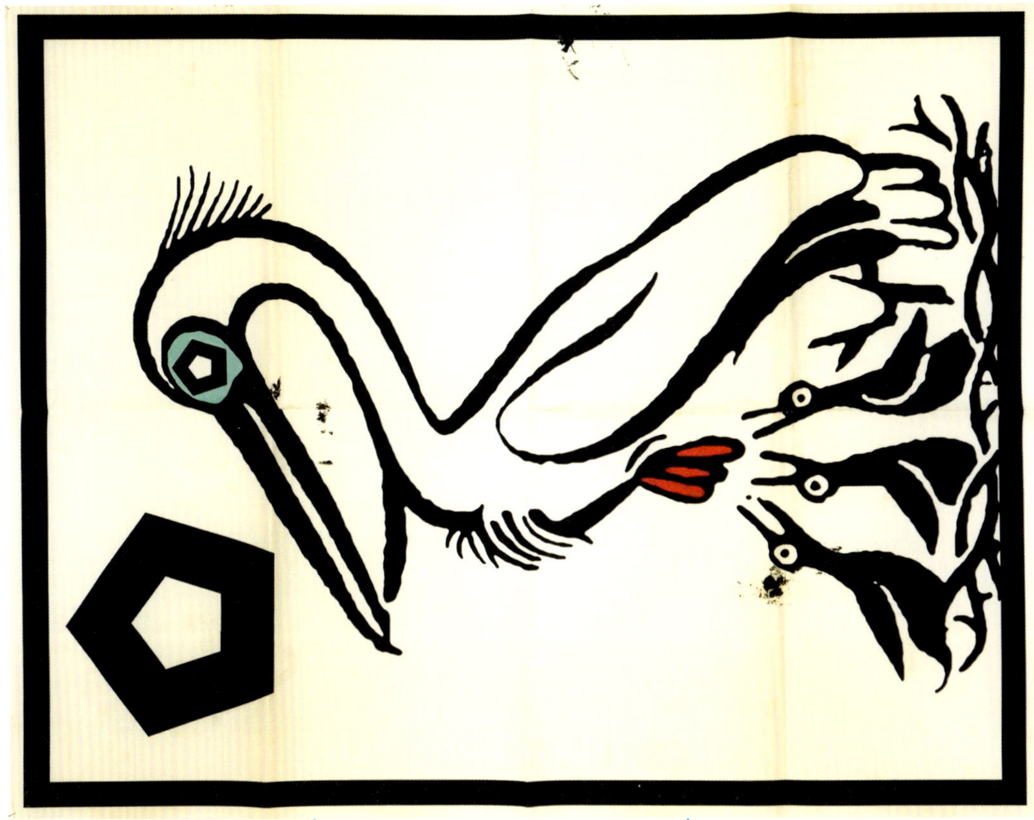

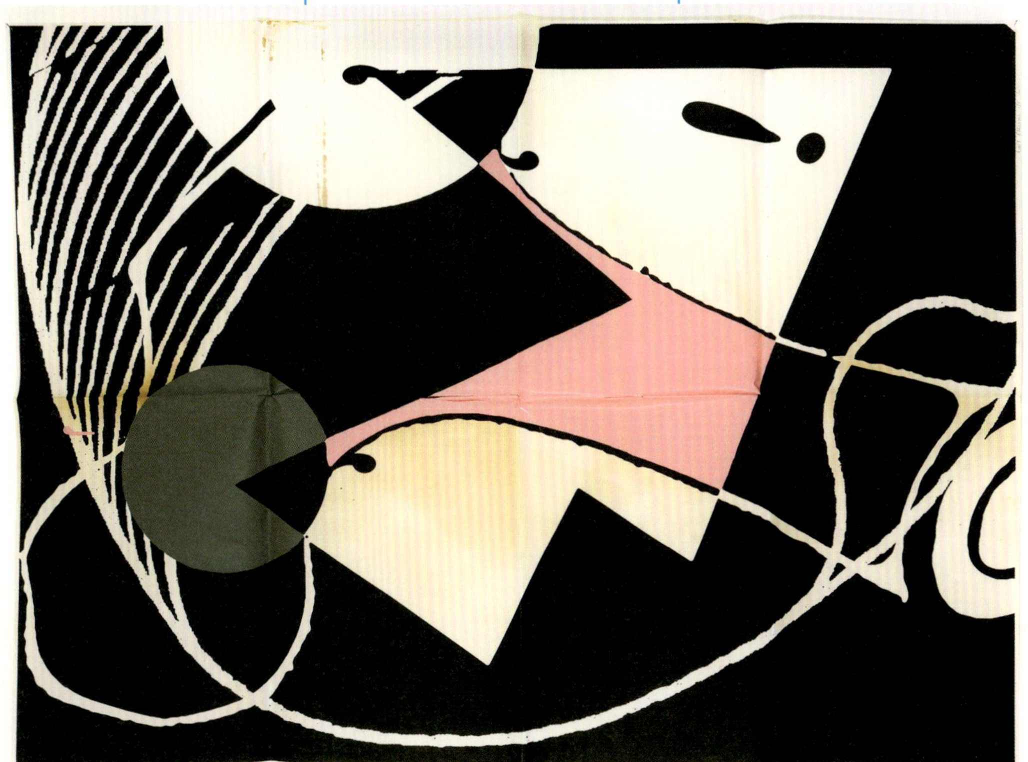

The Pelican in her Piety
2005
Print and enamel on paper
118 x 83.5 cm

Clouded Idol
2005
Print and enamel on paper
118 x 83.5 cm

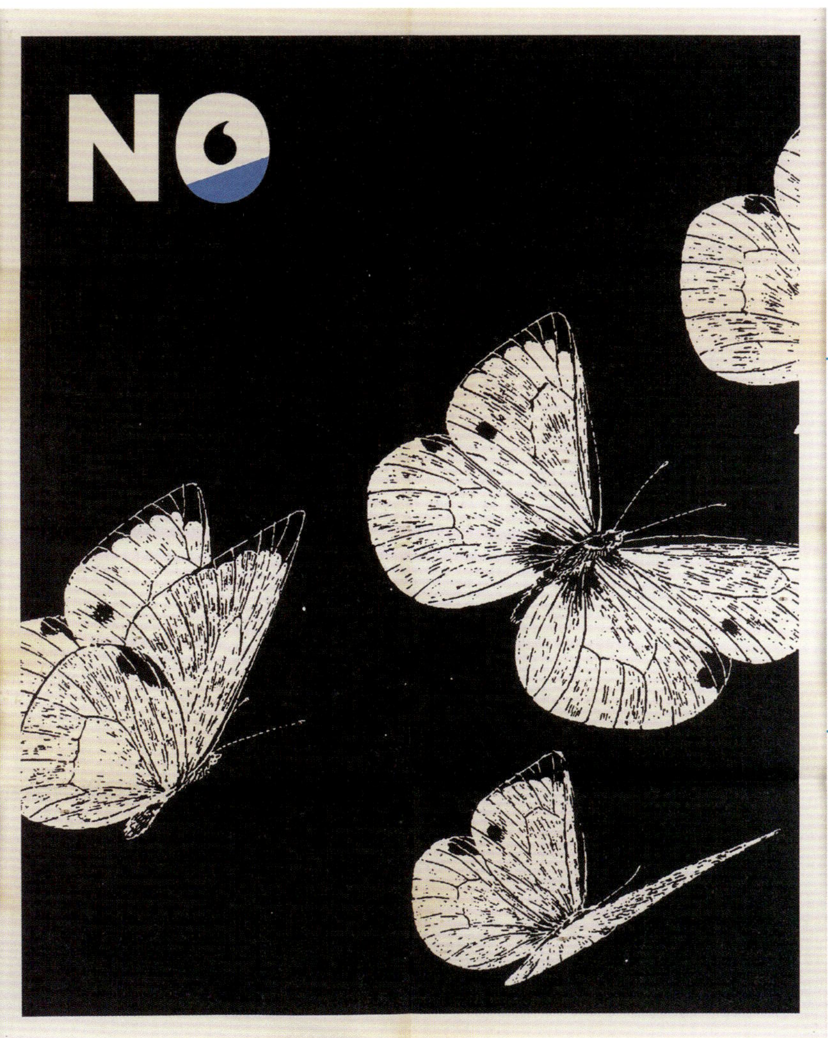

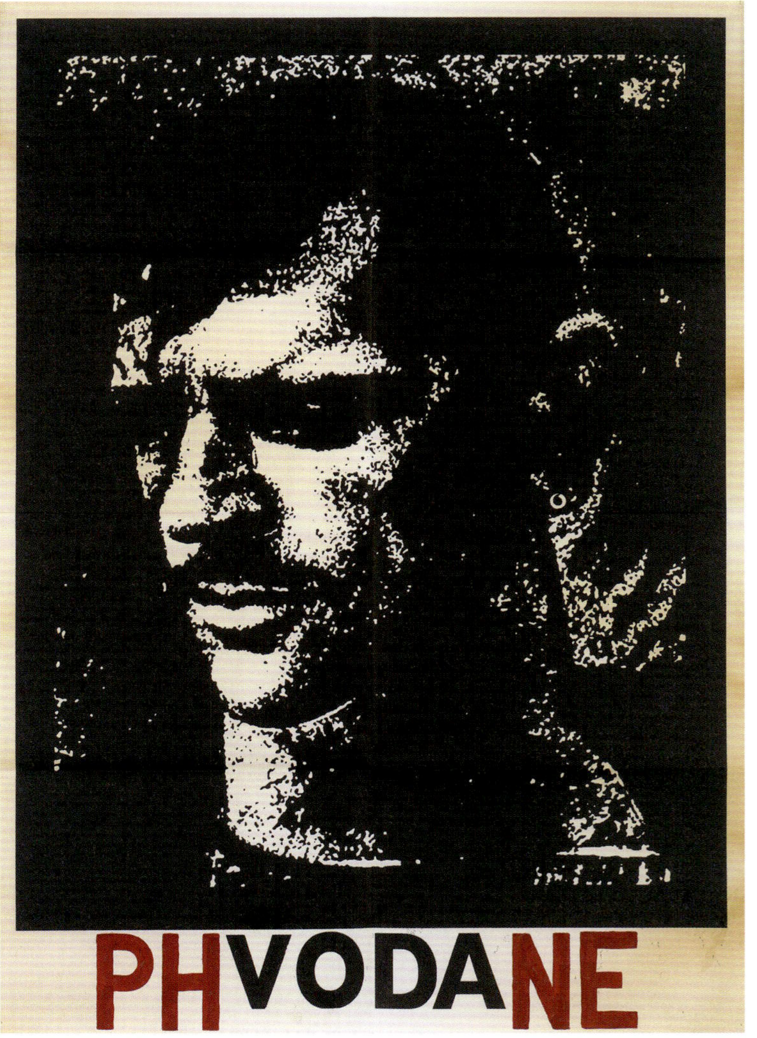

Negative
2005
Carbon print and enamel
90 x 60 cm

Phvodane
2005
Carbon print and enamel
90 x 60 cm

Doo (Chess)
2005
Carbon print and enamel
90 x 60 cm

Cluster
2005
Carbon print and enamel
90 x 60 cm

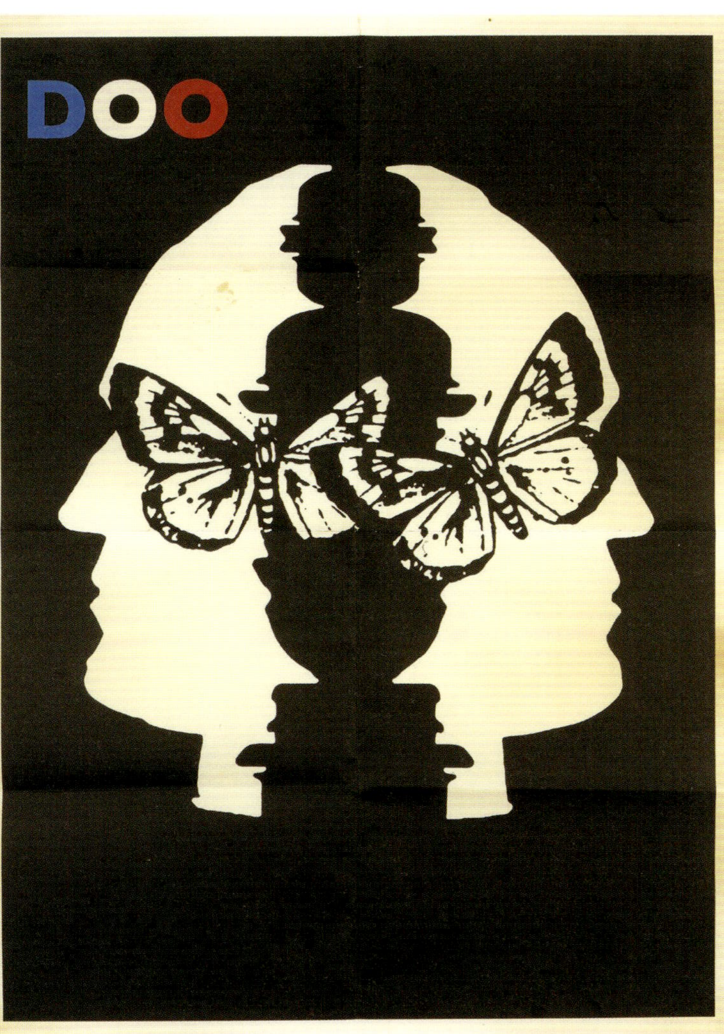

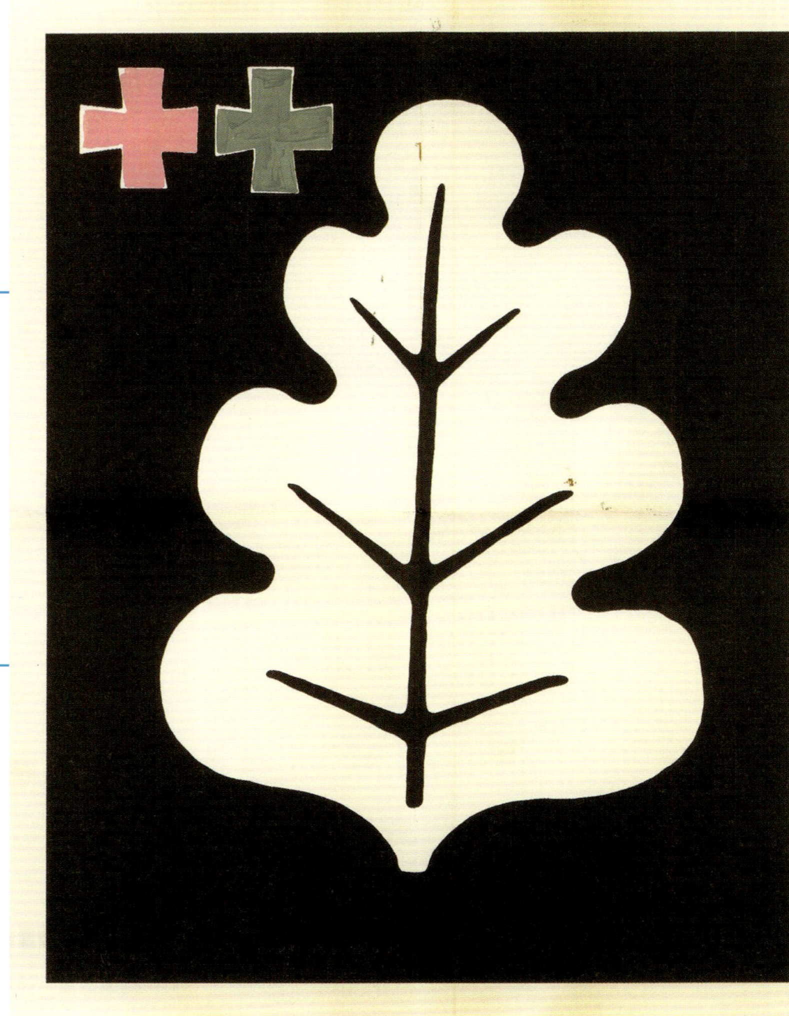

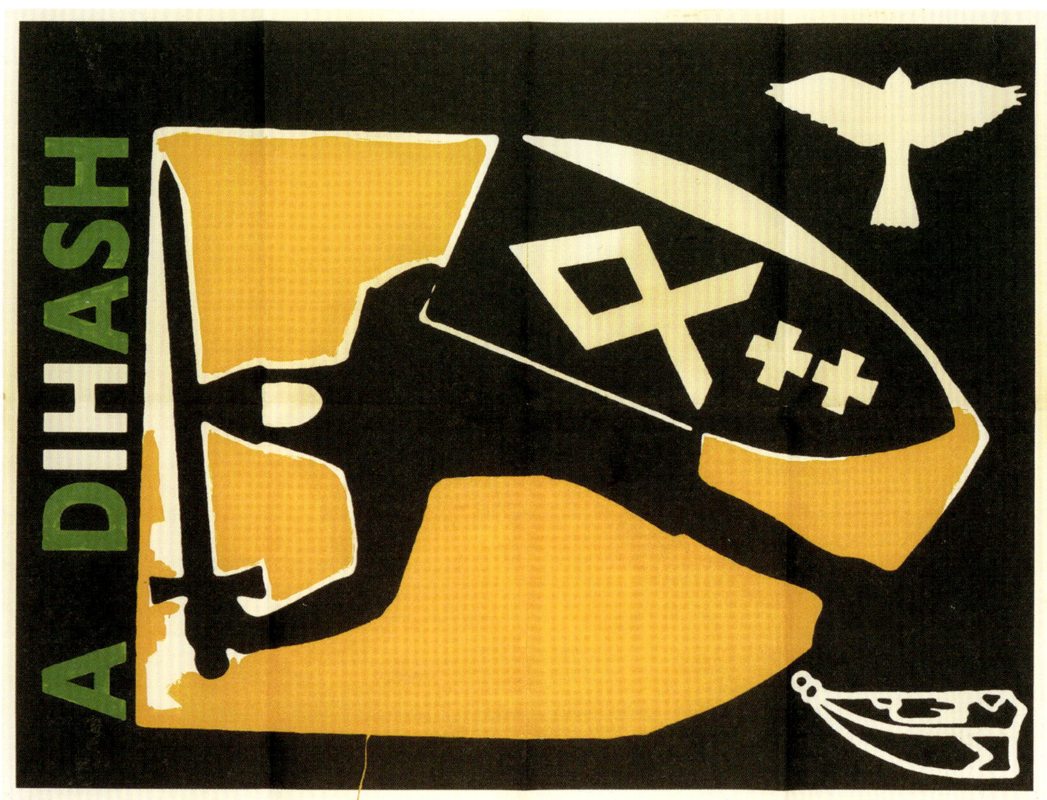

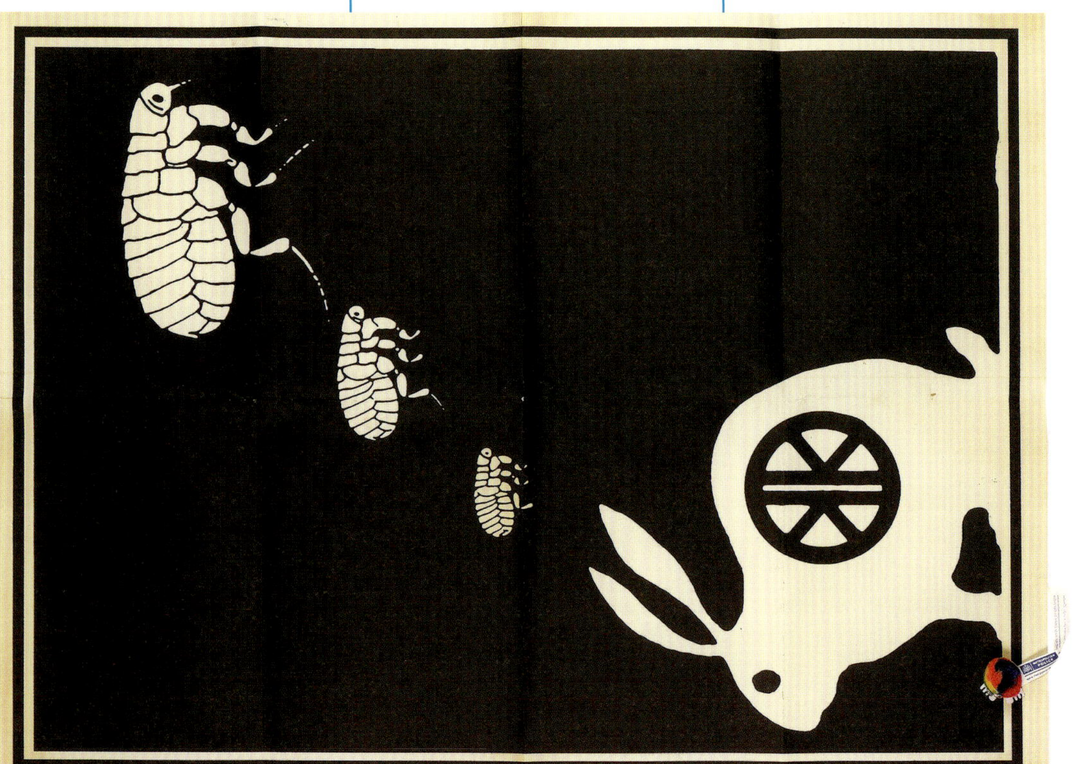

Solar Prop
2004
Carbon print and gonk
90 x 60 cm

A Dihash
2005
Carbon print and enamel
90 x 60 cm

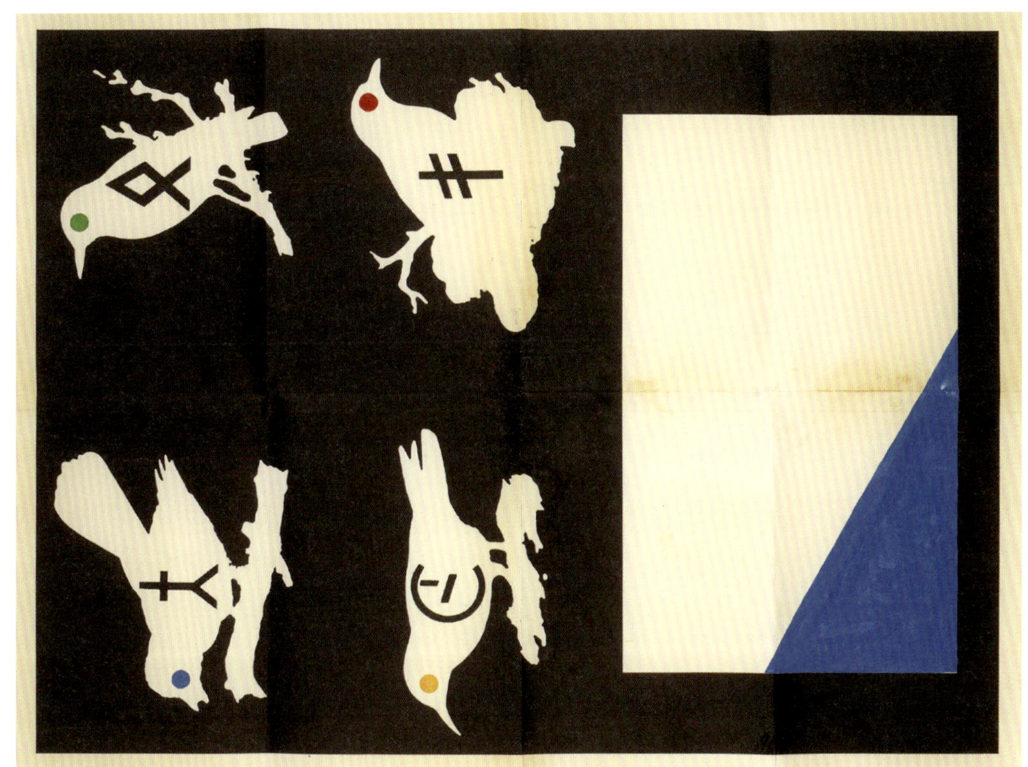

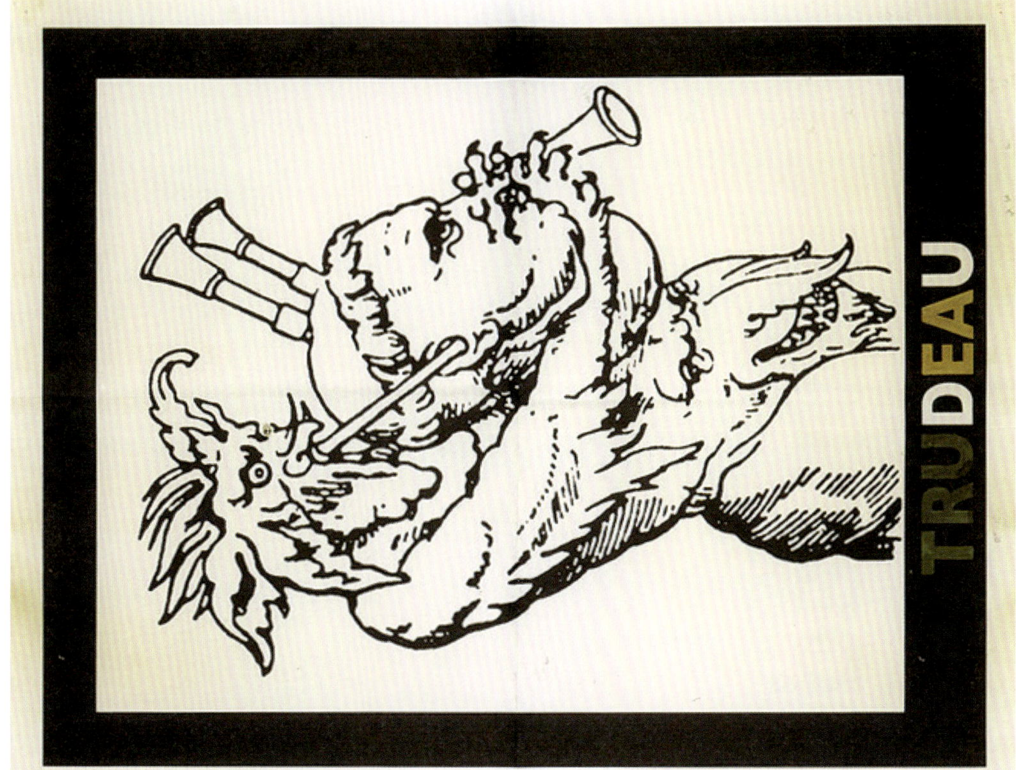

Trudeau
2005
Carbon print and enamel
72.5 x 58.5 cm
Photo: Ivo Faber

Unamiable Devices
2005
Carbon print and enamel
101.5 x 78 cm
Photo: Ivo Faber

Three drawings and a painting

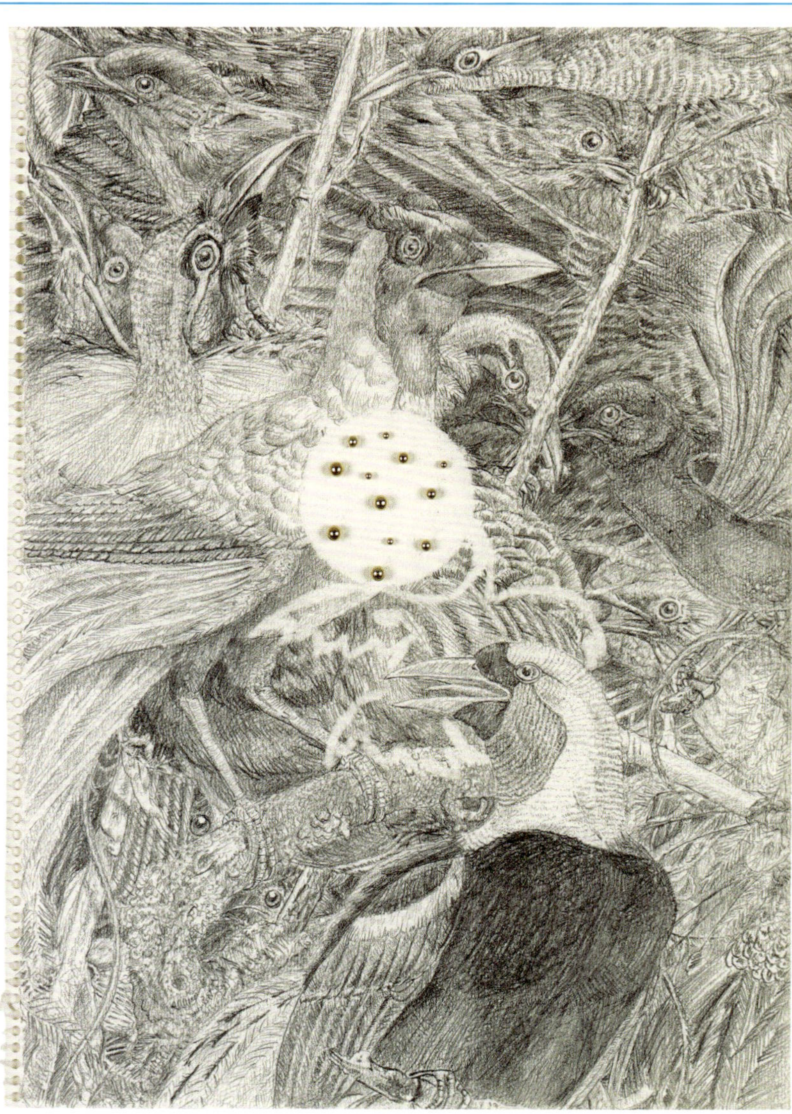

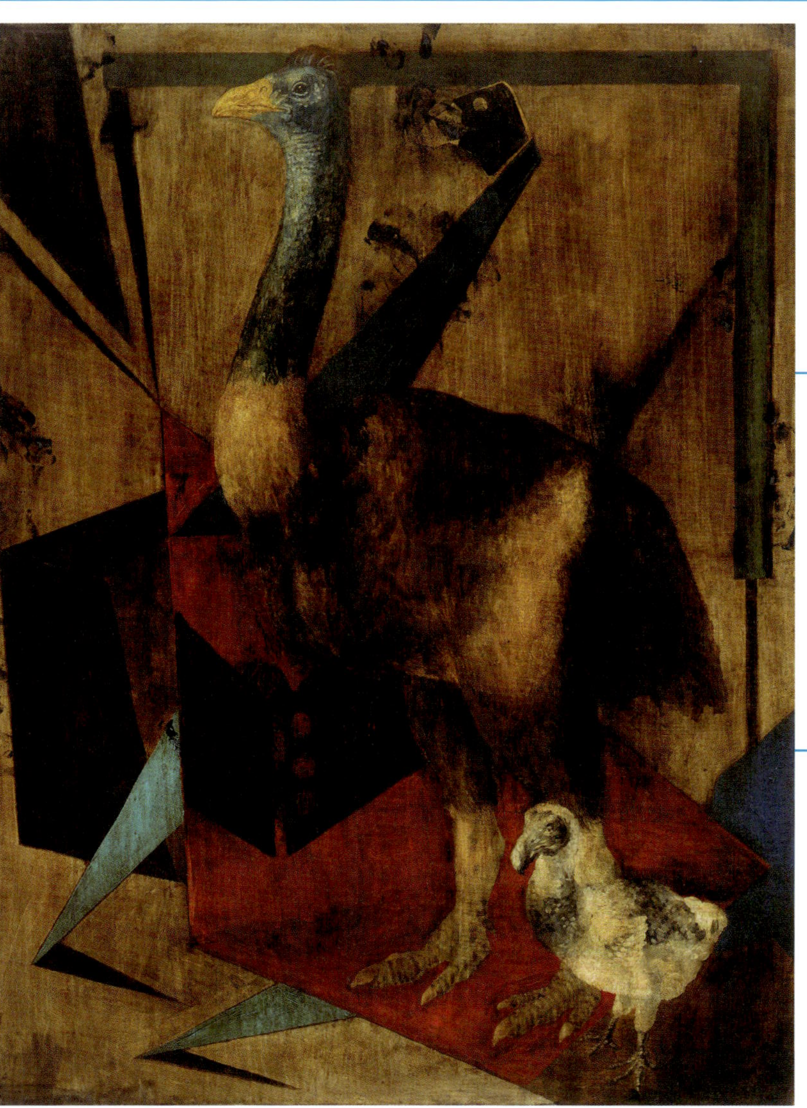

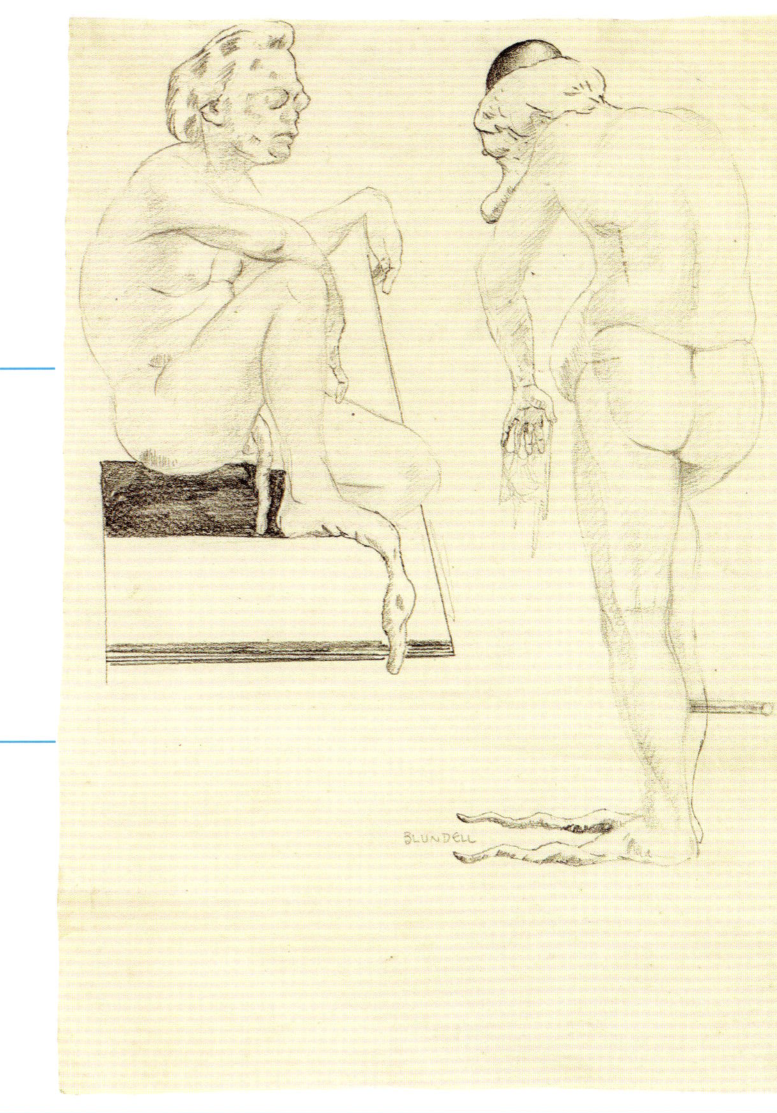

Strange Events Permit Themselves The Luxury of Occuring (Charlie Chan)
2006
Oil paint and make-up on canvas
100.8 x 75.9 cm

Drawing (they)
2005
Pencil on found drawing
36.5 x 27.8 cm
Photo: Ivo Faber

The Altruistic Birds
2005
Pencil and earings on paper
33 x 24 cm

Drawing (them)
2005
Pencil on found drawing
32.5 x 22.5 cm
Photo: Ivo Faber

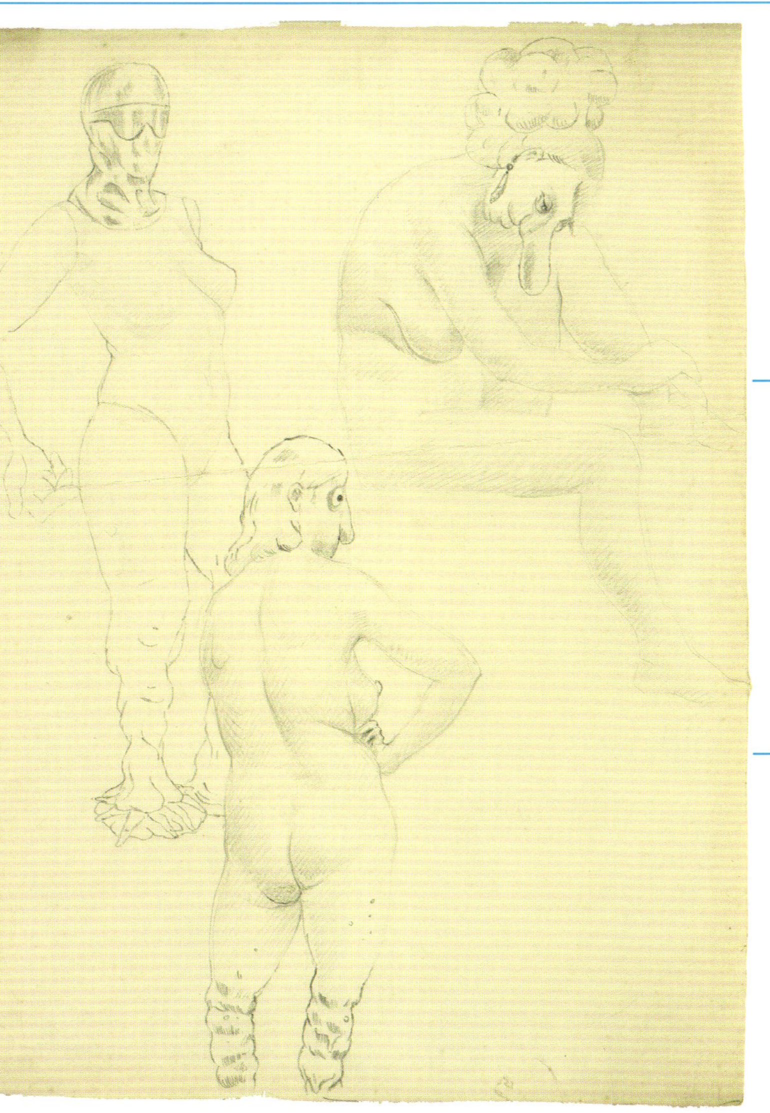

Seven heads

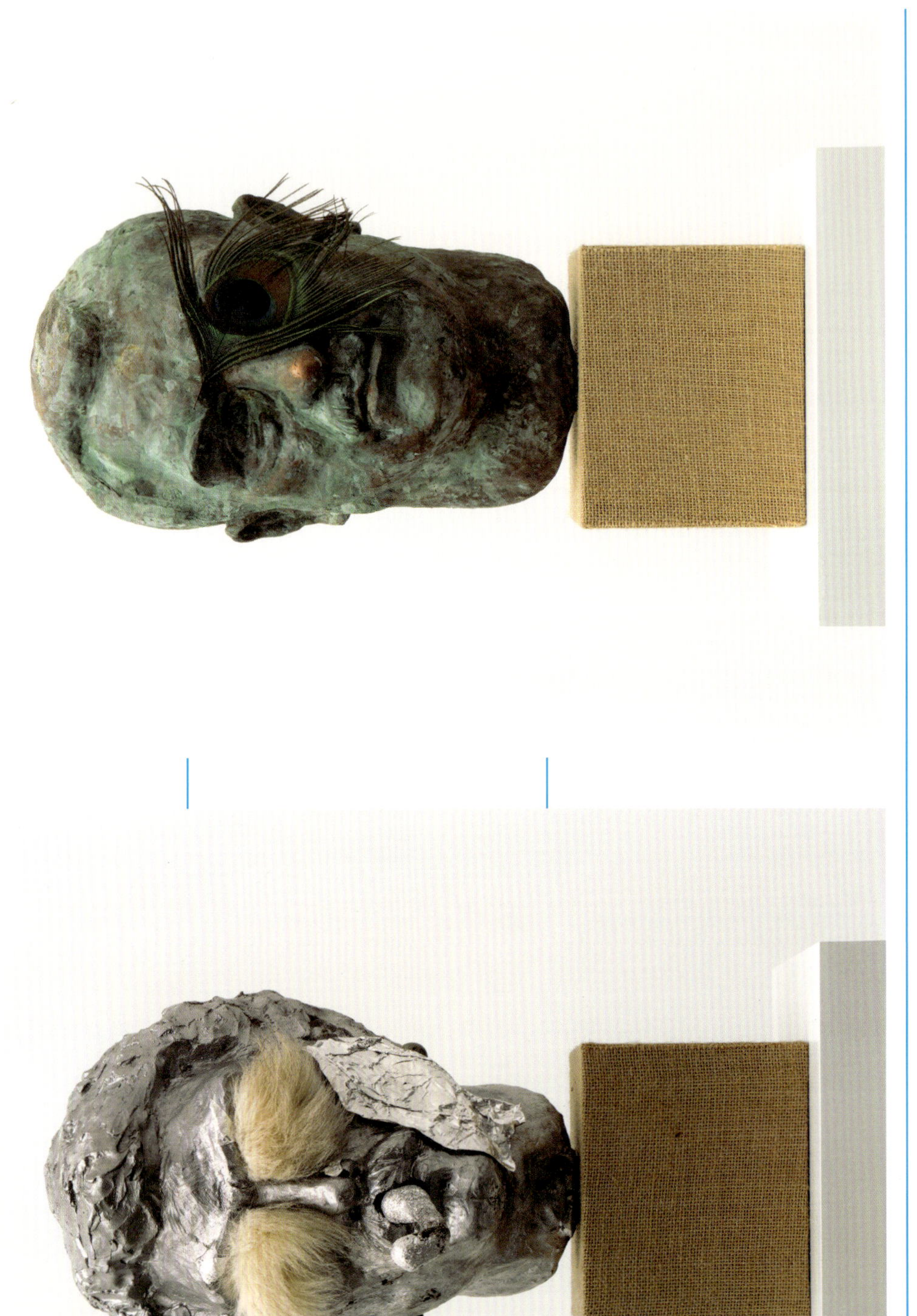

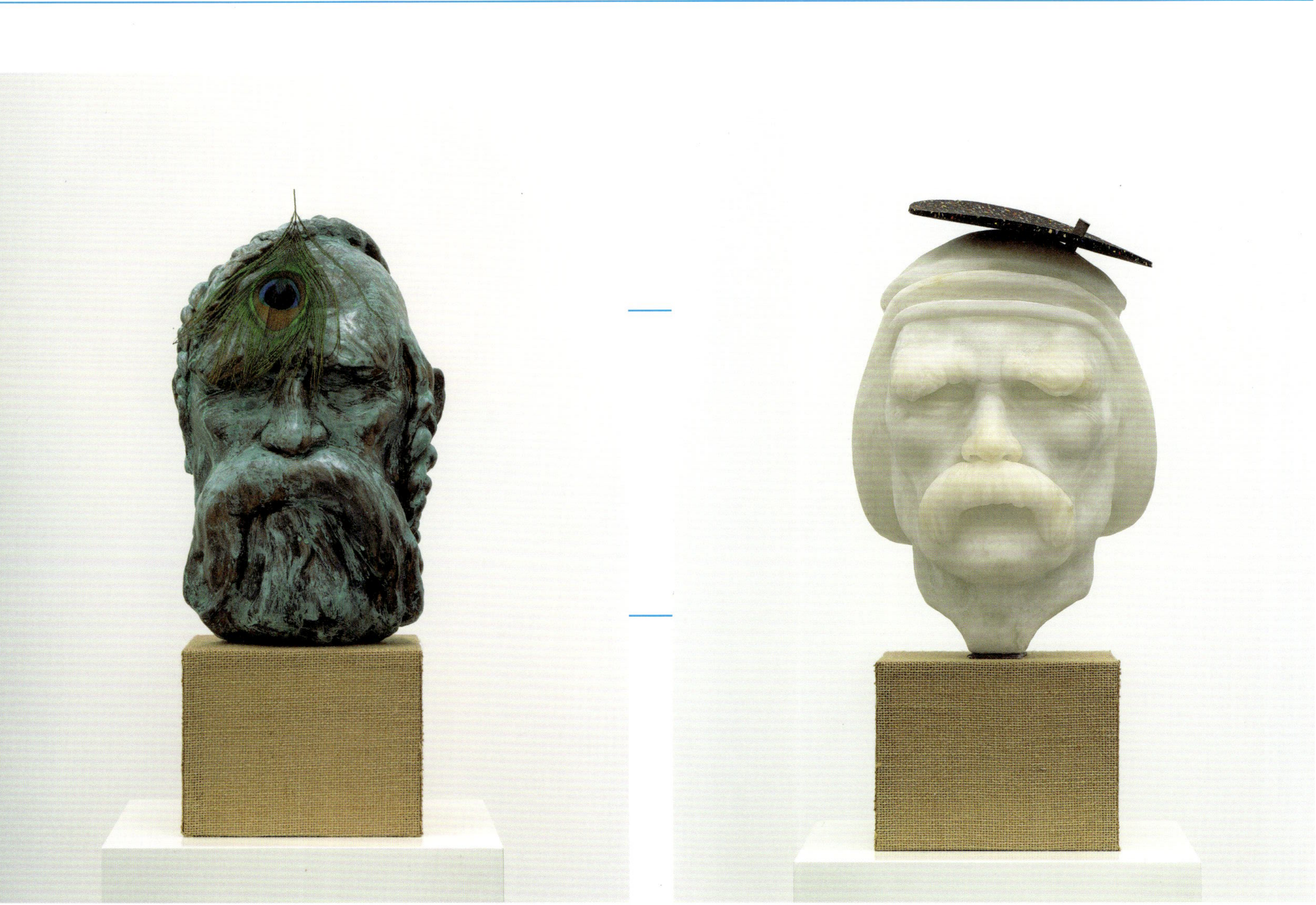

The Riven Murky Cloud
2005
Aluminium, fur, wax, wood, hessian
34 x 23.5 x 37.5 cm
Photo: Ivo Faber

Walkonian
2006
Polymer resin, copper powder in resin, peacock feather
34 x 21 x 26 cm
Photo: Ivo Faber

The Author of Mishap
2005
Copper powder in resin, peacock feather, wood, hessian, urine
36 x 21.5 x 23.5 cm
Photo: Ivo Faber

New Valkonian
2006
Onyx, resin, mixed media
30 x 28 x 38 cm
Photo: Ivo Faber

1- *Patrician*
2006
Polyester resin, steel
wire wool and bronze
38 x 38 x 34 cm
Photo: Ivo Faber

2- *Bauxite Maid Bauxite*
2010
Aluminium, plastic
grass skirt
80 x 35 cm

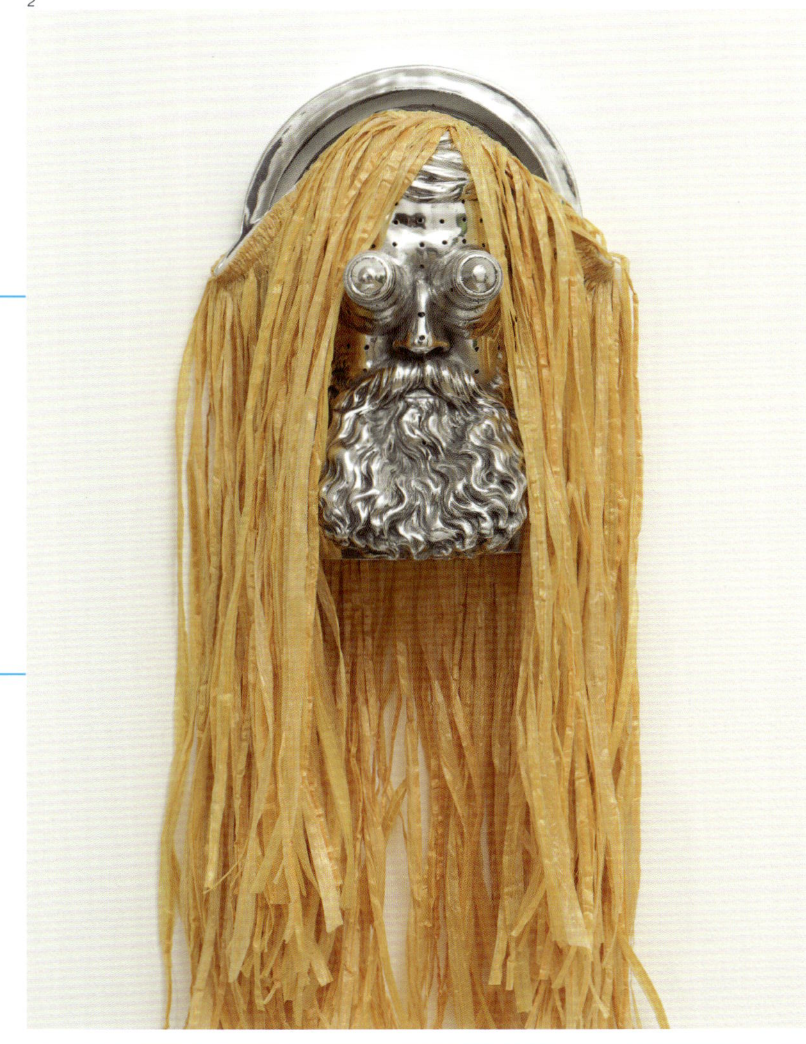

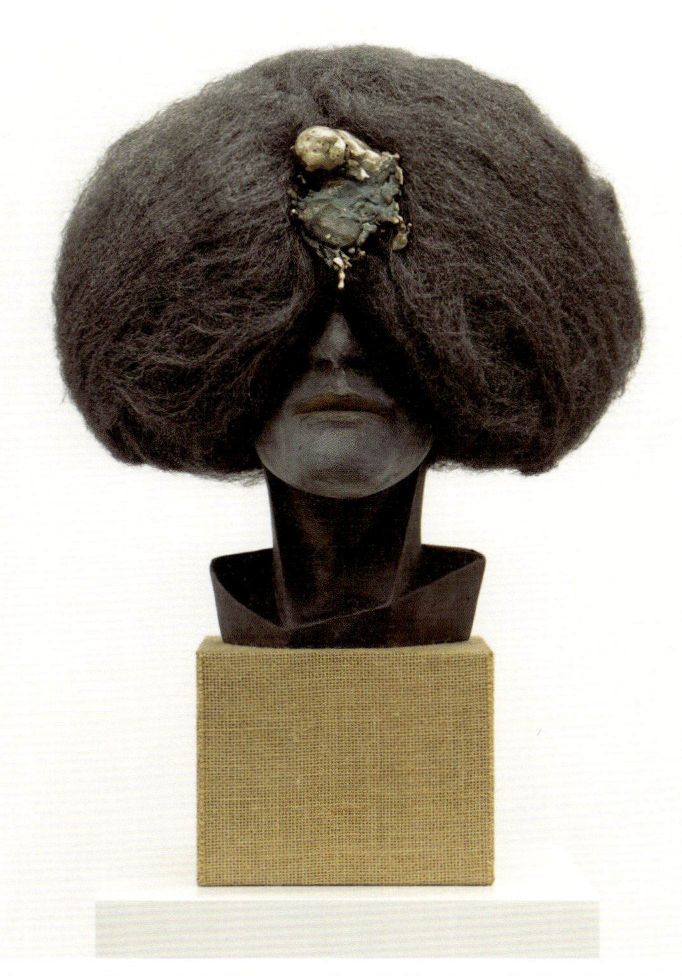

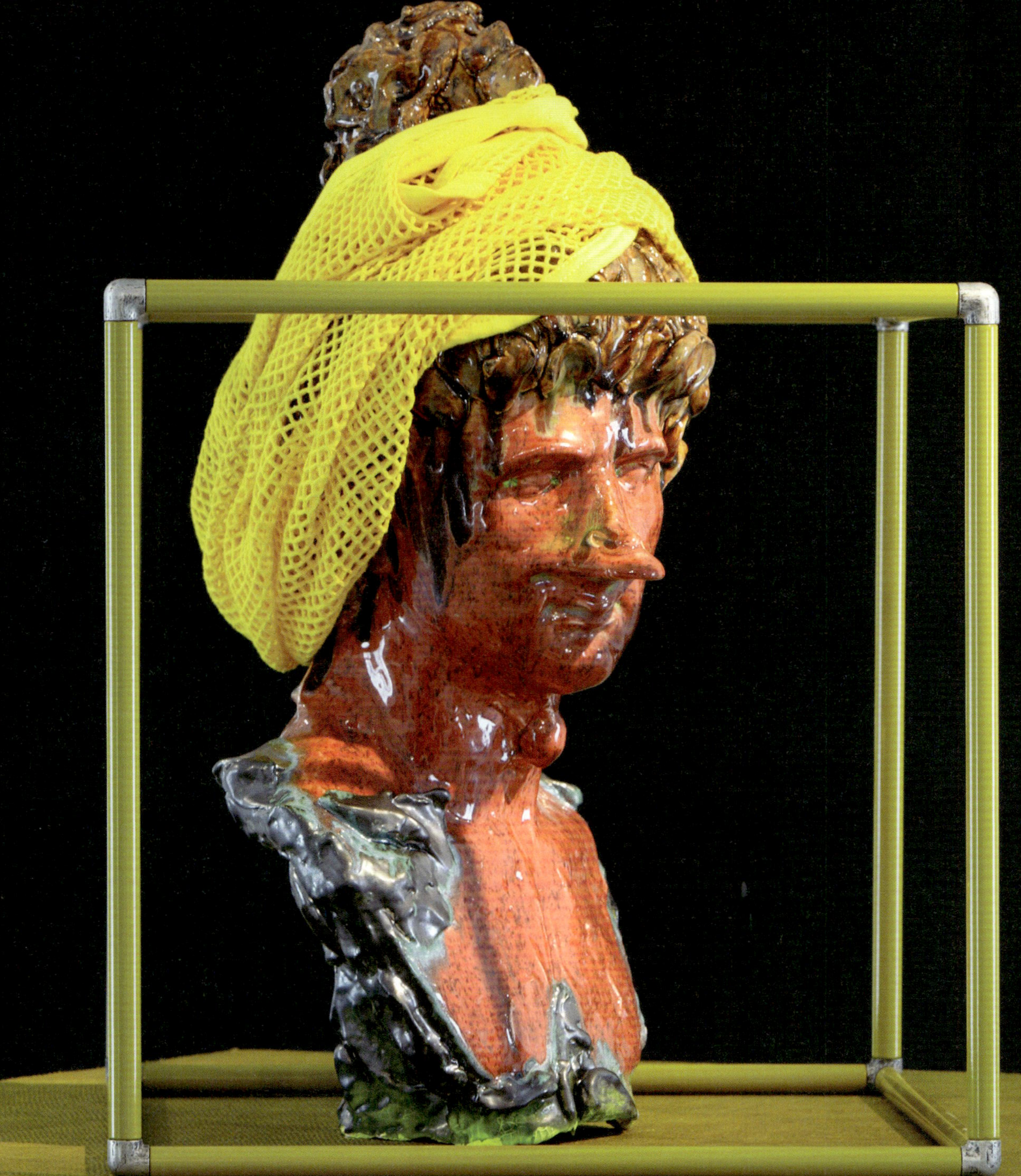

Omar (emergent), detail
2008
Ceramic, powder coated
steel, carpet, plywood,
starched hessian, found
objects, aluminium
189 x 125 x 125 cm
Photo: Claus Langer

Basel Statements
The Glidded Baumn

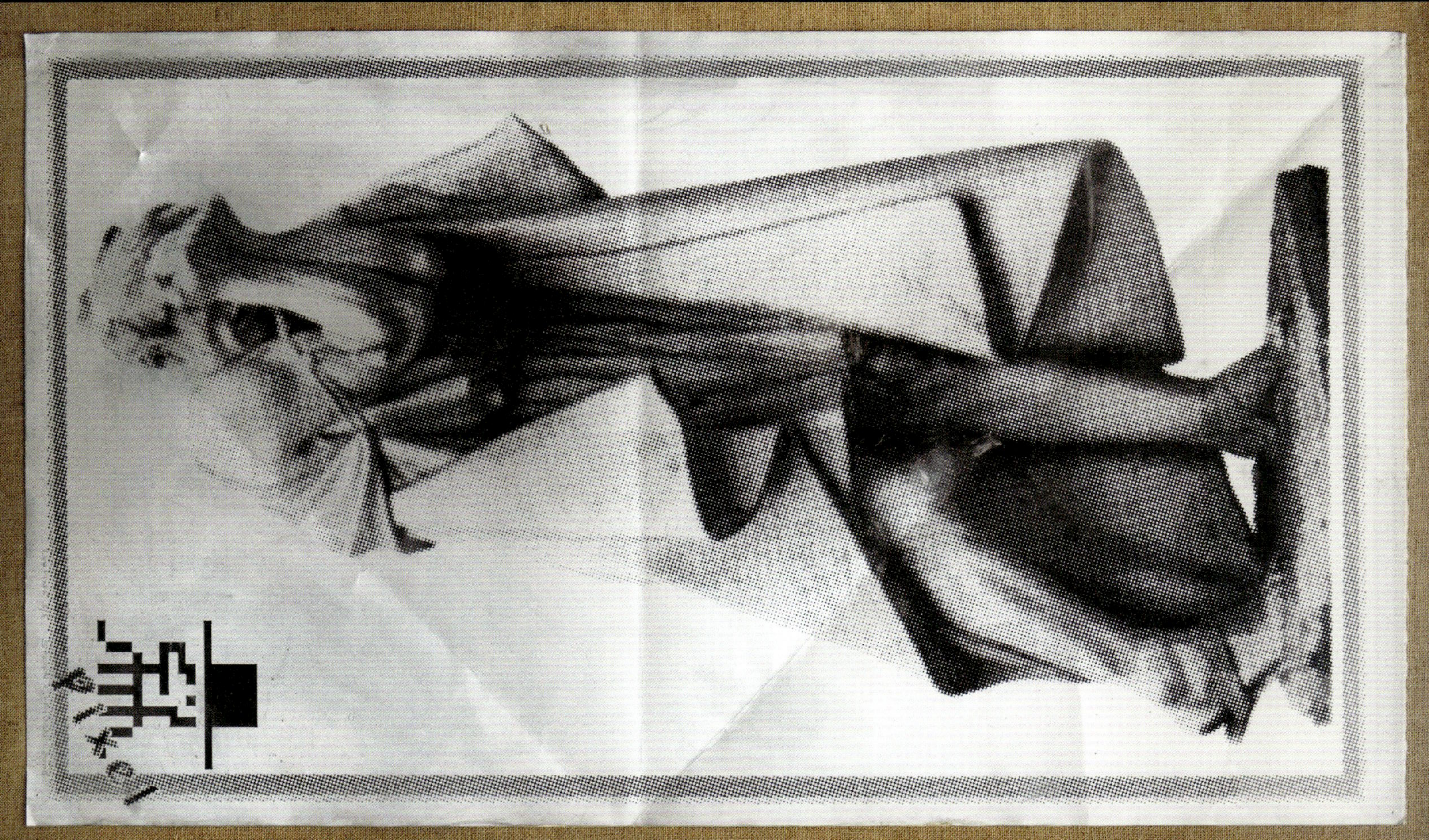

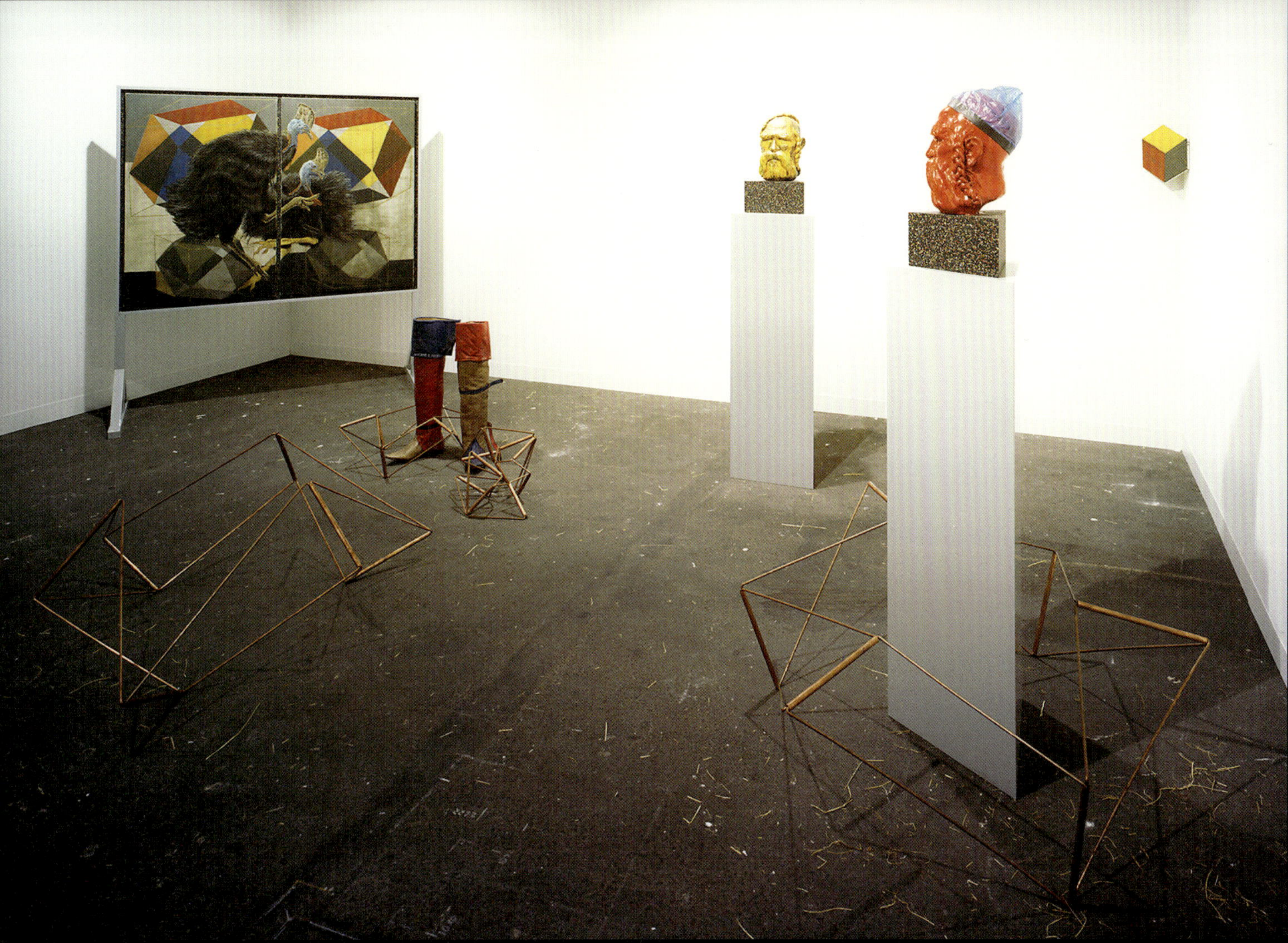

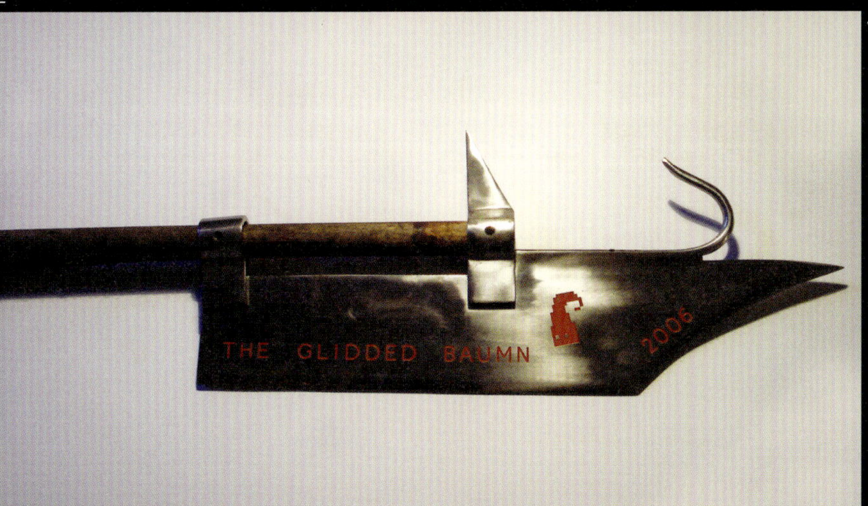

2

3

1- *Low Pixel (Beneath Contempt)*
2006
Screen print on archival paper, framed with Plexiglas on hessian-mounted MDF
155.5 x 92 x 10 cm

2- *The Glidded Baum*, installation view
2006

3- *The Glidded Baum*
2006
Wood, engraved steel
23 x 93 x 4.5 cm

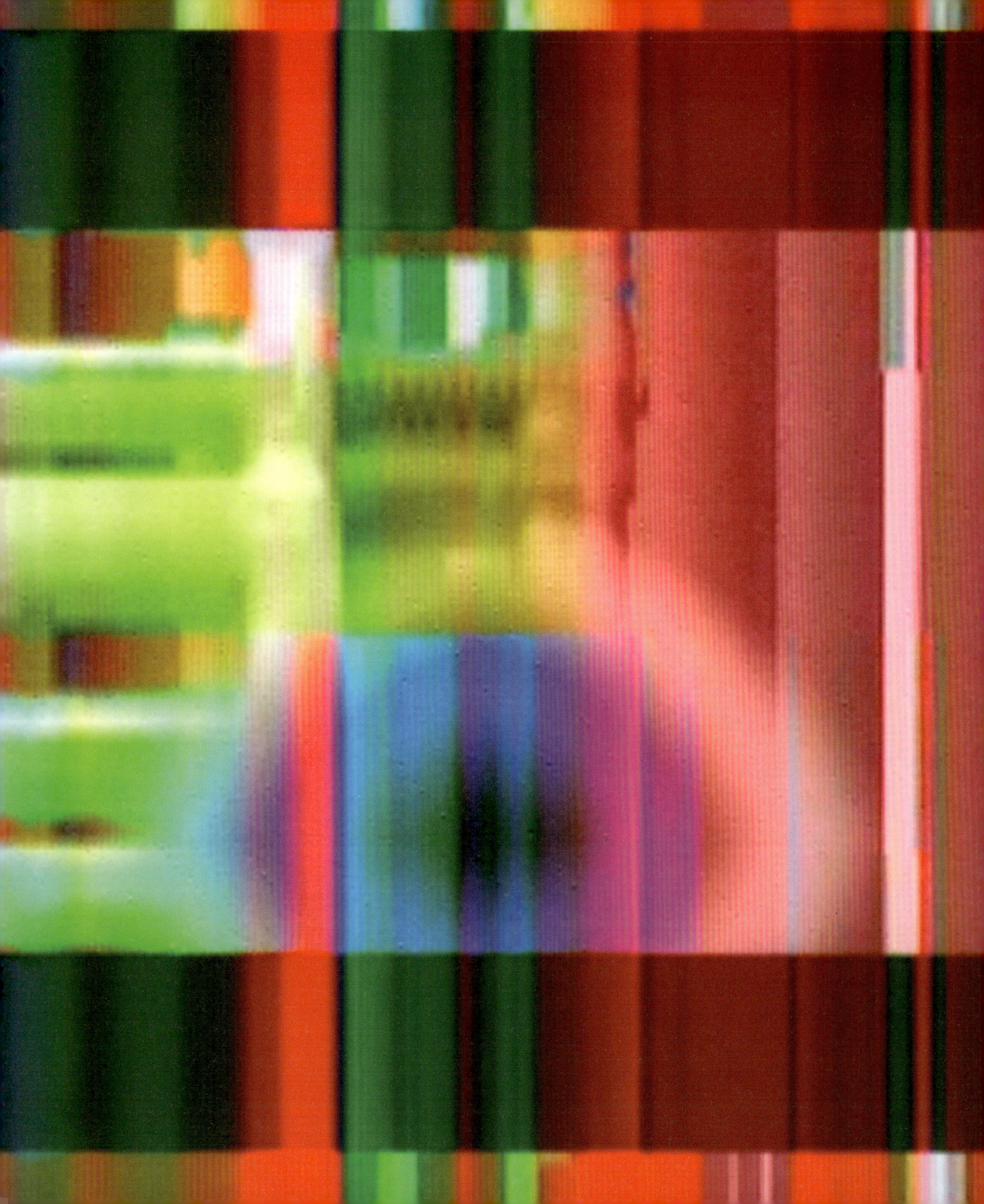

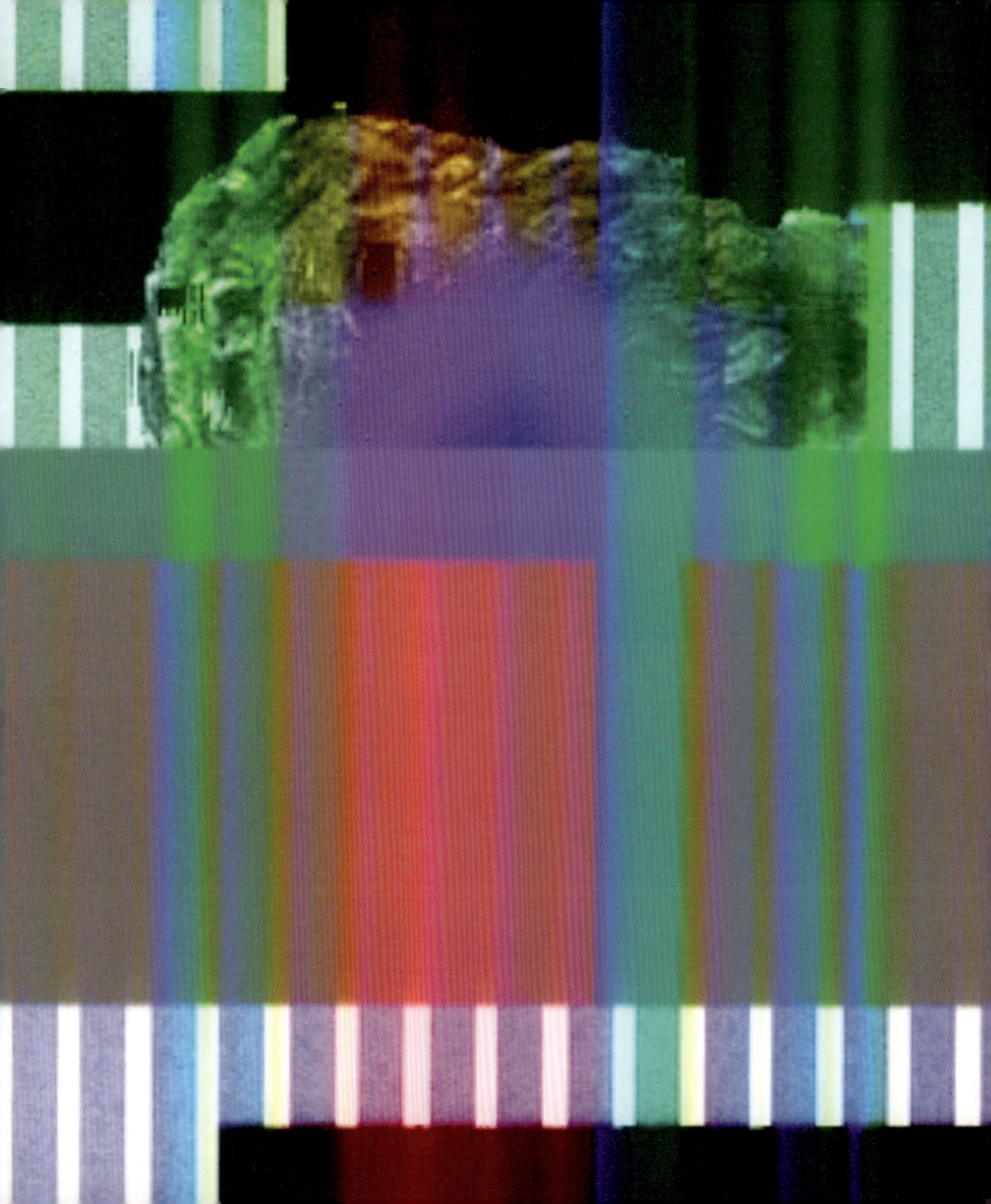

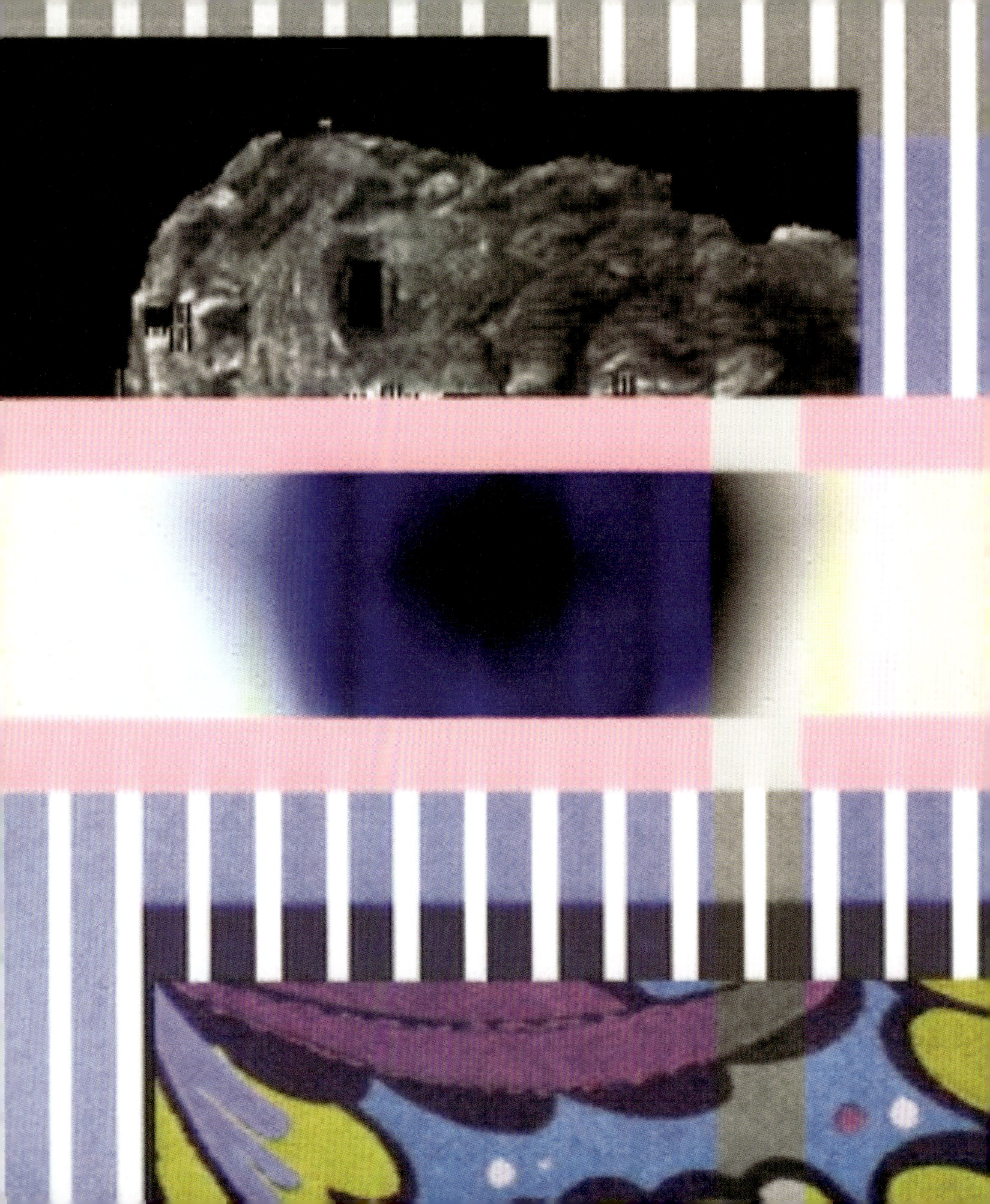

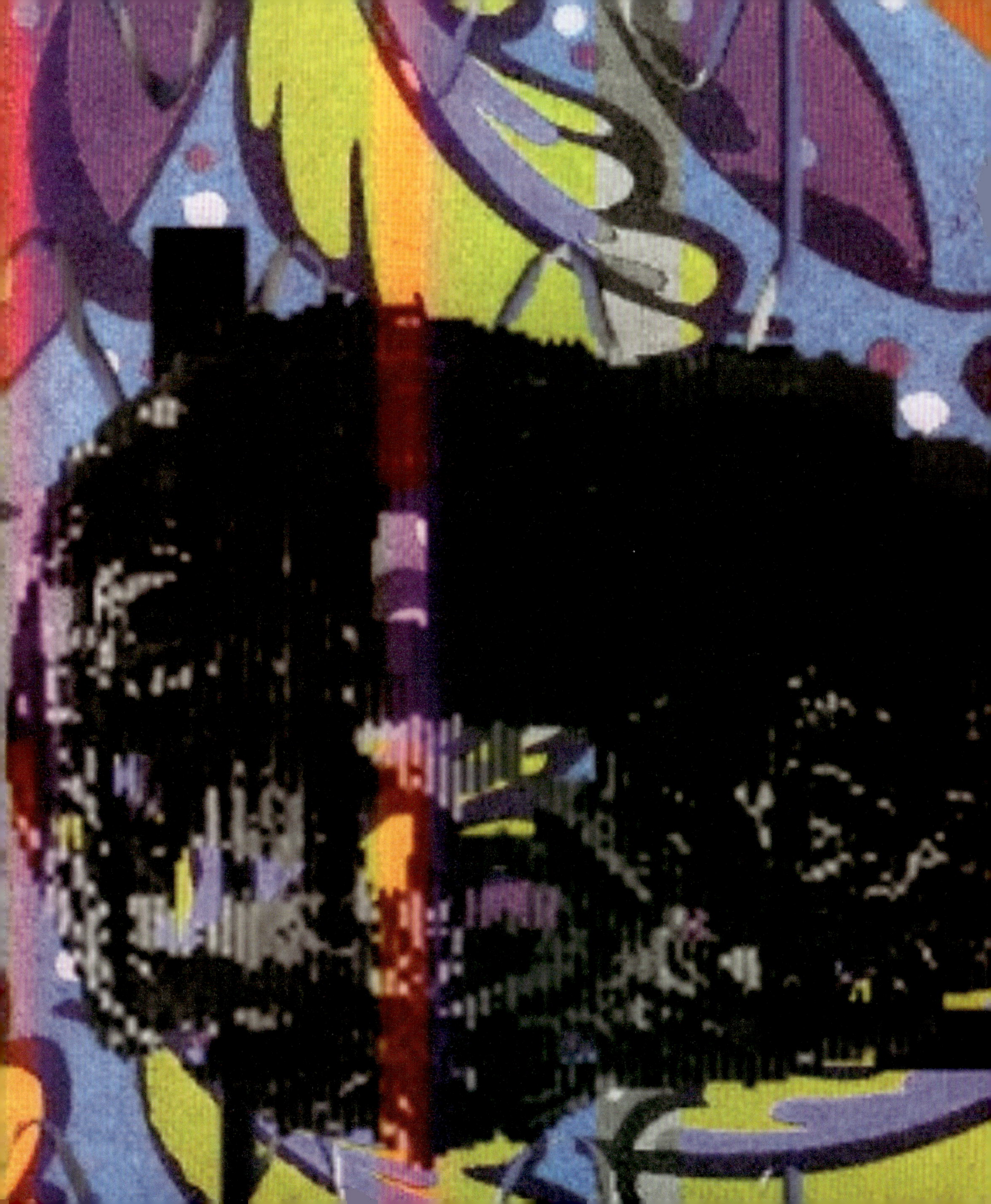

Martin Clark in conversation with Steven Claydon

Bloomsbury, December 2011

MC I remember you talked to me a number of years ago about a sort of mythos that you had created – a kind of parallel space for your works to inhabit, or perhaps be dislocated from. I think you called it 'New Valkonia', based on a Polish phrase you saw on a T-shirt, something already incomprehensible and which you kind of deliberately misappropriated or misread in a way.

SC At that time, I felt it might be useful to concoct a spurious or fictional cultural framework in which to house these, perhaps believable, perhaps ridiculous, but ultimately paradoxical objects or things. So I employed a fictive narrative as a means to catalyse a re-reading of things we encounter ordinarily and the cultural conditions and terrain they inhabit. For instance, public sculpture or museum artefacts or a piece of text or even a digital transmission. I see all of these as being relative, part of a contextual array and very purposefully contrived in order to suspend our disbelief. I'm interested in how you might use an object as a vehicle, a homunculus amongst other operational things, what anthropologists call social agency. But of course our relationship with things is not one-sided. That's why I was interested at that time in exploring something like early modernism and swan-song modernism, because it had been co-opted or neglected. We can talk about narratives as objects, about histories as objects, you could probably talk about how you could objectify – through an accretion of material and subject matter – a movement. So you could rely on received or modified information and say, ok, well modernism was a left-leaning, rational, humanistic project, but it doesn't take very much effort to realise that it was anything but, with its retrogressive recesses and catastrophic mutations, seances, exorcisms, knifings, bite marks and polychrome horror. With *New Valkonia*

I tried to glibly manufacture a spurious ritualised state modernism by misappropriating a Polish phrase that I casually came across in a flea market held in an overgrown Soviet-era stadium in Warsaw. It was populated with socialist-realist stone athletes, fake Nike goods, machine guns and other fertile miscellanea. I saw this phrase 'nie wal konia' crudely screenprinted onto a black T-shirt. It actually means 'stop beating the horse', i.e. 'stop masturbating'. In a way, as an artist, I associated that reference to onanism with artistic production, as well as more broadly with production and surplus in global trade systems and artificially maintained sovereign economies.

MC In the 'New Valkonia' work there's a sense of a modernism gone awry, or a modernism that's taken a different path, a series of wrong turns? I've been interested in looking again at early modernism, before it became an international style, before all the rough edges and eccentricities had been rubbed off it. The kind of modernism you are dealing with in your work seems much closer to that early moment, before it was rationalised, sanitised; when it was much more associated, or perhaps contaminated, with esotericism, mysticism, the arcane. We've talked before about modernist writers like TS Eliot and Ezra Pound, their relationship with esoteric, classical, even occult thought (as well as with a much more problematic right-wing ideology), but until quite recently it's always been a kind of hidden history – seen as embarrassing or awkward at best.

SC I suppose the irony is that I have always considered myself to be a proselytising rationalist, out to debunk all superstition and esotericism, but I can't keep away from stupidity and I absolutely appreciate the strange seductive value of those purple hubristic things I collude

with. I think the last thing that any sort of progressive project should do is to describe itself by its extremities and become prohibitive: 'if you're not with us you're against us'. I think the understanding of materials, perhaps from a much more arcane perspective, from systems of pre-Socratic Greek thought for instance, is beginning to feel very pertinent again. The idea that materials are not necessarily benign extended substances – in a Descartian sense. I think that we understand, right down to a kind of quantum level, that there are relationships between particles and between substances that would sound esoteric if they had been posited 50 years ago, but are now part of a mainstream scientific and secular cultural rationalism. This is all part of the unravelling of the physical phenomena of material substrate. So, my somewhat flawed manual would be Lucretius' *De Rerum Natura* (On the Nature of Things), where he writes this epic poem to describe to a pantheist the beauty and the peculiar corpuscular nature of the thing – from carrier particles, photons, light, to the cosmos at large. But it is always approached from a very rational, recognisable and relatively scientific standpoint. As much as I love and sometimes employ that kind of ritualistic, esoteric aspect, it's really because I think that these eccentric things exist within the realms of the rational inspection of earthly entities. Not in a condescending way, nor a sang-froid anthropology, but as a laymans means of better understanding the world of complex interactions between seemingly unknowable things and their schizophrenic environment. I guess there's an epistemological aspect to my work, but for me it is equally as credent as my interest in bird shit. I used to have a book called *Ornithological Dejecta* that helped you to distinguish the species of bird by photos of shit on car windscreens.

 In your work that investigation of the materiality of objects is one of its most present aspects. It feels like a fundamental part of the work is an ongoing enquiry into how materials, substances and objects hold or carry meaning, a kind of hypersensitivity to matter or stuff. It's a very formally sculptural enterprise in one sense, but it also feels like there is an almost tangible attention to sensation as well as comprehension in the way you put your work together – that somehow all of these aspects are disrupted or muddled or put into play in both a very physical as well as a very intuitive way.

SC I'm very aware of the fact that there is a palpable dual, or multiple, nature to a thing. One of the pieces of writing that I like very much, which was perhaps the first piece of writing in western philosophy, is called the Anaximander Fragment. Anaximander was what we retrospectively call a pre-Socratic philosopher, a natural philosopher I suppose. From his statues he looks like a geography teacher with extra beard rations. He was interested in trying to understand the nature of 'stuff' and 'being' within the world. So it was a rational pursuit, but also metaphysical. Anaximander states that it's entirely understandable that when things come into being they should also anticipate their destruction, as payment for this precocious happening, for breaking away from what he called *apeiron* – which is the kind of cosmos of general substance, or matter, or dust, which he considered everything came from. When matter enters into this contract – into the vanity of forming or becoming an object – it is only natural that it should somehow ultimately decompose. What I like about this is that he affords stuff a kind of conscience or culpability. In the everyday we rely on the usefulness of our relationship with a thing, we create hierarchies

and taxonomies from this perspective with respect to matter's equipmental nature, and we can't help but anthropomorphise it. Little do we know of the self-becoming nature of things. So a thing's material is always caught in a kind of asymmetrical internal struggle, on the one hand knowing that material has this springy potential, this potency, without actually necessarily giving forth in the anthropocentric realm, without becoming useful; it has this potential and then it has its ascribed meaning – through reference and our experience with it and the relational pact that humans make with an object or event. So a thing is entirely dual, even multifarious, but certainly nefarious. Martin Heidegger's view was that something is equipmentally or latently active, internally energetic, and objects have a worldly relationship in the realm of reference and interaction. He talks about equipmental nature, by which he basically means 'use value'. What I prefer to consider is something's potential or potency, because I think that is the root, the physical origin, of the 'thingly'.

MC In the museum or gallery there is a kind of ocular hierarchy, we know things and their properties through how they look, we look very closely. So glass is different from wood is different from metal is different from plastic. We ascribe a difference to things through whatever sensory relationship we are afforded; if we can only look then it is ocular, if we can touch then we have a tactile relationship; if we have the science to break something down then we have an even more complex understanding. But all of this is in relation to our own human/sensory encounter and the limits of that encounter. It's interesting that you are talking about stuff, about things, having a kind of inherent sensibility. But a material has no ocular, or tactile, relationship to itself or to other materials, it cannot have

this kind of sense of itself. Instead there is a necessary blindness or dumbness?

SC Well people call it an inertness but the activity is rhetorical. Within a thing it has its own properties, and within that thing its properties abound. So it doesn't mean that just because we don't have an intimate relationship with those properties that this thing doesn't have some kind of efficacy or inter-thingly agency. It's important to us once we unlock those properties. Prior to that it is just a stone, rather than bauxite, or flint rather than a scraper or spear or whatever. A digestible world of simplistic categorical designations. But this is precisely the relationship to objects that I have been trying to redress. I am interested in asking, 'well what is this?', besides its superficial material state, besides the fact that we have a facility to understand it as a cultural artefact, characterised by a genre or category. We ascribe a quick-fix meaning to things without wanting to properly understand them or the subtle emissions issuing forth, unexpectedly, from their thingly depths.

MC So, very simply, is that something you're trying to do in the work? To try and allow things to reveal themselves, to 'issue forth'?

SC I think so, but, you know, I end up resorting to all of the tricks that anyone else uses. So I'll work with the notion of museum furniture and I'll think about what the bleakest outcome for an actual object would be, like, a musical instrument ends up in a glass case and is unplayable, or something like that. I'll use some shorthand myself in order to get a thing across, but my relative perspective is paradoxical and flawed too, and within my appraisal of the thingly there is some autobiography. I understand there is actually a cruel beauty in the act of playing with the properties of things. I've been involved in music and the idea that an instrument could be deprived of its utility as it is transformed into a culturally potent artefact has both a self effacing charm and a worldly profundity.

SC Well, as much as I think that is one of the most insightful texts that has ever been written about objects, I also kind of find it flawed. Because I think an object has those oscillating qualities of visibility and invisibility anyway, prior to its broken state. But I agree that a fragment may possess a very different ontology. I think Heidegger would probably not designate a broken or fragmented art object like Edouard Manet's painting, *The Execution of Maximilian* (c. 1867-8) in the same way, and I think that perhaps in his later work when he wrote *The Origin of the Work of Art*, he had real problems trying to remove the artwork from the broken tool model. He thinks that a work of art has agency and voracity and that there is a kind of revealed work in the work of art despite its usefulness. I think that this was truly insightful, despite the fact that

I would say that the tool, once broken, doesn't really change its ontology as revealing, contingent material. It may just alter its dual resonance as fragmentary artefact perhaps. I think it is still gurgling, still setting forth.

SC Well, yes and no in a way. The things I make are not out of the ordinary, they contain everything we might understand or expect about a human interaction with a thing. They have formality, they have substance, they employ seduction (and repulsion), they have potential equipmental use, they have a context that they may or may not operate within, but they also have an intrinsic value all along the way. I mean some kind of potent quantitative, auto-referential qualitative beingness. But what I try to do is quite brutal. I'm employing shorthand too, I understand the notion of a vessel, for instance, in a very obvious way. The vessel as a container, as a metaphor or prop, a vehicle for the suspension of

disbelief, as an anthropomorph, as a lowest common denominator (in its relation to commerce), as something that may be qualitatively inferior to the thing it contains until time or cultural factors render it otherwise. It is all these obvious things and none of them. Also I like to think that a vessel is one of the most subtle and peculiarly abstract things that we encounter as human individuals.

SC Yes. Sometimes they're impossible vessels that I manufacture, because they're solid or something, sometimes they're found objects like the Kibbo Kift 'solar propaganda' vessel I found in a charity shop in Dalston, and sometimes they're purchased as scrap or from antiquarian dealers. They're historical things and redundant things. I've got, for instance, this peculiar ceramic piece from the Mohenjo-daro proto-civilisation in the ancient Indus valley that I'm going to modify and employ in a work for the Firstsite show. I like conversion, transfiguration. And then I'm using olive barrels from contemporary Kalamata that are, either ironically or cynically, manufactured in earthenware-coloured plastic to ship olives around the planet. So I'll play with that, cast it in solid foam or deploy it in a happenstantial or quasi-formal way with an actual Roman olive oil vessel, in sympathetic disjuncture. These things can be seen as very obvious casual equivalences, but what I really want to do is create compound conjunctions or climates of things, because I wouldn't want any of these encounters between things to exist as a purely binary dialectic – they're too complex for that, they've got too much going on to permit themselves the luxury of a closed illustrative system, they've got too much materially and socially vested in them to represent a simple analogue. The polarities are held in configurations like DNA, chirping like DNA. They are physically dissolute things that get coerced into a-parallel contexts. You know, for me when I go to a gallery or museum now and I see the way a fragment is captured within a Perspex and steel 'context-structure', I don't find it a depressing example of institutional colonialism, that it is re-contextualised or stripped of context. In fact I find it totally elevating, and the more arcane and mismanaged the object the better, because I think in a way objects should be equipped to manage that kind of relative association with other emergent things. You can't get anything as beautifully simple-complex and completely impossible as a physical or elemental embodiment, artificial or otherwise. And anything you confer on it, like: 'that's a fragment of a sculpture', 'that's a lost earring', or 'that's a rubber johnny in the street', could never properly describe the very peculiar nature in which things find themselves. People get excited if they find 'the face of Jesus' in a tomato or something like that. A tomato in itself, as a thing that happens, is just way more fucking perverse and extraordinary than anything you can confer on it or derive from it.

SC The practice is based on the investigation of the nebulous passage of materials from the atom or corpuscle through to cultural anthropocentric object. When I talk about a model, like the climate of signs or 'stuff', or when I appropriate Charles M. Schulz's Pig-Pen

98

as an emblem, I'm trying to illustrate that. So when I began to think about the notion of this 'climate of stuff', I was reminded of a piece of writing that I must have read many times before but which suddenly gained some sort of asymmetrical meaning for me. At the beginning of Joseph Conrad's novel *Heart of Darkness* there is a passage about a boat sailing down the Thames. Conrad describes the crepuscular, dawn light, and the yarns of the seamen. He likens these stories, in fact any good story, to a nut. The nut has a kernel and it has a carapace, but we associate the nut with its carapace, its shell. A good story never touches down on the kernel, it just weaves a shell around itself. We identify it by its extraneous properties. The internal, indwelling, concealed part of it has all of those properties too, but it never busts that open. It's a bit like a good work of art not being an illustration. It's like that, but it's not that, it's better than that.

SC In my work I think about casual equivalences, and then I think about how an equivalence might start as casual and then become arrested into a concrete relationship. Then it becomes kinetic and starts to orbit a subject, it performs peripatetically and somehow creates a climate or shell around an errant or invisible core. I think that draws attention to the fact that objects do have an inherent contingency without the designation of humans. Because we create all of that around the thing, we create the shell, we create the etymology, we call it a thing, but really there is this very peculiar way in which we designate and make things subjective. Within them, at the core of that, like a bubble in a glass, there is a particle of magnificent stuff. For me Pig-Pen is emblematic of that, of the subjectivity that

accretes around a thing, becomes a thing itself. And it's a mouthing thing, it's trying to talk of individual relations and semantic confluence, of descriptive powers of speech outside of human ingenuity, language or literature. But then it starts to become something else, it starts to become an object, an ossified but energetic sentence or a corpuscular narrative, a sentient shell, a reference to the kernel but discrete in symbiotic disjuncture. So you can lose the boy, lose Pig-Pen – the climate is the object now.

SC …I think it can be an unknowable thing…

SC I think it's the only kind of conclusion you can come to. Everything garners social provenance and 'thingly' reference regardless of whether it's designated the most meaningless or the most superior object in the hierarchy of things. I'm only accentuating that climate, that accretion of subjectivity or intimate relationship between abstract things and the physical thing. So the whole practice is very simple, it's only really exacerbating our ability or our facility to understand a thing up to a certain point. We surely only understand our contemporary selves with the conceit of hindsight; we only ever configure things around our own canon and around ourselves, with the past as a naïve precursor to our position at the 'zenith' of understanding and ingenuity. So even the bravest or most radical investigations into things and science and what-have-you replays a kind of canonical onanism, an attempt to put our current position at the fulcrum of learning. I think that we have lost so much by employing this ultimately destructive conceit.

SC Well, I think maybe the most obvious thing to say about the vessel is that they are primarily produced to contain something. So the object itself could be construed to be secondary to the thing that it contains. But then there is a duality again, where the vessel can either become an aesthetic object or a kind of lowest-common-denominator object. I am very interested in those kinds of objects or things: things like the pixel or the brick or the atom. I would also consider something like a barrel as a lowest-common-denominator object and, ironically, incredibly important as a conduit, an agent of commerce, a symbolic emblem, an artefact and a kind of material punctuation.

SC Yes, in the passage of materials there are heirarchies and subtleties that often escape the radar of subjectivity. Fundamentally valuable things that are invisible by necessity of their nature as denominators of conveyance or assembly. So, vessels have this duality too. And also, maybe because they are voluminous, or fat, they start to resemble something anthropomorphic. That universal 'will' to anthropomorphise an object is something else that is at the core of my practice. Throughout history we constantly try to characterise things. In my meandering through London's museums I've encountered this tendency again and again. A good example is the face jug. These jugs appear in British ceramics, in European ceramics, and possibly every human civilisation. In Britain you find examples in Neolithic pottery, and it's very common amongst Roman jugs, some found in Colchester. In fact there's one that I've always been drawn to in the British Museum, a face jug, very rudimentary, with 'Colchester' written right underneath its ugly mush by some cheeky Georgian or Victorian antiquarian vandal.

SC Apparently, Aztec priests used to get drunk the night before their rituals – often rituals involving human sacrifice – in order to be closer to that kind of corpuscular interface with things. As anyone who has had a hangover will know, the last thing on your mind is making any kind of complex environmental assessment; it becomes much more a sort of exploratory, experiential, existential state.

SC It was entirely about the hangover, about holding open the open and keeping it there.

SC …it's a kind of fizzing. The air's palpable. In a way that's what I want the work to do. The idea that somehow, in the glut of stuff we are surrounded with, you can engender a reading that is separate from mundane correlation. I want to create the possibility to phase into the stuff you are looking at, rather than employ this highly loaded equipment, the baggage of received information that we carry. Gustave Flaubert knew a thing or two about that.

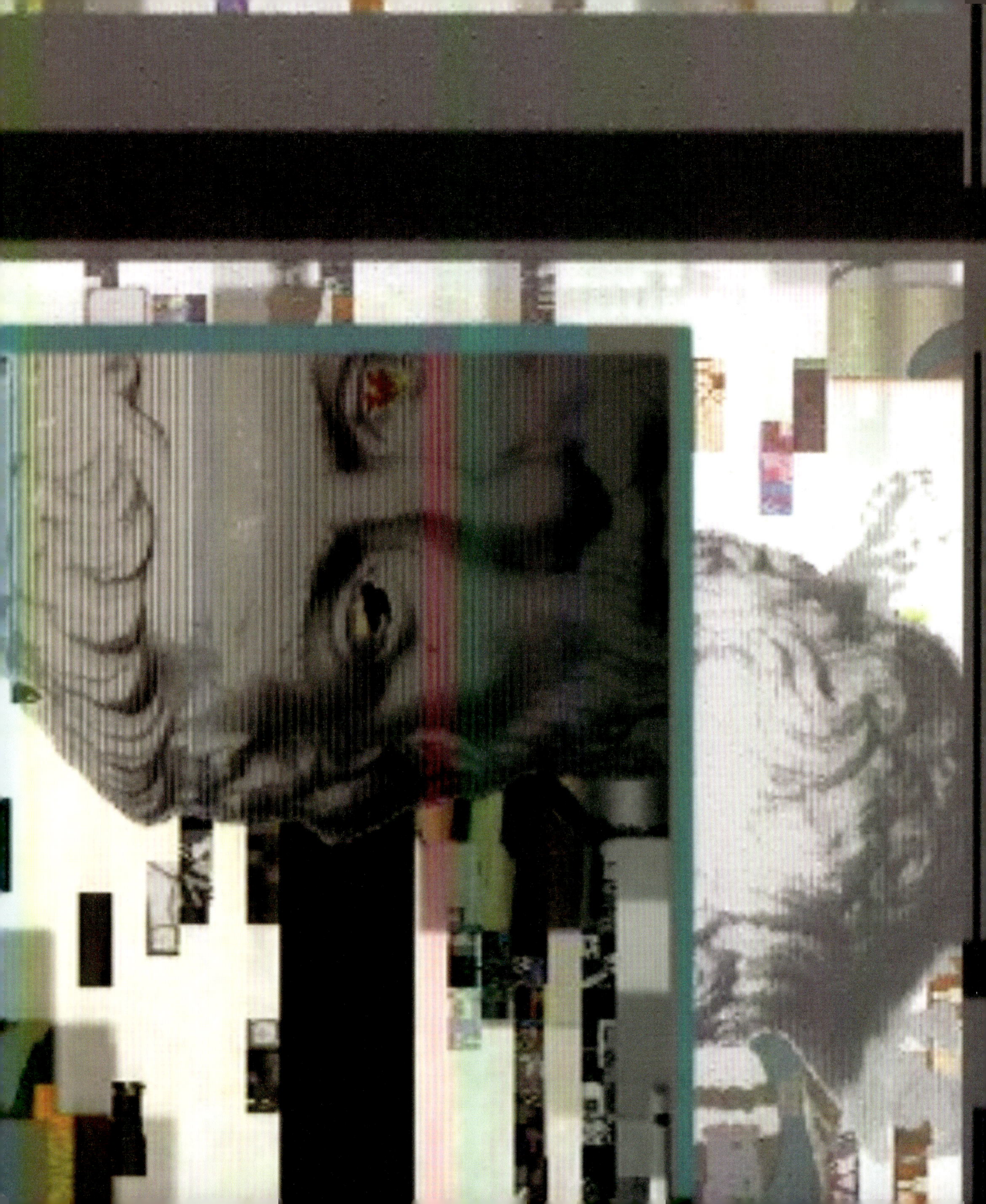

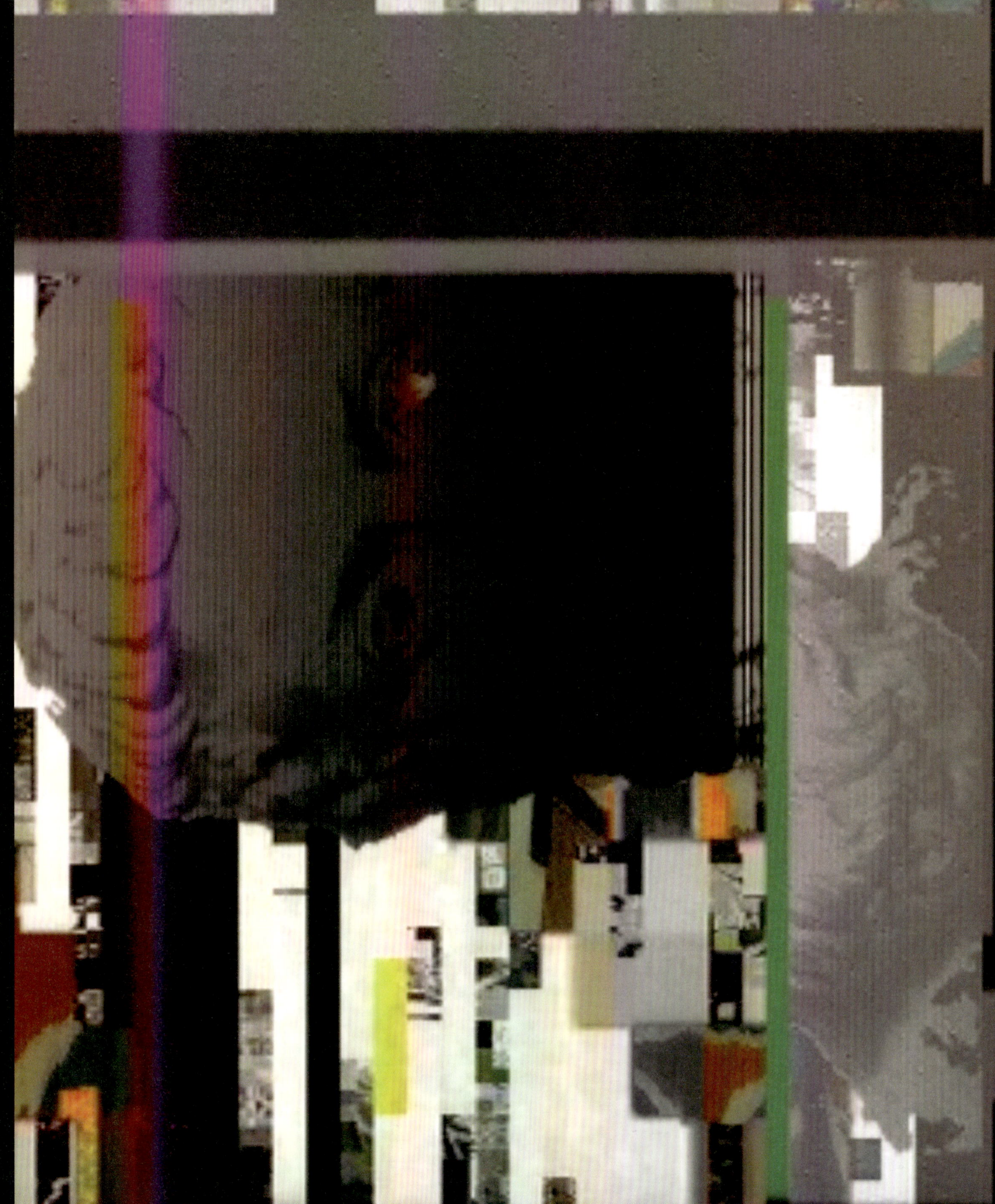

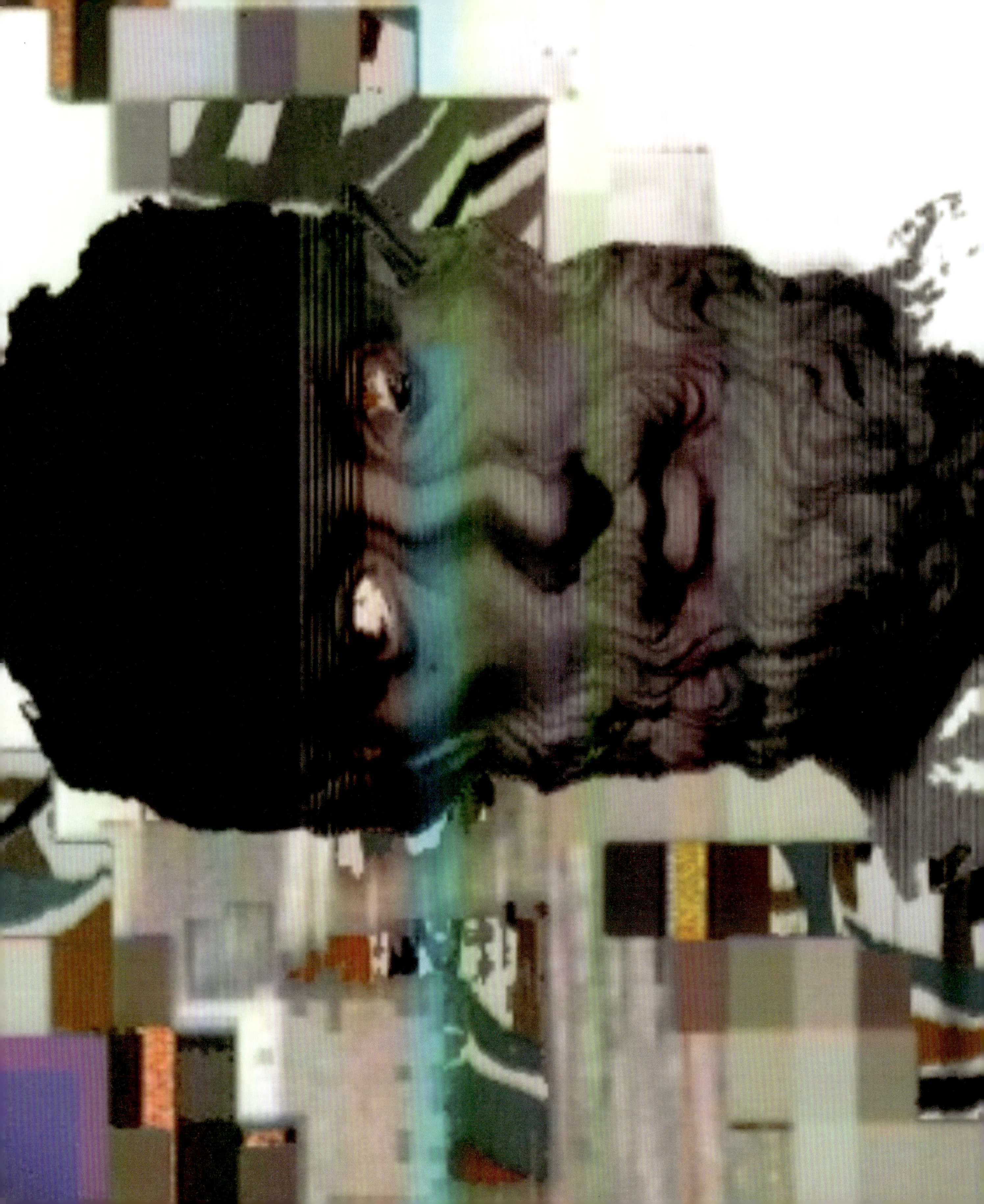

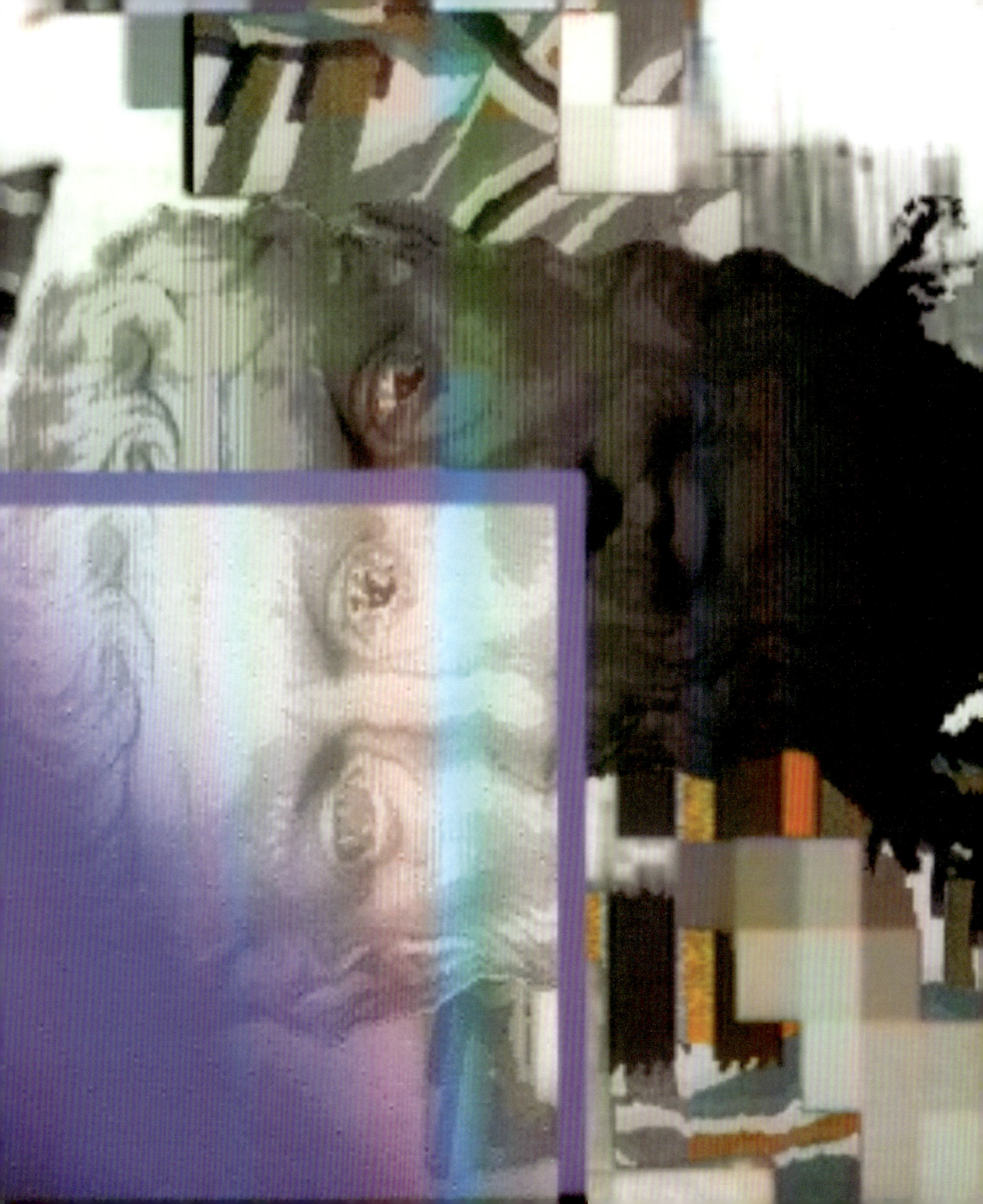

From Earth

2005
Video
4 minutes, 27 seconds

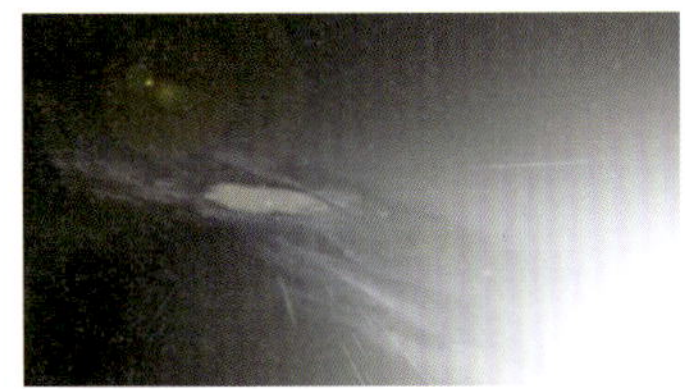

Stony carpets. Rimmed and buttressed basins. Tears of terraces. Matted filaments and curds. Thick leathery sheets brilliantly coloured, the intensity of hue varying as colonies wax and wane. Rotten eggs. The arrival of the blue greens. Stony cushions, teetering columns and spiky armour. A ring of teeth. An endless variety of shapes, rays of light, trumpet-shaped mouths and elongated bodies. Packets of chlorophyll. Thrashing tails and giants. A mass of flailing threads and bulging-out fingers. Ornate vases and bottles. Concentric spheres fixed by needles. Gothic helmets, rococo belfries and spiked space capsules.
A creeping speck of grey jelly. A hollow sphere. A tiny ball. Needles meshed together to form a scaffold. A flower basket. A million tiny splinters or an intricate and beautiful lattice. An unfortunate woman who was loved with the god of the sea and as a result had her hair changed by a jealous goddess into snakes. An enemy, solitary, glued

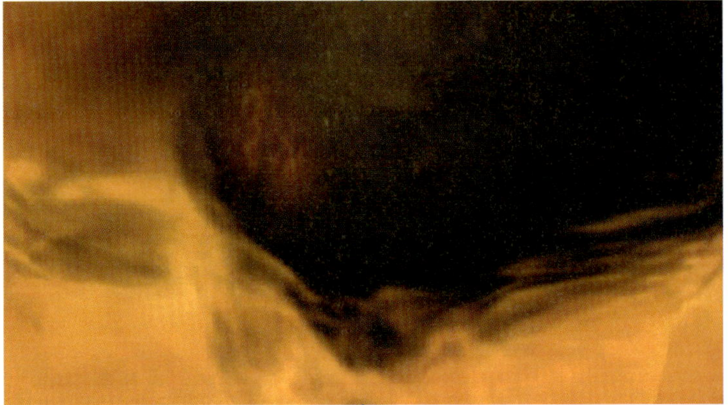

to the rock. Very odd shapes. A buttercup. A rose. Ghostly waves of light, writhing arms, a skeleton of stone, deposits of ooze. Domes, branches, antlers delicately tipped with blue. Organ pipes that are blood red. Mysterious turquoise shapes. Phosphorescent purple eyes. Patterned rosettes unfurl a flat ribbon, stripped yellow and scarlet. A simple maze. Slight electric shocks. A few light-sensitive spots. A collar with slits in. A simple pyramid and a ribbon-shaped tongue covered with rasping teeth. A kind of

Three films

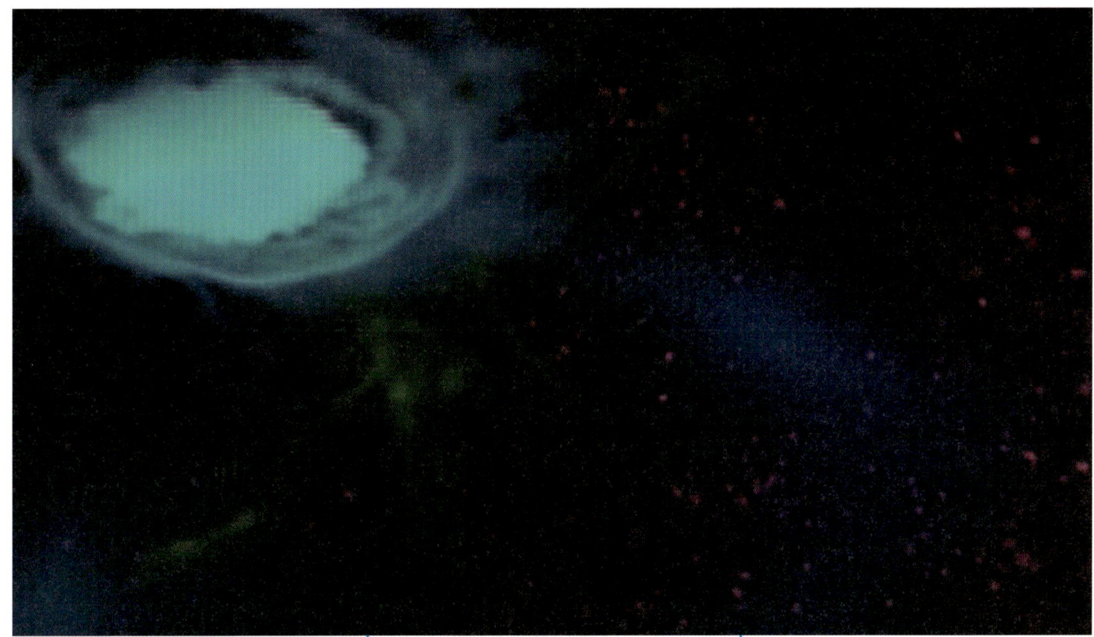

gun and a tiny glassy harpoon of the most delicate proportion and colours, banded, stripped and patterned in many shades. Secondhand weapons complete and unsprung. A zigzag of brilliant green flesh, spotted with black and a line of small brilliant eyes. A miniscule animated globule. Gas-filled flotation tanks. A floating chalice. Bead-like discs. The gutter. The five-fold symmetry of the hydrostatically operated tube. Imps of darkness, sprightly cousins, sausage-like with fleshy lips. A slow but unstoppable flood of sticky tubules pours from the anus. I am struggling in a mesh of filaments. Does this represent a blind alley or a planned progression? A crescent-shaped head equipped with bristles and a pair of feathery appendages, a gut, a large blood vessel and a nerve cord. In the dark stagnant waters there are no signs of tracks or burrows, just a turbid cloud

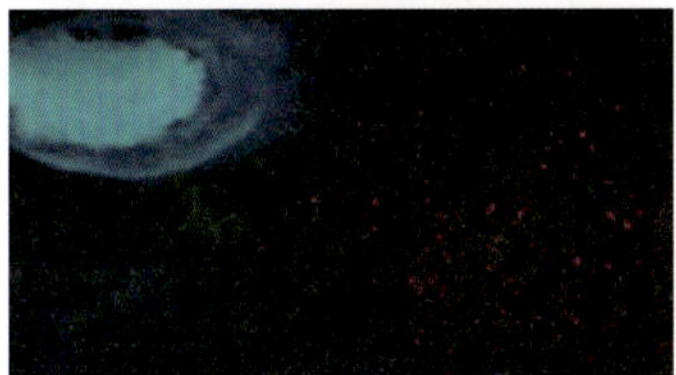

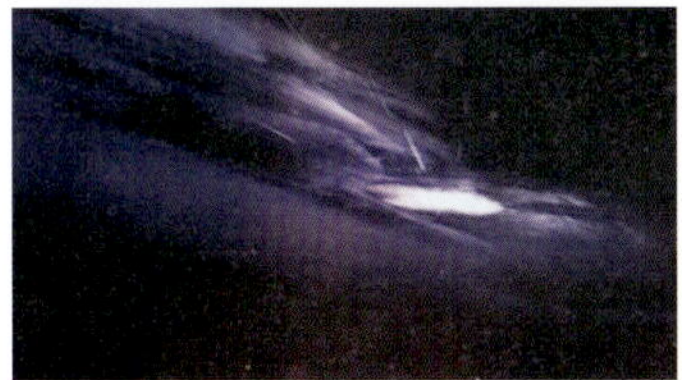

of oxygen to fuel the process of decay. Tiny carcasses. One had fifteen segments, a trunk in front of its mouth and five eyes, one pointing upwards. Another had seven pairs of limbs beneath and seven tentacles waving above, each of which apparently ended with a mouth. They seemed to be experiments. The body armour was constructed partly of lime and partly of a horny substance. These empty suits of armour are a cluster of separate components, each with its own lens of crystalline calcite trying to correct the spherical aberration. A huge dome shield, bean-shaped with a roughly rectangular plate hinged to the back of the shield, which carries a sharp spike

large and flat like the leaves of a book, a continuous strip like a causeway of giant cobbles. It appears this dynasty came to an end to take up a static life. Soft wrinkled skin, outgrown armour, a translucent ghost of its former self. Black tides of larva lie split over its flanks like slag from a furnace. Steam hisses between the blocks caking the mouths with sulphur to form a waxy covering that wards off desiccation but does not totally emancipate. Pools of liquid grey, yellow, blue, bubble creamily. No speck of green relieves the desolation of the black, empty planes. This is the debris.

Semi-phonetic script for
The Fictional Pixel

2008
Video
9 minutes

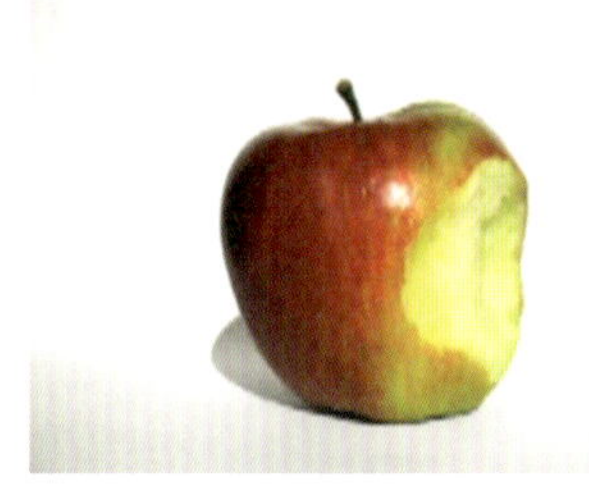

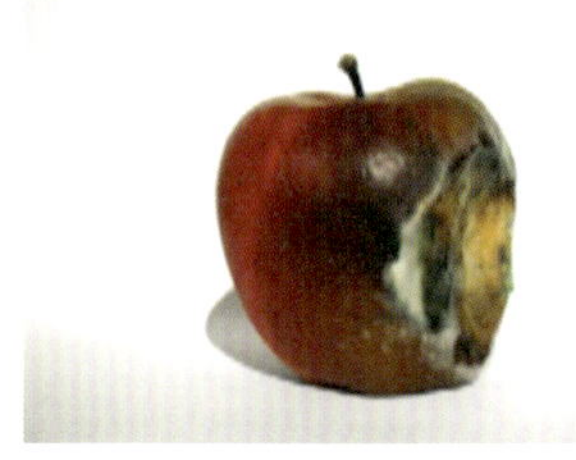

Alex:
ORIGINAL MATTER, AND
ENDURING UNDERLYING STUFF

Alex and Vicki:
And she whom they call Iris, this
too is by nature cloud, / purple
red, and greeny yellow to behold.

A picture element is the smallest
piece of information in an
image. Pixels are arranged in a
two-dimensional grid represented
by dots or squares; Allowing
for the unconcealedness of the
digital kernels. Each pixel is a
sample, of an original image. A
pixel is generally thought of as the
smallest single component of an
image. The more pixels used to
represent an image the closer the
result can resemble the original
apparition. We can also speak of
pixels in the abstract as a unit of
measure.

The word pixel is a compound,
composed of two fragments, the
first based on a contraction of pix,
for picture, and the second, el, for
element. The origin of the word is
obscure. dwelling in the blue, and
gloomy penumbra of sylvan
Arcadia. but was first published in
relation to picture elements in
video images transmitted from the
moon and mars.

The Atom is the smallest particle
that constitutes a chemical
element. Seed-like, tiny. An atom
consists of an electron cloud
composed of negatively charged
electrons that surround a dense
nucleus. This circle is a virtuous
circle not a vicious circle. Atoms
form about 4% of the total mass
density of the observable universe,
the remainder of the mass is an
unknowable dark matter. The first
atoms were theoretically created
during an eepoc, known as the
recombination.

Most of the atoms that make up
the Earth and its inhabitants were
present in their current form in
the nebula that collapsed out of a
molecular cloud to form the solar
system. The rest are the result of
molecular decay and barefaced
invention.

Vicki:
The concept of the Atom as an
in-divisible component of matter
was first proposed in the 6th
century BC, way before
H'err-odditus. Who's eye was in his
ass-hole. His spurious combination
creatures inhabited an altogether
more polyglot spectrum.

Alex:
In the 17th and 18th centuries,
natural philosophers provided a
physical basis for this idea by
showing that certain substances
could not be further brokendown
conceptually or by chemical
methods. Later it was revealed
that the village was divided, as
physicists discovered sub atomic
components and structure inside
the atom, thereby demonstrating
that the atom was not in-divisible.
The principles of quantum
mechanics were used to
successfully model the thingly
character of the Atom.

As mentioned earlier, the Idea that
matter is composed of discrete
units and cannot be divided into
arbitrary tiny quantities has been
around for millennia. These ideas
where founded in abstract,
philosophical reasoning. To
understand a thing we must think
the Being of beings. The nature of
atoms in philosophy varied
considerably over time and
between cultures and schools of
thought. Sometimes possessing a
spiritual element. A vacillation
between secular and mythical,
revealing and concealment, earth
and world.

In approximately 450 BC,
D'moc-retus coined the term,
Atoma, which translates as
uncuttable or the smallest

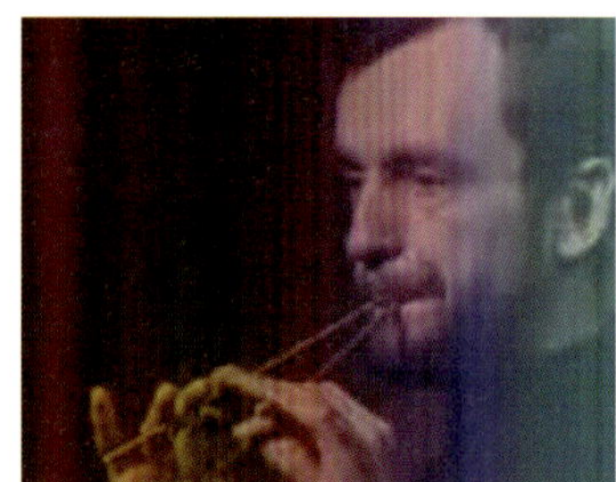

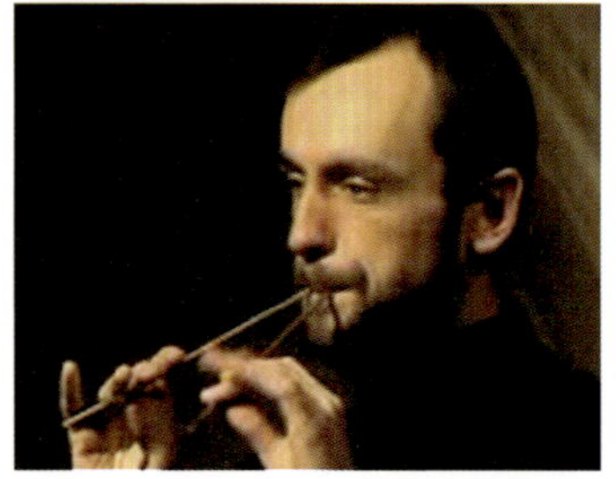

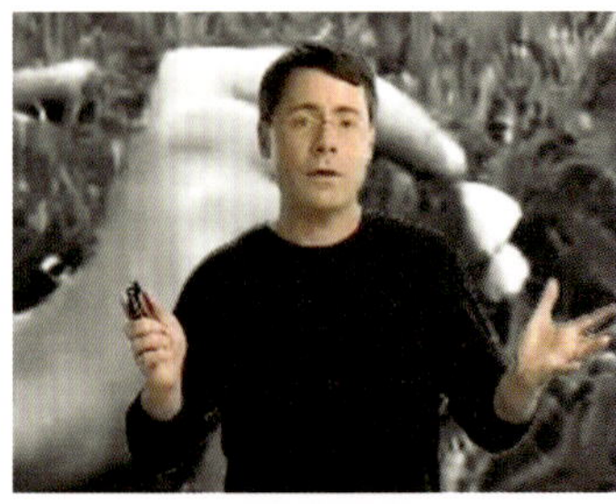

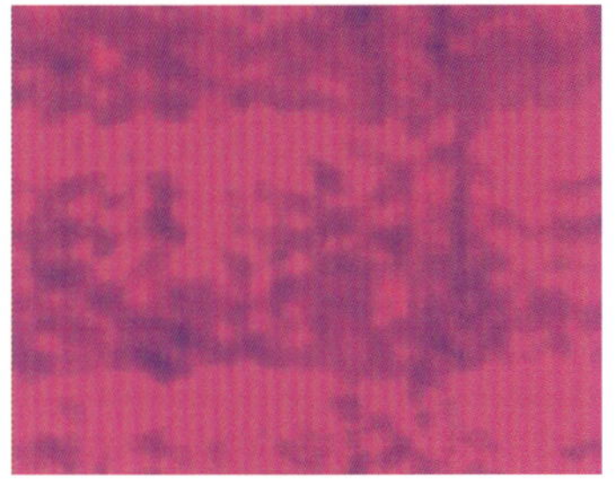

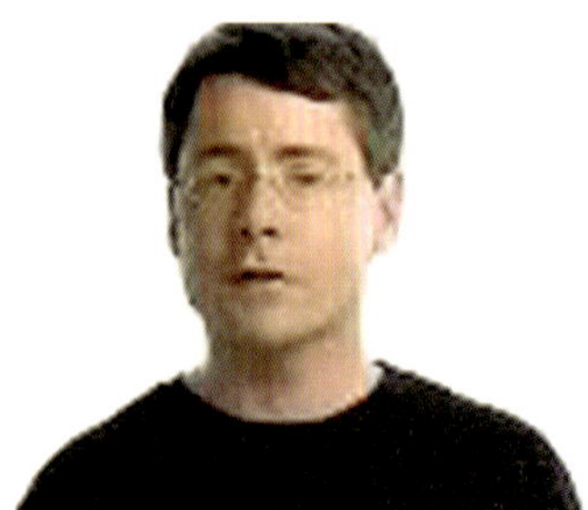

in-divisible particle of matter.
Something that cannot be
divided. In 1661 one of those
natural philosophers argued that
matter was composed of various
corpussles. rather than the
tanaycious classical elements of,
air, earth, fire and water, thereby
resuscitating a 2000-yearold
notion. The term element was
later defined to mean a basic
substance that could not be further
brokendown. The idea of the atom
has been more recently adopted
by scientists, because it elegantly
explains new discoveries in the
field of chemistry and holds open,
the open of the world.

Vicki:
There are two forms of knowing.
One genuine, the other a bastard.
To the bastard belong all these:
Sight, hearing, smell, taste, and
touch. The GENUINE, has been
separated from these.

Alex:
Pre-Soakratic philosophers

rejected traditional mythological explanations for the phenomena they encountered, in favor of more rational explanations.

To explain the origin of things; they sought to discover or describe one primary, material substance as the base or elemental foundation of all natural objects. Much of their thought remains completely obscure, elusive and impenetrable, for instance, for the Pythagoreans, the one thing that formed the substrate of all the infinite things in the universe was; NUMBER.

The audacious atomists held that void, space without matter, exists, and that this void contains an infinite number of in-divisible units, which are undifferentiated in material. By random movements they form vortexes, in which atoms come together and form the sensible, terrible world. The shapes of the atoms and their arrangement with respect to one another give physical objects their apparent characteristics. The earth tends to draw the world into itself and keep it there. This is its nature as concealing.

Vicki:
There are fragments that proclaim the unity or identity of opposites. Moving blocks. BARBARIAN MATTER

Alex:
Nature in the cosmos was fitted together out of unlimiteds and limiters. The unlimitids are unstructured stuffs and continua. The limiters impose structure on the unlimiteds. Things become knowable because they are structured in this way. Stutter, stutter, stutter. Mouth the words. Repeat after me;

What seem to be generated objects are instead temporary mixtures of ingredients. The original state was one of universal

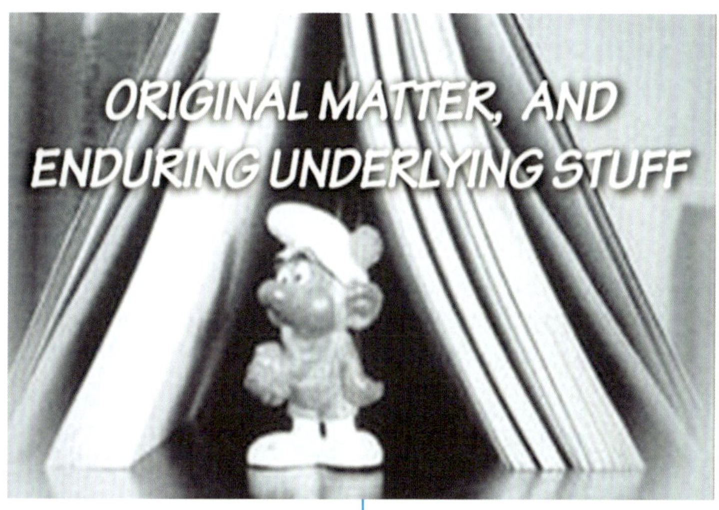

mixture. All things were together, unlimited both in amount and smallness, for the small too was unlimited. And because all things were together nothing was evident. This is the intimate struggle between world and earth.

As a rotation spreads out through the unlimited mass of indistinguishably intermingled ingredients, the rotation causes a winnowing or separating effect and the cosmos as we know it emerges from the mixture. Moreover, not only were all things together, they are even now together, in a different way, despite the differentiations now achieved. Everything is everything in some proportions, however small or great. This is a move to prevent even the appearance of; coming-to-be, from, what-is-not.

Appearances are a sight of the unseen.

Alex and Vicki:
A fictional group; small, sky blue; somewhere in the woods.

Vicki:
The cast has a simple structure: all characteristics essentially alike, Very short ("just three apples tall") Blue skin, white trousers with a hole, white hat in the style of a Phrygian cap.

Alex:
Like alchemists they configured

the notion of original matter and enduring underlying stuff. "Does the original stuff persist through the changes that it undergoes in the generating process?" They conclude that it does. Material monists, committed to the reality of a single material stuff that undergoes many alterations but

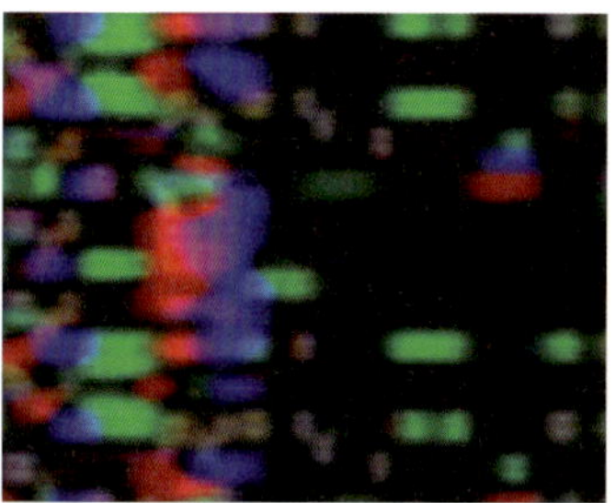

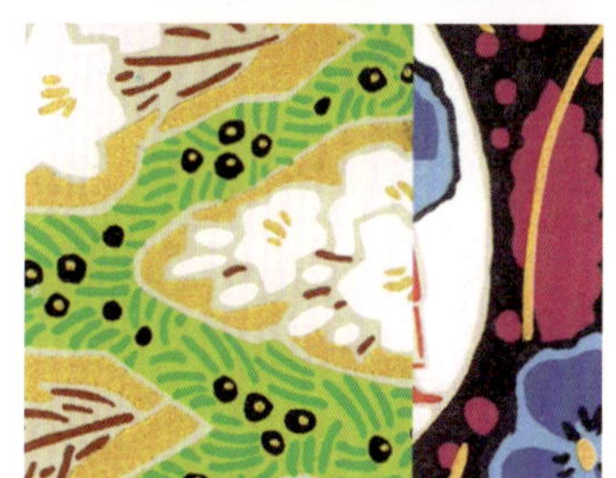

persists through the changes. Original matter from which the world is formed. Seminal transforming material pips that endure as a singular substratum. An irreducible pluralism of stuffs passing on their qualities to items constructed from them. The atomists consider all phenomenal objects and characteristics as

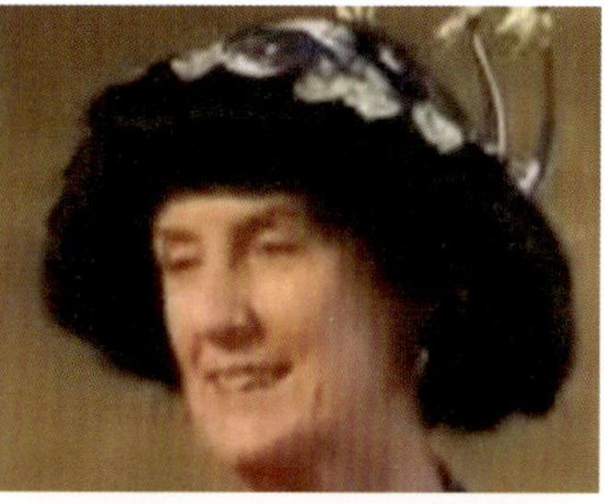

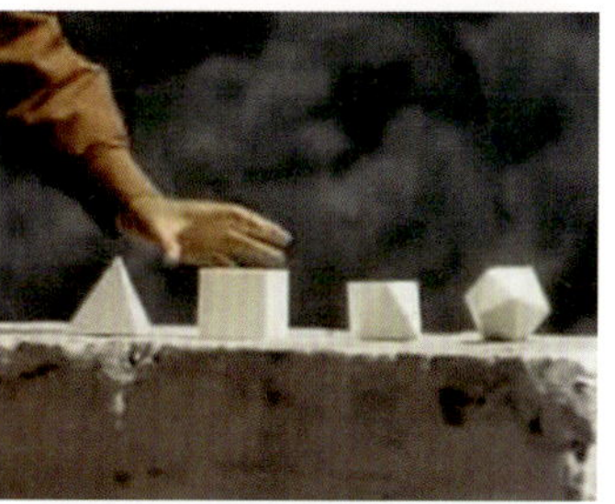

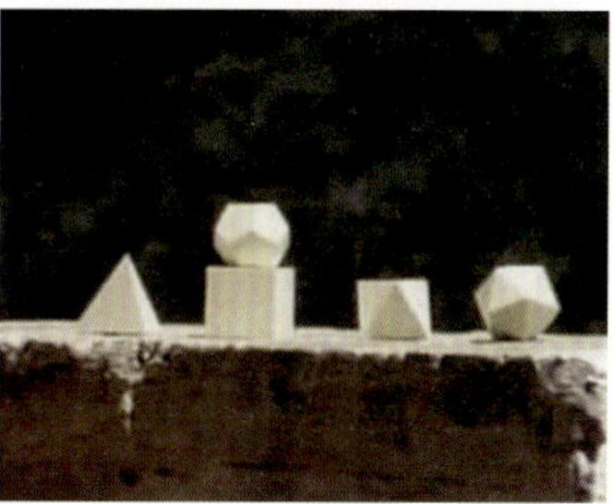

emerging from their background mixture.

Every thing, constructed of; spiralling elements, corpussles, atoma and VOID.

Vicki:
To create is to cause something to emerge.
What is real is an infinite number of solid, uncuttable units of matter, uniform, differing only in position, arrangement, followed by their numerous monotonous peers who look exactly alike. Agents of nothingness enthusiastically endorsing the reality of the empty.

Vicki:
By convention sweet and by convention bitter, by convention hot and by convention cold, by convention colour: *in reality, atoms and VOID.*

Alex and Vicki:
All phenomena are clouds, coloured, moving, incandescent.

Cluk Cluk

2006
Video
5 minutes, 34 seconds

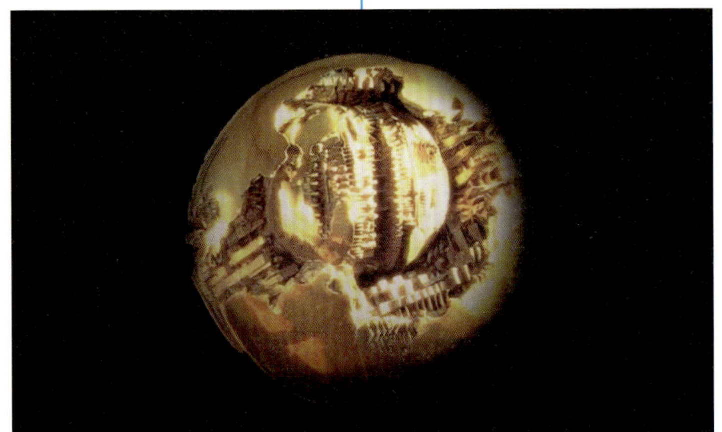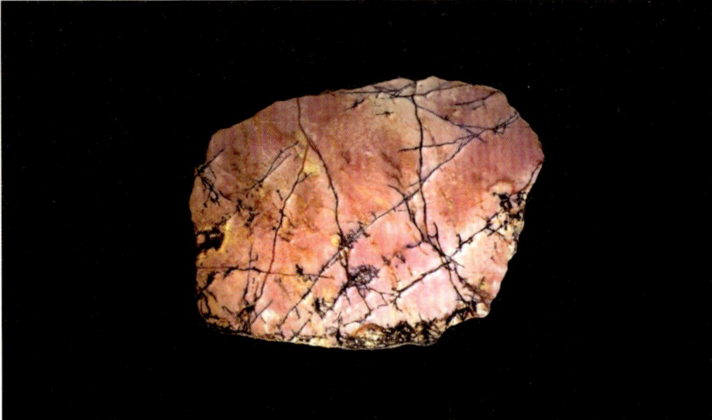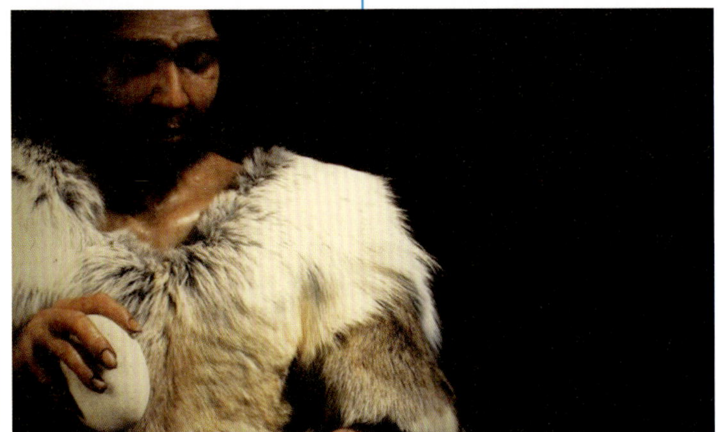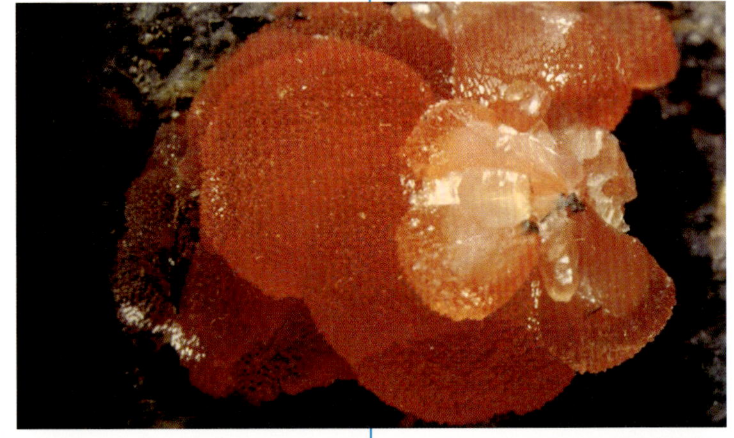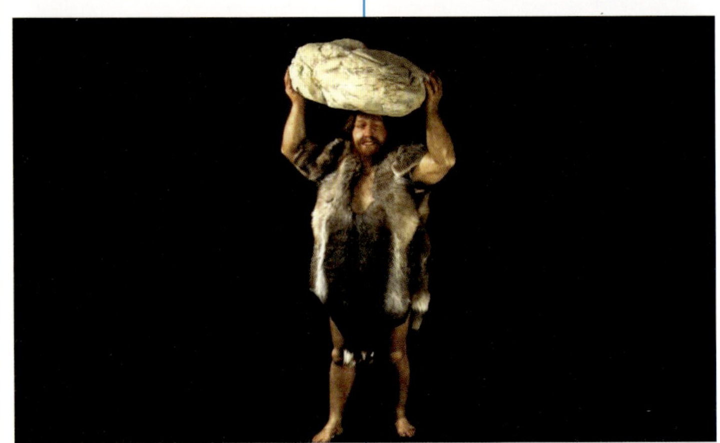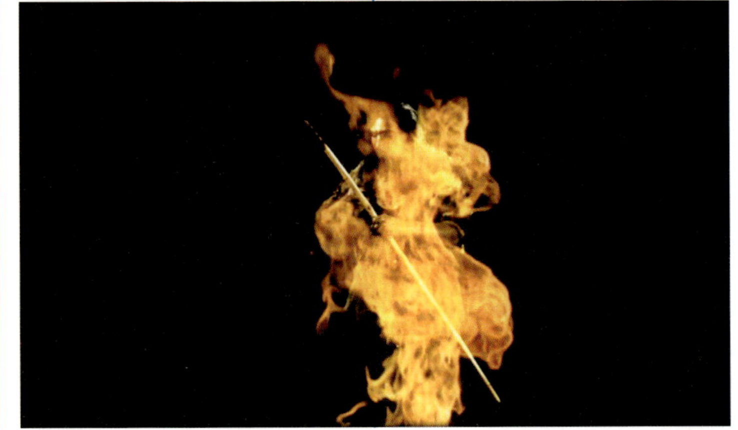

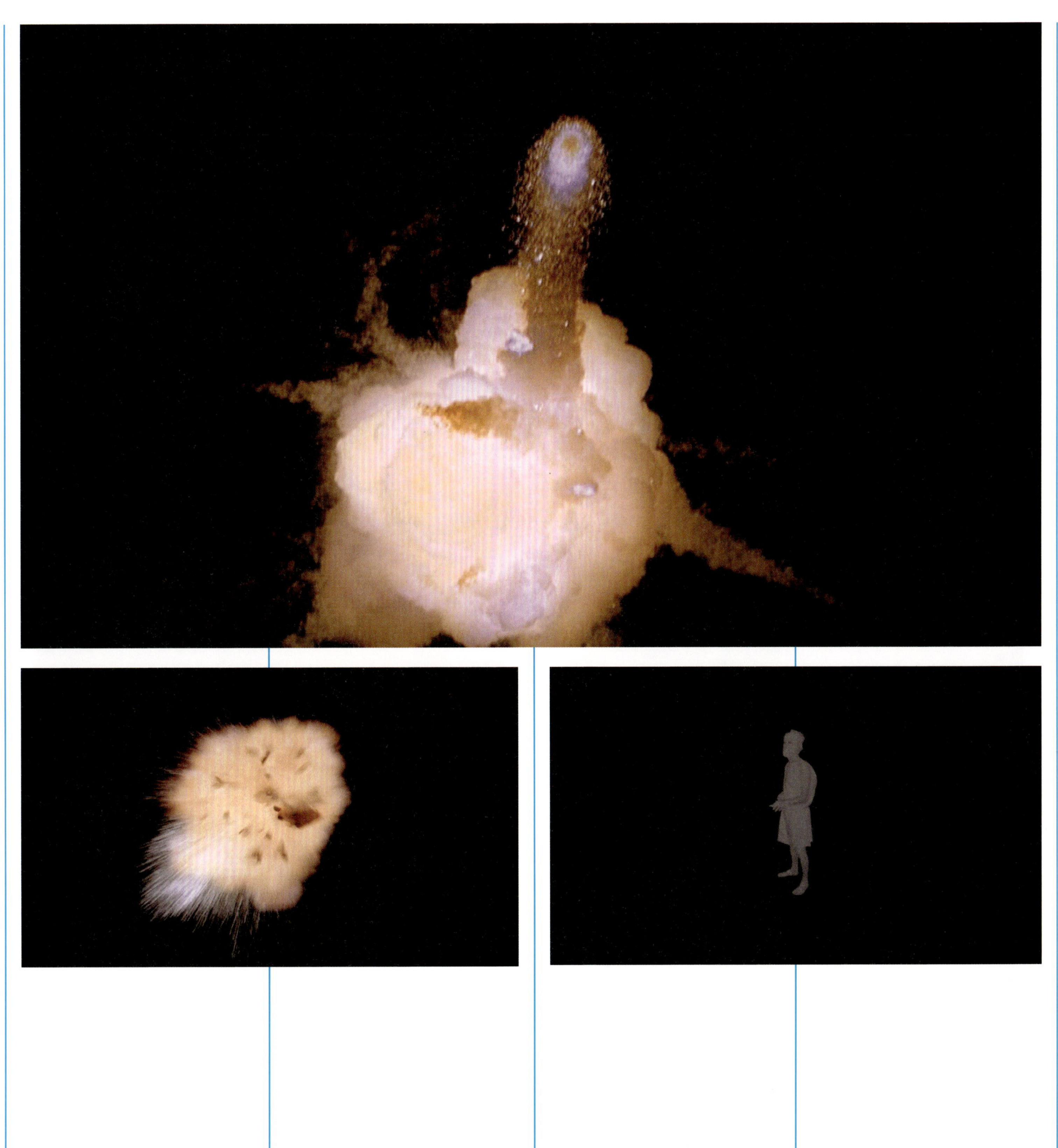

Forward-facing Lemon Yellow Eyes

Hayward Gallery, London
31 March 2011

Photos: Mark Blower

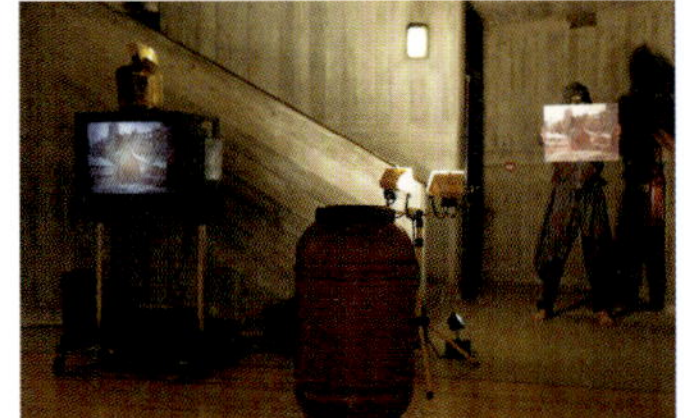

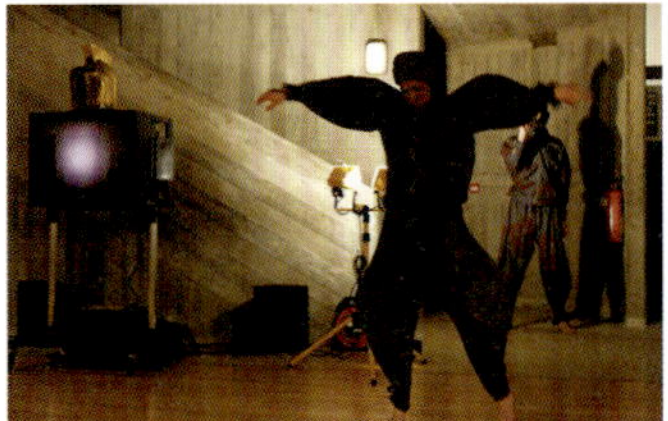

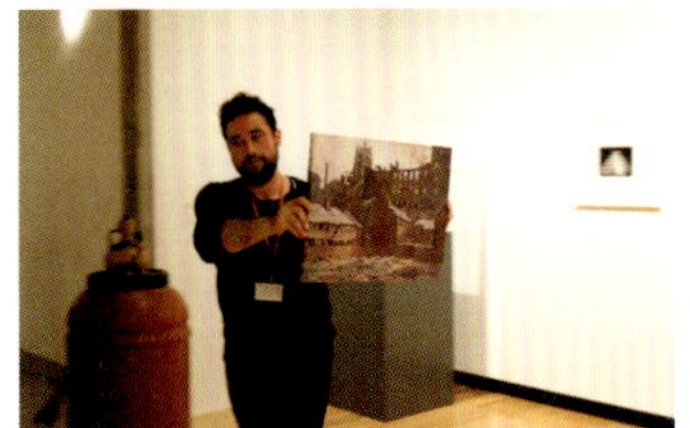

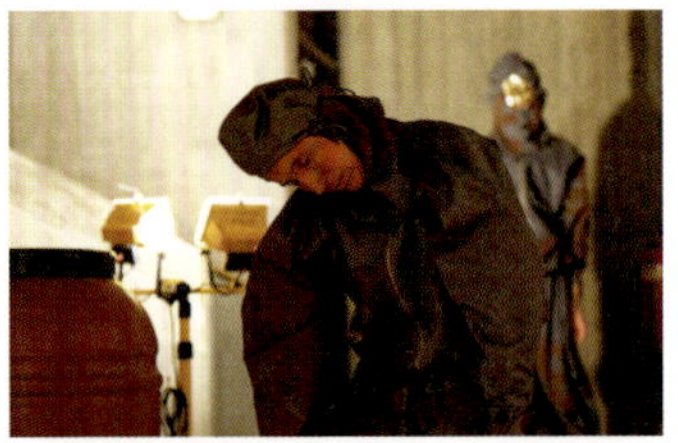

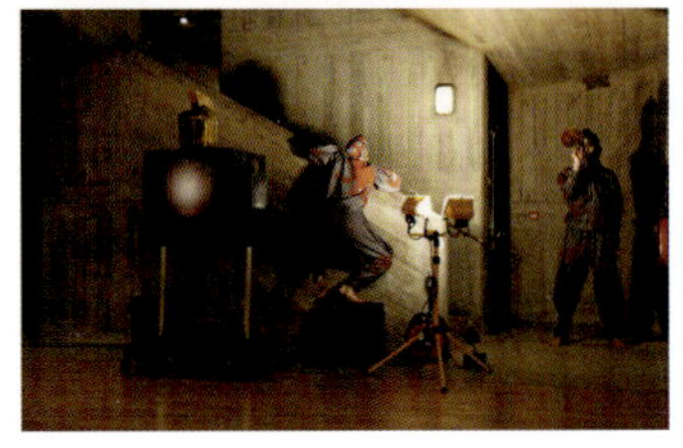

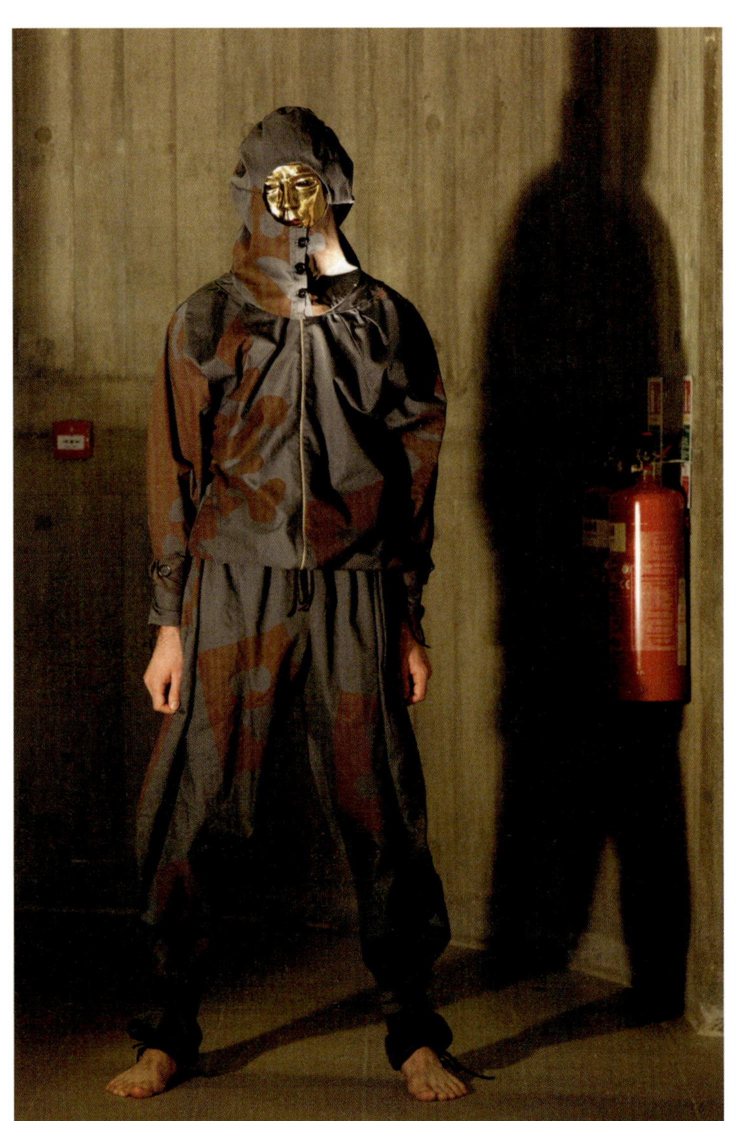

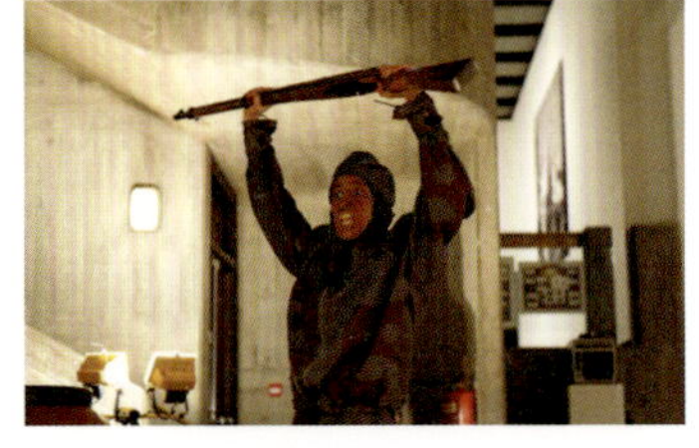

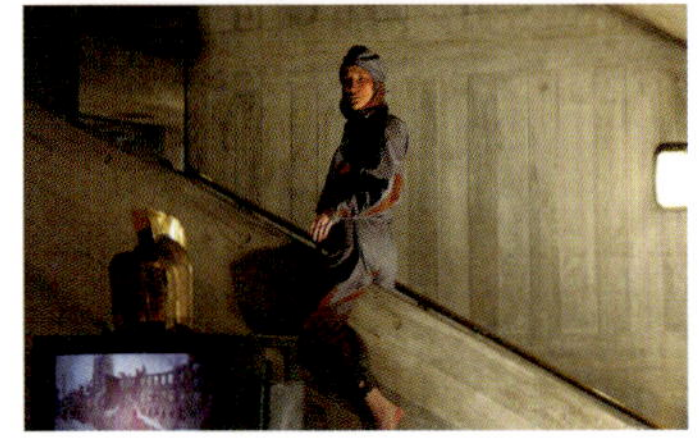

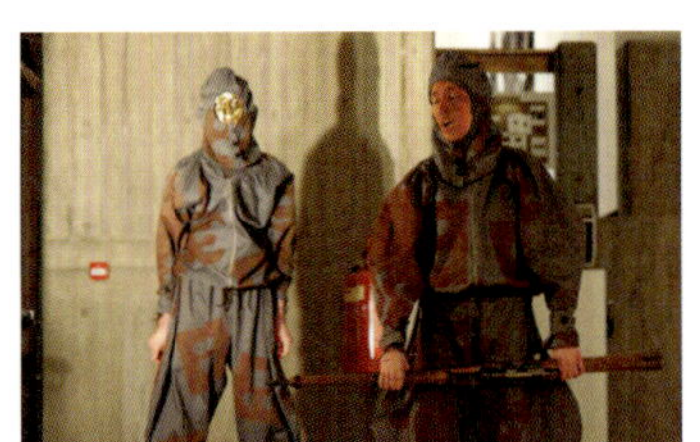

An Equivalence Propelled

Royal William Yard, Plymouth
17 September 2011

Photos: Simon Keitch

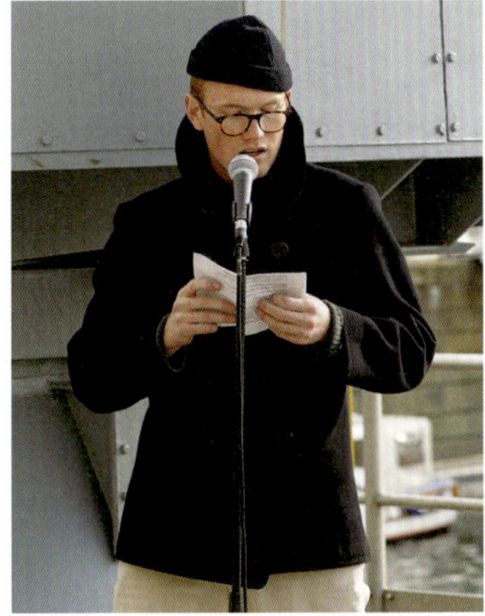

Eh, så.. Dette, dette er tingen.
Tingen holdt oppe.

Opp. Opp. Opp.
Høyt, Høyt, Høyt.

Høyt oppe. Appollo-høyt.
Høyt opp over underlaget. Gjørma.
Over den straffeskyldige jorda.
Høyt oppe over alt under.
Den grunnleggende medskyldige
til det gitte.

Til det som jeg vil si. Å-tilskuer.

Her er en ting, som andre ting.
Tatt på fersken.
En annen legemliggjøring av
fastfrosset ekvivalens.

Tatt likefremt ut av lomma, Min
lomme, eller fra lagerrommet.
Transfigurert fra ditt lagerrom.
Akkurat som redskapet fra
kjelleren, eller potetene fra
kjelleren,
eller trestammer i skauen,
eller pixler,
eller, for den saks skyld, Blekk.
Svart blekk fra den blekksvarte,
blekkspyttende jordlige
blekkskriver.

Blekk som, tross alt, er akkurat
som hvasomhelst og ulikt alt annet.

Dette er det "tingliges" natur, og
det er også stoffets natur.

Brettet ut av eteren, ut av
det underliggende og inn i
rundtomkring.
Det surround-sound-rundtomkring.
Det opp-høyt-rundtomkringe av
det verdensrundtomkringe.
Avdekkingen av bortgjemmingen.
Det vinkende anus.
I dette størrelsesforholdet er
utganger bare forvirrede innganger.
Og…

Vel.

Betrakter! Betrakt!

Pixler er her i verden. Harde pixler.
Jævla harde. Tro meg!
Elektriske pixler og ørsmå,
uendelig små neutronpixler.
Tonnevis av pixler sammensatt til
oppstillinger.

Sammensettninger så komplekse
som hva som helst du kan
forestille deg, dypt nedgravd i
dritten.
Hvilken som helst gammel dritt.
Helt ærlig, det er sannheten om
den saken.
Det kuttbare-ukuttbare og det
ukuttbare-ukuttlige.
Partikler og atomer. Omstokkede
målinger og legioner av diabolske
systemer.

Her ligger tingens virkeevne.
Selvfølgelidelse, hvorfor ikke?
Virkeevne framfor medfølelse.
En koføderasjon av fenomener og
tillagte metaforer,
nok til å stille vår bunnløse tørst for
skrekk og adspredelse.
Det tilforlatelige materialet som
hamrer verden inn i klarhet.
Effekt øker affekt.

Ahh men.
Her også bedrageri.

Jeg holder et ark i hånda.

Jeg holder dette arket i hånda.

Dette arket holdes oppe av en

hånd som er min egen hånd.

Denne tingen inneholder sin egen
tilblivelse, og det er bedrageri i den
tilblivelsen.
Dette er redskapet og prosjektilet.

Å konsumere de sammenvevde
virkeevnene av jord og verden. Det
kanibalens virkelig humane rite.
Å kastrere de selvreplikerende
skaperkraften av robot-tingen.
Å gnafse, gnafse, gnafse i vei på
over.
Og å gnafse, gnafse, gnafse i vei
på under.

Å gnage på denne tingen og dette
dokumentet og dens egne, lumske
selvtilblivelse.
Det er handlingens retning og her
lurer sannferdighet.

Derfor, som konklusjon, har jeg
bestemt meg for å handle, å sluke
tingen og sluke dens verden, å
forlate den,
og å forlate deg, åh betrakter.
Og således talte jeg fra Det og det
gjennom meg.

Er det noen som har noe salt?

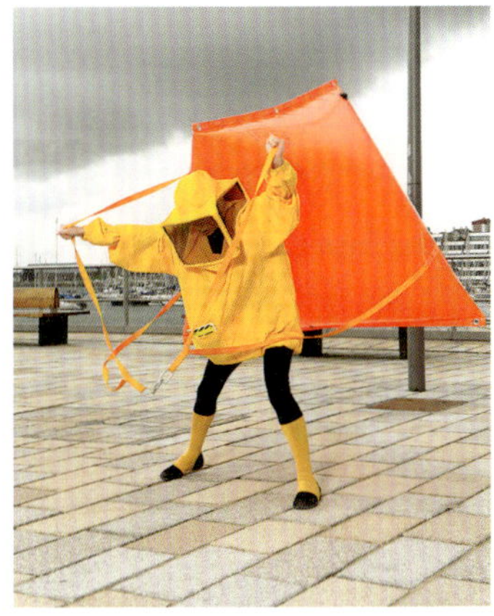

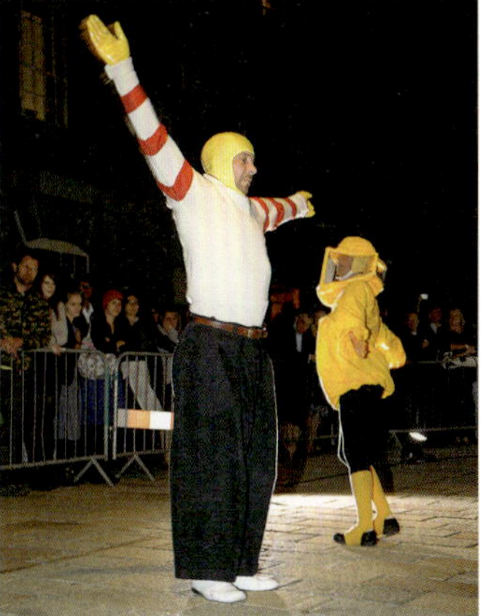

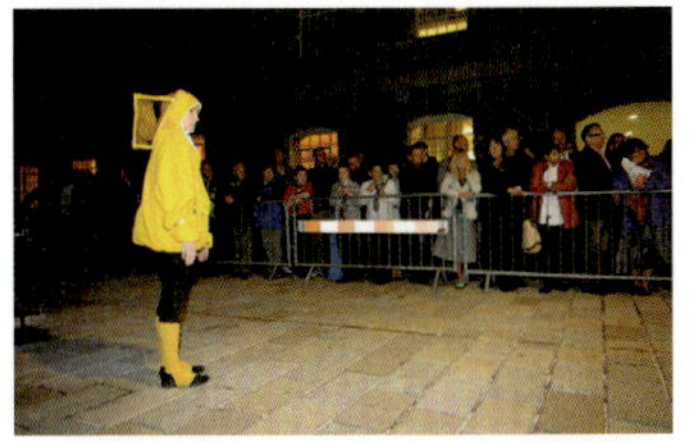

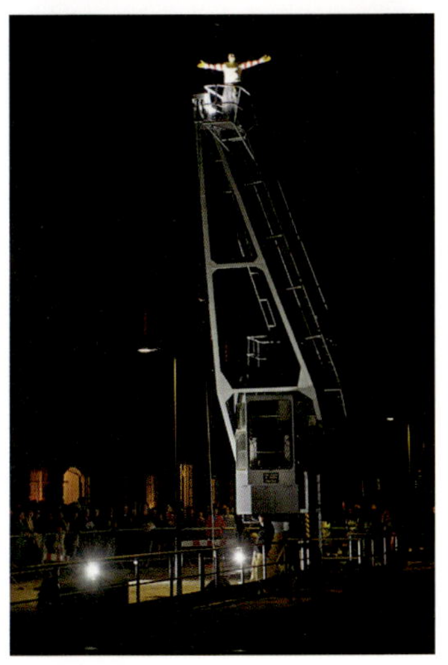

Bestiary!

Cavallerizza Reale – Manica Corta
Accendere l'ascolto Artissima 16
8 November 2009

Photos: Vieri Brini

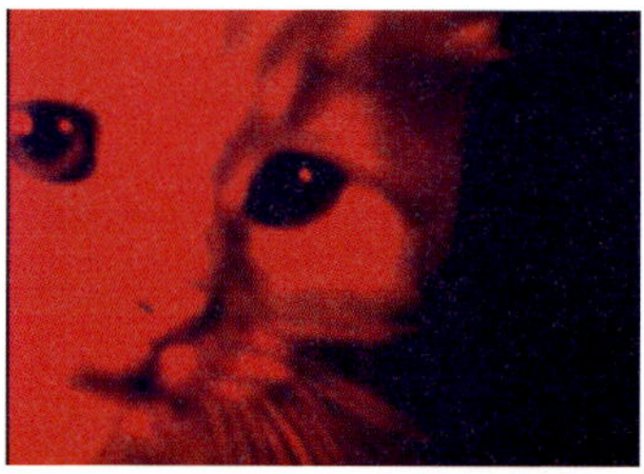

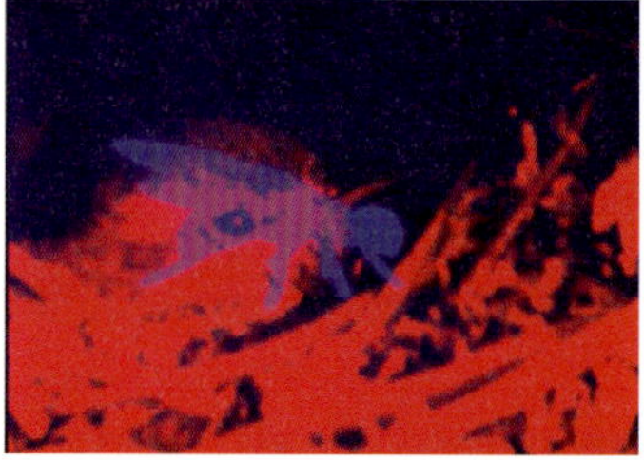

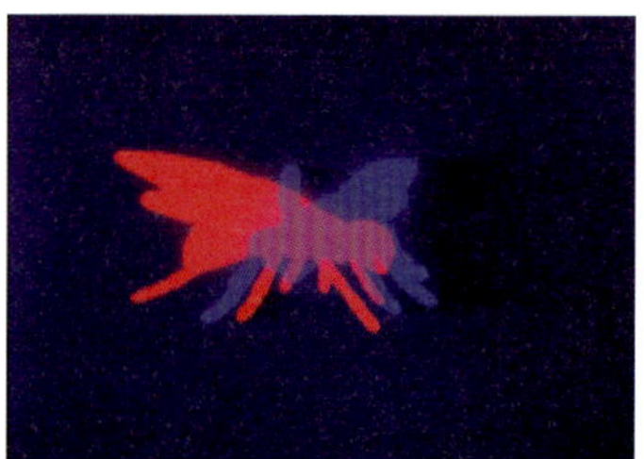

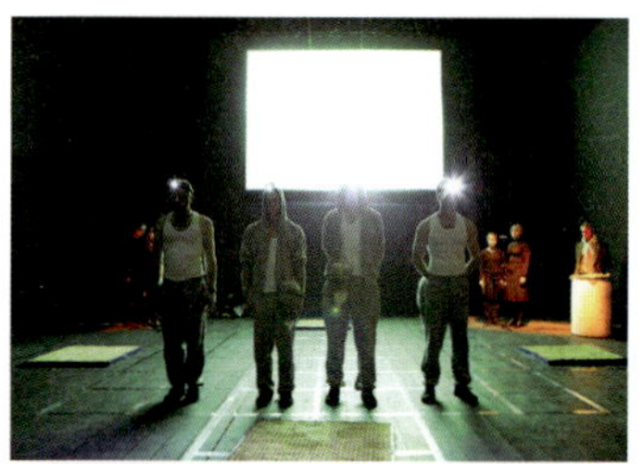

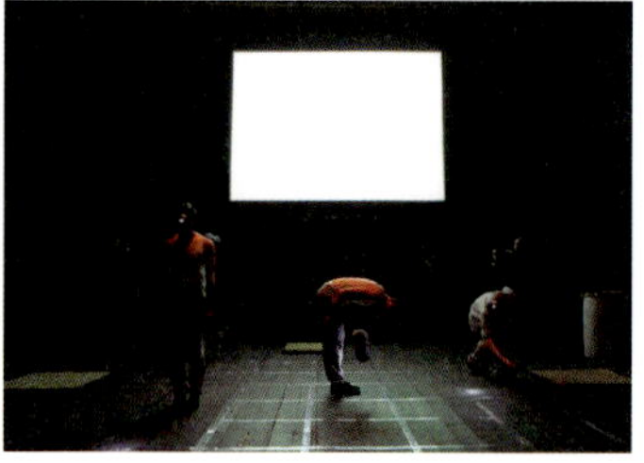

Narrator:
Bestiary!… the darkling and the growing pale.

Bestiary is a game with dice, not unlike our game of Ludo.
The codec shows four players sitting on the ground, or on mats round a table in the shape of a cross and divided into squares.

Prior to commencement players are awarded symbolic zoomorphic characteristics. The characters are wasp, kitten, wren and mouse. Vespula Vulgaris, Felis Catus, Trogloditas Troglodytus, Mus Musculus. At one side of the board, watching over them, is a God. The Tutelary Deity of dancing, music and gambling.

For dice, the players use beans marked with a certain number of pips… and according to figures obtained at each throw, they move small coloured stones from square to square on the board.

The course of the game is communicated via heralds to players outside the city boundaries, who enact the motions in accordance with traditional rules of interpretation.

The winner of the game and the stakes is the one who first comes back to the square he has started from.

Bestiary, like all things, has a hidden meaning.

There are fifty-two squares on the board. That is, the same number as the years that are contained in divinatory and solar cycles.

The sky, it seems, is a sacred gaming board… upon which divine beings play with stars as their pieces.

In the everyday life of laity, the game is the pre-text for huge bets in which great quantities change hands… it is, especially, a game for great men, and for some, it ends in ruin and slavery.

Numerous tales tell of an emperor who played against a lord, and laid as a wager the city's market place against a garden belonging to that lord… He lost!

The next day, soldiers appeared at the palace of the fortunate winner, and while they saluted him and made him presents, they threw a garland of flowers around his neck with a thong hidden in it… and so killed him.

The rule book goes no further than warning those who were born under certain signs that they will be great gamblers, and that in gambling they lose all their possessions. Through all this, the game is played with great enthusiasm. Opponents are martialled and assembled for commencement of the game.

The outcome of the game is impossible to auger. Stakes are high, potential plays are modelled, but never forecast for fear of reprisals pending the possible defeat of the favourite.
The ground is good.

Destinies hang in the balance, like morning mist over a fast-moving and turbulent river. Ready to evaporate or fall prey to the swirling eddies and currents below.

The game commences as night falls, disturbed creatures register their alarm with howls and cries. As the contestants rally to the conch's clarion call, and initial perfunctory pays lip service to decorum, but quickly degenerates into a scramble for pole position… and, a customary chaos ensues.

Roleplay, shadow play, the players enter a dark place, a darkling slow phase. Here, all moves are murky and inconclusive.

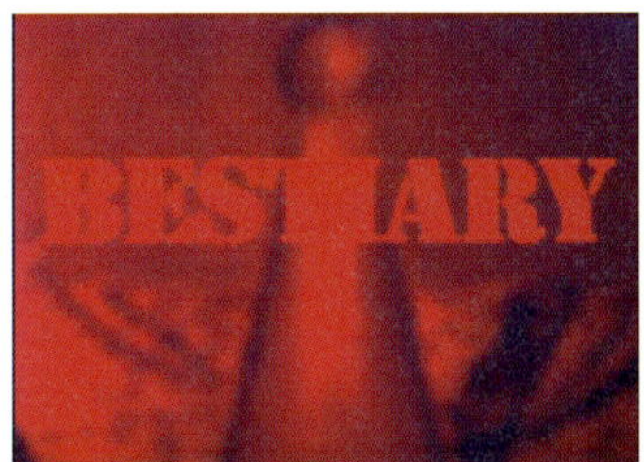

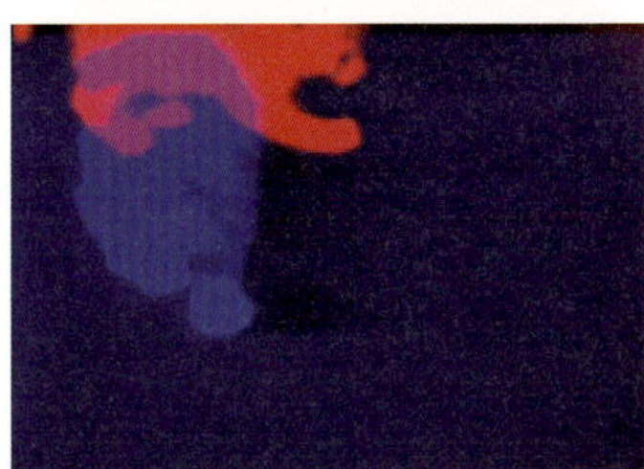

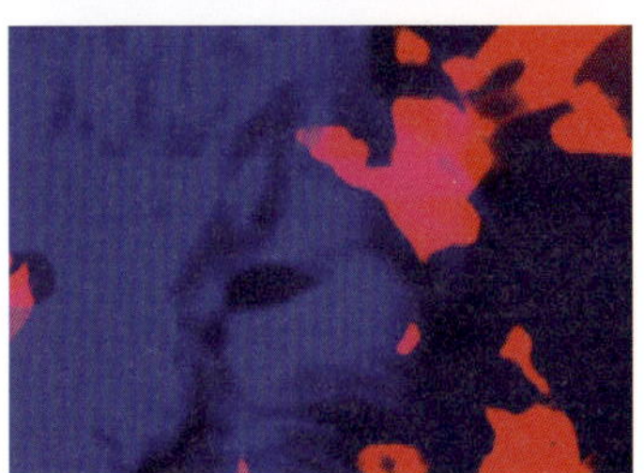

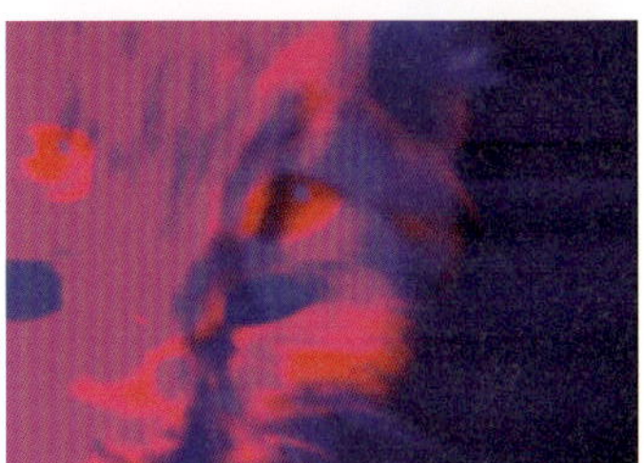

A stalemate seems imminent, a martinet takes the field, deliberate, cautious and precise. Then a subtle shift suggests collusion, the power balance alters, the aggressor is pushed back, a number of pieces are lost or forfeit.

My territory is your territory... My earth is your earth... Your square is my square... Your sequence is my sequence.

The final square is occupied. Now the game is won. The victors come together and sing! All are awarded garlands, all are penalised and obliged to sacrifice pieces, all lose their lives. Mean are the rewards, spartan the parameters.

The sky above the volcano grows pale, the morning star shines with the brilliance of a gem, and to greet it the wooden gongs beat on the temple tops and the conchs wail. There are still wafts of mist over the water in the icy air of this altitude, but these dissolve in the first rays of the sun. Day has begun, and as the morning develops, figures return to the city carrying as trophies the heads of the animals that have been killed the previous night.

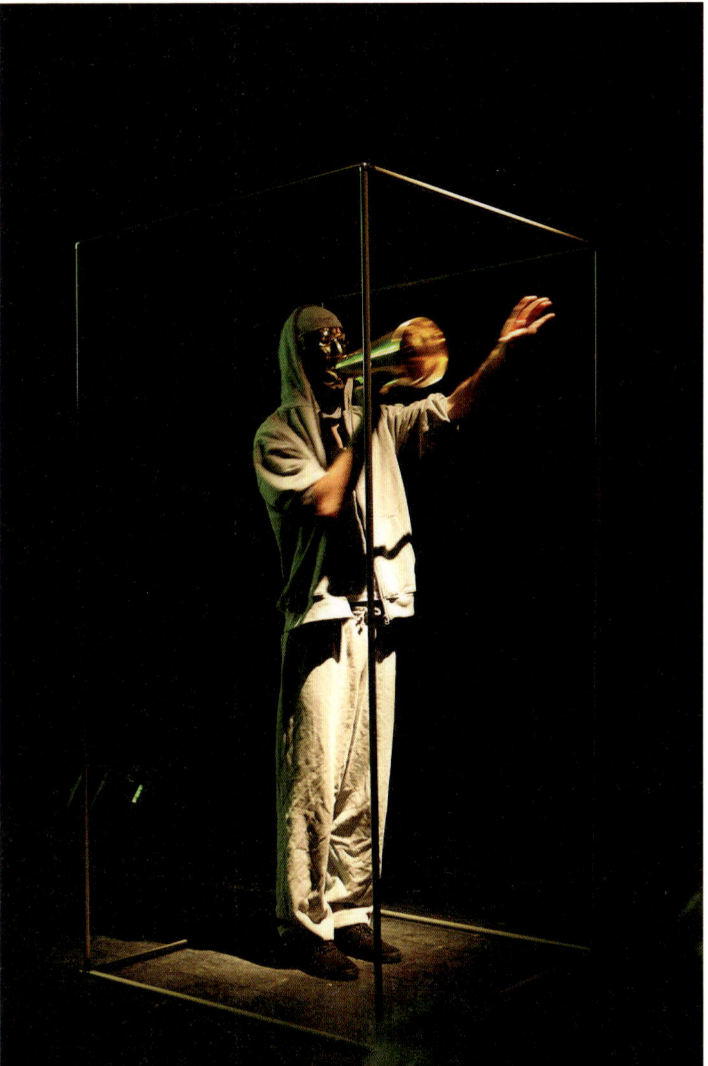

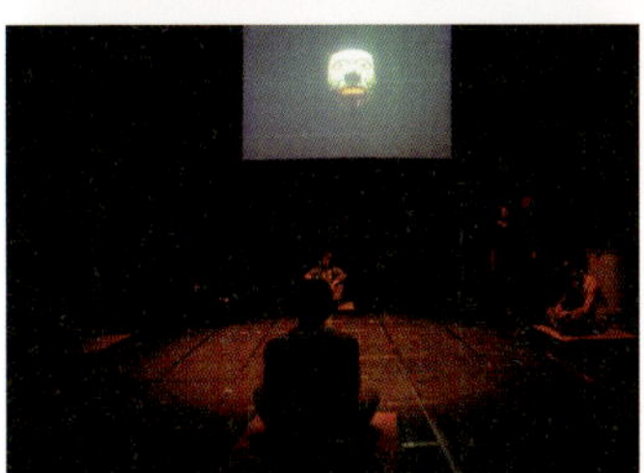

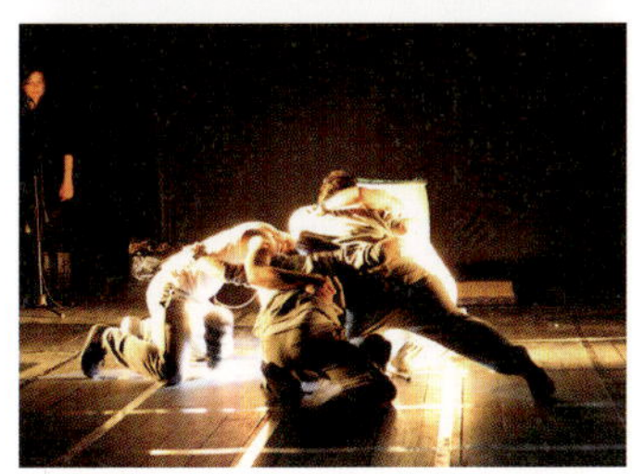

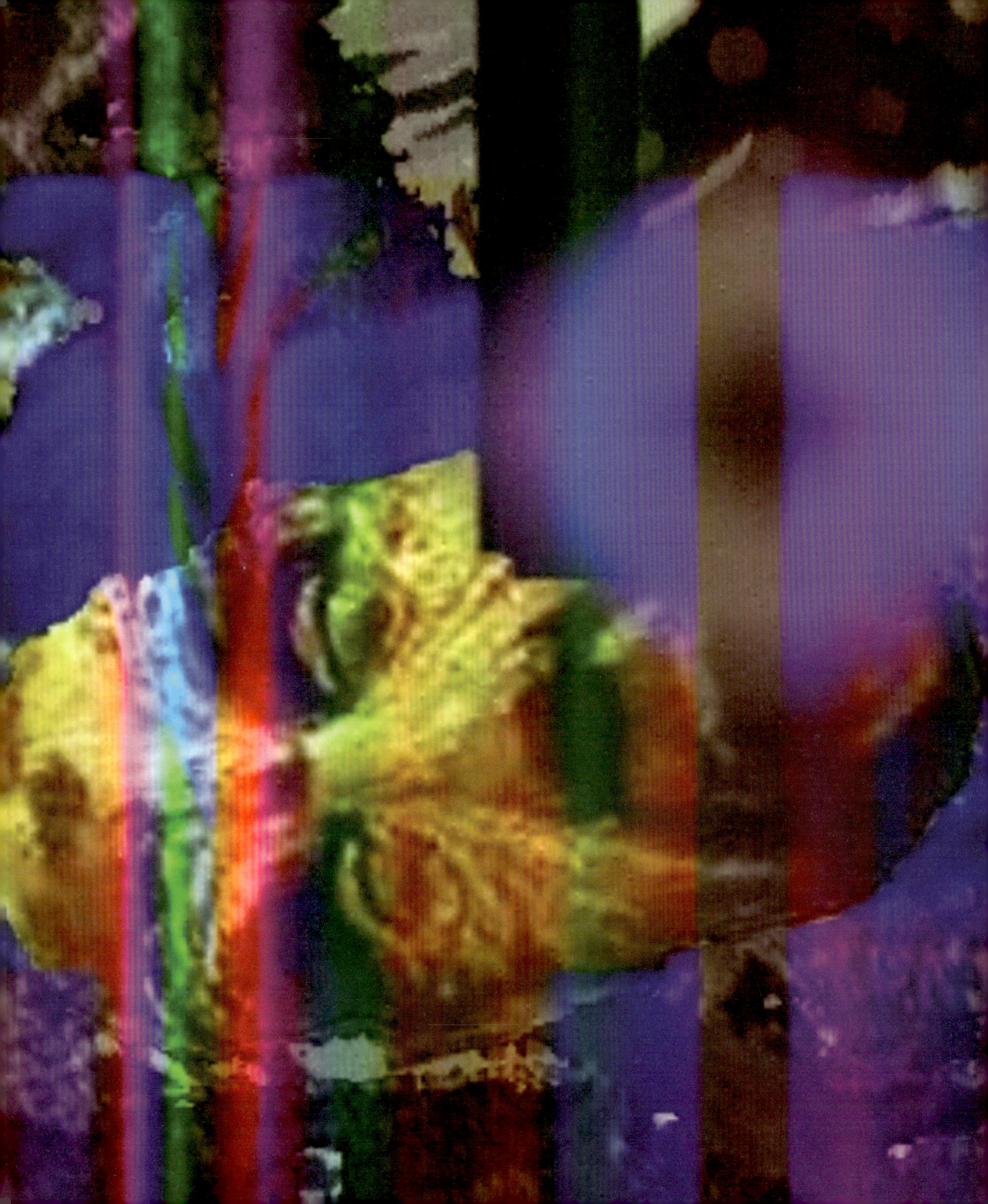

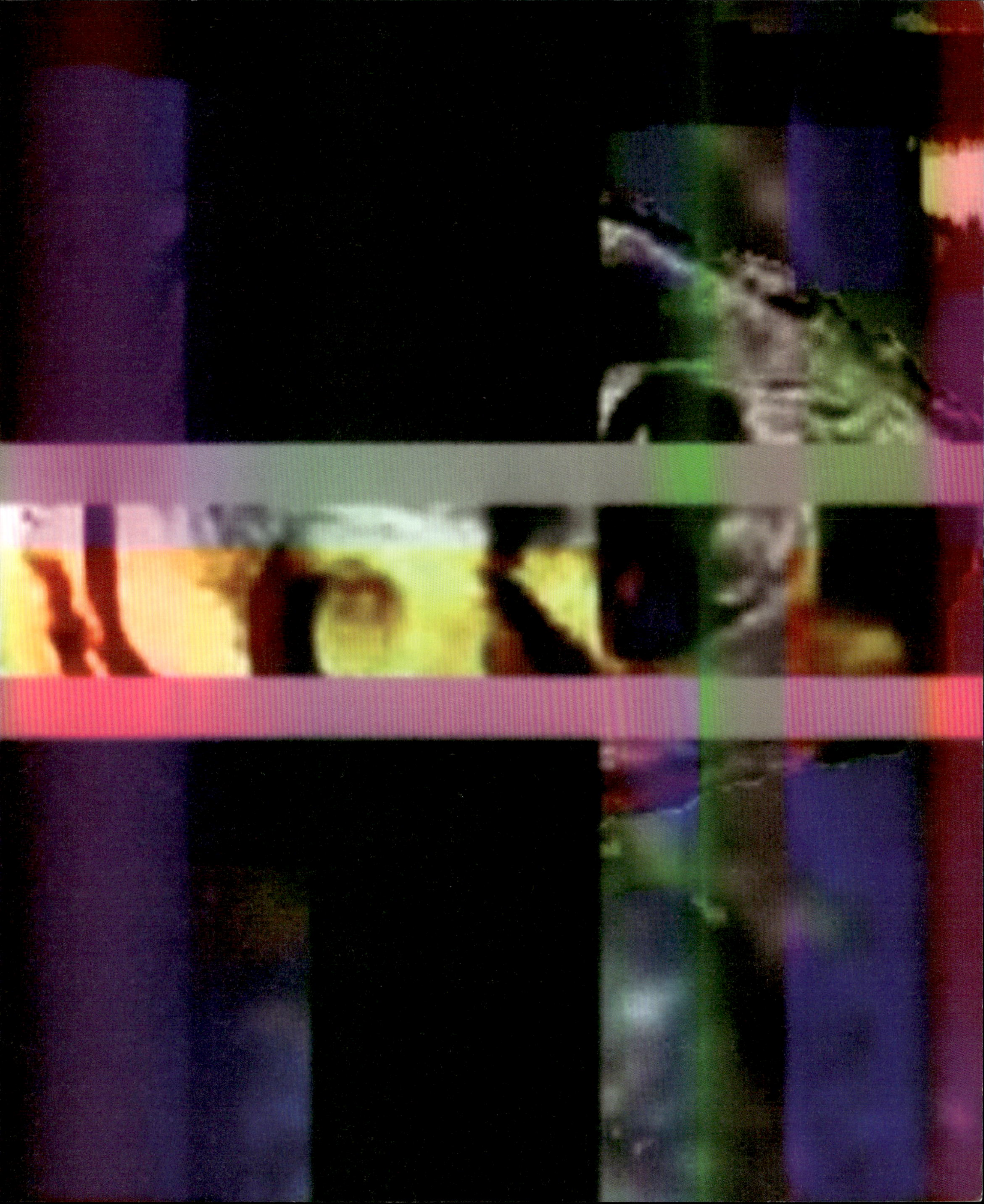

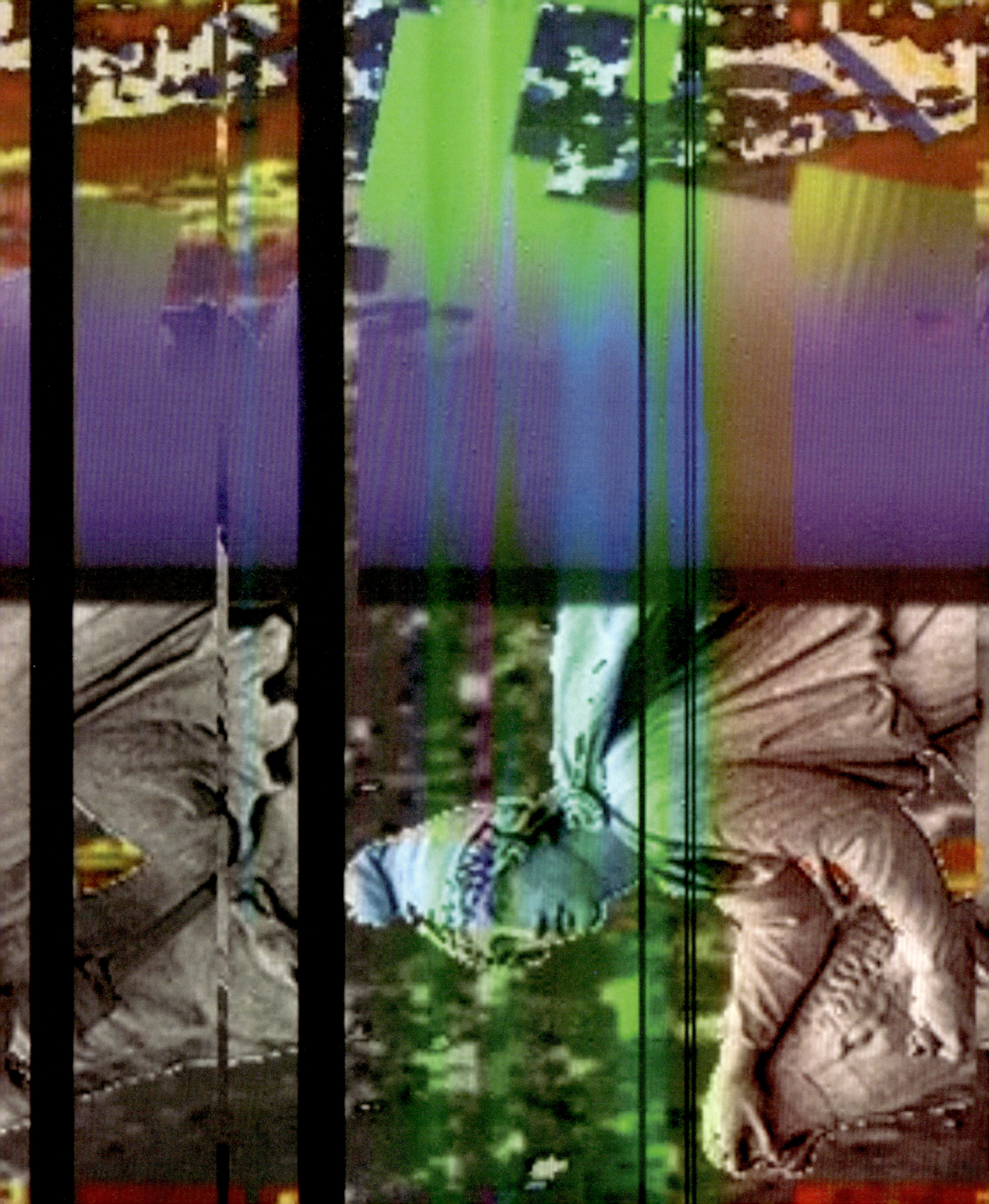

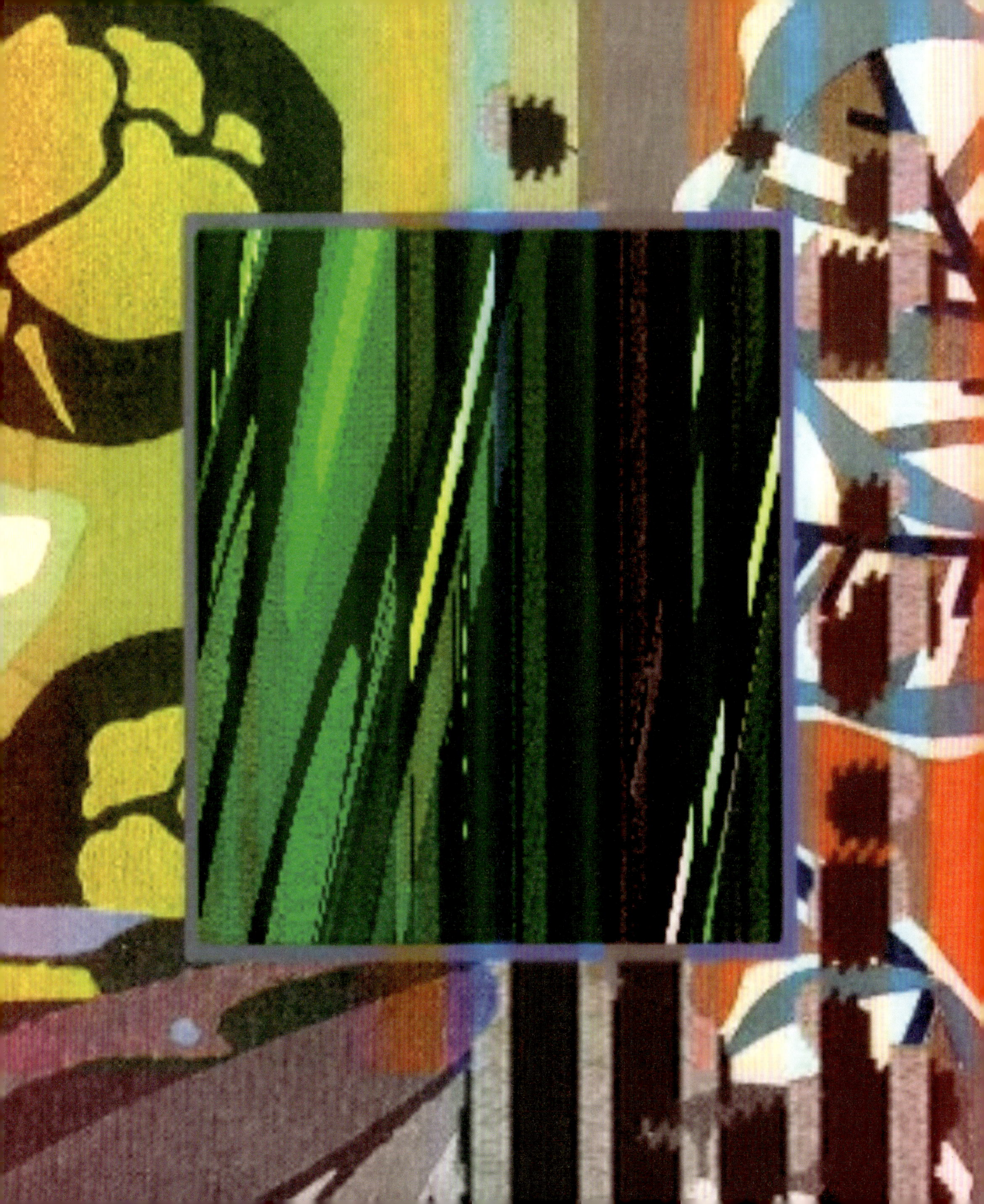

Anthropocentric vessel

Photograph taken through the window of a cable car, near Zurich

Photograph taken through the window of a cable car, near Zurich

Photograph taken through the window of a cable car, near Zurich

Jack too Jack, Dundee

Russian nuclear suit

Snoopy videogame, Snoopy Flying Ace, Smart Bomb Int.

Buoy © Matt Probert Photography

Add N to (X) 12" cover by Paul Noble, 2000

Removed memorial plaque, Bristol

Disney lightbulb. Digital photo manipulation by Deborah Davidson

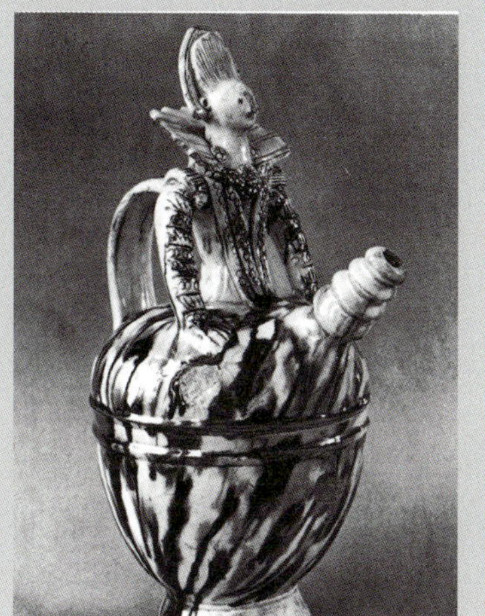

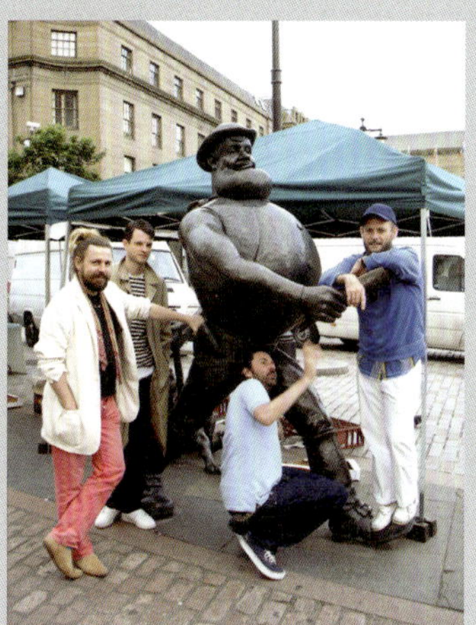

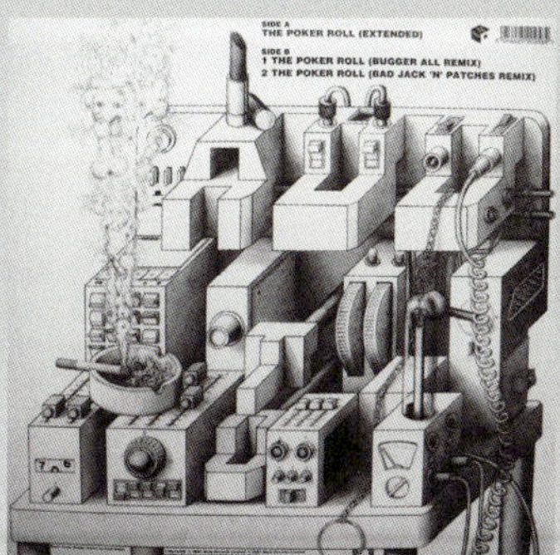

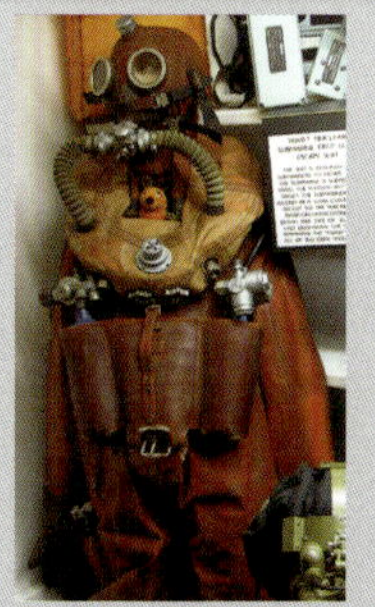

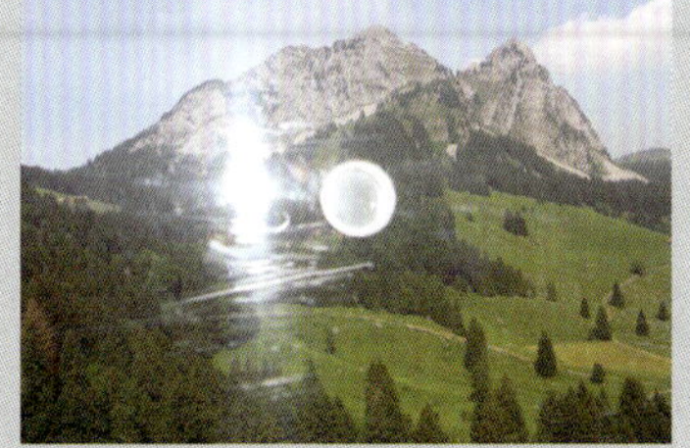

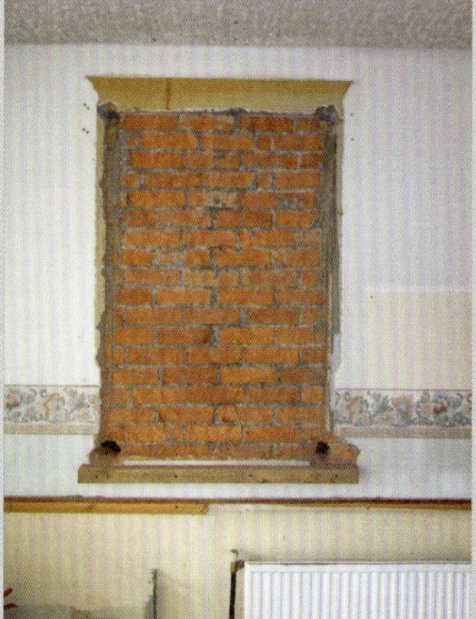

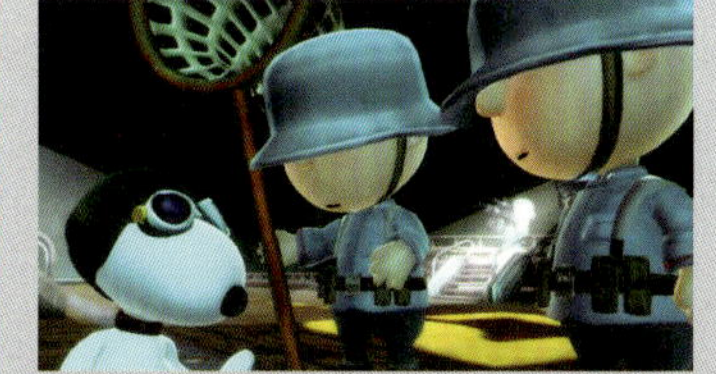

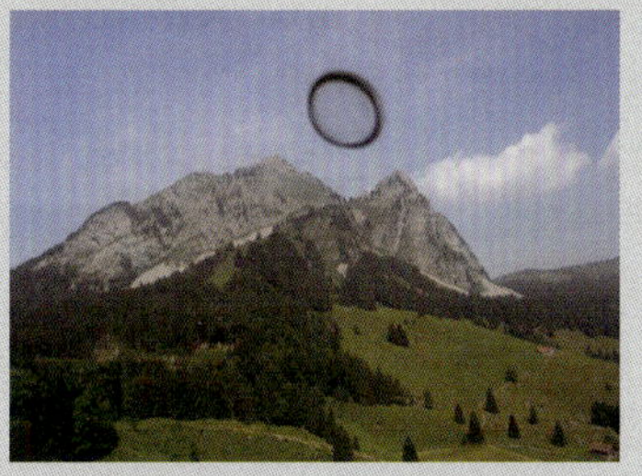

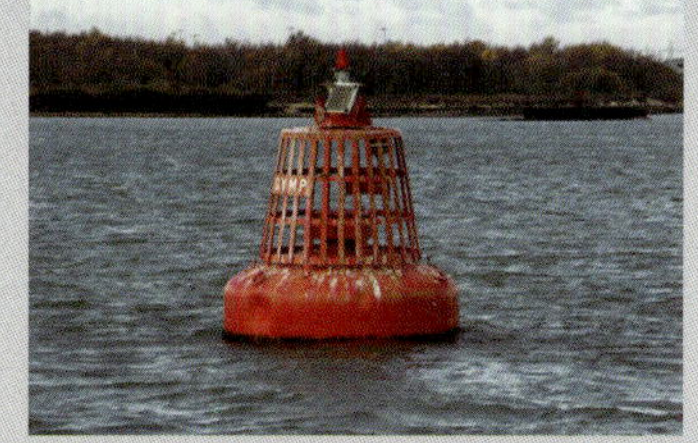

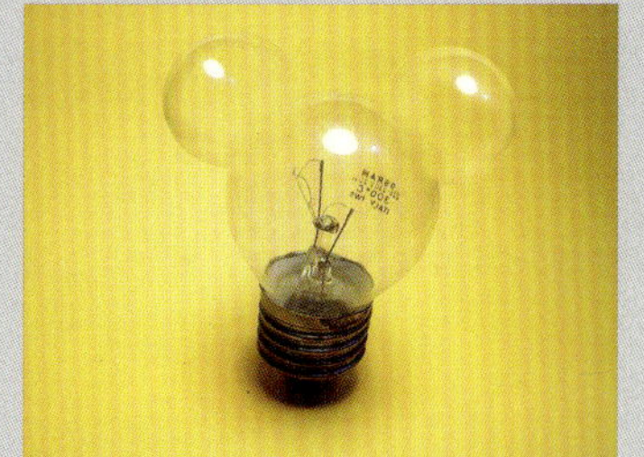

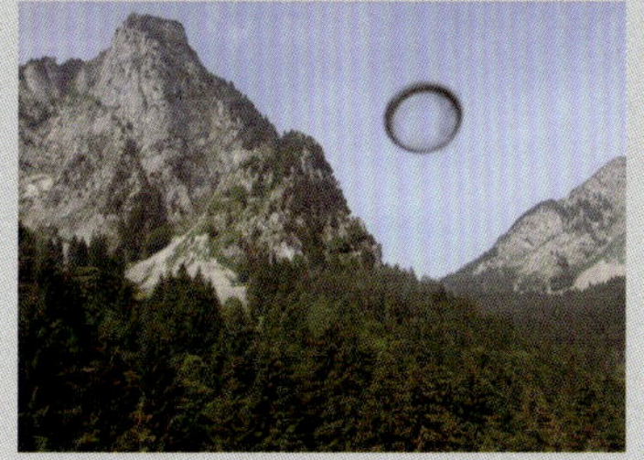

Zardos 2

Ettore Sottsass

Degraded film emulsion
© University of Kentucky

Luis Buñuel

Snoopy hat

Giant African land snail

Casts in the Skulpturhalle, Basel

Casts in the Skulpturhalle, Basel

Snoopy helmets

Smoke machine

Carlo Carrà, *The Drunken Gentleman*, 1916, oil on canvas © DACS 2012

Napolean's cart

Steven Claydon/Hotel exhibition invitation, 2008

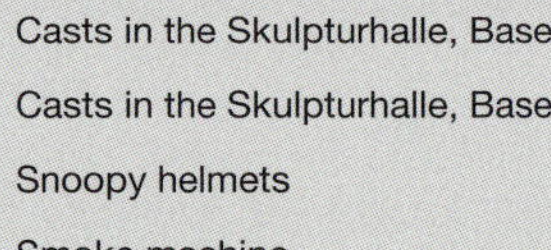

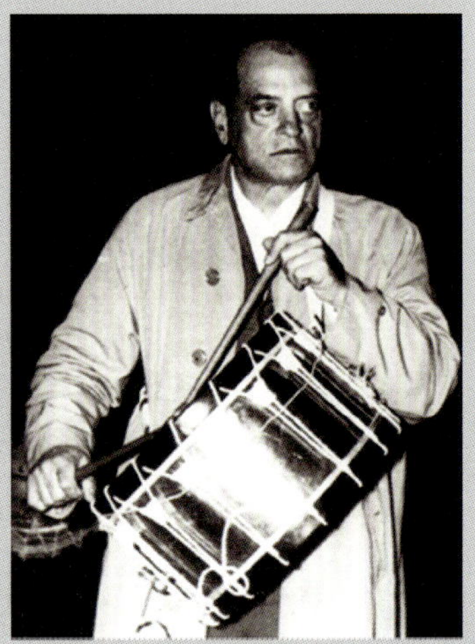

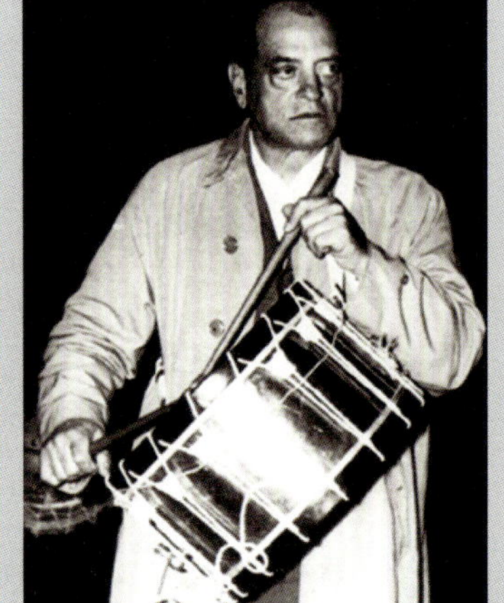

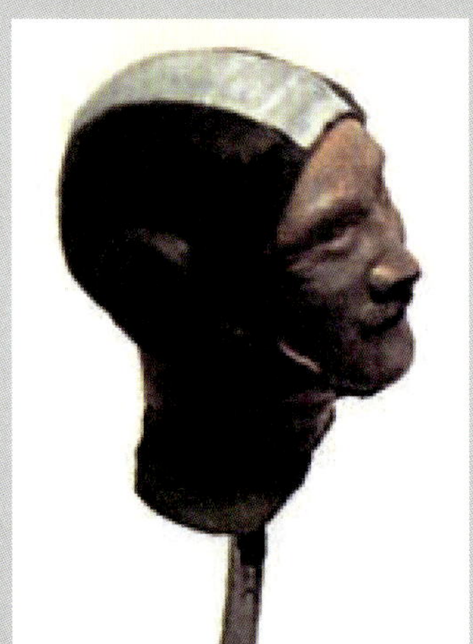

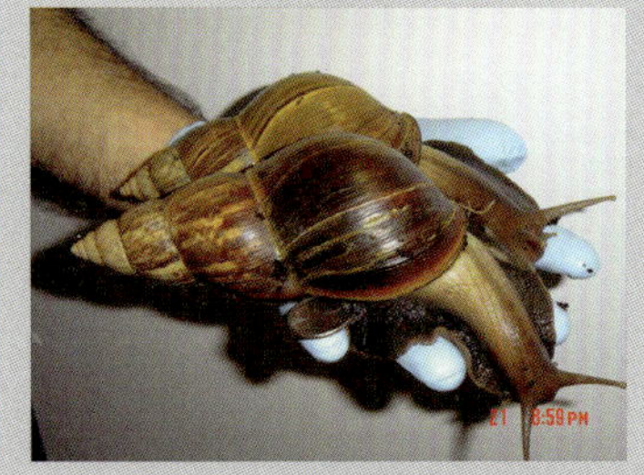

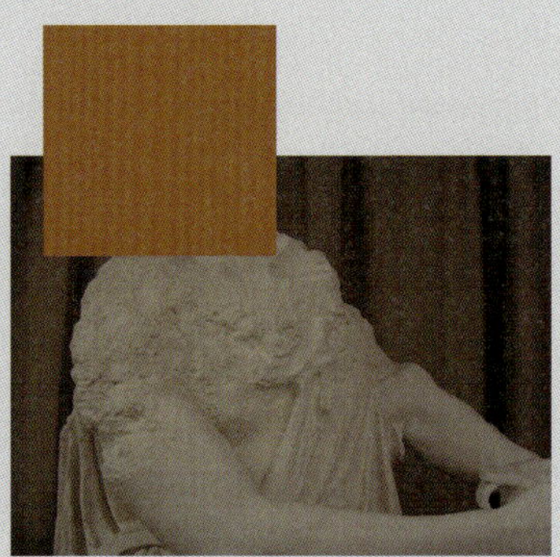

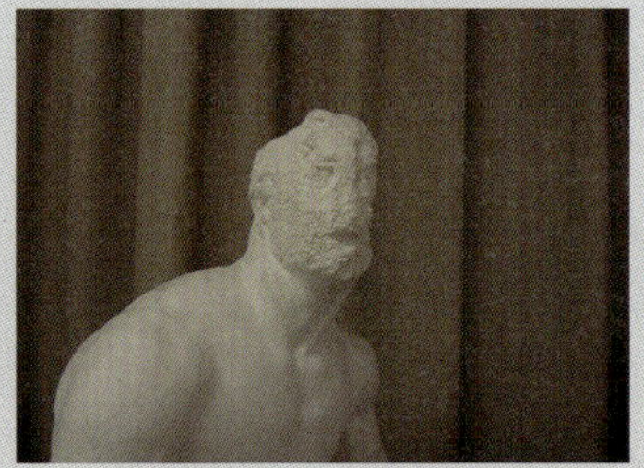

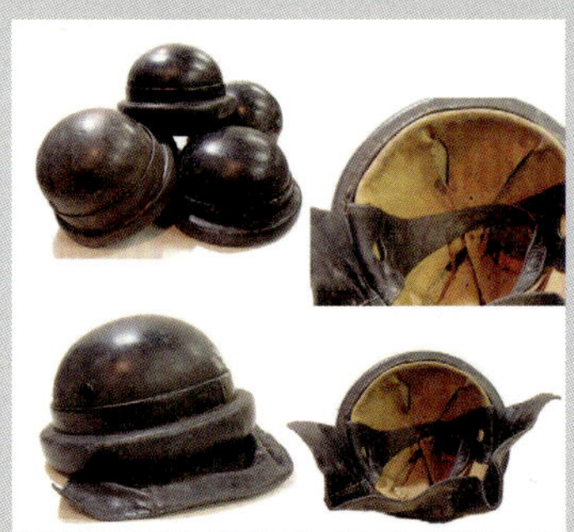

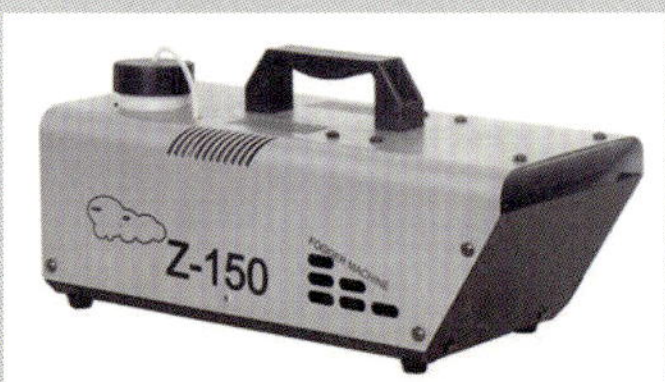

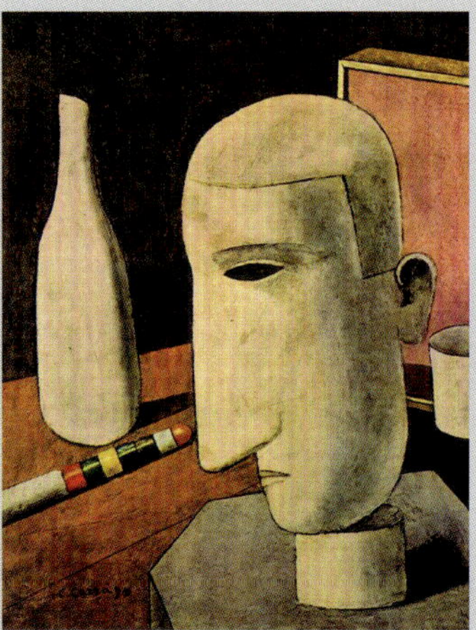

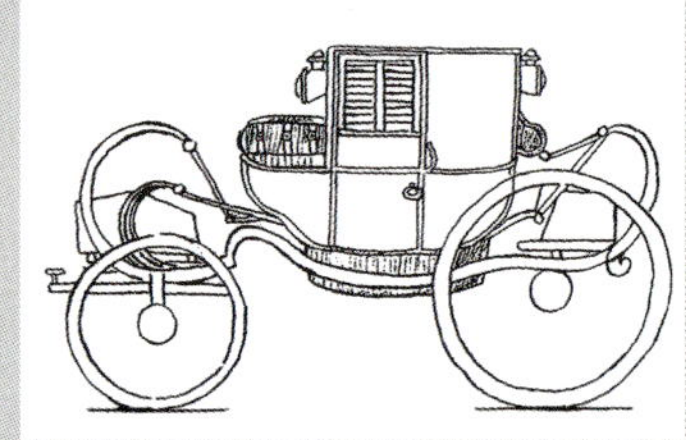

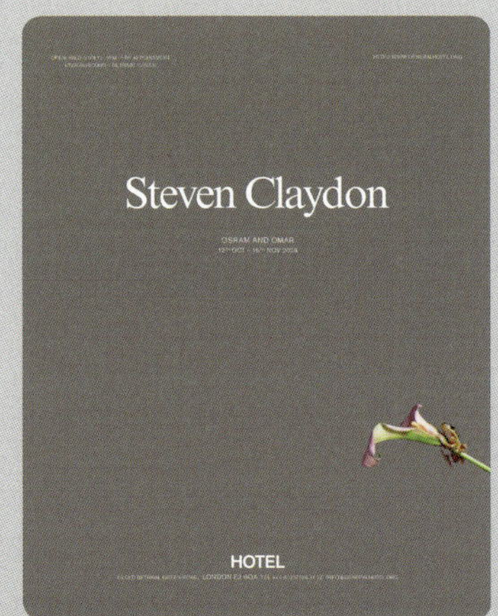

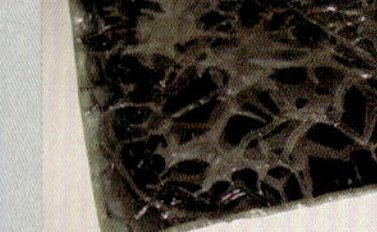

Found sculpture

Claytec clay bricks; unfired hand-pressed earth bricks made from a mixture of clay, sand and straw

Example of copper plating
© Copper plating by Nitec UK Ltd.

Cristopher Dresser double-spouted pot

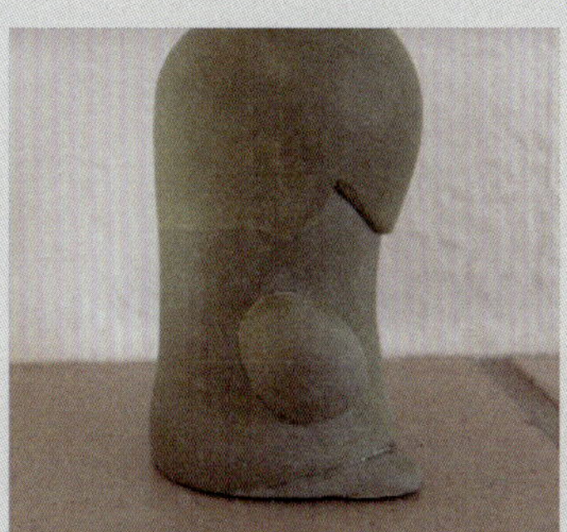

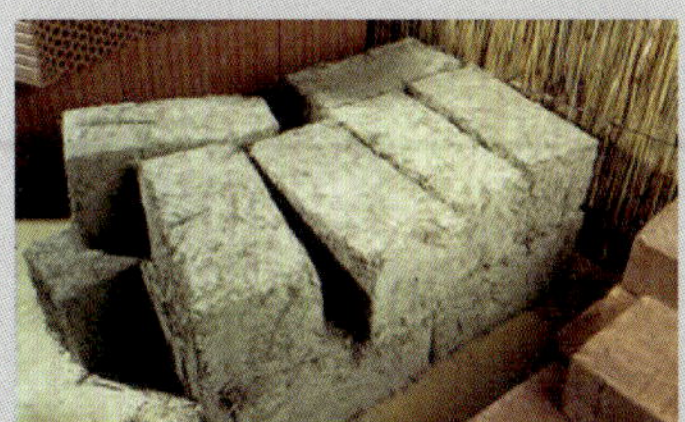

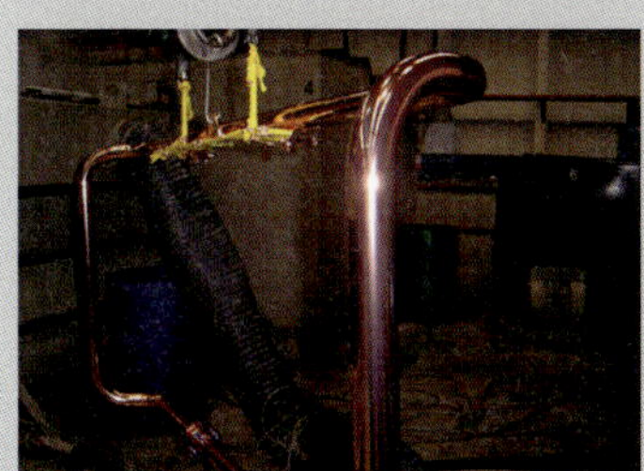

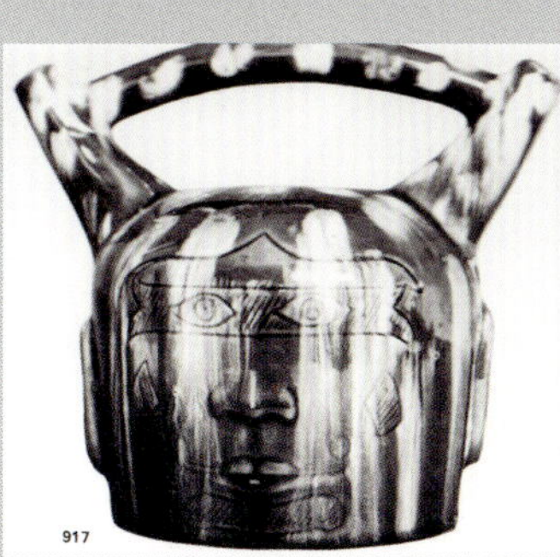

Barry Taylor of Walsall as a caveman

Firewall

Climber in the Dolomite mountains, Italy

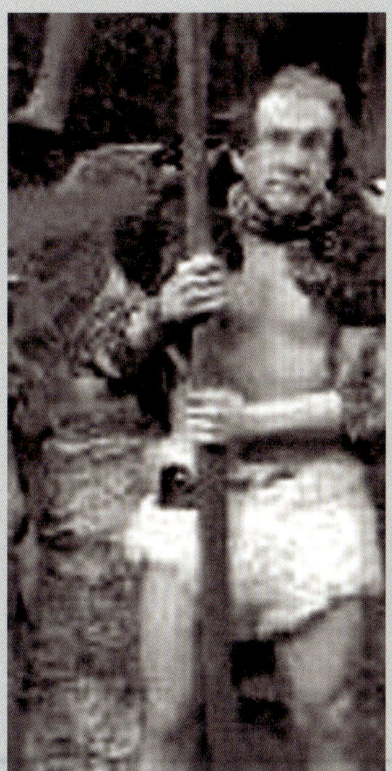

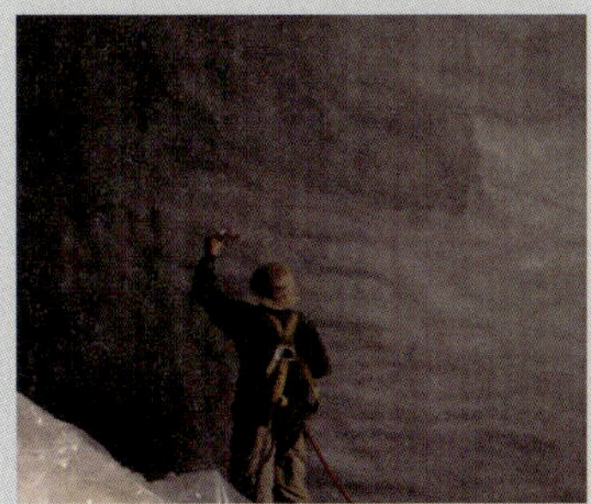

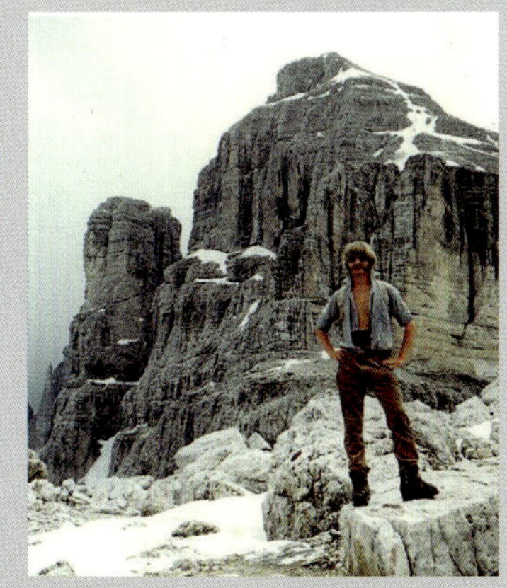

Differentiated creature. Photographer: Sonke Jonsen © Operation Deep Scope 2005 Expedition: NOAA Office of Ocean Exploration

Oboe cleaner

Steven Claydon, booklet cover for Serpentine Gallery, 2008

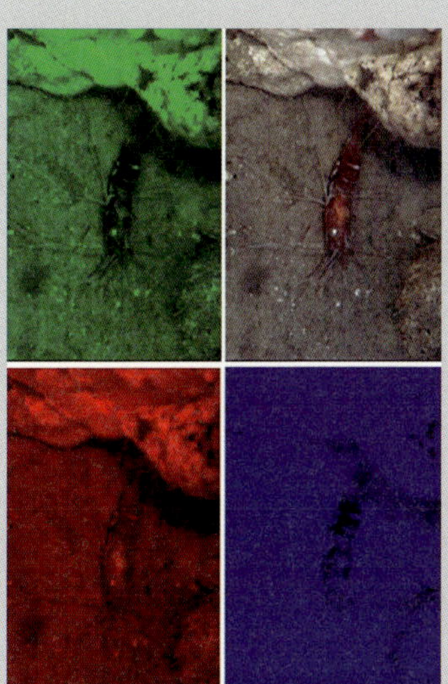

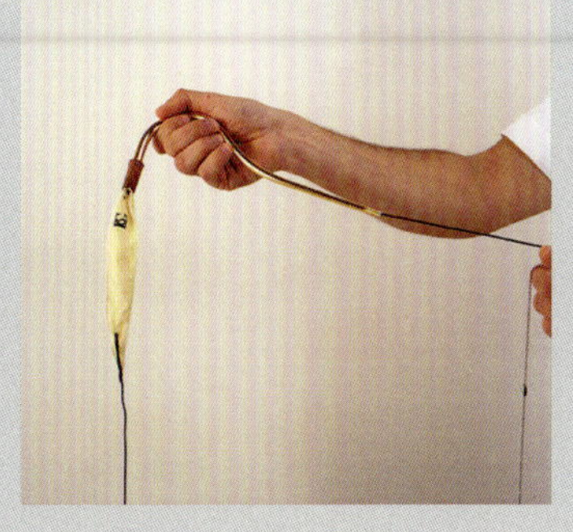

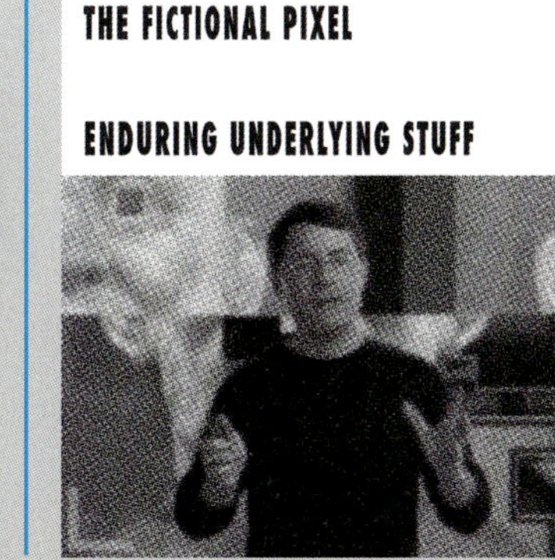

Harpsichordist Michael Monaco (l) and Peter Redstone pose with the harpsichord that Redstone built for the St. George Tucker House. The instrument is a reproduction of a harpsichord made by the English craftsman Thomas Barton in 1709. © The Colonial Williamsburg Foundation

Plan for a sculpture for Coshum Hospital, Bristol, Steven Claydon, 2011

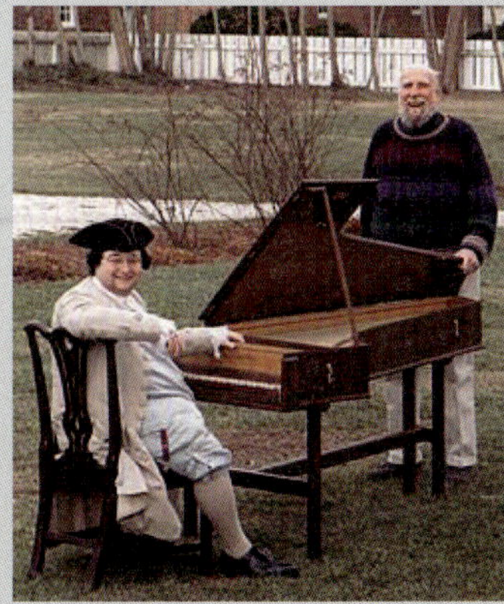

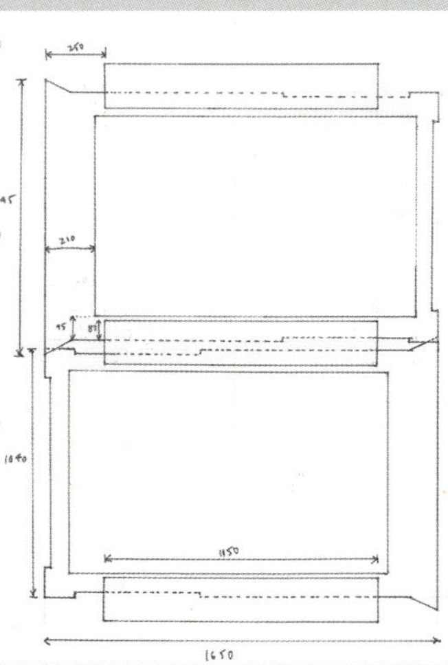

Henry vacuum cleaner plant pot

CNC drawing

Heidegger tent

Slow loris

Satellite © OAR/ERL/National Severe Storms Laboratory (NSSL)

Bell Laboratories logo designed by Saul Bass, 1969 © The Porticus Centre, Beatrice Technologies, Inc., Subsidiary of Beatrice Companies, Inc.

Pig-Pen © Peanuts Worldwide LLC

English Face jug © Michael Holford

Ikebana

Apollo snoop

Landing Signal Officer

Japanese doll

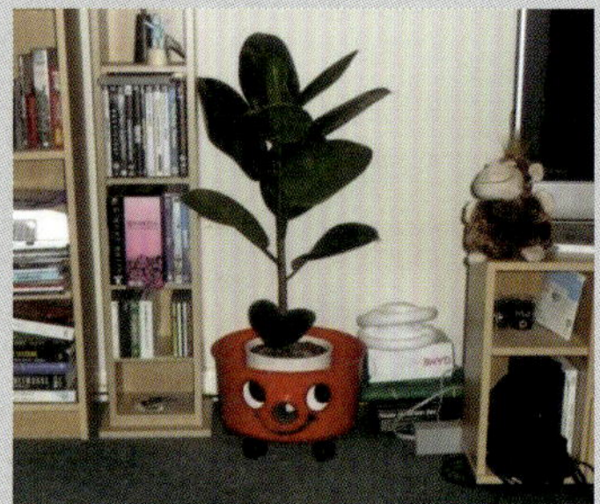

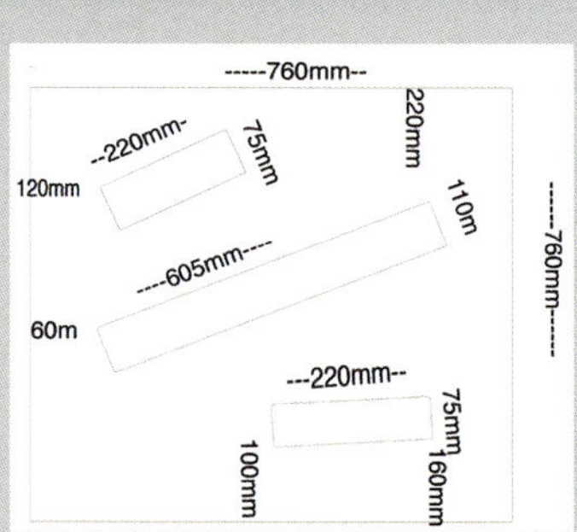

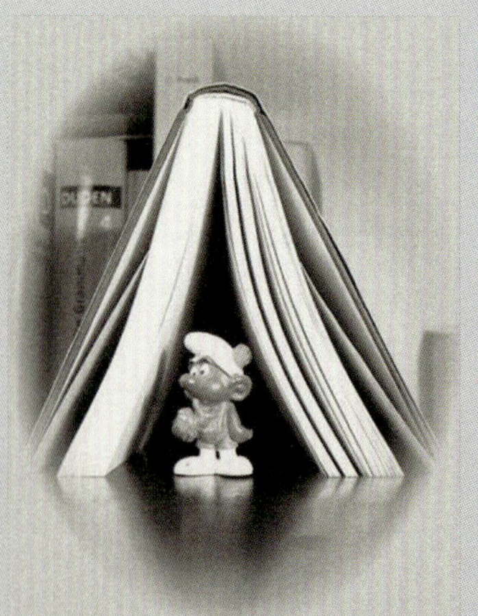

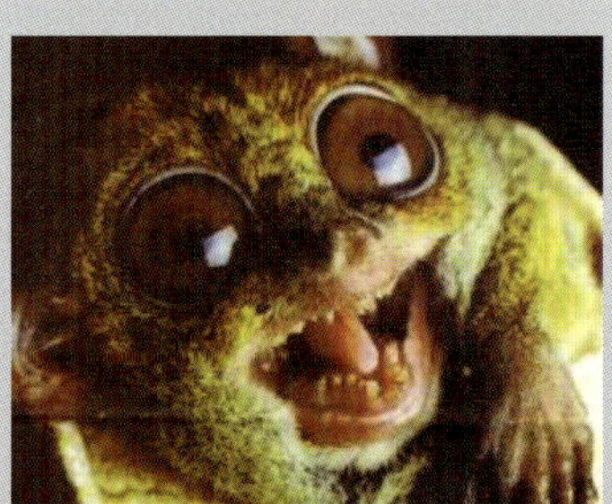

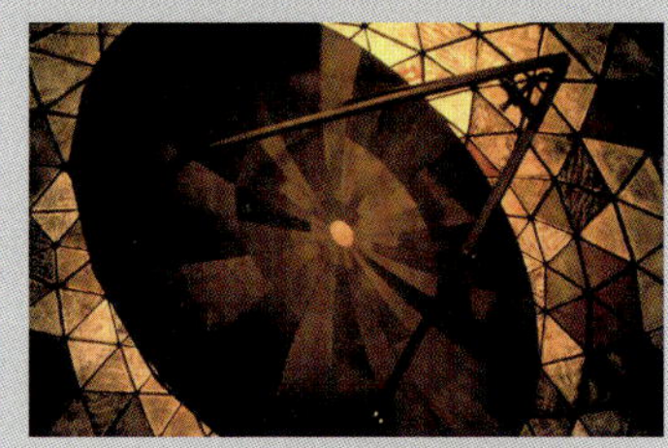

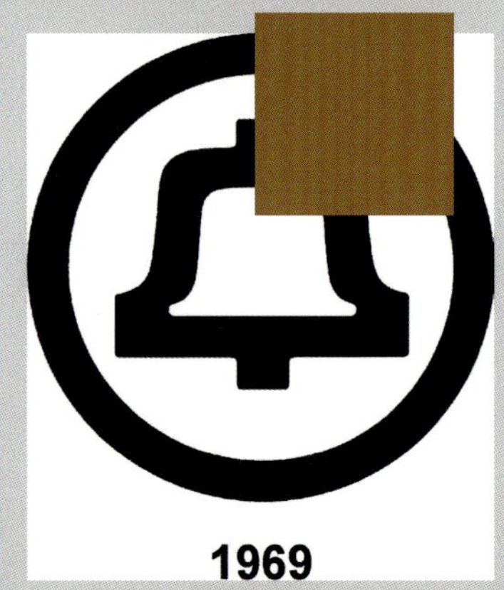

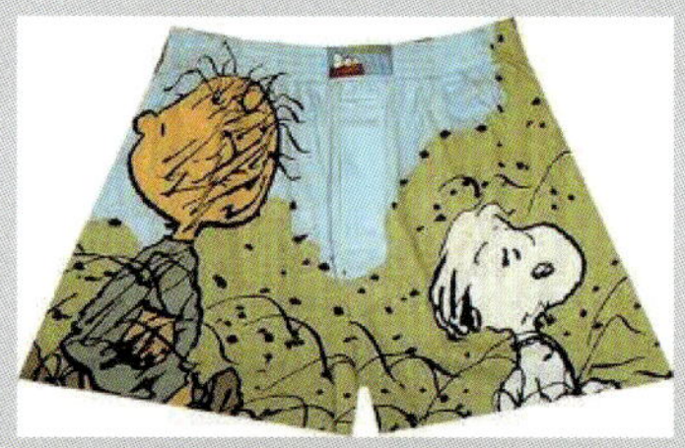

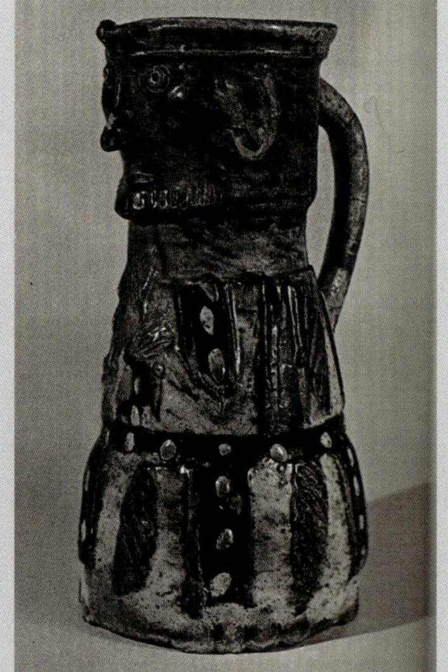

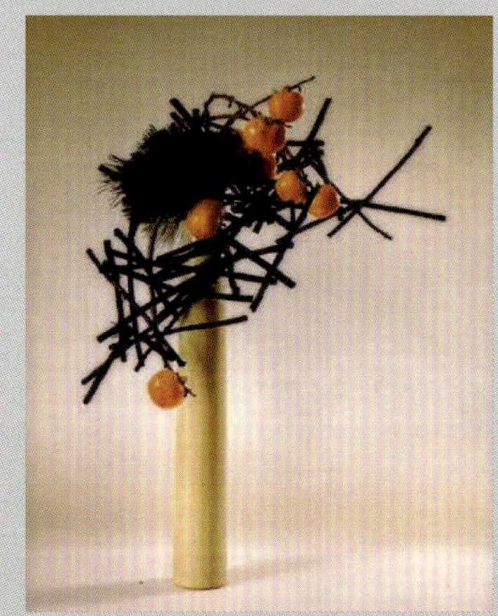

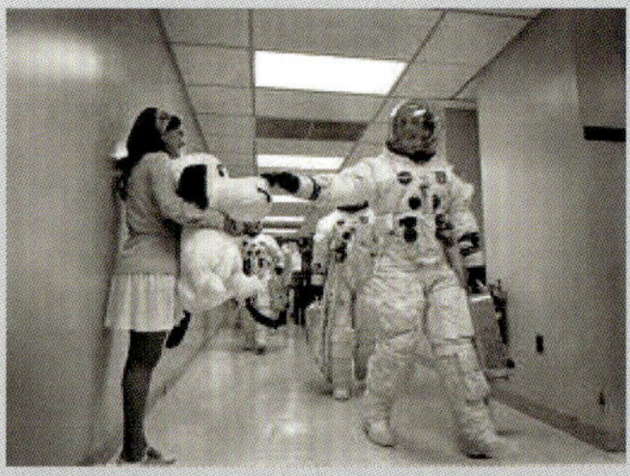

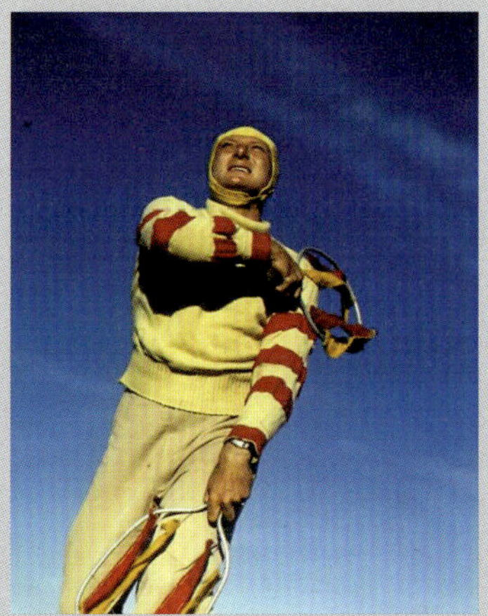

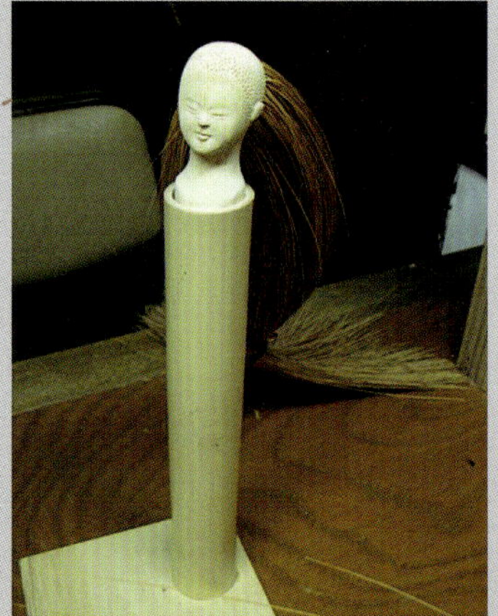

Captive wicker Harley

Frogs Five

Graphic icon

Jack too Jack airborne

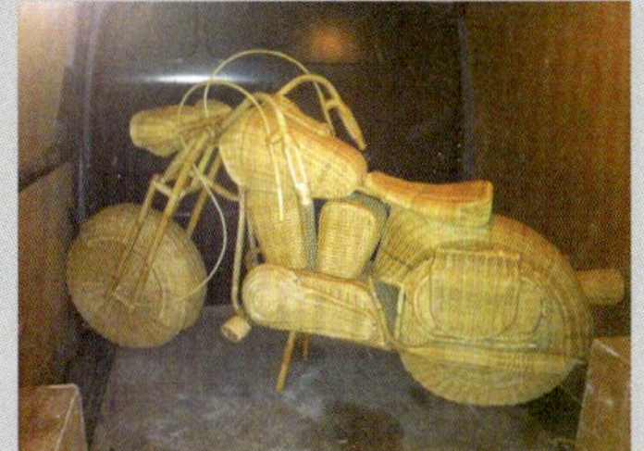

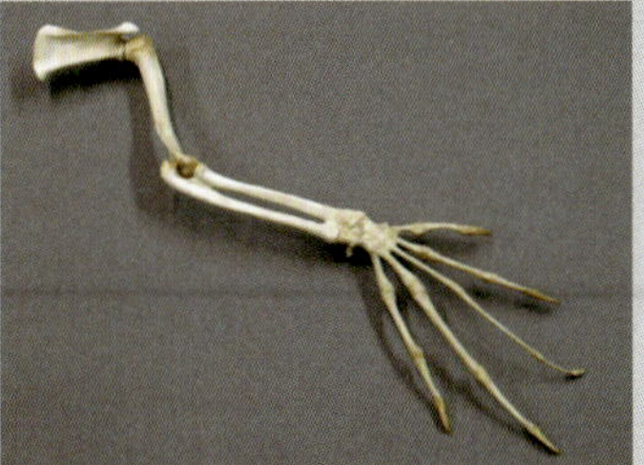

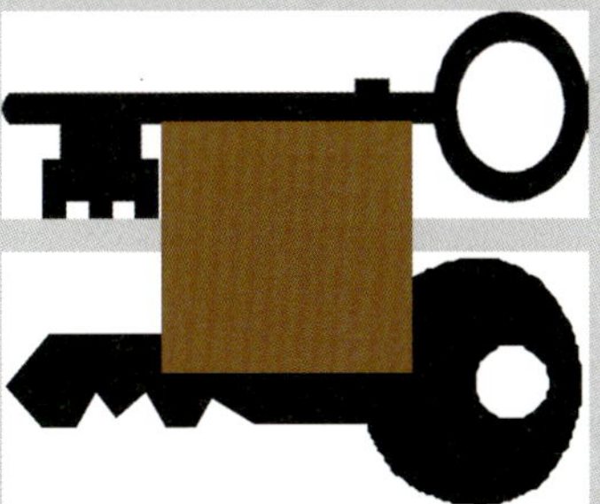

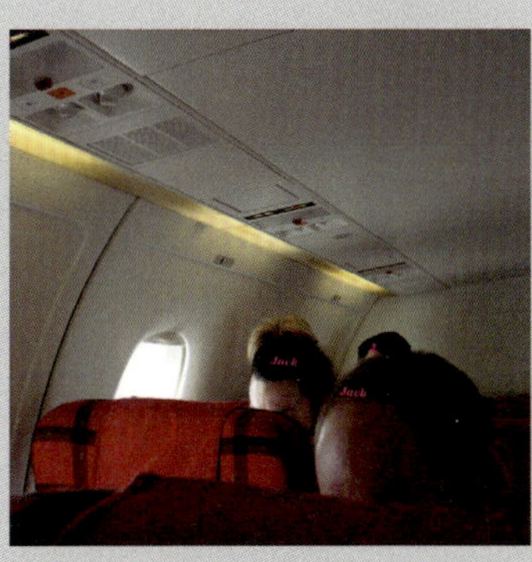

Japanese itinerant monk

Bauxite

London bomb

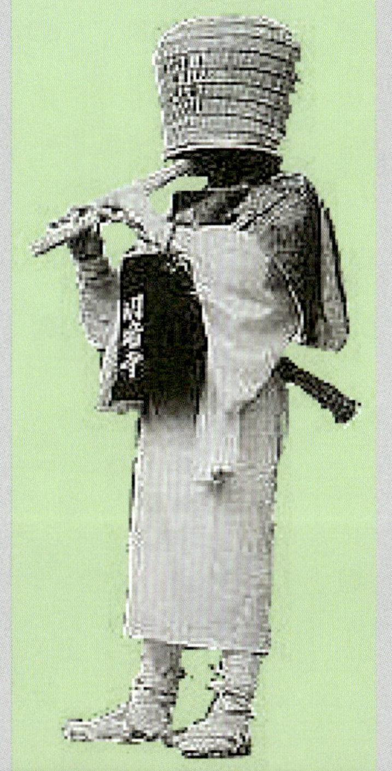

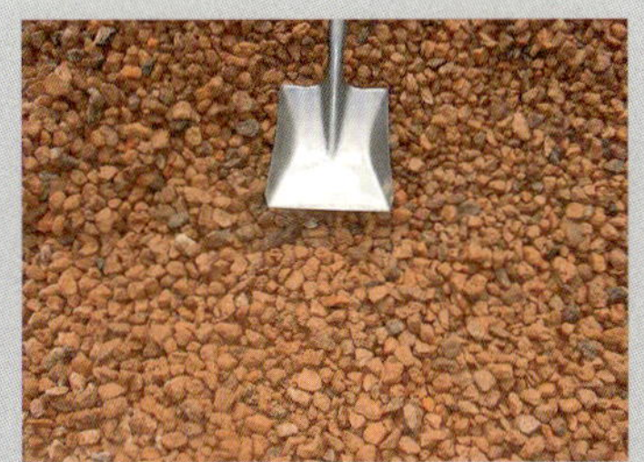

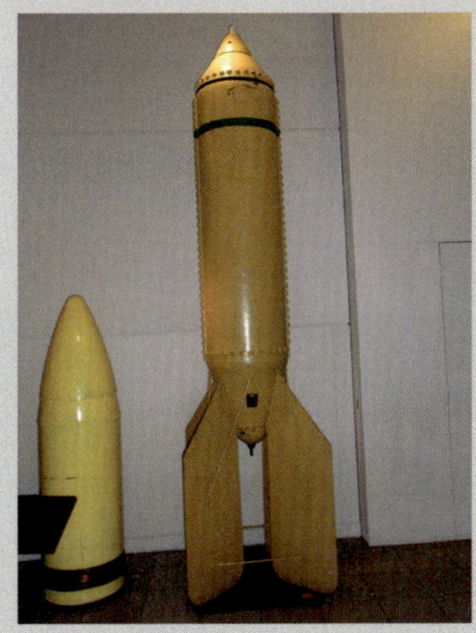

Landing Signal Officer

Mylar compound

Satellite drone
© Press Tyrol

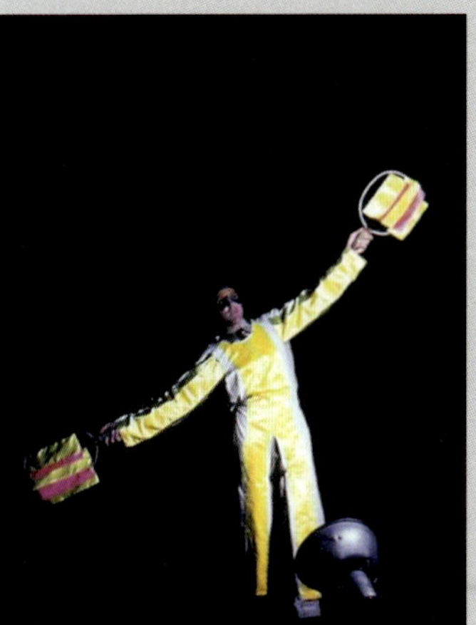

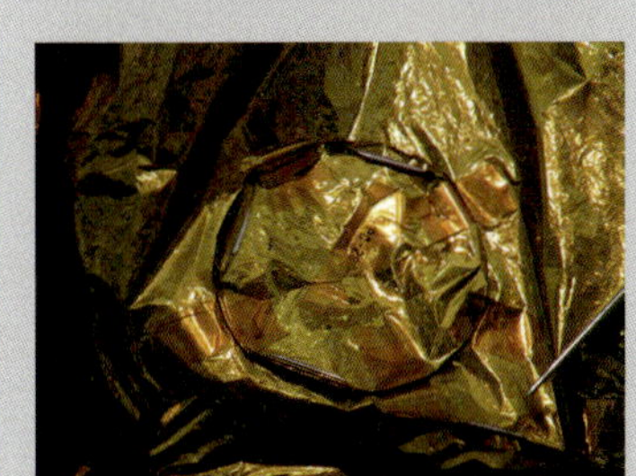

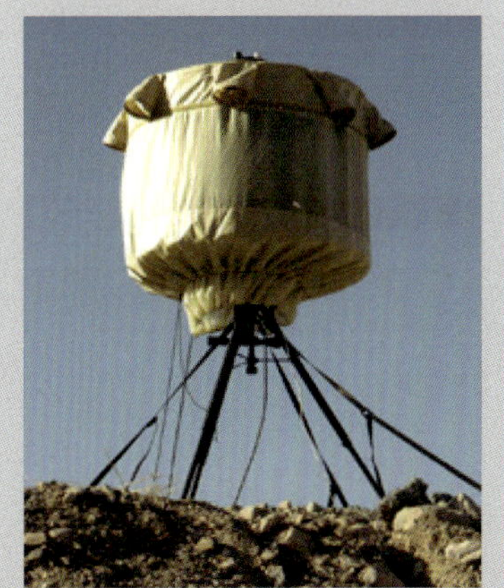

English slipware

The evolution of repetition

Long Meg

Long Meg

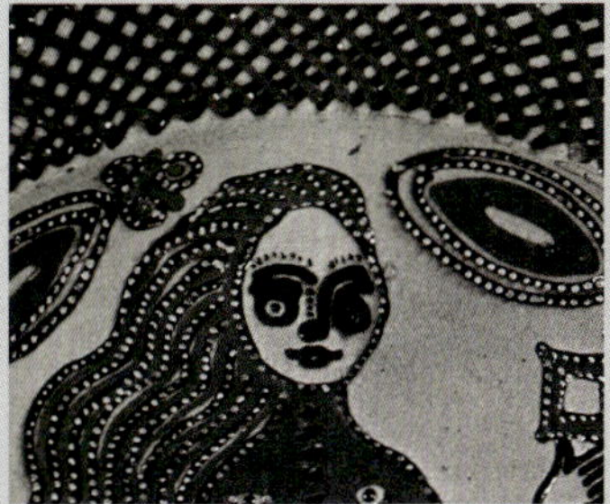

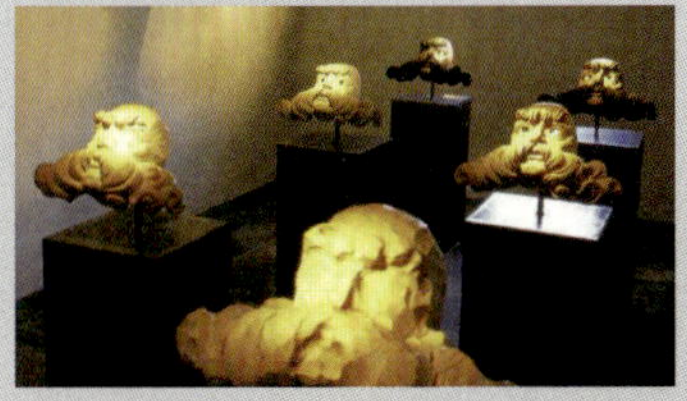

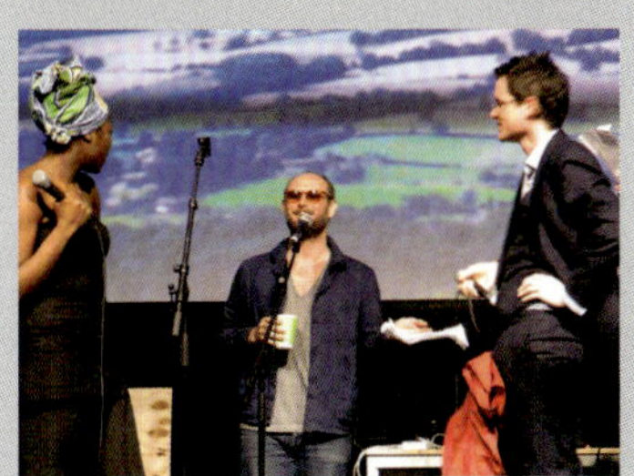

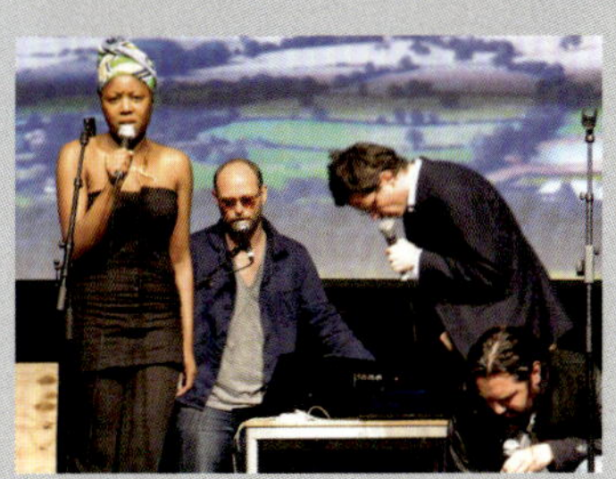

Ocean nuts

Ocean buoy

Add N to (X) promotional material

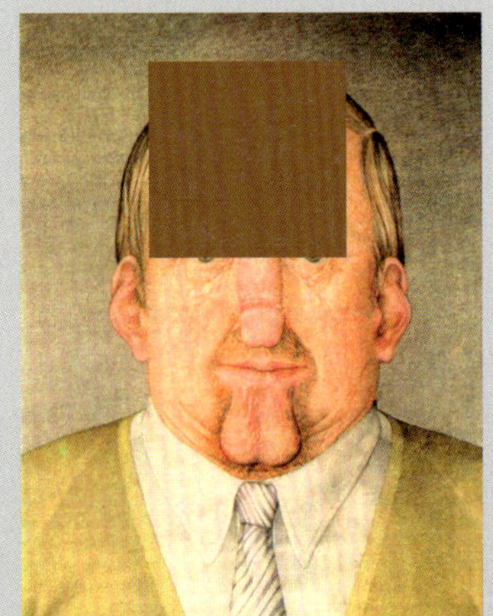

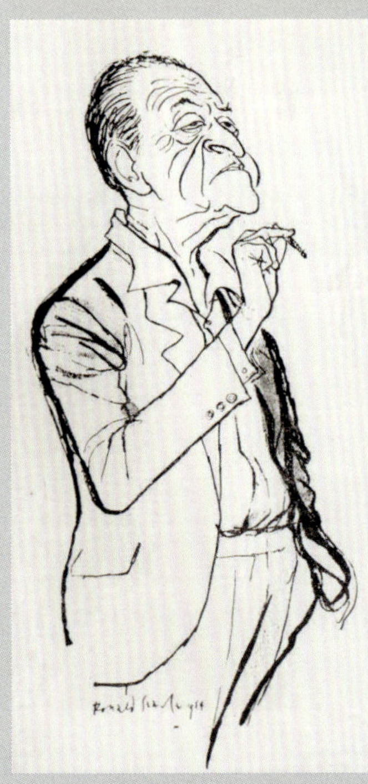

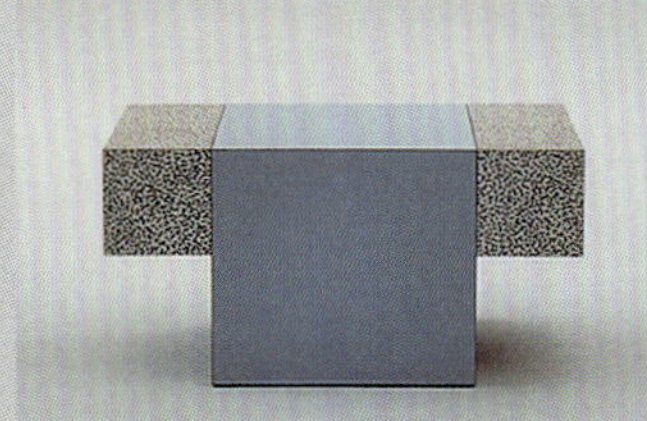

Nobnose

William Somerset Maugham drawing by Ronald Searle

Memphis bench

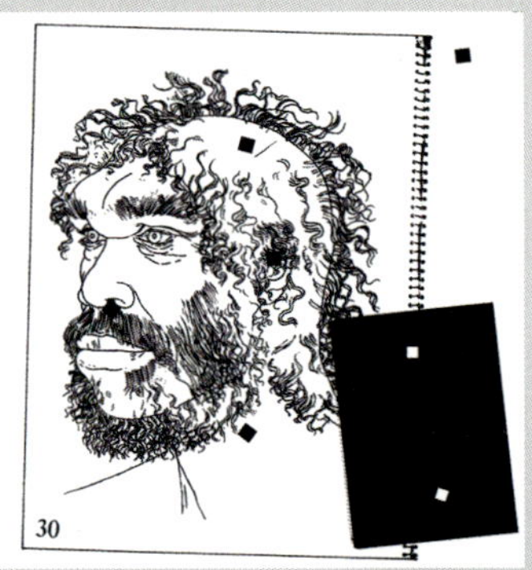

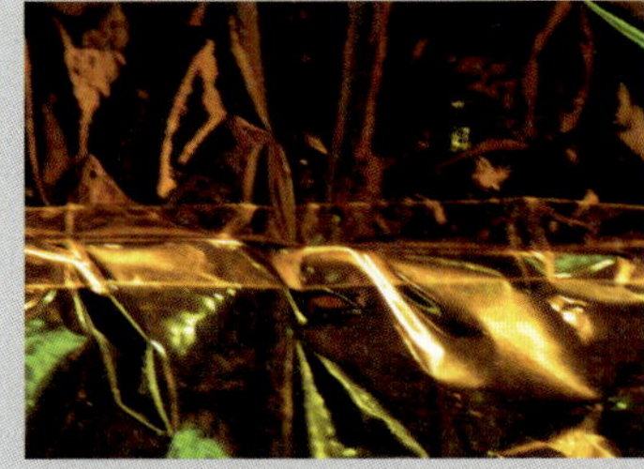

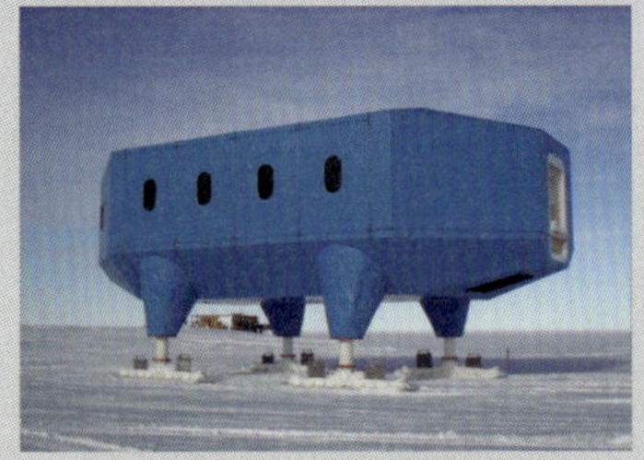

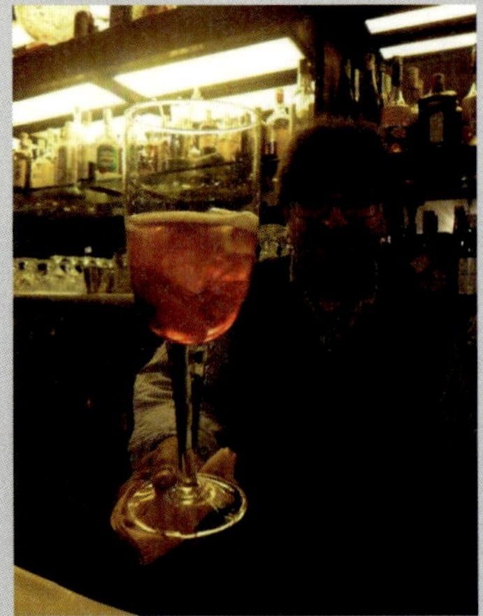

Preparatory drawing for the Foliage of Poor Judgement, 2009/10

Mylar and Kapton

Accommodation Module, Halley 6 Research Station, British Antarctic Survey by David Goulden

Maurizio with a Negroni Spagliatto, Bar Basso, Milano

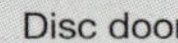

Disc door

Russian sniper

Luis Buñuel

Censored Neanderthal

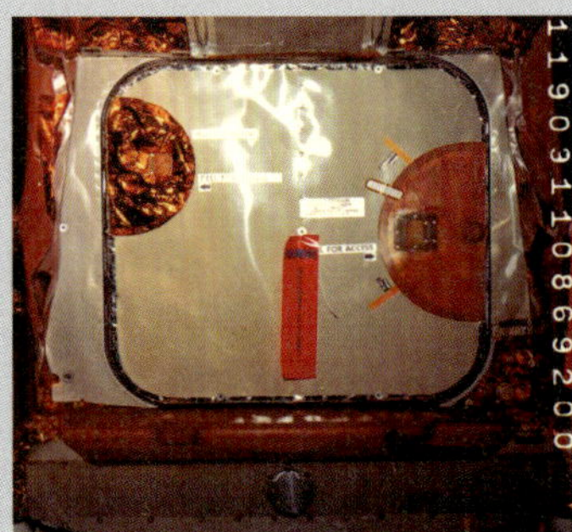

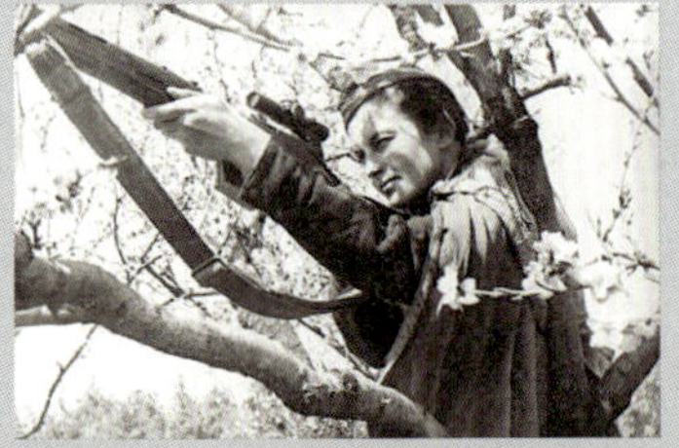

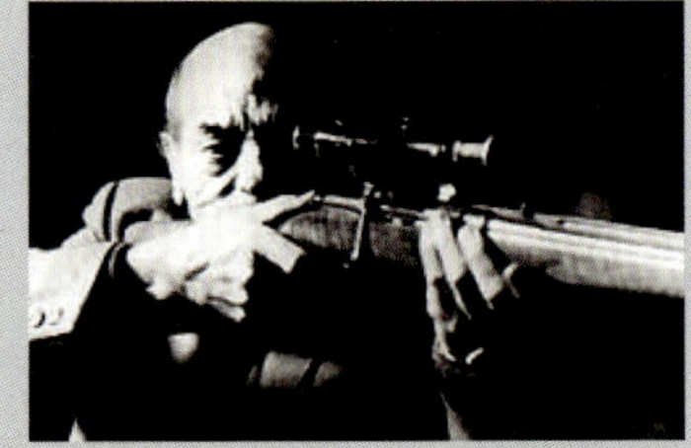

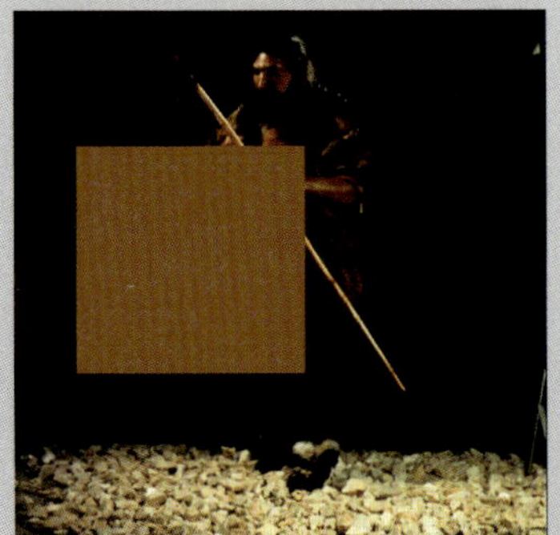

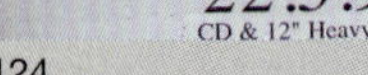

The here and now © WAG Screen,
www.wagscreen.co.uk

Mask © The Cleveland Museum of Art

Dog chew

Landing Signal Officer

Drones in orbit

Diagram of fractal properties of
analysed images: the random set
of HIRES files (crosses), HIRES
images of ruin-like formations (black
squares), and aerospace photographs
of terrestrial archaeological objects
(opened squares)

Quarry

Bee vest © Blue Bell Hill Apiaries

Mud pump

Diorama depicting drilling for oil at
the State Historical Society Museum,
Montana

Pig-Pen X-ray
Pig-Pen © 2011 decalboy.com

Poster for Long Meg. Artwork: Kieron
Livingstone

Brown square

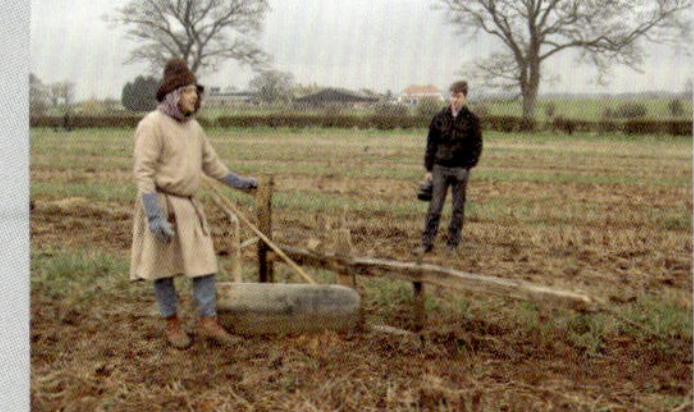

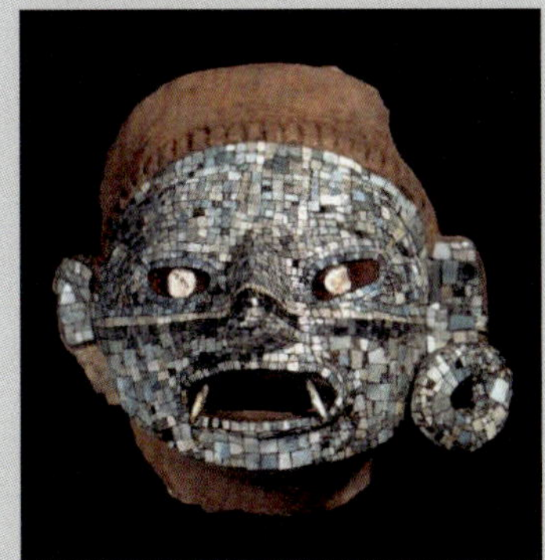

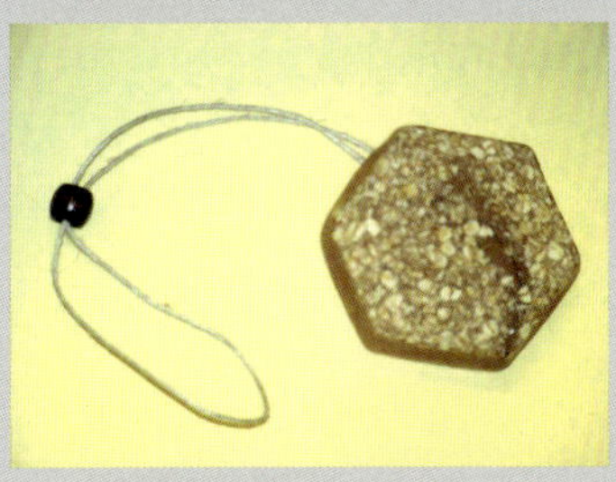

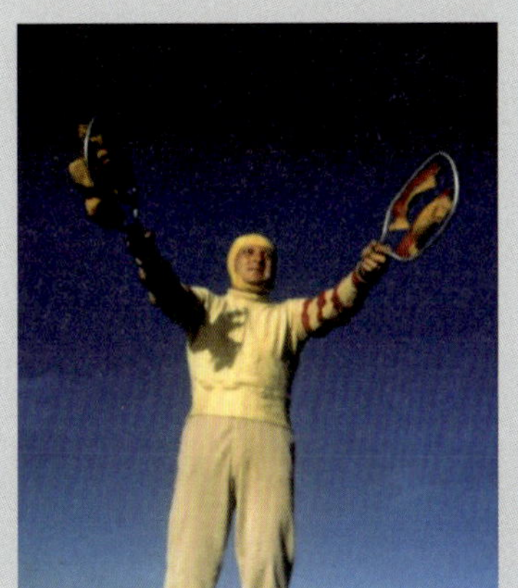

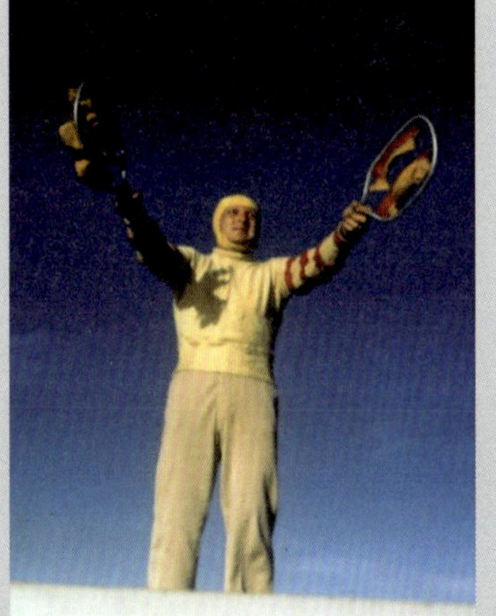

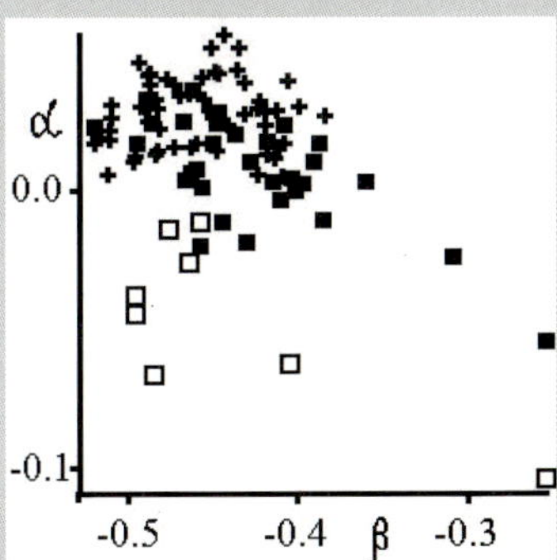

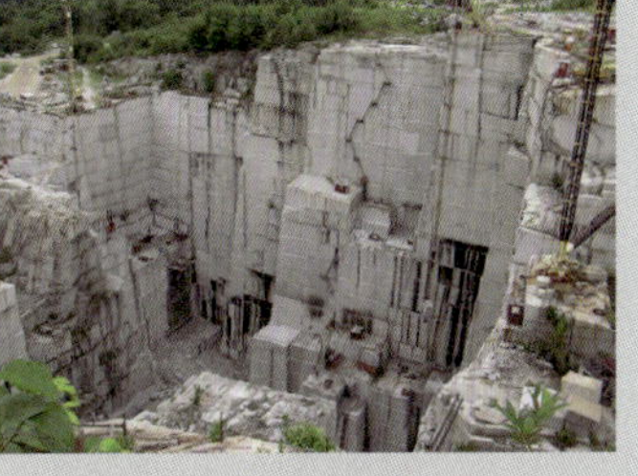

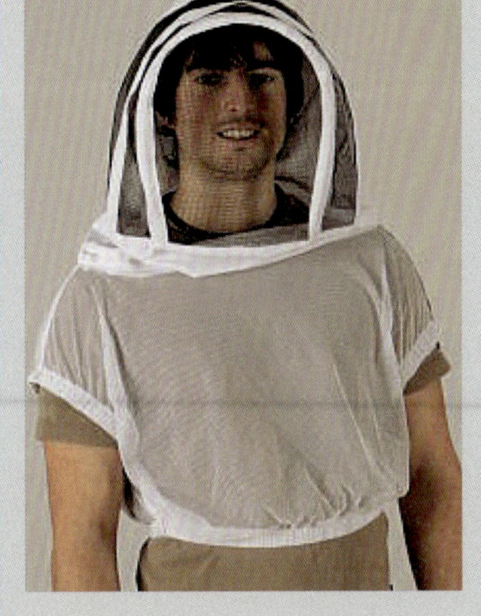

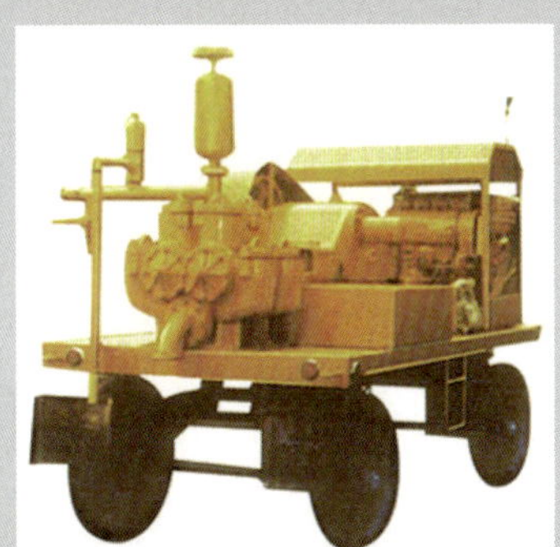

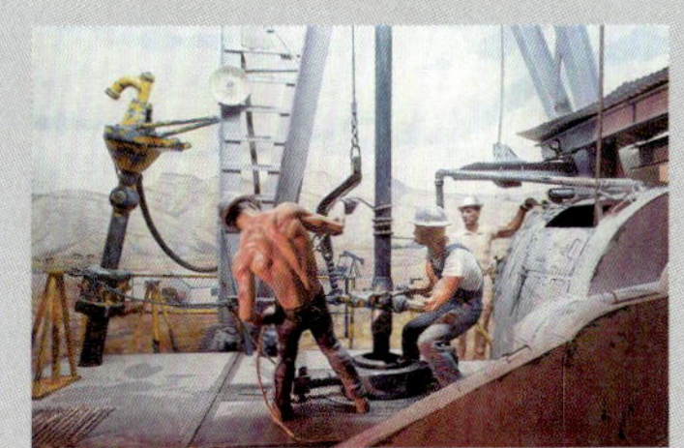

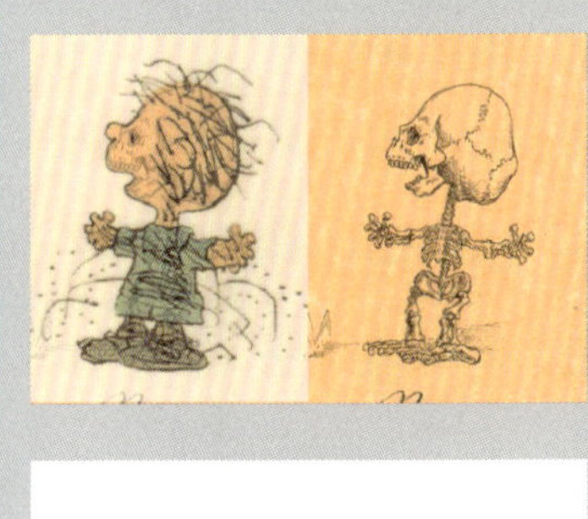

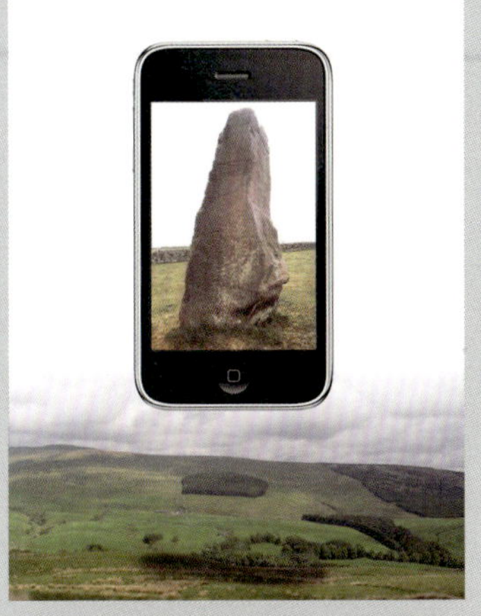

Jacques-Yves Cousteau

Rivers of magnesium

Poster for Long Meg. Artwork: Kieron Livingstone

A stringed musical instrument ('une sorte de mandoline'), two rattles made of polished seed pods, and two bells collected by the French explorer Robert Hottot in 1906. Photographer: A. Robert Hottot © Pitt Rivers Museum, University of Oxford

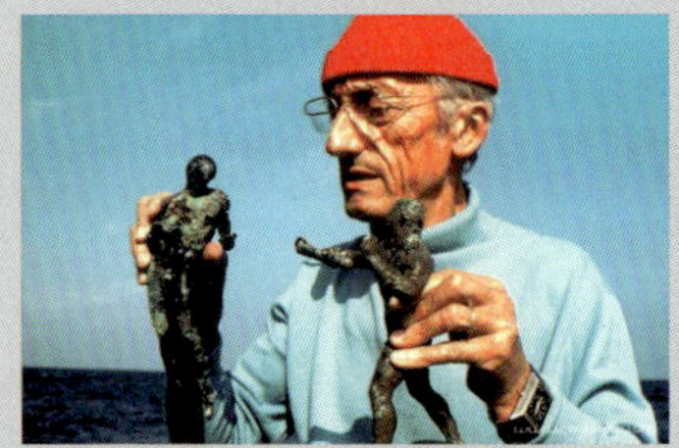

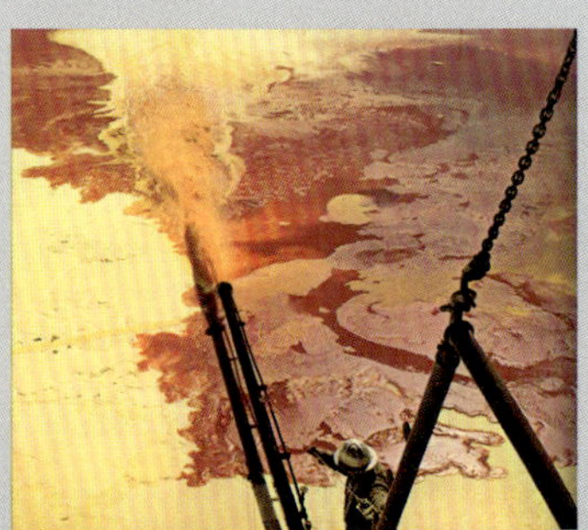

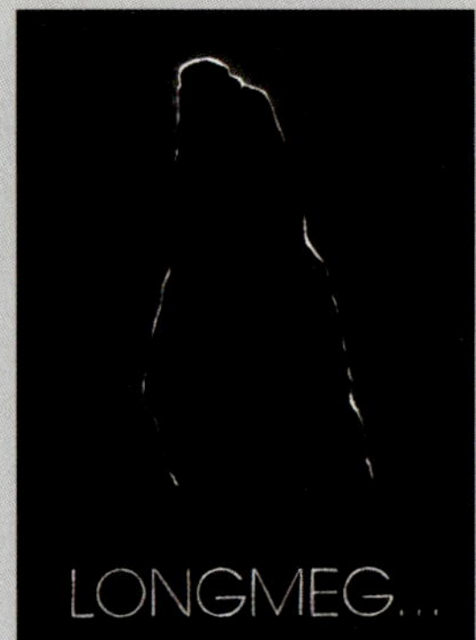

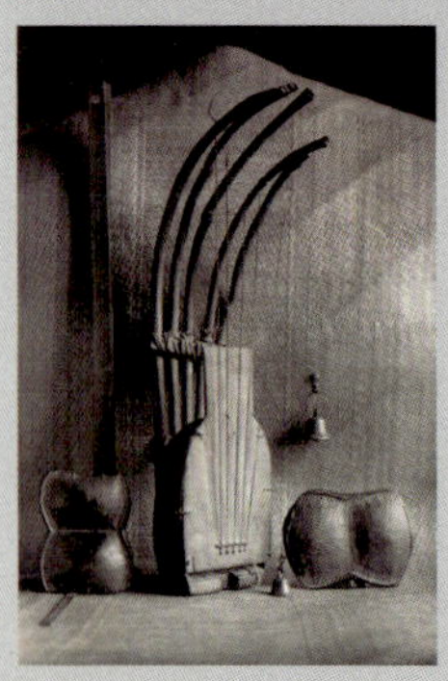

Forward-Facing Lemon Yellow Eyes, Steven Claydon, Hayward Gallery, 2011

Coper pots for copapods. © Reproduced from Hans Coper by Tony Birks, Stenlake Publishing

Rhineland stoneware

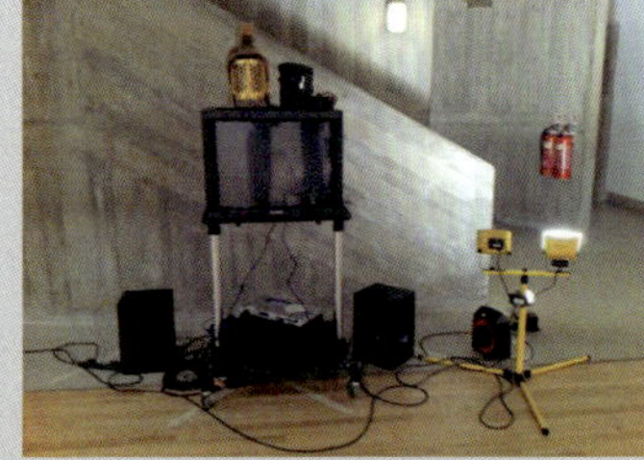

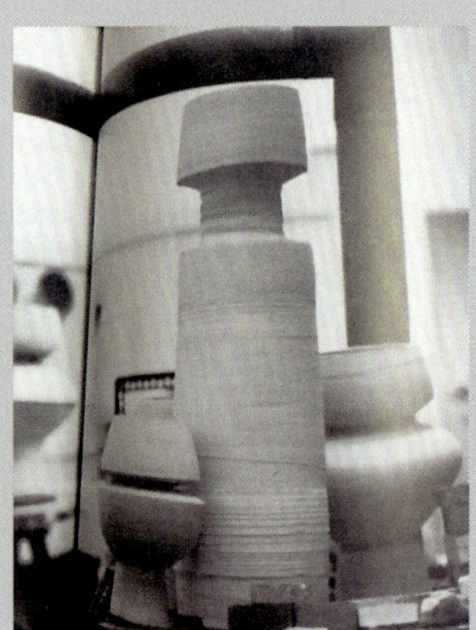

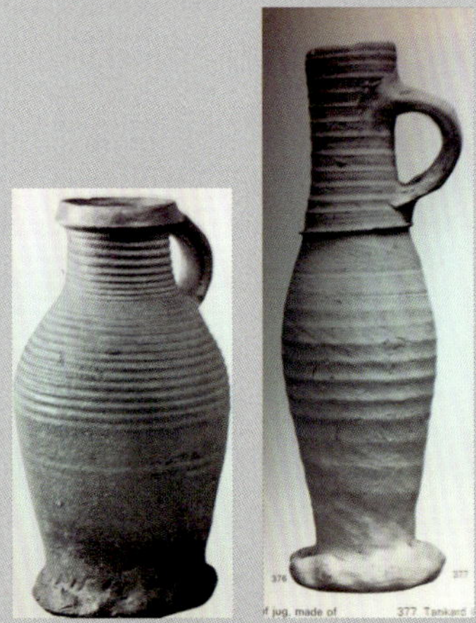

Your rubber roof

Toad Shakos

Barclays, Angel, Borough of Islington, London

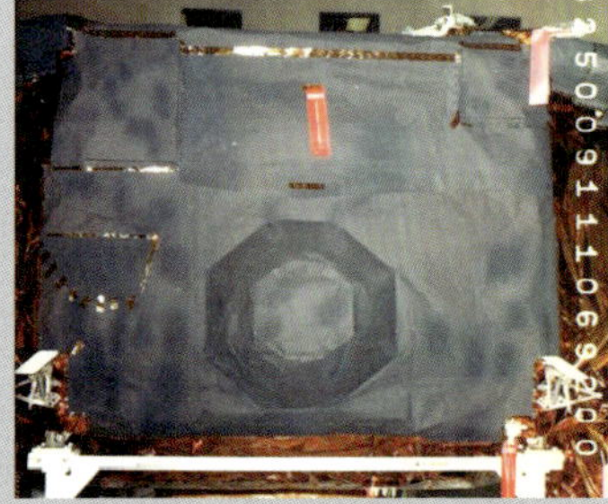

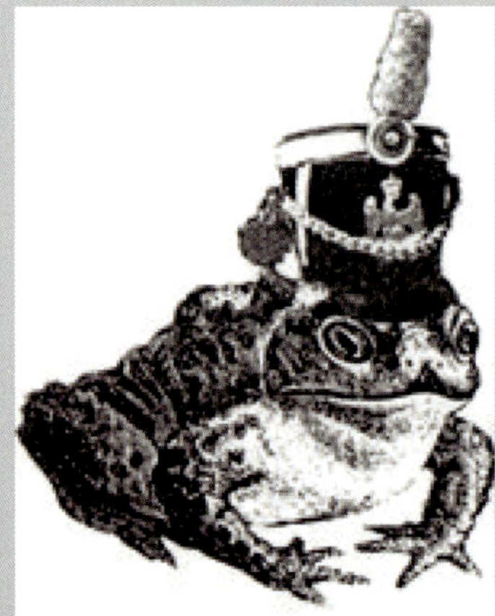

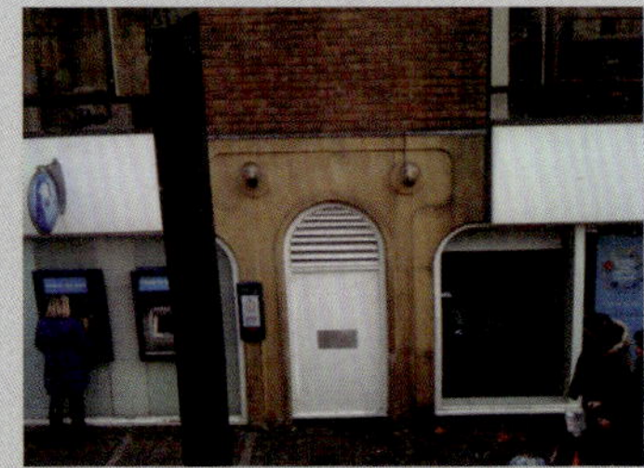

Climate © Peanuts Worldwide LLC

Lumps of rock

David Munrow © 2007 Viking New Media

Maurice Wilson

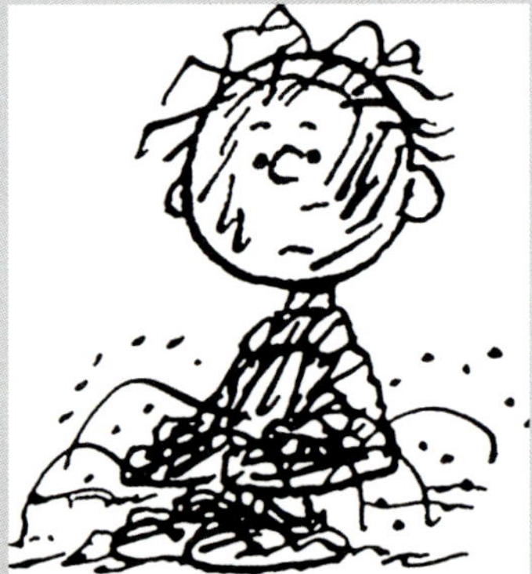

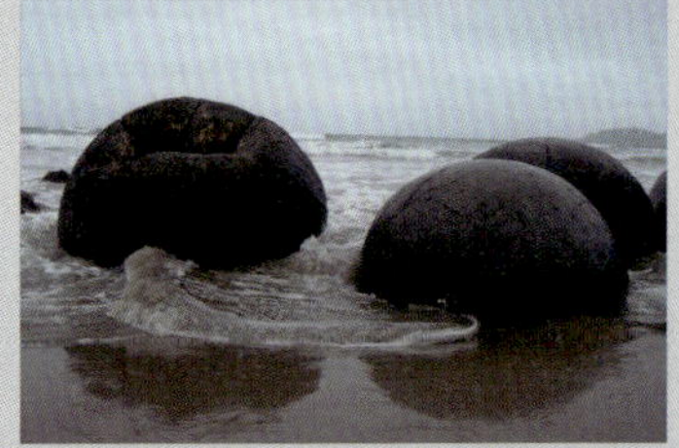

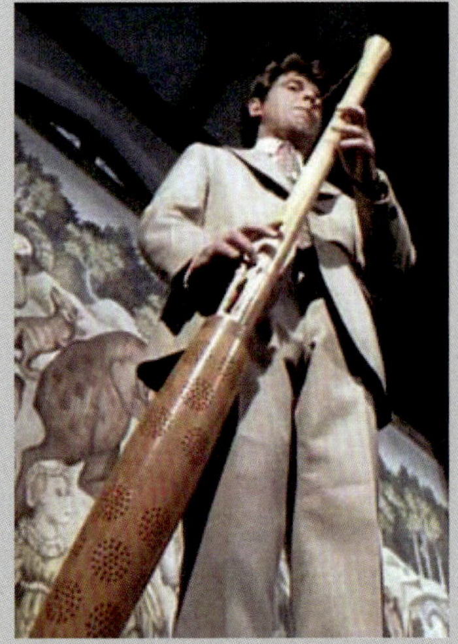

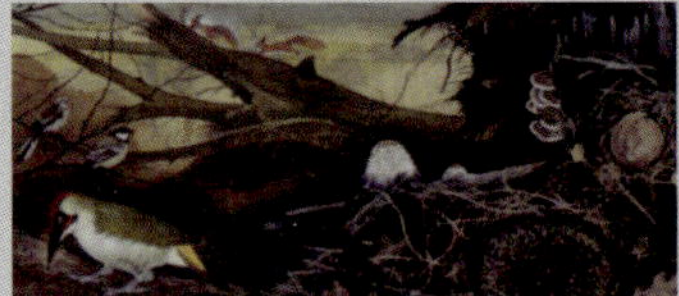

Cottage industry

Enter trom

Bulb head © Matt Welsh

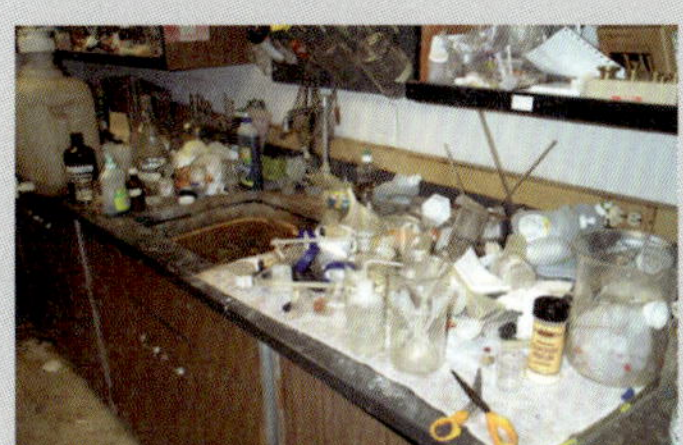

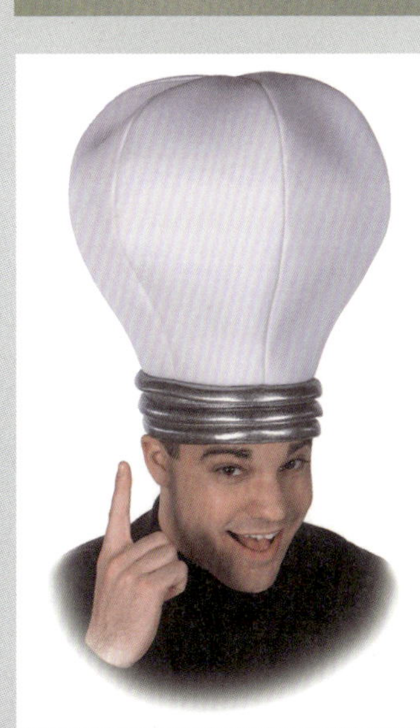

Bulbous bow on a container ship
Bulwark bulkhead © Hadag
Seetouristik und Fährdienst Ag

Anthony Blunt

St Paul's trom

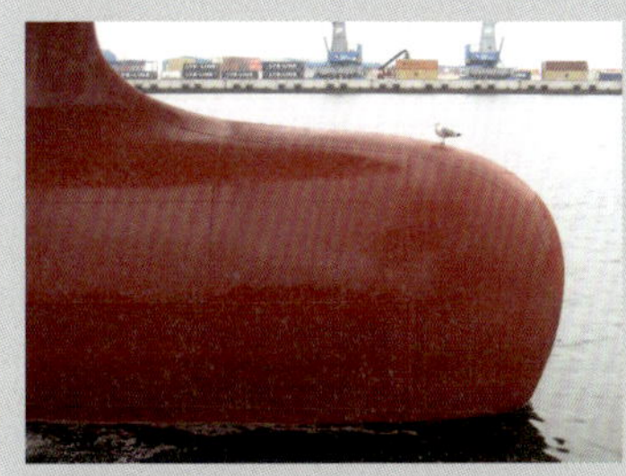

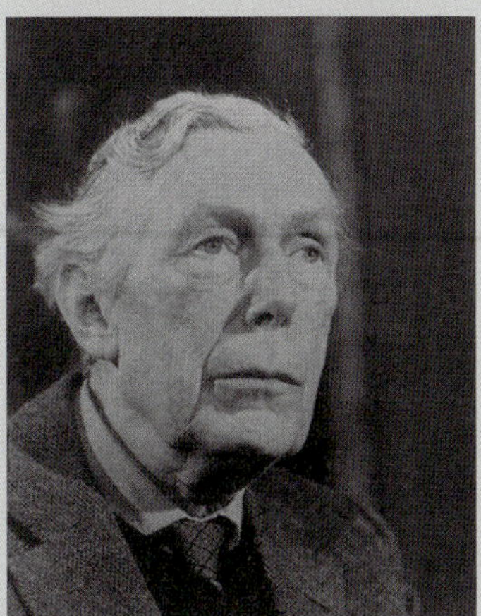

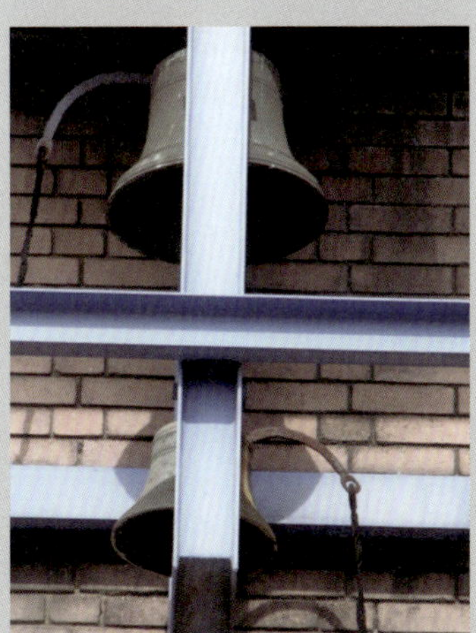

Whitechapel Bell Foundry

Plan for a sculpture for Coshum
Hospital, Bristol, Steven Claydon, 2011

St Paul's trom

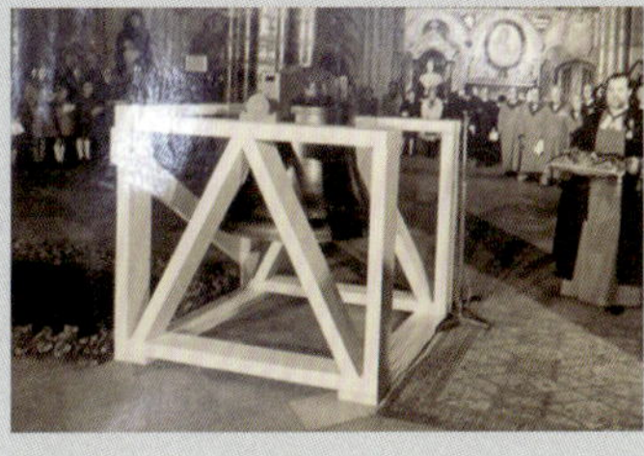

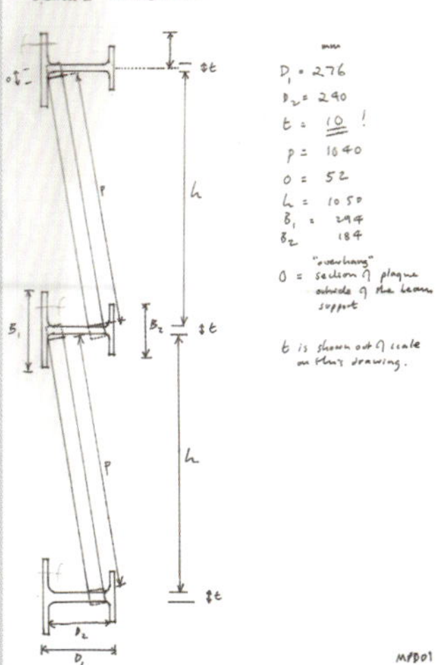

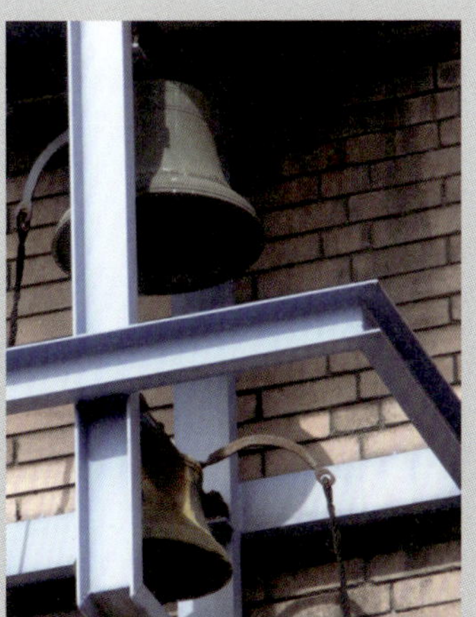

Pictures in a museum, Svolvær,
Norway

Pictures in a museum, Svolvær,
Norway

Pictures in a museum, Svolvær,
Norway

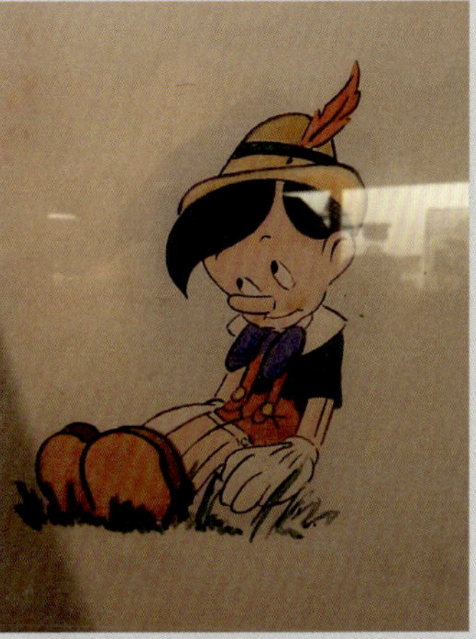

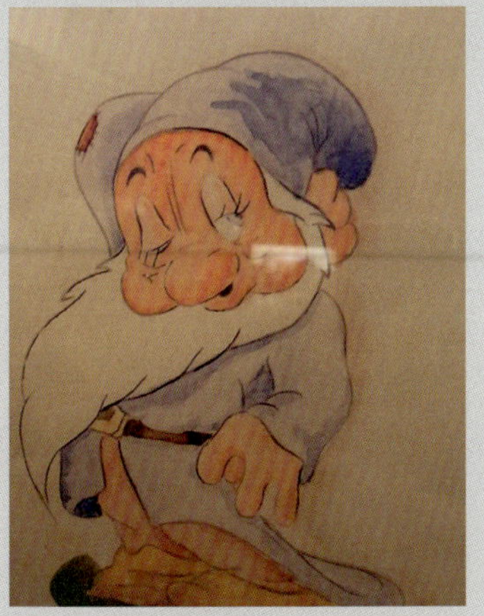

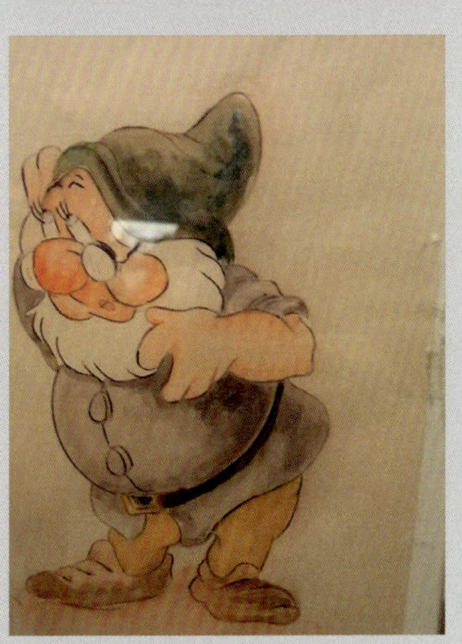

Snail sex

Intruder

In the country

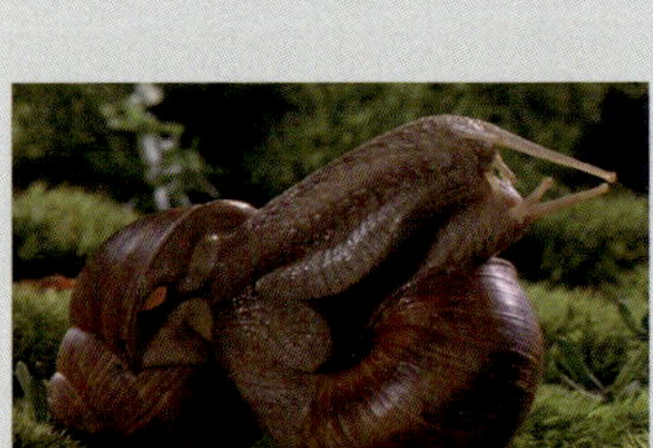

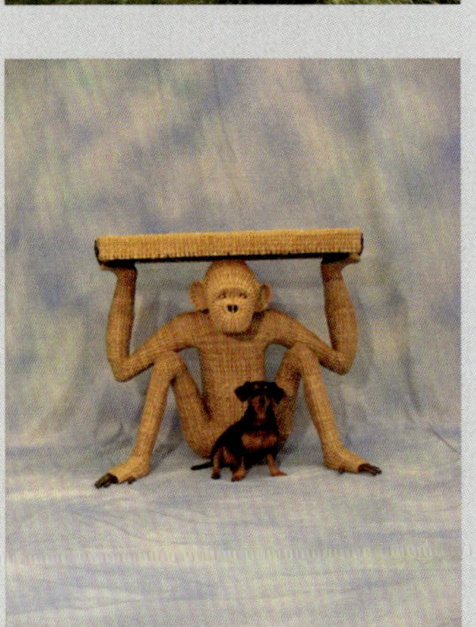

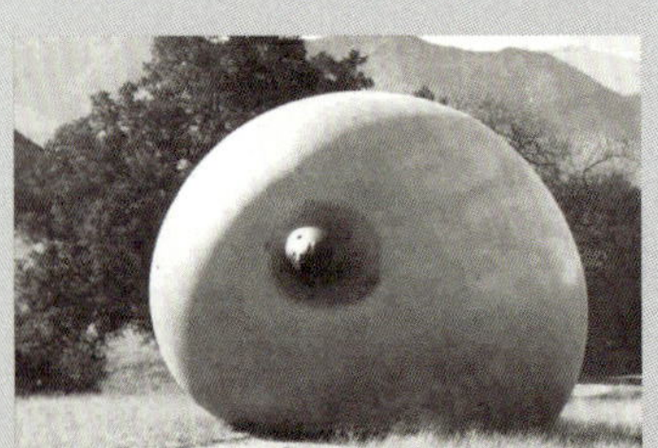

Brew Boy

Drawing by Frank Brangwyn © David Brangwyn

Wolfgang Amadeus Mozart's *The Magic Flute*

Bulb

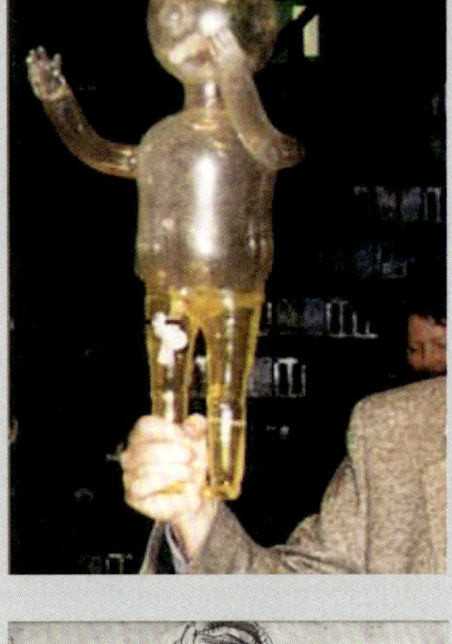

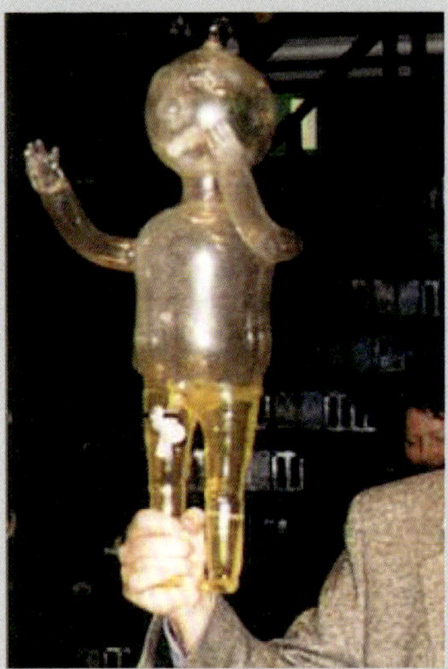

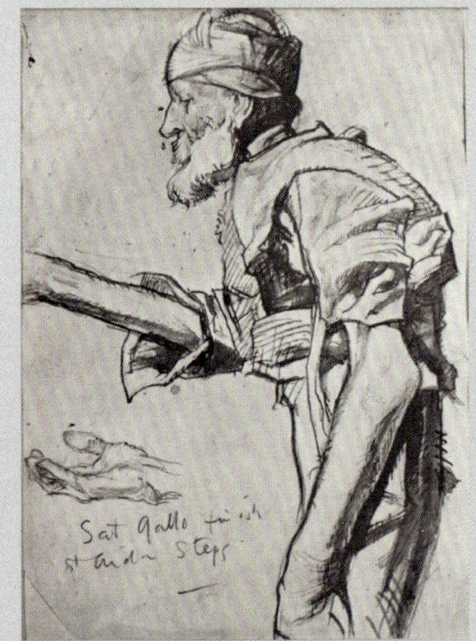

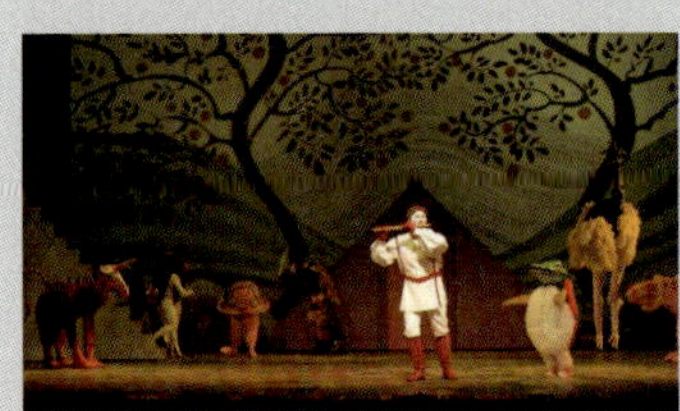

Snoooooopy

Snoopy sub

Enter trom

Study centre

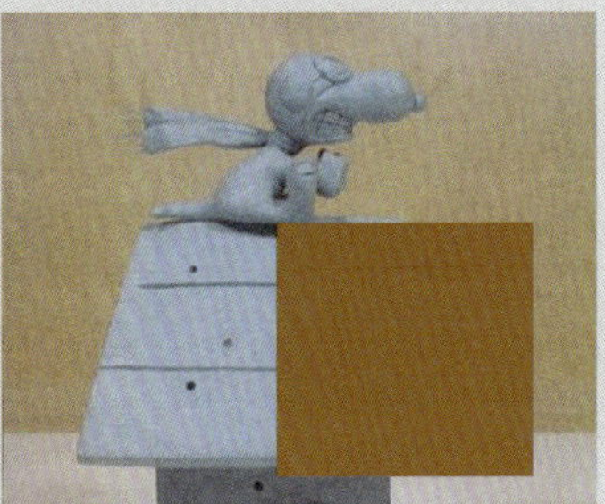

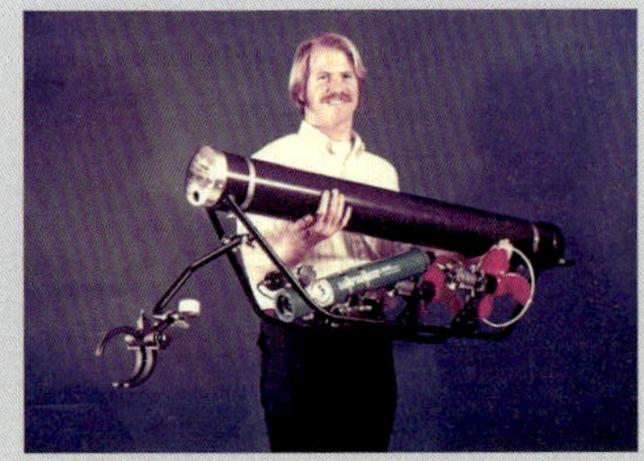

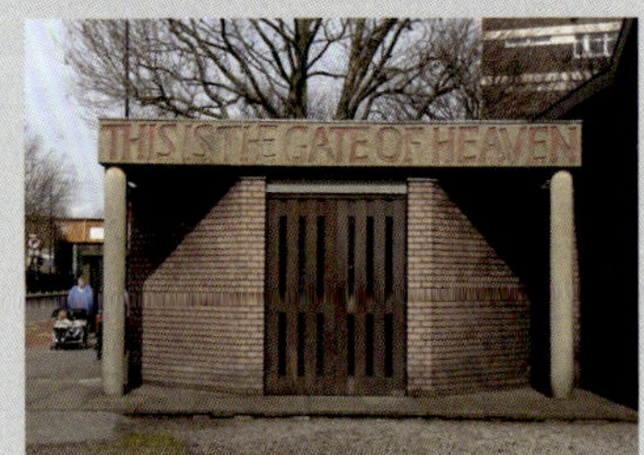

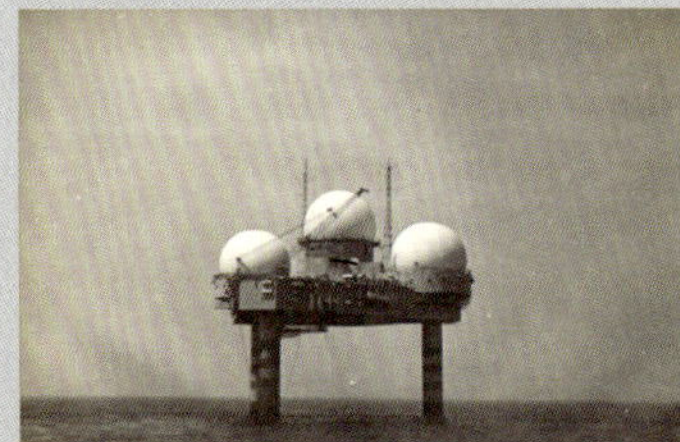

The carapace eight

Desperate deiter

Roman cavalry helmet

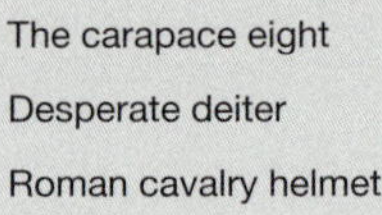

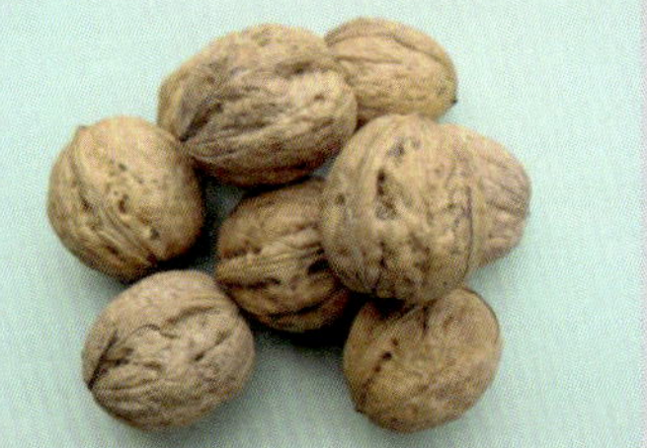

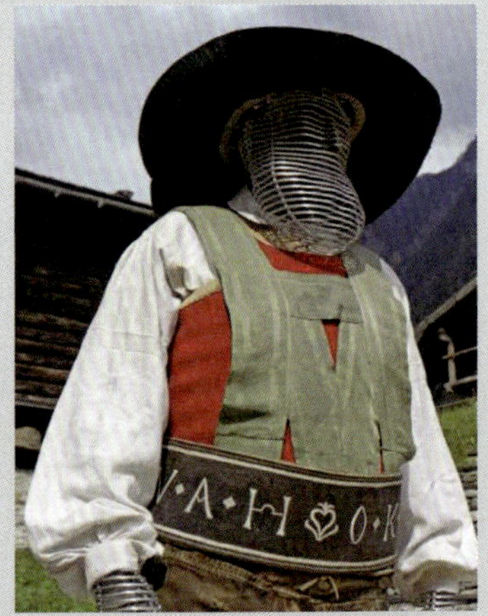

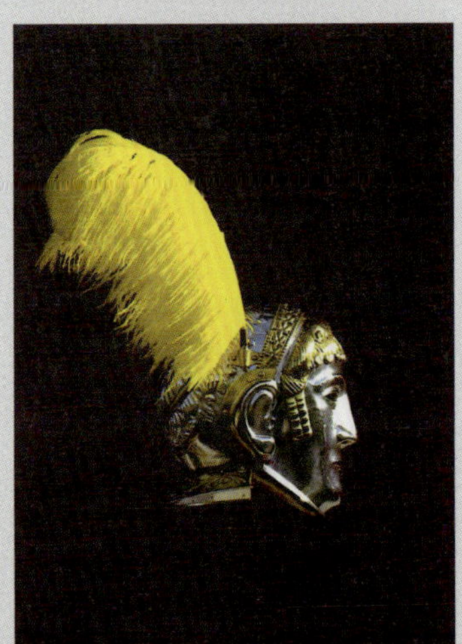

Small abstract I

Small abstract II

Stepney bell

The medieval shoes

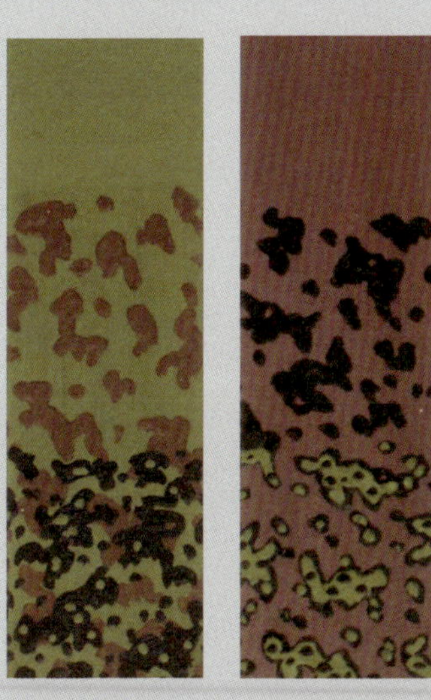

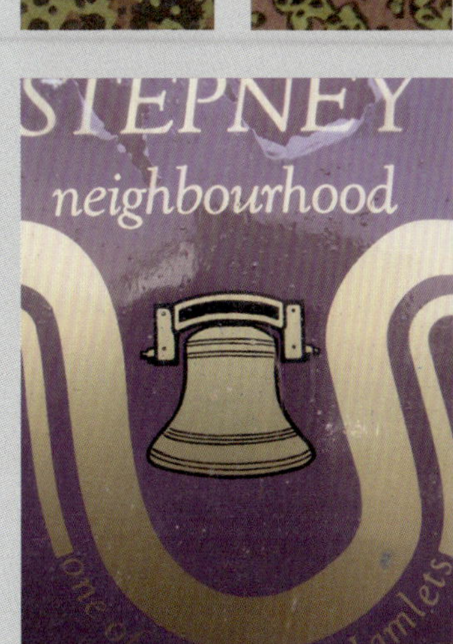

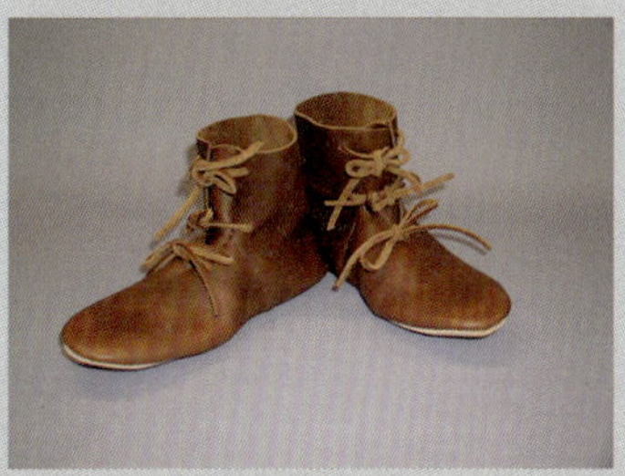

Mailbox

Amazon snake scan

Luminous dials

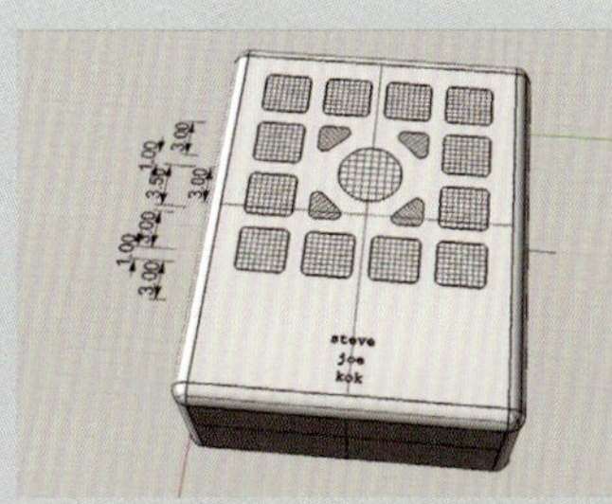

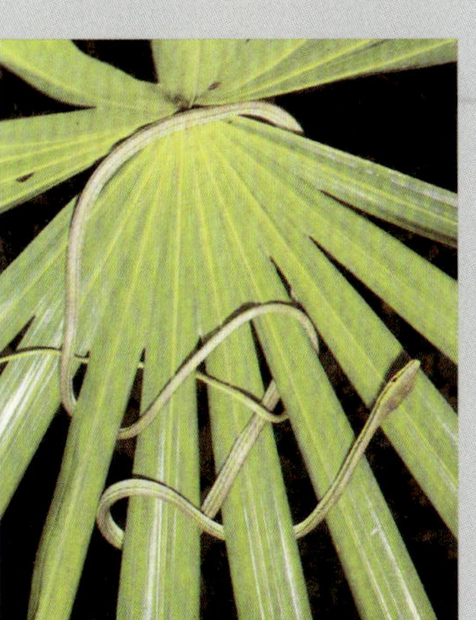

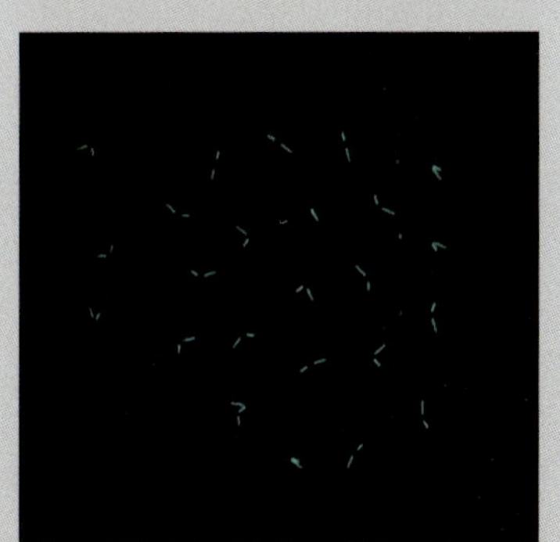

Add N to (X) promotional material

Dolomites

Inflatable mark buoys

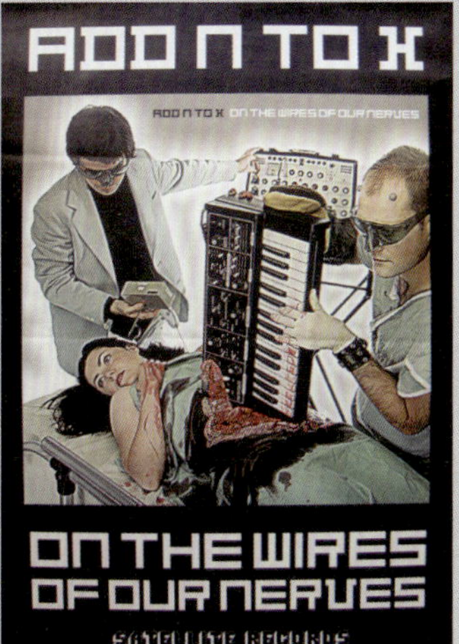

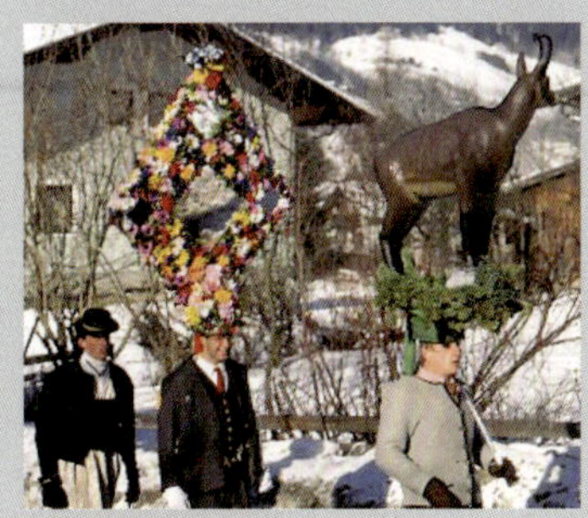

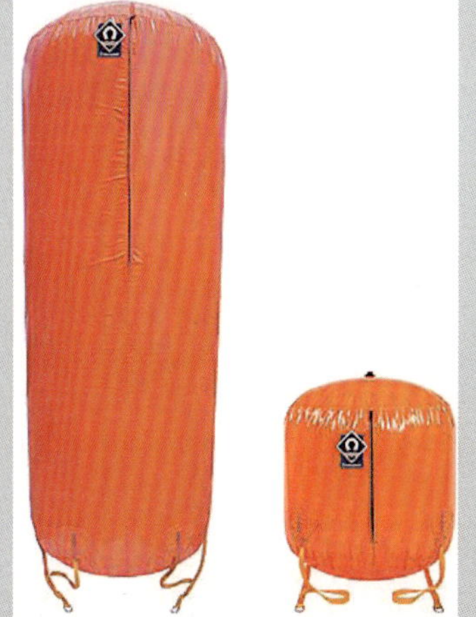

Graphic icon © Inkwina

Watermelon carving

Monocular

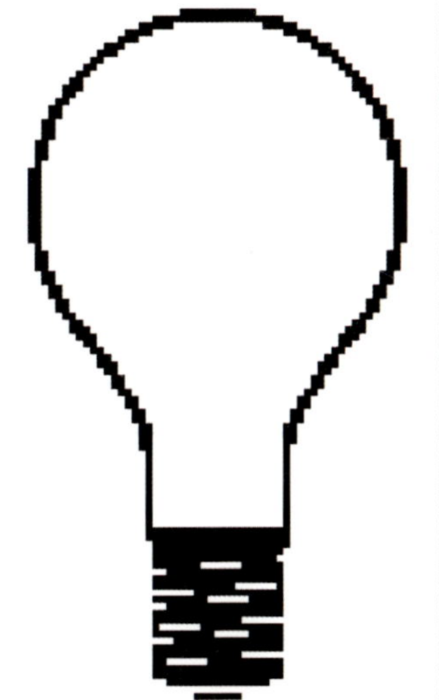

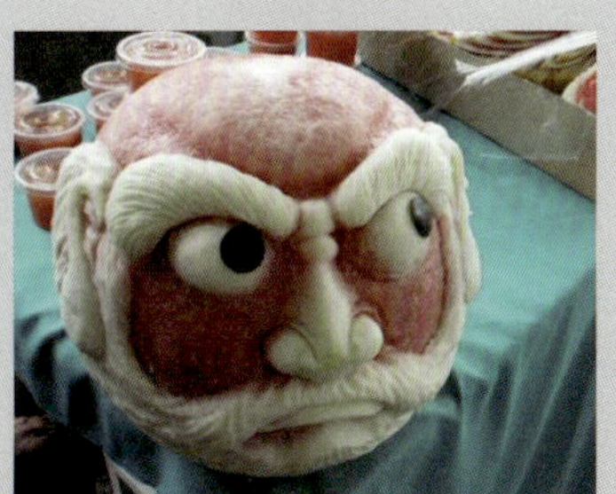

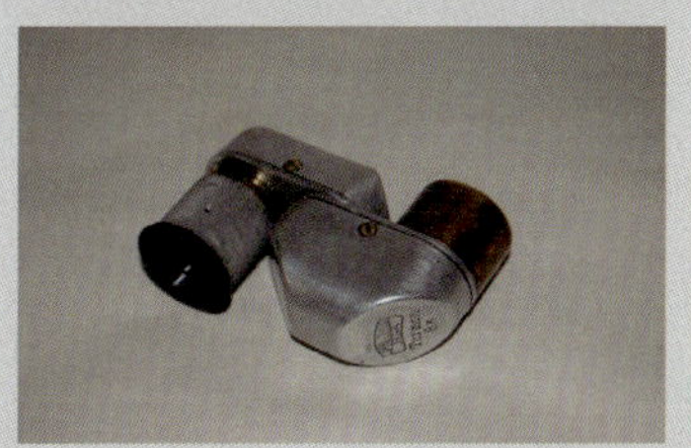

I say ding dong! © I Say Ding Dong

Occluded vitrine

Arthur Abraham, the 'Boxing Smurf'

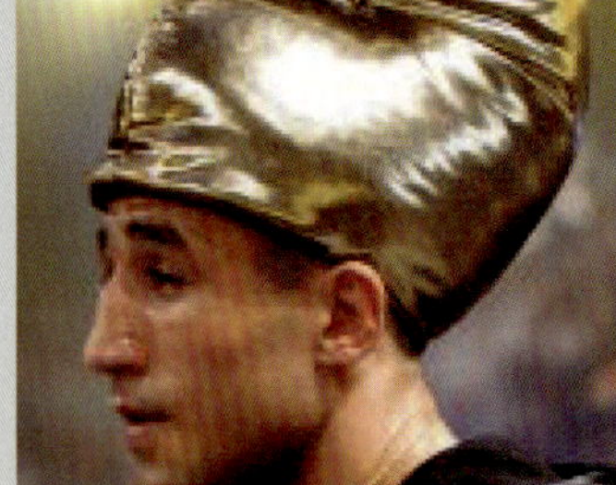

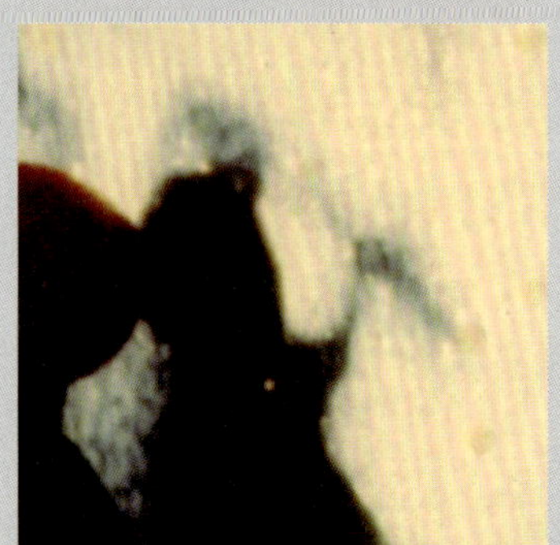

Whitechapel Bell Foundry

Whitechapel Bell Foundry

Degraded celluloid film

Image showing degradation of photographic emulsion

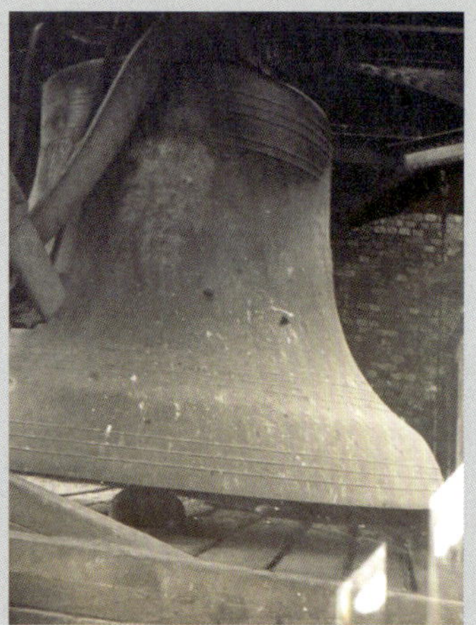

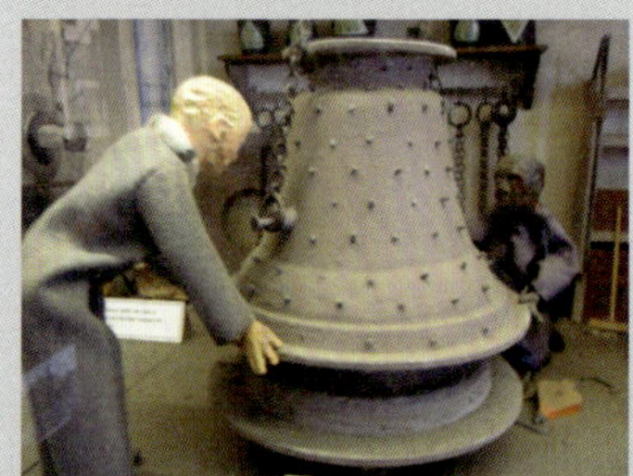

Tyrolean carnival masks

Tyrolean carnival masks

Tyrolean carnival masks

Bell profiles © Richard Offen/CCCBR

Sentinels

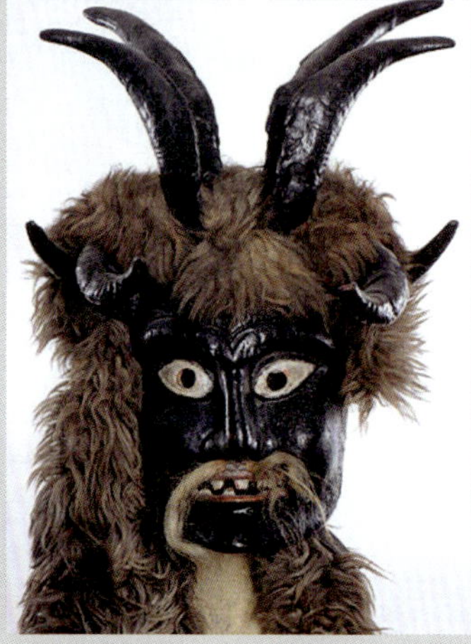

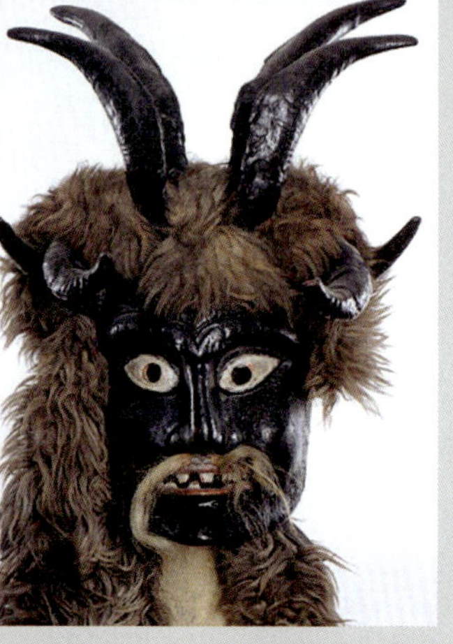

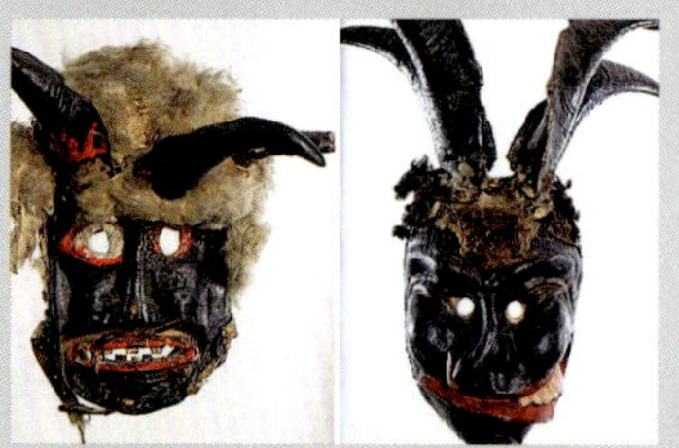

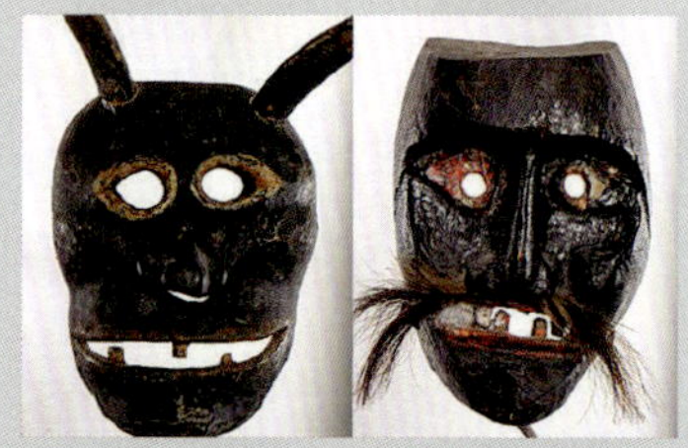

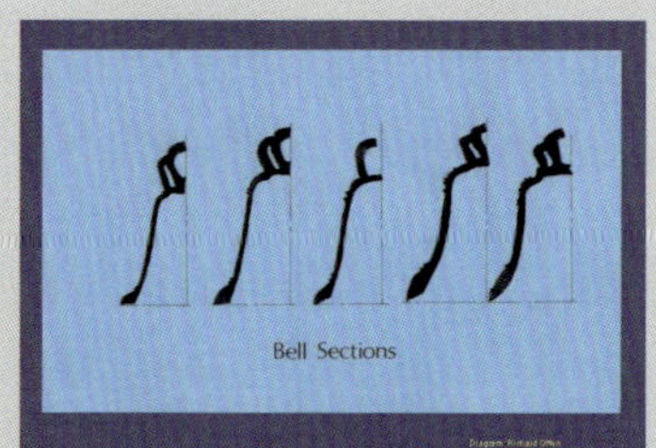

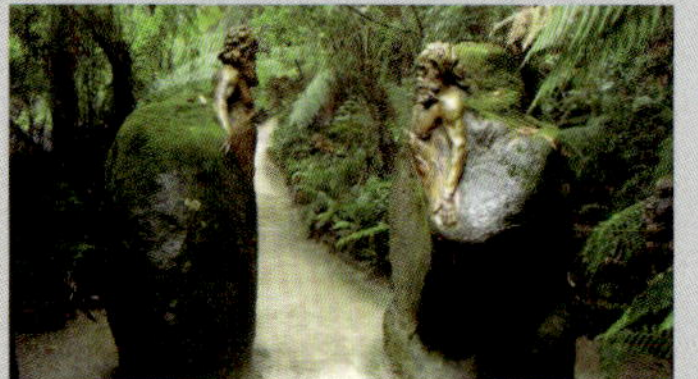

Down Syndrome Girl © Heather Spears

Prop from the 1982 film *Bladerunner* © www.bookofjoe.com

89 butterfly

Pure gum rubber

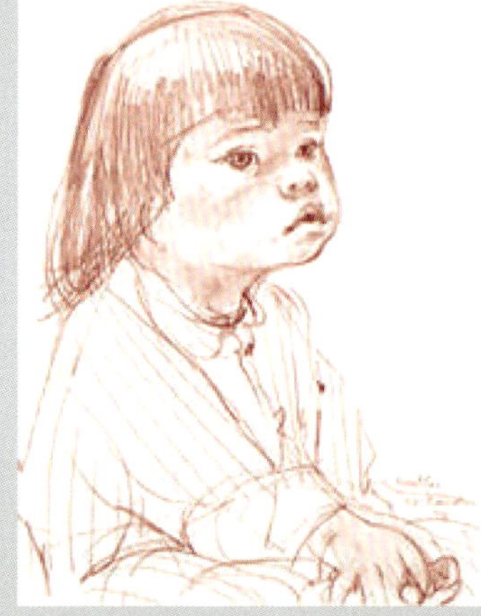

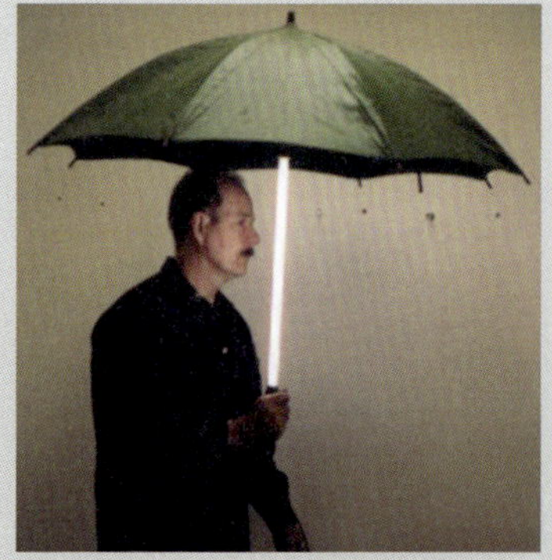

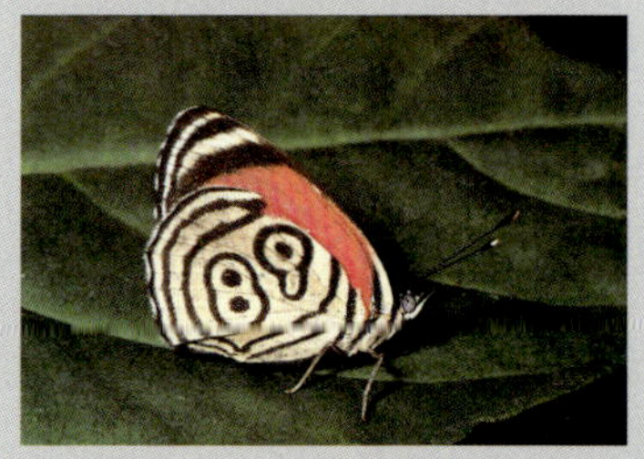

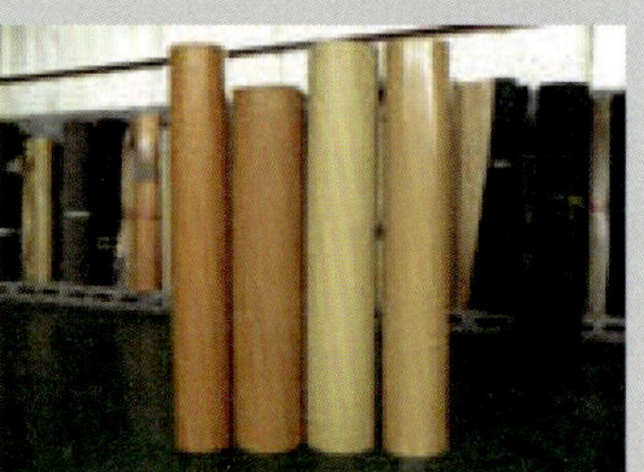

David Kordansky

Early daylight bulb

Detailed plan of the wall surface of the north and south galleries in the Haus der Kunst, Munich © Haus der Kunst

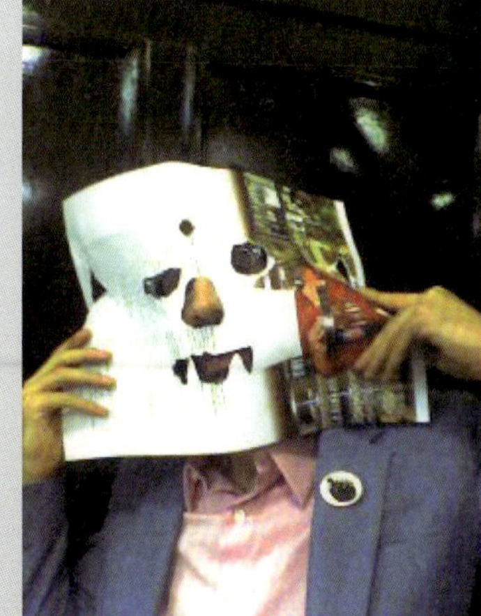

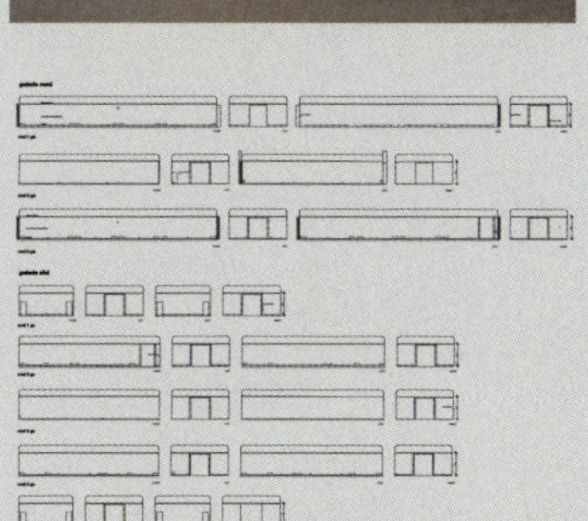

Incredible instruments

Pure gum rubber

Concrete bunkers, Guernsey © G.C. Carr

Horatio Sanz as Pig-Pen from *Peanuts* on *Saturday Night Live*, NBC, 2006

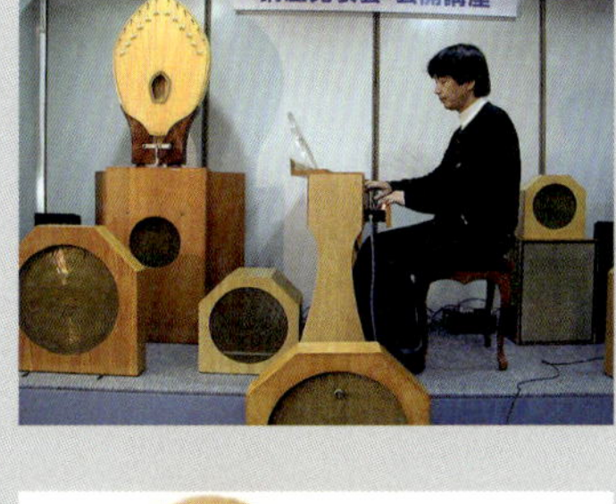

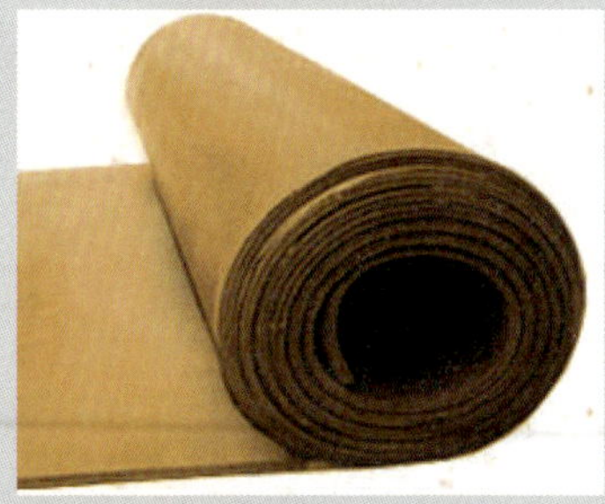

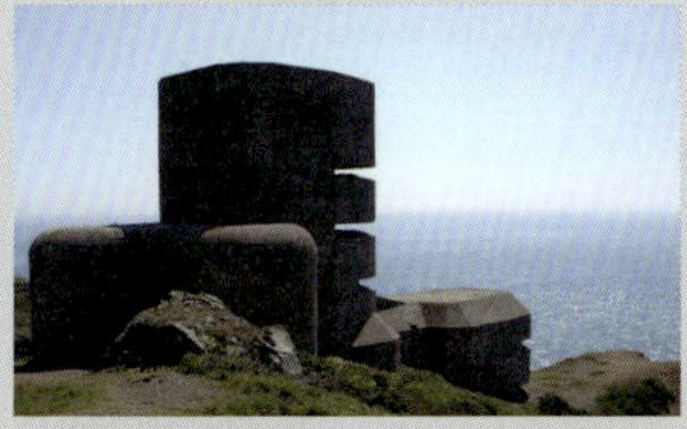

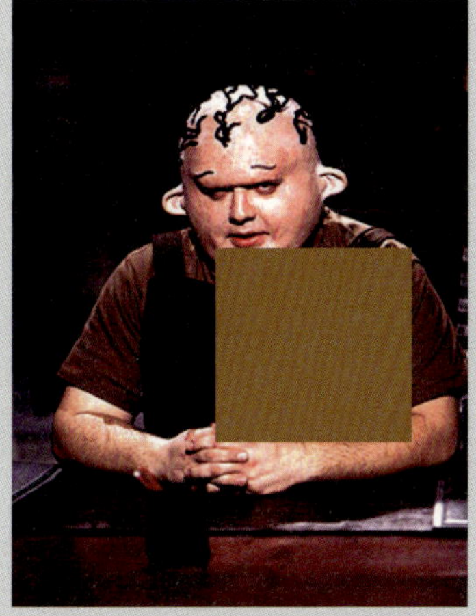

Russian sniper

Secular conjurer

LSO semaphore

The Lemur

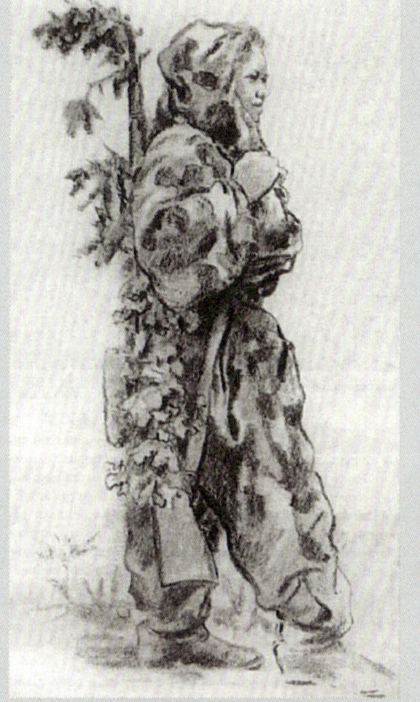

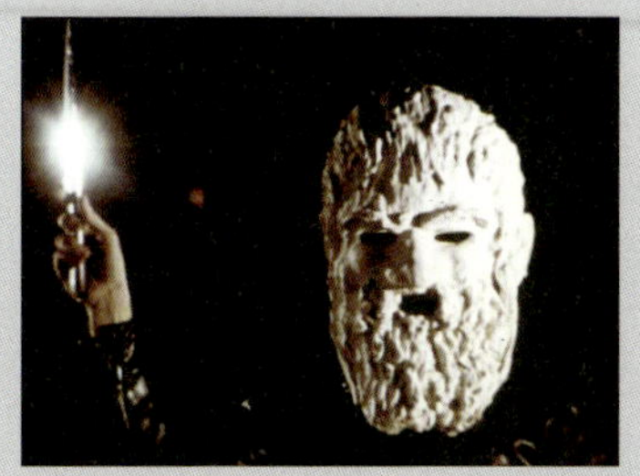

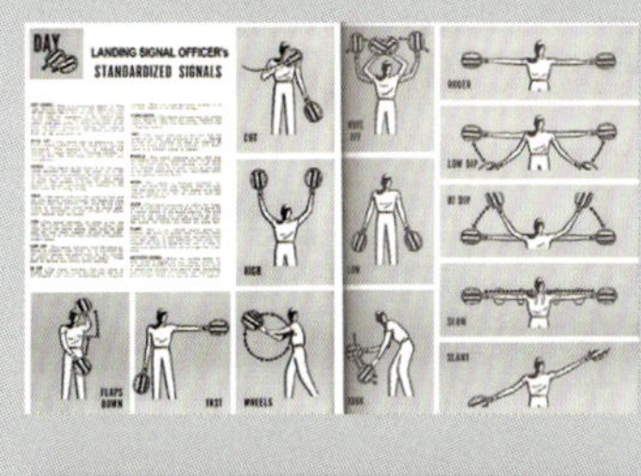

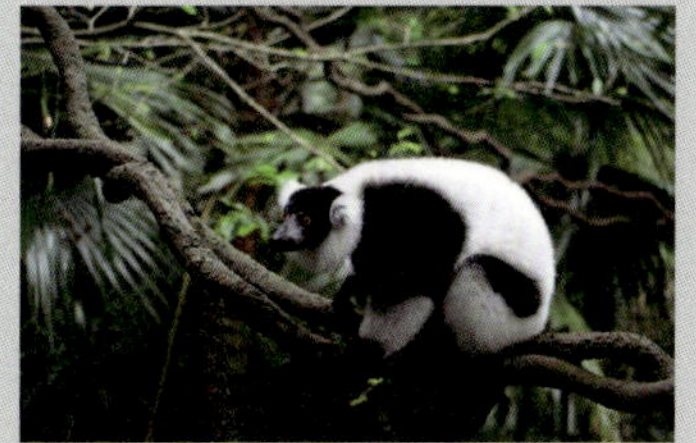

RAL 1027 Curry Yellow

Cosmonaut orange

Antiproton emulsion

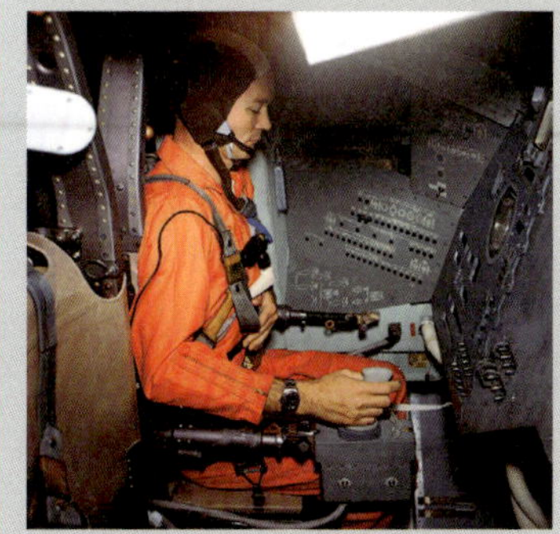

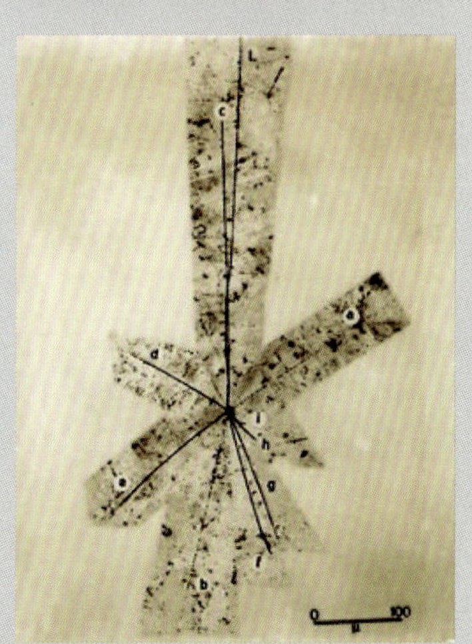

Photograph of particles © Dehautenbas

Landing Signal Officer's cap

Landing Signal Officer's cap

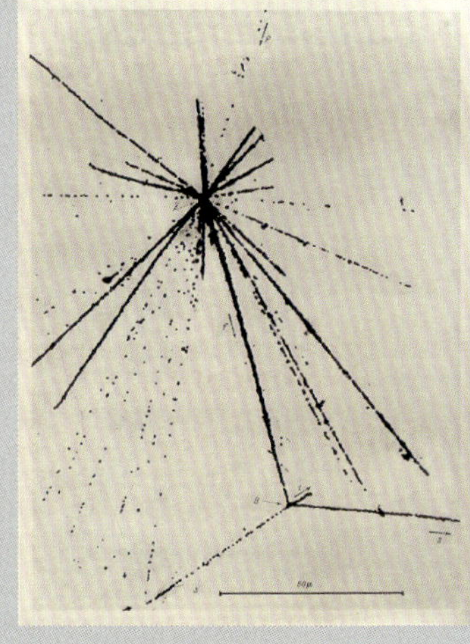

Landing Signal Officer's cap

Your son

Landing Signal Officer © 2000-2010 All Rights Reserved, Eric Rymer

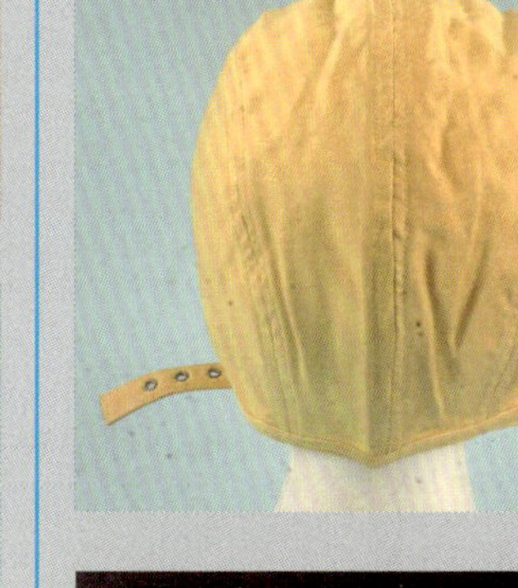

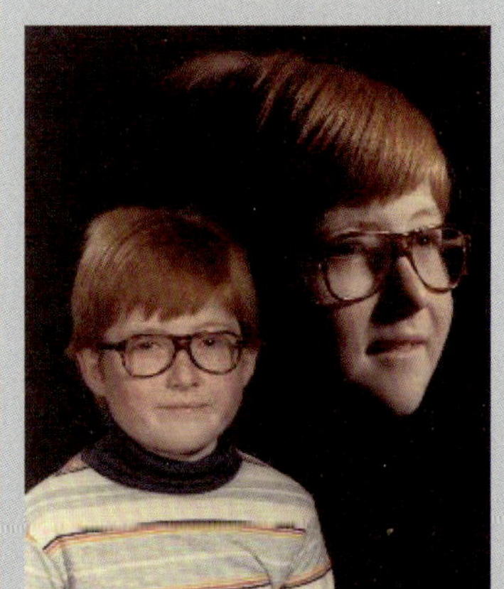

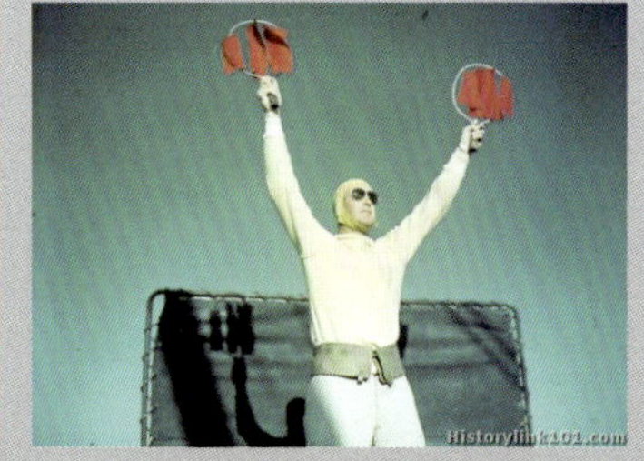

Photograph taken in central London, 2010

Bulkhead light in social housing, Borough of Camden, London

Photograph of removed hoarding, central London

Neolithic bone carving

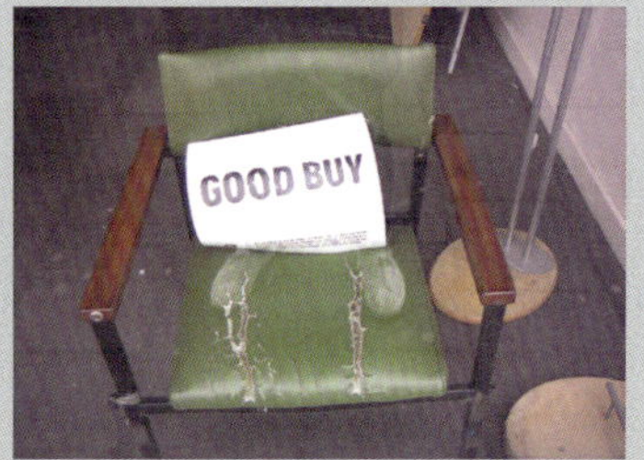

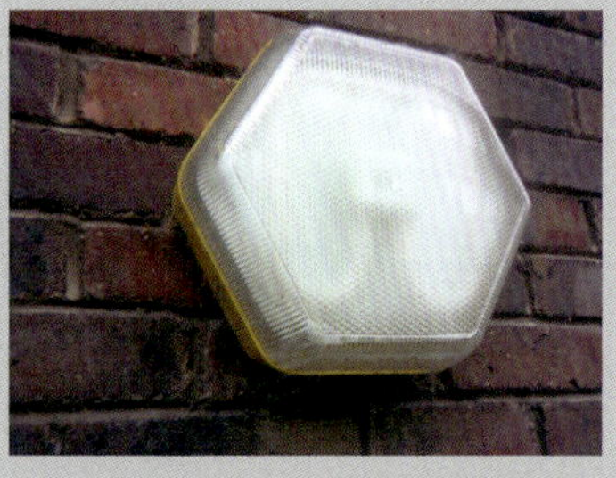

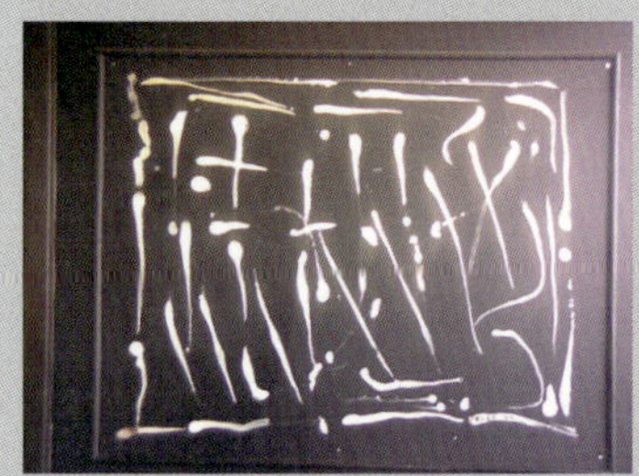

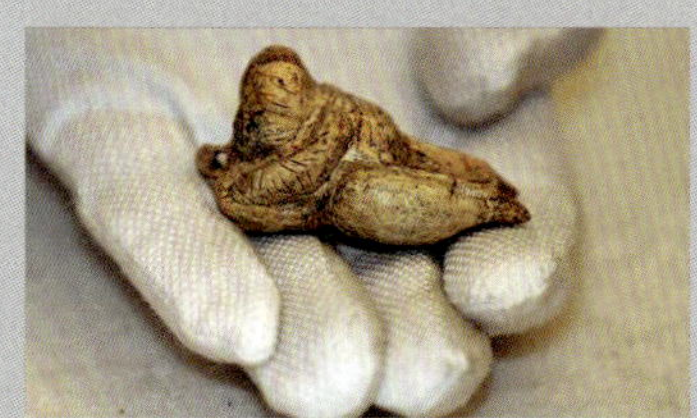

Assface © Frank Ly et al 2004-2010

Diagram showing the international standard paper sizes, ISO 216 A series © Bromskloss

Astronaut Thomas P Stafford, commander of the Apollo 10 lunar orbit mission with Snoopy mascot. During the Apollo 10 lunar orbit operations the Lunar Module was called Snoopy when it was separated from the Command/ Service Modules

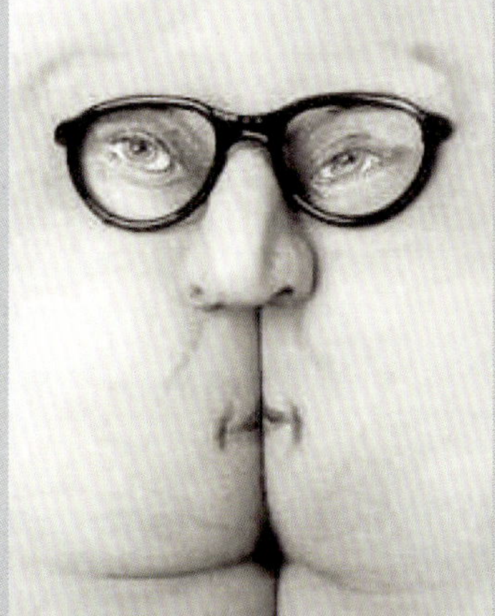

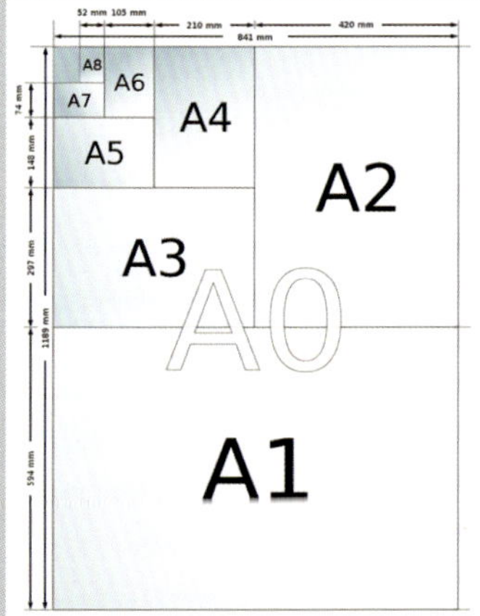

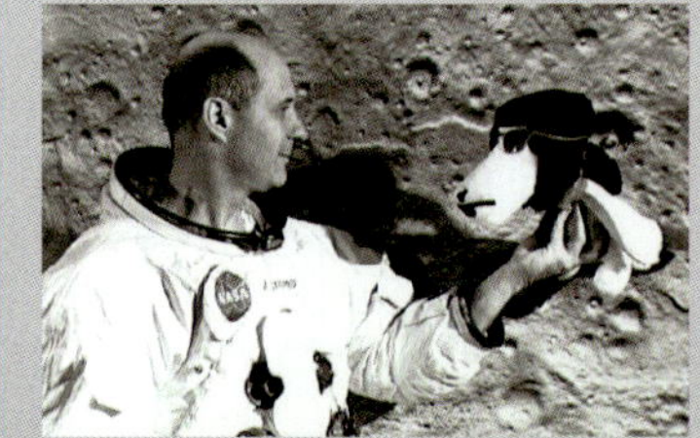

Weaver's hand

Small weaver

Woven small

Soviet space suit © Martin Belam,
currybet.net

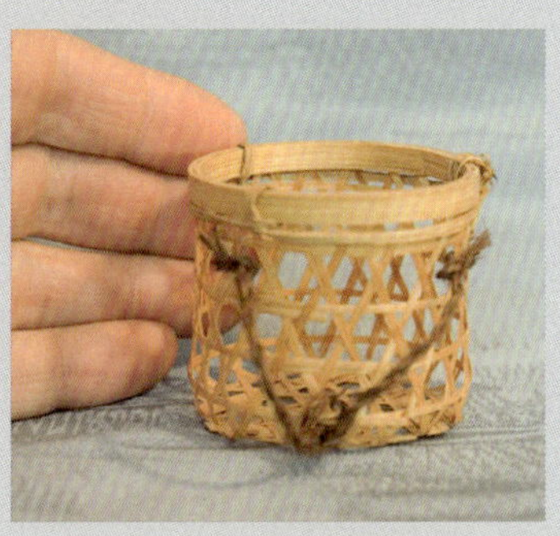

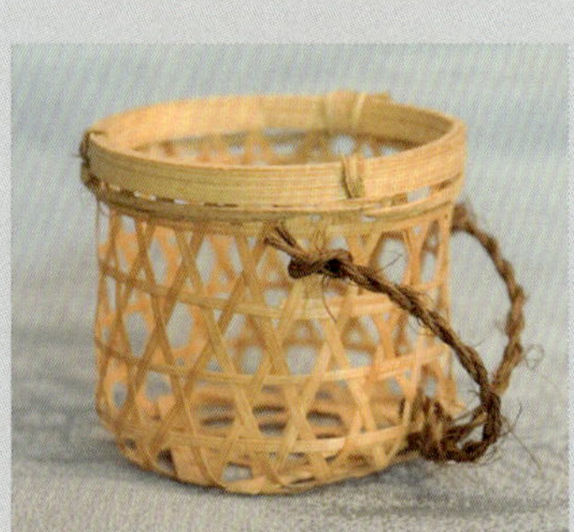

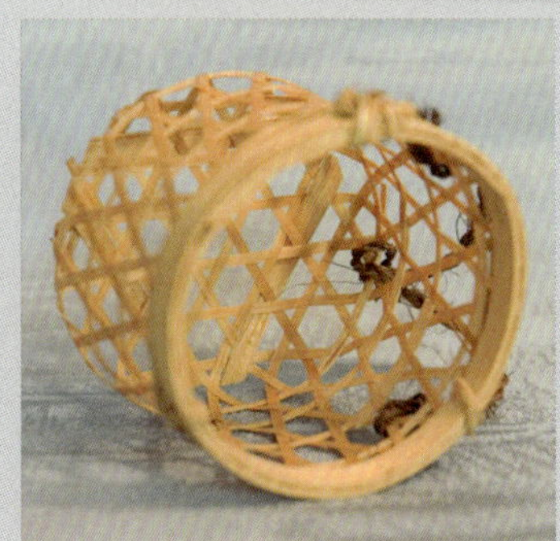

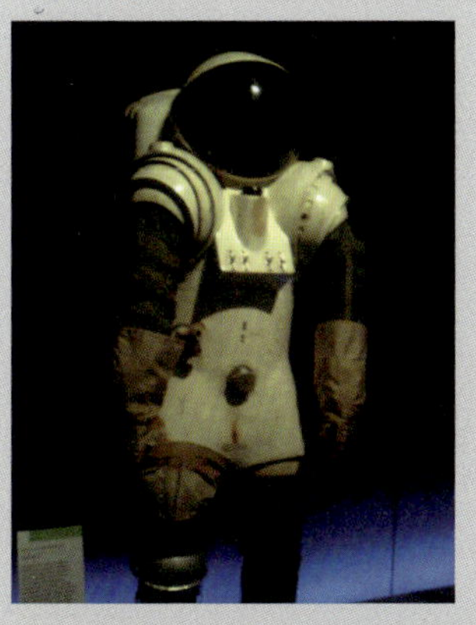

STIMPI (Short TImescale Motion of
Pancake Ice) buoy in the Weddle Sea

Occluded vitrine

Steven Claydon cover design for
Ancient Set exhibition booklet, 2008

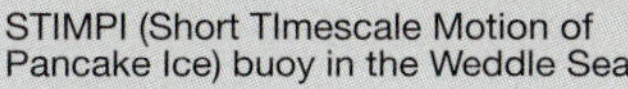

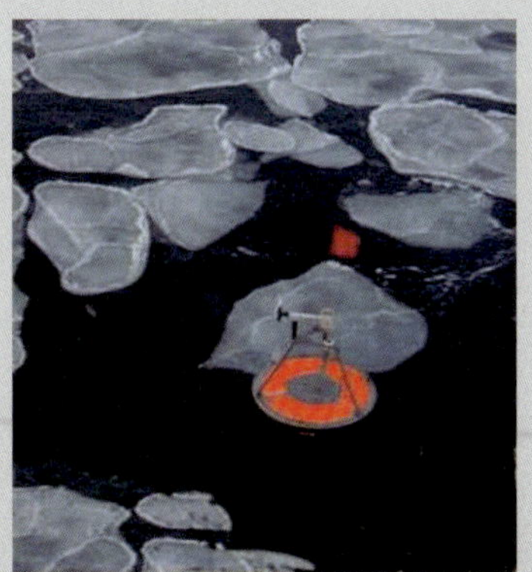

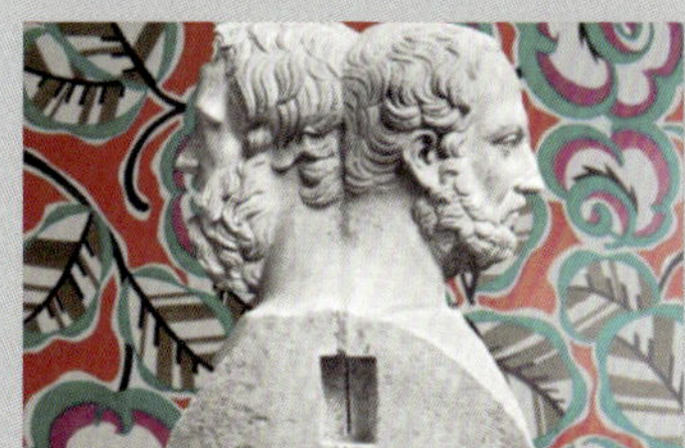

North Pole pellet

Still from A Clockwork Orange,
directed by Stanley Kubrick, 1971

Jack too Jack promotional flyer

Climbers in the Dolomite mountains,
Italy

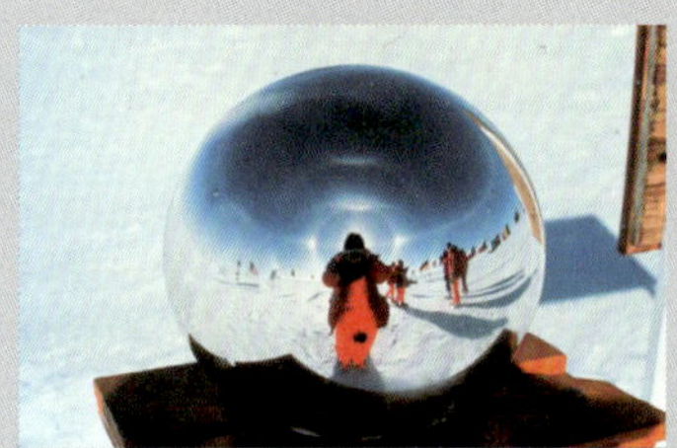

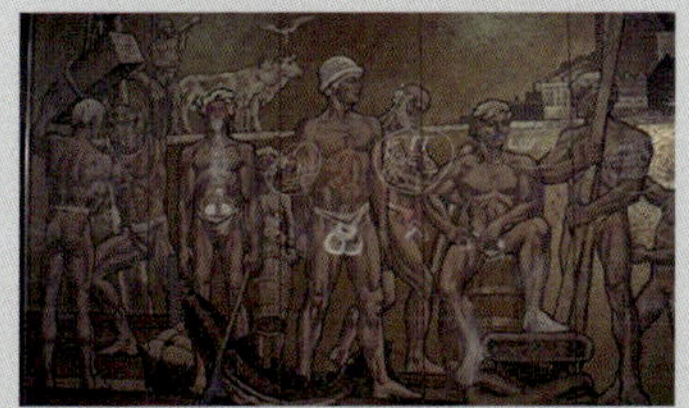

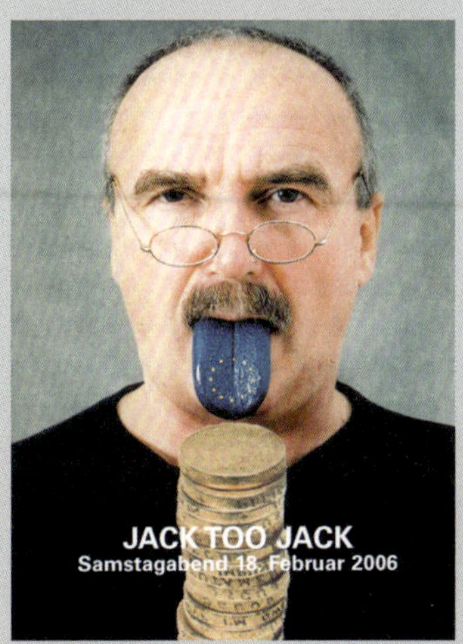

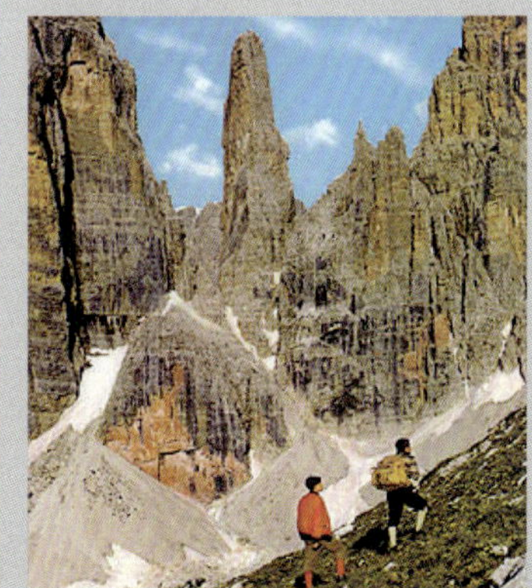

Automobile adapted with cardboard

Automobile adapted with cardboard to
imitate a SDKF2 halftrack tank

Steven Claydon/Galerie Rüdiger
Schöttle exhibition invitation, 2009

Us

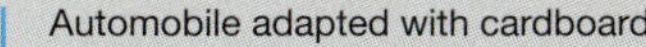

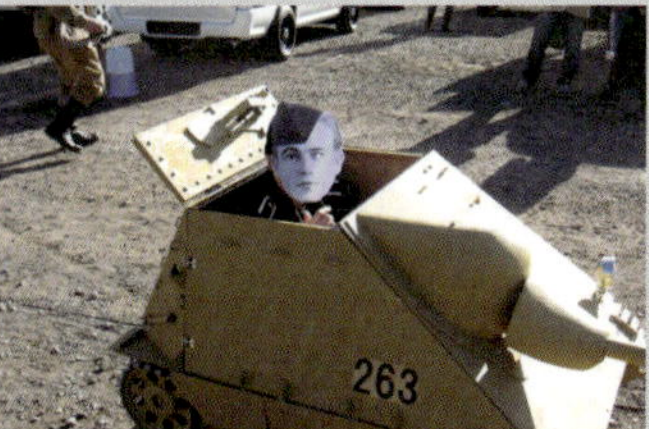

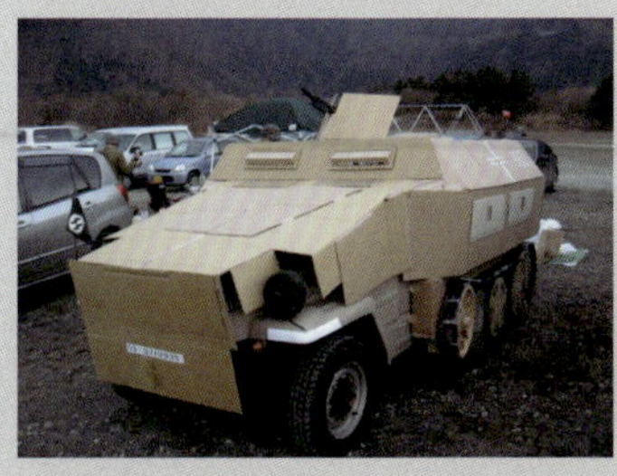

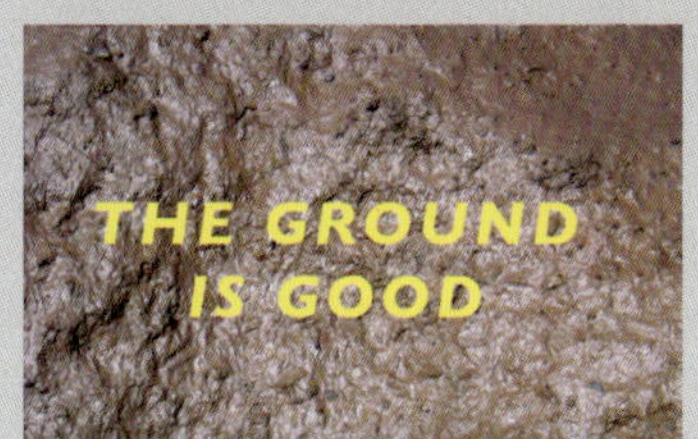

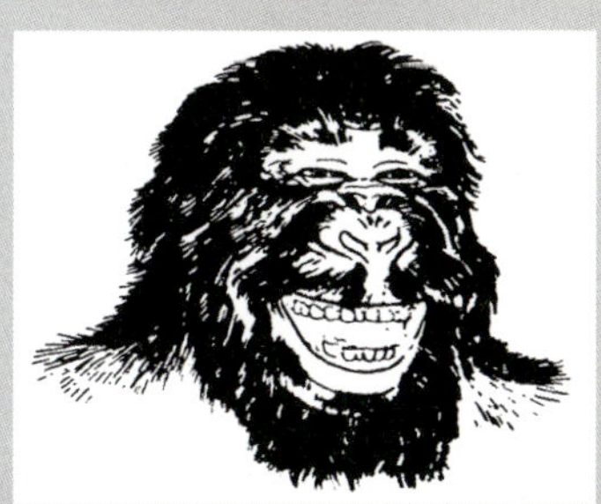

Steven Claydon

Year		Solo exhibition	Group exhibition	Text/publication/catalogue	Artist text	Curated exhibition	Performance	Residency	Screening
2012	*The Dan Cox Library for the Unfinished Concept of Thingly Time*, Cubitt, London		•						
	Culpable Earth, Firstsite, Colchester	•		•	•				
	Transmitter/Receiver: The Persistence of Collage, The New Art Gallery Walsall, Walsall; Usher Gallery, Lincoln; touring in 2013 to Aberystwith Art Centre, Aberystwith, and Tullie House Museum and Art Gallery, Carlisle		•						
	'Steven Claydon on Walter Sickert's Queen Victoria and her great-grandson', *Tate Etc.*, Issue 24, Spring 2012				•				
2011	*Alma Mater*, LUX touring programme, various venues								•
	Mon Plaisir...Votre Travail..., La Salle de bains, Lyon	•							
	Something in the Way, LIAF 2011, Kabelvag		•						
	We Will Live, We Will See, The Zabludowicz Collection, London		•	•					
	Transmitter/Receiver: The Persistence of Collage, Middlesbrough Institute of Modern Art, Middlesbrough		•						
	Secret Societies. To Know, To Dare, To Will, To Keep Silence, Schirn Kunsthalle Frankfurt, Frankfurt; CAPC de Bordeaux, Bordeaux		•	•					
	Twickenham Garden, Kimmerich, New York	•							
	Time Again, Sculpture Center, Long Island City		•	•					
	Moulène, Claire, 'Les céramiques stupéfiantes de Steven Claydon', *Les Inrockuptibles*, 31 May			•					
	Savage Messiah, Rob Tufnell, London		•	•					
	Steven Claydon: Forward-Facing Lemon Yellow Eyes, Hayward Gallery, London					•			
	British Art Show 7: In the Days of the Comet, London; Glasgow; Plymouth		•	•					
	'Carol Bove and Steven Claydon: Material Fidelity', *Flash Art*, January/February			•					
	Beauman, Ned, 'British Art Show 7', *Frieze*, Issue 136, January/February			•					
2010	*British Art Show 7: In the Days of the Comet*, Nottingham Castle, Nottingham		•	•		•			
	Alexandra Bircken, Carol Bove, Steven Claydon, Kimmerich, New York		•						
	Trom Bell To The Bow Draps, Hotel, London	•							
	Rappolt, Mark, 'Steven Claydon', *Art Review*, October			•					
	Morton, Tom, 'Out of the Cave', *Frieze*, issue 134, October			•					
	Rive Gauche/Rive Droite, Marc Jancou Contemporary, Paris		•	•					
	At Home/Not at Home: Works from the Collection of Martin and Rebecca Eisenberg, Center for Curatorial Studies, Bard College, Annandale-on-Hudson		•	•					
	Goldene Zeiten (Golden Times), Haus der Kunst, Munich		•						
	Newspeak: British Art Now, Saatchi Gallery, London		•	•					
	Cotton, Michelle, 'The Dark Monarch', *Frieze*, issue 128, January/February			•					
2009	*Newspeak: British Art Now*, The State Hermitage Museum, St. Petersburg		•	•					
	The Dark Monarch, Tate St. Ives, Cornwall		•	•					
	Alejandro Jodorowsky's 'Dune': An exhibition of a film of a book that never was, The Drawing Room, London		•						
	Remote Memories, KAI 10 Arthena Foundation, Düsseldorf		•	•					
	Smaldone, Andrew, 'Steven Claydon', *Art Review*, May			•					
	Le Sang d'un poète, Sant-Nazaire Biennale, Frac des Pays de la Loire, Carquefou		•						
	The Ground is Good, Galerie Rüdiger Schöttle, Munich	•							
	Two Times New Horizon, Galleria Massimo de Carlo, Milan	•							
2008	*Osram and Omar*, Hotel, London	•							
	Novel, Bibliothekswohnung Anna-Catherina Gebbers, Berlin		•						
	Homage to Modern Art, Galleria Massimo de Carlo, Milan		•						
	Heroes and Villians, Marc Jancou Contemporary, New York		•						
	Busan Biennial, Busan		•						
	Morton, Tom, 'Back to the Future', *Frieze*, issue 118, September			•					
	The Ancient Set and The Fictional Pixel, film installations and performance, Serpentine Pavilion, London						•		•
	The Ancient Set, International Project Space, Birmingham	•		•					
	A & not A, Galerie Dennis Kimmerich, Düsseldorf	•							

Year		Solo exhibition	Group exhibition	Text/publication/catalogue	Artist text	Curated exhibition	Performance	Residency	Screening
	In Geneva No One Can Hear You Scream, Blondeau Fine Art Services, Geneva		●	●					
	Morton, Tom, 'Strange Events', *Frieze*, issue 113, March			●					
	Withers, Rachel, 'Strange Things Permit Themselves the Luxury of Occurring', *Artforum*, March			●					
	Ascari, Alessio, 'Interview', *Mousse*, issue 12, January			●					
	Glover, Michael 'Inside the curious world of Steven Claydon', *The Independent*, 7 January			●					
	Ward, Ossian, 'Gothic Art Revival', *Time Out London*, 2 January			●					
2007	*Strange Events Permit Themselves the Luxury of Occurring*, Camden Arts Centre, London					●	●		
	Nueva Dimension, Hats Plus, London		●						
	Day, Charlotte, 'Rings of Saturn Tate Modern', *Art & Australia*, vol. 44, no. 3, Autumn			●					
	Effigies, Stuart Shave/Modern Art, London		●						
	Sympathy for the Devil, Art and Rock and Roll Since 1967, Museum Of Contemporary Art, Chicago		●	●					
	Old School, Hauser and Wirth Colnaghi, London; Zwirner and Wirth, New York		●						
	New Valkonia, David Kordansky Gallery, Los Angeles	●							
	Come Into The Open, Projekt 0047, Oslo		●						
	Jack too Jack, Arnolfini, Bristol							●	
	Pale Carnage, Arnolfini, Bristol; Dundee Contemporary Arts, Dundee		●	●					
	Gallery Swap, Hotel at Guido Baudach, Berlin		●						
	Me.di.um, St. Barthélemy								●
2006	Coomer, Martin, 'Introducing: Steven Claydon', *Modern Painters*, December 2006/January 2007			●					
	The Metal Bridge, Sorcha Dallas, Glasgow		●						
	Deep Into That Darkness Peering, Galerie Kamm, Berlin		●						
	Courtesy Of The Neighbourhood Watch, White Columns, New York	●							
	Rings of Saturn, Tate Modern, London		●						
	Keep Passing The Open Windows Or Happiness, Galerie Gisela Capitain, Cologne		●						
	Dereconstruction, Gladstone Gallery, New York		●	●					
	The Glidded Baumm, Art Statements, Basel	●							
	Writing the Strobe, Dicksmith Gallery, London		●						
	Too, Jian-Xing , 'Le Voyage Intérieur', *Art Review*, February			●					
	Morton, Tom, 'Looking Back: Emerging Artists', *Frieze*, issue 96, January/February			●					
	Fox, Dan and Simon Reynolds, 'Music 2005,' *Frieze*, issue 96, January/February			●					
2005	*Time Lines*, Kunstverein für die Rheinlande und Westphalen, Düsseldorf		●						
	Odiseado Tra Tempo, Peter Kilchmann Galerie, Zurich		●						
	Paris – Londres: Le Voyage Interieur, Espace Electra, Paris		●	●					
	All Across the Thready Eye, Galerie Dennis Kimmerich, Düsseldorf	●							
	Flies Around the Fury Flotsam, Curators Space, London		●						
	Wood, Catherine, 'Fear of a Planet at Hotel', *Frieze*, issue 93, September			●					
	Post no Bills, White Columns, New York		●						
	Lightbox, Tate Britain, London		●						●
	Fear of a Planet, Hotel, London	●							
	Lack, Jessica, 'Fear of a Planet at Hotel', *Guardian Guide*, 19–25 March			●					
	Even a Stopped Clock Tells the Right Time Twice a Day, ICA, London		●	●					
	Clouds of Witness, Islington Town Hall, London		●						
	Jack too Jack, Portikus, Frankfurt						●		
	Jack too Jack, Inverleith House, Edinburgh						●		
	Jack too Jack, Rio Cinema, London						●		
	Remixed Water, Manchester						●		
2004	*The Third of the Third*, Hoxton Distillery, London	●							
	The Last Supper, Hoxton Distillery, London		●						
	The Poster, The Show 1,2,3..., Hoxton Distillery, London		●						

Year		Solo exhibition	Group exhibition	Text/publication/catalogue	Artist text	Curated exhibition	Performance	Residency	Screening
	Jack too Jack, *Shades of Destructors*, Prince Charles Theatre, London						•		
	Jack too Jack, *Shades of Destructors*, Gavin Brown Enterprise, New York						•		
	Jack too Jack, *Shades of Destructors*, Humanist Society, London						•		
2003	*The Sum of the Earth*, Hoxton Distillery, London		•						
	Nibs., Hoxton Distillery, London		•						
	Strange Greeny from The Sum of the Earth, Kunstwerk, Berlin								•
	Total All Out Water, edition, box set, SHOWstudio				•				
2002	'Architecture in Architecture', *Sleazenation*				•				
	'Sometimes Leather', Underwood Audio 2				•				
2001	*It Grows Away, collaboration with Neil Chapman*, The Hoxton Distillery, London		•						
	'Twinterview: Interview with Steve and Paul Claydon, *Untitled,* no. 25, Summer			•					
	Loud Like Nature, ADD N TO (X), La Box, Borges		•						•
	'Autointerview', with Neil Chapman				•				
2000	*Five Works in Lieu of a Particle Accelerator*, Greengrassi, London		•						
	One Geocrab, film screening as part of Night Stop Cinema, The Week of Small Miracles, London								•
1999	ADDING N TO (X), Villa Noailles, Hyeres		•						
	The Opposite of a Good Idea, live performance with Neil Chapman, *Inventory*, vol. 3, issue 2; launch, Guy's Hospital, London						•		
	'The Approach', with Neil Chapman, *Inventory*, vol. 3, issue 3				•				
	'The Opposite of a Good Idea', *Inventory*, vol.3, issue 2				•				
1998	*Shrimp-Ice Briefing*, with Neil Chapman, ICA, London		•		•				
	It's A Curse Its A Burden, Approach Gallery, London		•						
	ADD N TO (X) Dinner Music for Electronic Quartet, ICA, London						•		
	ADD N TO (X) music for *A Page of Madness*, silent film by Teinosuke Kinugasa, in collaboration with Barry Adamson, Nick Cave and Pan Sonic, Royal Festival Hall, London						•		
	'The Fullness that Fills up the Pulse of Durations: The Ambassadors', collaboration with Chris Ofili, CD Box Set				•				
1997	*Peripheral Visionary*, Eindhoven, Netherlands		•						
	'Carousel', with Neil Chapman				•				